OSAMA

OSAMA

The Making of a Terrorist
Revised Edition

Jonathan Randal

I.B. TAURIS
LONDON · NEW YORK

New edition published in 2012 by I.B.Tauris & Co Ltd
6 Salem Road, London W2 4BU
175 Fifth Avenue, New York NY 10010
www.ibtauris.com

First edition published in the United States in 2004 by Alfred A. Knopf,
a division of Random House, Inc., New York
First published in the UK in 2005 and reprinted in 2006 by I.B.Tauris & Co Ltd

ISBN: 978 1 78076 055 1

A full CIP record for this book is available from the British Library

Printed and bound by CPI Group (UK) Ltd, Croydon, CR0 4YY

Book design by Robert C. Olsson

To Geneviève

Contents

Acknowledgments

I have taxed the limits of old and new friends who have helped me over the past five years. They include many journalists, academics, diplomats and businessmen, as well as other sources accumulated over five decades as a foreign correspondent in and out of the Muslim world. I owe them all my thanks. But I owe special thanks to two friends—Wade Greene and Don Larrimore. They know why.

Preface to the New Edition

I am an old retired reporter who covered wars for a living and often sleeps poorly. In the hours before dawn I regularly turn on the radio to the BBC World Service, which for many decades before the digital age was the foreign correspondent's most reliable and constant friend. But just before 5 a.m. Paris time on May 2, vestigial habits of a professional lifetime jolted me wide awake; the World Service was reporting that Osama bin Laden, the world's most elusive terrorist, was dead, killed in Pakistan in a daring night-time helicopter raid carried out by elite U.S. Navy commandos known as SEALs.

As I made my first coffee of the day, my head still a jumble, I listened to President Barack Obama inform my fellow Americans and the world about the high-risk operation ending the longest and most expensive manhunt in modern history. I confess I had my own very personal reasons for celebrating the death of the man whose name is destined to remain associated with the hijacked airliners sent crashing into the twin towers of New York's World Trade Center and the Pentagon on September 11, 2001.

Starting in late 1998, I had spent more than five years chasing down many a blind alley researching and writing, indeed rewriting, a book on Osama. (I had all but completed a manuscript on 9/11, but decided to start all over again and that exercise took almost three more years.) But now I was shot of him. I prayed an emboldened president would seize on Osama's death to accelerate the inevitable recessional from Washington's endless wars with the Muslim world and start winding down the fighting in Afghanistan.

Barack Obama certainly risked his presidency, as is evident in photos of the tense White House situation room as he and his aides anxiously awaited the SEALs' terse thumbs-up message: Osama's thrice-repeated codename, "Geronimo", a curious choice given the Apache chief's long defiance of the U.S. Army in the late-nineteenth century, followed by "E" for enemy and "KIA" for killed in action.

My mind raced back to April 1980 when, as the Washington Post's correspondent in Iran, I covered an earlier risky military mission, a botched operation in the Iranian desert to rescue 52 American diplomats held hostage by Iran's Islamic Revolution. That failure doomed the presidency of Jimmy Carter. Now by killing Osama, the president could turn conventional wisdom on its head and call the self-serving bluffs of our often-unreliable and corrupt Afghan and Pakistani partners who have manipulated our national obsession with the Al-Qaeda leader to keep us subsidizing their own agendas.

Americans have a weakness for personifying their enemies. That explains why Osama at large was such a problem. By killing Osama, in American parlance, the president had "nail(ed) the coonskin to the wall"— President Lyndon Johnson's vain plea to his troops during the Vietnam War—and provided Americans with a cathartic sense of immanent justice for 9/11. Nearly ten years later Americans were not just getting even for that day's nearly 3,000 dead. Osama's death also helped repair the trauma inflicted by the breaching of Fortress America (especially its financial and military citadels) for the first time since the British burned the White House in 1814.

America's exhilaration of revenge soon subsided and the nation waited anxiously. Could the president, would the president, devise a way out of Osama's deliberately laid trap for getting the world's only superpower bogged down in these debilitating, asymmetrical conflicts? The stage seemed set. At long last Americans were willing to face reality. The staggering bill for a decade of dubious battle in Afghanistan and Iraq was ruinous (around $4 trillion and more still, counting veterans' benefits), blood (more than 6,000 soldiers killed), prestige and honor (the shameful horrors of the Abu Ghraib and Guantanamo prisons). Nor with the regularly renewed restrictions of the Patriot Act and other security legislation had America's democratic institutions emerged unscathed.

By the time of Osama's death, Americans were weary of George W. Bush's wars and feeling the pain of their own devastated economy and ballooning national debt. A distant and mocking memory was a former French foreign minister's critical description of America as the world's only unchallenged "hyperpower" in the period following the Soviet Union's collapse and the end of the Cold War. The national mood had changed so much that the Republican Party was split wide open, ranging from the ever-bellicose neo-conservative Bush wing to penny-pinching Tea Party isolationists and others convinced the United States could not afford the $120 billion annual cost of the Afghan war.

What would the president do? Finally, almost two months after Osama's death, on June 22, President Obama, often criticized by both domestic friends and adversaries as indecisively lawyer-like, seized the main chance. He announced 10,000 troops would leave by the end of the year, followed by 23,000 before the end of September 2012 or just five strategic weeks before the next U.S. presidential and congressional elections. All 100,000 American soldiers would be out in 2014.

The contrast with the autumn of 2009 could not have been greater. Then the president had dithered for three anguished months before giving in to Pentagon insistence that without a 30,000-man surge the war would be lost. Seizing on what passed for a vague face-saver at the time, the president reluctantly justified the surge in terms of fighting Al-Qaeda, and promised an undefined number of troops would start heading home in the summer of 2011. Thanks to the Al-Qaeda leader's elimination, suddenly Obama, the commander-in-chief who had never worn a uniform, was commanding. The scurrilous attacks on America's first black president, questioning whether he was really native born and legally qualified for the White House, abruptly ceased.

So now the president could cut the Afghan Gordian knot. His decisions clearly displeased his generals. They made plain they wanted to maintain troop levels to exert maximum pressure on the far-from-defeated Taliban. If the war suddenly took a turn for the worse, if Al-Qaeda staged some new spectacular attack on the United States or the Taliban again began sweeping all before them, the brass politely intimated, the president would be held responsible. He accepted the risk, seeking to reassure by noting that 68,000 American troops—or twice as many as before he took office in January 2009—would remain after the surge ended just in case.

The military were not the only senior officials displeased. Secretary of State Hillary Clinton worried about the implied abandonment of ambitious, if unfulfilled, nation-building programs, including her cherished program for educating girls long deprived of schooling under Taliban rule. The president also kicked the regional anthill, serving notice that Osama's death had changed the entire calculus of the war. Shorn of his carefully calibrated diplomatic wording, his statement signaled that the United States was heading out of Afghanistan, and sooner rather than later. For the first time United States officials were saying out loud what had before only been whispered; armed, unmanned drones had killed more than half the top 30 senior Al-Qaeda cadres in Pakistan and only 50 to 75 Al-Qaeda fighters were thought to be active in Afghanistan. That was scarcely enough to justify spending an unsustainable $10 billion a month on a war, now America's longest, deemed both unwinnable and not really worth trying to win after Osama's death.

After all, a desire to punish Al-Qaeda and Osama were the reasons the United States had reacted to 9/11 by invading Afghanistan and defeating them and their Taliban protectors even if the quarry was allowed to escape to Pakistan to fight another day. So, mission accomplished, or almost (were it not for Pakistan's messy jihadi politics and worrisome nuclear arsenal). Osama dead also meant that for the first time in a decade the United States could deal with two untrustworthy partners in Afghanistan and Pakistan who no longer could rely on the Al-Qaeda factor to keep Washington's billions moving in their direction.

In Afghanistan, reducing its military footprint meant the United States was signaling the end of an open-ended commitment to the inept, corrupt and back-biting regime of Hamid Karzai. Bye-bye nation-building. Karzai was put on notice that Afghanistan's own fledgling army and police soon would have to fend for themselves. As for Pakistan, no longer would the United States pretend that the spies of the Pakistani army's Directorate of Inter-Services Intelligence were not involved in all kinds of skullduggery, including very possibly helping Osama hide for five years in a high-walled, three-storey compound within a mile of the national military academy in Abbottabad. (A foolproof way, some conspiracy theorists argued, to control Osama's slightest movements.)

For a decade and a half Osama had been at the center of long-festering friction between the United States and the ISI, which perhaps in whole (or more likely in part) wittingly tolerated, sometimes encouraged and occasionally, to please Washington, cracked down on Al-Qaeda and its master. The Abbottabad hideout was hard, but not impossible, for the ISI to explain away. In any case, the deeply embarrassed Pakistani military command, considered so untrustworthy that the United States did not inform Pakistan until the raid was completed, looked humiliated, foolish and incompetent.

The army, the most revered institution in an otherwise often incorrigibly corrupt state, was visibly reeling from unaccustomed public criticism and rumblings within its ranks against the army commander judged too subservient to the United States. Not since its loss of East Bengal, now Bangladesh, at the hands of the Indian army in 1971 had the Pakistani military experienced such a crisis of confidence. The Pakistan army's top brass maintained it had not known about Osama's bolt-hole, had not detected the U.S. raid while it was under way and was unaware the American intruders were violating Pakistani sovereignty until their helicopters had left Pakistani air space. They took with them his body and a treasure trove of DVDs, audio and video tapes, computers and hard disks, thousands of printed pages, thumb memories and even some digital pornography (which inspired the tabloid New York Post headline: "Osama bin Wankin").

The admissions by the Pakistan army brass amounted to a devastating confession. But to have pretended otherwise risked even greater embarrassment for a military establishment so mired in decades of double- and triple-dealing that perhaps its present leaders no longer quite remembered, much less fully understood, what at each past step had seemed a reasonable choice. More humiliation was to come several weeks after the raid. The Americans let it be known that they had gleaned the next best thing to the proverbial smoking gun from the cornucopia of captured documents described as worthy of a small college library. An incriminating telephone number of a leader of the ISI-connected Harakat-ul-Mujahedeen jihadi group was found in the memory of the captured cell phone belonging to the courier who unwittingly led the Americans to Osama's hideout. Harakat was well known as virtually a fully owned ISI subsidiary, one of the many jihadi groups used as ISI fronts in Pakistan's battle with India over disputed Kashmir. (Harakat militants training alongside Al-Qaeda recruits had died when U.S. cruise missiles struck a joint training camp in Afghanistan in 1998 in retaliation for Al-Qaeda's attacks on U.S. embassies in Kenya and Tanzania.)

So, finally the Americans had established, or at least decided to go public with, what looked like a direct link between Osama and the ISI. Suddenly the rules of the game had changed. As long as Osama was on the loose, Washington paid the Pakistani army—currently the bill came to $2 billion a year—ostensibly to fight Al-Qaeda. But much of the money was in all likelihood squirreled away to fight the only real adversary that counted in Pakistani eyes—India. And now?

The ISI long ago convinced itself that using Osama to keep stirring the Afghan pot was worthwhile against the inevitable day when Washington would tire and Afghanistan could become Pakistan's strategic depth against a richer and more populous Indian arch enemy. That was what Pakistanis called their "forward policy." It had never suited the ISI's purposes to clarify its own relations with Osama. Not quite straightforward, but what did the Americans have to complain about? Had they not walked away from Afghanistan after the defeated Red Army left in 1988 and had they not allowed Pakistan virtual control of the Taliban before 9/11?

IN THE HIGH stakes world of South Asian realpolitik, concerned with what the Pakistanis call "ground facts," the game had changed after 9/11. Osama alive remained important, but arguably less as a player in his own right and more as a chip to be bargained away at the right time. Perversely, the more the Americans pursued Osama, the more he became a Pakistani pawn and kept American dollars flowing. Only the Americans, for "coonskin" reasons, had attached paramount importance to killing Osama to justify the elaborate SEAL Team Six raid, complete with state-of-the-art stealth helicopters and dangerously exposed CIA surveillance operatives operating from a nearby safe house.

A detached observer might have questioned such zeal (and looked askance at some aspects of the official American version of the raid which almost certainly were fudged to protect still secret tradecraft.) Still, there was a crowning irony hiding in plain sight, much as Osama himself had spent the last five years of his life hiding in plain sight holed up in an old Raj cantonment town. And that was that, by the time he died at 54, Osama had become irrelevant.

Some of his irrelevance could be charted by the dogged statistics of modern counterterrorism, grown vastly more efficient since 9/11 thanks to billions of dollars spent for that purpose. Ten years ago the CIA, the FBI, the lavishly funded Defense Intelligence Agency, the National Security Agency (so secretive it once was nicknamed "No Such Agency") and other barely known intelligence organizations often did not even exchange information, or least not efficiently. Because the FBI and CIA computer systems were not compatible, famously some members of the 9/11 suicide bomber teams slipped into the United States despite red-flag warnings designed to deny them visas. Such obvious lapses had been remedied.

New tools kept coming on stream: armed unmanned drones in ever more sophisticated and deadly iterations, stealth helicopters capable of eluding radar detection, cloud-piercing radar and electronic sorting and tracking techniques for listening to telephone conversations, intercepting Internet traffic and analyzing the contents without having to resort to the tedious, time-consuming hands-on analysis of yore. Only a decade ago one specialist said tackling Al-Qaeda was like "looking for a needle in a needle stack." Just as crucial was vastly improved international cooperation on counterterrorism among the world's specialized services—and reduced feuding by rival national experts.

Before 9/11, with the notable exception of France, ever vigilant to prevent spillover from jihadi violence in its former Algerian colony, Western intelligence organizations were not seriously focused on Islamist extremism. Britain was still primarily worried about the Irish Republican Army, for instance, and Spain concerned with the Basque separatists of ETA. And in the United States, even after Al-Qaeda's deadly simultaneous attacks in 1998 on American embassies in East Africa and a U.S. destroyer in Aden in 2000, the incoming Bush team had brushed aside the outgoing White House counterterrorism czar's insistent warning of impending operations against the United States itself.

In the wake of 9/11, the "Alliance" system was established in Paris as a major international clearing house for sharing data on jihadi terrorism. So important were these exchanges that they worked smoothly even during the serious crisis between the Bush administration and President Jacques Chirac, who had publicly opposed the American-led invasion of Iraq in 2003. For Osama, the upshot was that it became simply too dangerous in the drone era for him and his senior cadres to move around once-safe tribal areas in the badlands along the Afghan-Pakistani border accompanied by a cohort of bodyguards. Osama the accomplished equestrian, the tall athletic Islamic hero on his white stallion in obvious emulation of the Prophet himself, Osama the famous marksman, Osama who liked to pop up unannounced to visit his followers, the scarlet pimpernel of jihadi terrorism, that is, Osama the accomplished self-publicist—all that was finished. Too dangerous. There was always that $25 million American bounty on his head to worry about.

Indeed, the price for his staying out of America's vengeful grasp had come down to living like a hermit (if being surrounded by two wives and children in the Abbottabad compound can be so described). Gradually, that famously bearded face, once ubiquitously seen on Third World walls, T-shirts and posters, faded away. Sahiba, Al-Qaeda's clandestine news agency—aptly named "the clouds"—did its best to keep up pretenses by producing infrequent video and audio clips of Osama, who dyed his white hair and beard for such performances. Osama became dependent on a trusted trilingual courier for episodic communication with Al-Qaeda's steadily eroded remnants among the surviving inner circle in Pakistan and those further afield in unruly Yemen, anarchic Somalia and the equally unwelcoming sands of the Western Sahara.

To prevent American electronic eavesdropping , the Abbottabad compound had no telephone line or internet connection. These precautions finally came to naught. The Americans eventually identified the tradecraft-wise courier who was careful enough to remove his cell phone batteries miles before he came to or left Osama's compound, but uncharacteristically had used a cell phone to call a third person on the U.S. watchlist. Deprived of the vital oxygen of easy access to the media and direct contact with his inner circle, Osama fell victim to a contemporary strain of Gresham's law governing pop culture heroes and villains in our Andy Warhol world of evanescent notoriety.

Isolated in his compound like Gloria Swanson's ageing movie queen in Sunset Boulevard, the white-bearded Osama, wrapped in a blanket like an old man suffering from rheumatism, was reduced to contemplating his former glory as he watched footage of his younger self on an ancient television set. What a comedown for a man who had delighted in the most recent electronic gadgets. And didn't just the Americans enjoy releasing that footage seized when they killed him! With the passage of time Osama commanded less obedience from those Al-Qaeda clones in Iraq, Yemen or the Western Sahara than McDonald's central ownership expects from the fast-food chain's worldwide franchisees.

In my mind's eye, I imagined Osama consoling himself by insisting his first name still was instantly recognized even in the world's meanest hamlet.

But the true measure of his irrelevance came out of the blue shortly after the New Year.

Abruptly, the long-frozen Arab world began shaking in ways that no one had predicted—not Western officials, not political scientists, and certainly neither Osama nor the equally startled long-enthroned regimes suddenly under threat. Barring a miracle, nothing he could do would restore his place in the imaginations of those he sought to impress: the West, especially the Americans, the Arabs and Muslims everywhere.

Starting in Tunisia of all places, North Africa's smallest state, spontaneous upheavals began sweeping Muslim societies from the Atlantic Ocean to the Persian Gulf. Final results from what became known as the "Arab Spring" are far from in. Their infrequent successes at best are still too unstable to lay claim to durability. Yet, at least pace-setting Tunisia and Egypt, where peaceful mass demonstrations drove out long-ensconced autocrats, kept pushing. They installed fledgling democratic institutions despite a lack of experience and seriously damaged economies deprived of essential hard currency receipts from now skittish foreign tourists.

What was clear was that the thousands who died demonstrating in often still uncertain struggles from Bahrain, Yemen and Syria to Libya and Morocco gave their lives for what they conceived as democracy, democracy plain and simple, not the "guided," "Islamist" or "peoples" varieties. Rarely, if ever, mentioned at the onset were jihad, Al-Qaeda, or even Islam, those essential touchstones for Osama. (Only in chaotic Yemen, and after several months of violent anti-government street demonstrations, did pro-Al-Qaeda jihadis start appearing and then in often confused circumstances suggesting that the beleaguered regime may have egged them on in hopes of rallying Western, especially American, support.)

Osama never had hidden his contempt for people power, elections and all the other trappings of democracy that the demonstrators so volubly championed. His strategy called for his "sworn" men, his phalanx of jihadi followers in Al-Qaeda, to reunite the umma, or Muslim faithful, by re-imposing the religious rule of the caliphate abolished in 1924 by Ataturk, the quintessentially secular founder of the Turkish republic. When you came down to it, Osama and the peaceful demonstrators for democracy shared but one thing: a desire to get rid of incumbent Muslim regimes they considered corrupt.

Osama wanted to do it by force and force alone—and certainly not by peaceful street demonstrations organized in part by Westernized, educated young men and women expert in the use of Twitter, Facebook and the Internet and aware of radical American academic theories about maximizing the influence of crowds. Bush in his time had talked the talk about necessary democratic reforms in the Muslim world, but stopped when rebuffed by conservative regimes warning "it's us or Osama." Early in his presidency Obama had held out his hand to Muslims in major speeches in Istanbul and Cairo, generating real, but short-lived, enthusiasm. That promise foundered on hard realities ranging from a stolen election in Iran to a rightwing Israeli prime minister who thwarted timid White House initiatives designed, among other things, to demonstrate that the United States could act decisively in the Middle East. But despite such manna for standard jihadi propaganda, opinion polls showed Muslim support for Al-Qaeda dropping, albeit without much improvement in America's abysmally low approval rates.

What had happened? Muslims now realized that by far most of Al-Qaeda's victims were fellow Muslims, killed, for example, in Iraq in the name of ancient hatreds reignited by the now fallen traditional Sunni ascendancy against the Shia majority. No setback was more telling than Osama's failure despite determined efforts to overthrow the Kingdom of Saudi Arabia, the Land of the Two Mosques and the Kaaba—and his birthplace. Osama had only set his sights on the American "far enemy" as a way to take over the Kingdom by hurting its protector, but his efforts before and after 9/11 were repulsed. Gradually, Muslims in Saudi Arabia and elsewhere came to see Osama as a nihilist, incapable of providing a viable model for stable Muslim governance. Perversely, was God in Al-Qaeda's jihadi version of Allah turning out to be The God That Failed?

As if to underline Al-Qaeda's hard times, Osama's own death was quickly followed by the liquidation of two senior associates. One was killed in Pakistan by a CIA drone acting on good intelligence. The other, Fazul Abdullah Mohammed, died a victim of bad luck barely a month after Osama. With a $5 million bounty on his head for his part in the 1998 attacks on the East African embassies, Fazul became lost in bad weather in the dead of night and mistakenly attempted to drive through a trigger-happy government checkpoint near the Somali capital of Mogadishu. His five languages, his mastery of disguise, even a rumored plastic surgery-altered face, did not save him.

It is dangerous to draw conclusions from isolated cases, especially when it comes to jihadi terrorists. Still, clearly the once imaginative and seemingly unstoppable success of early Al-Qaeda operations — with their signature simultaneous attacks in 1998 and 9/11—did give way in later years to sloppy implementation. Osama and his operatives no longer seemed capable of organizing the seamless spectaculars that in their heyday had been their worldwide trademark. So was it just that Lady Luck on December 27, 2009 was no longer smiling on jihadi terrorism when a well-educated young Nigerian trained in Yemen failed to ignite his explosive-laced underwear as his transatlantic airliner neared its destination of Detroit? Similarly, the gods of terrorism abandoned a young, recently naturalized man of Pakistani parentage who imperfectly triggered explosives packed in a car he left parked in New York's crowded Times Square on Saturday evening May 1, 2010. When smoke emerged from the car, two street vendors alerted mounted policemen, who called in the bomb disposal squad just in time.

Even when luck occasionally had deserted Western cities, the deadliest jihadi attacks inspired by Al-Qaeda in attention-guaranteed locales never came close to emulating 9/11's near 3,000 victims. For example, the Islamist suicide bombers' morning rush-hour attacks on Madrid's Atocha railway station on May 11, 2003, and the suicide bombers' underground and bus blasts in London on July 7, 2006, claimed "only" 191 and 56 lives, respectively. They remained the most deadly jihadi operations in Europe of the decade. The record suggested that Al-Qaeda has yet to regain the clout of the critical five years before 9/11 when Osama left Sudan and basically hoodwinked Mullah Omar, the Taliban leader, into allowing him to use Afghanistan as a sanctuary for planning his spectaculars.

Certainly that did not mean that jihadi acts of terror would not strike Western targets in future. Terrorism, like the poor, was not about to disappear any time soon. Did not the French have a saying that warned "not to insult the future"? In any event, Al-Qaeda's modus operandi was soon copied by others (although a key terrorist invention—the use of suicide belts—was the brainchild of the Tamil Tigers.) And, of course, any large-scale attack triggered the raw memory of past operations. On November 28, 2008, for example, a minutely planned seaborne commando raid against a main railway station, two luxury hotels, a Jewish center and other targets in the Indian economic capital of Mumbai took 164 lives. The assault was quickly traced back to the ISI. One of the problems of terrorist attacks, it turned out, was that each successive operation logically had to be ever more devastating to shock and impress. So many victims were getting killed every day in fighting in Iraq and Afghanistan that even multiple deaths by car bomb or suicide operation became commonplace, boring, just white noise and no longer automatically pre-empted media attention. And since fellow Muslims accounted for the overwhelming majority of those killed, such victims attracted less attention even in their native lands than did foreign victims. Such is the curious, but durable, lesson of covering violence and wars.

Osama and Al-Qaeda had fallen victim to that cynical news agency rule-of-thumb of my youth for deciding how many words to devote to deaths related to an accident, natural disaster or battle in the Third World. If memory serves, one American was worth two Brits, three Frenchmen, 30 Russians, 400 Egyptians, 1,000 Indians and 5,000 Chinese. While I was writing my book about Osama, I sometimes imagined he really was the brand new herald of transnational terrorism, a kind of free-floating source of inspiration unbeholden to any organized state and nestling in my mind's eye in the heavens over Central Asia like the god of the Druze.

Now I rather think at the end of the day Osama had become a pawn in Pakistani hands. He had been useful to keep the dollars flowing. Doubtless he would have been amused to know that his death had served to worsen already-accelerating bad relations between Pakistan and the United States so that they were snarling at each other in public. Osama alive, Pakistan and the United States indulged in nods and winks and went through the motions as partners. Osama dead, Washington might have been tempted to walk away from Afghanistan and Pakistan. But one of the more frightening ironies of the Osama era was that Pakistan showed increasing signs of coming apart because of its devotion to the jihadi groups it had deemed essential for pursuance of its "forward policy." Another failed state in theory could be lived with. But in 1998, just months before Osama's first big terrorist operation, Pakistan had exploded the first "Muslim" nuclear device and later was busy building bombs.

As tempting as it might be for the United States to walk away from "AFPAK," Washington's term for Afghanistan and Pakistan, the nuclear bombs, cutout jihadi groups and a military establishment shot through with sympathy for jihadi ideology made that impossible. So the United States would have to soldier on, albeit with the hope of a vastly reduced military footprint in South Asia and elsewhere. In the months immediately after Osama's death, the United States openly challenged a humiliated Pakistani army, stepping up the very drone attacks the ISI specifically wanted curtailed and cutting military aid a hefty $800 million to underscore Washington's displeasure with Pakistan's broken promises. A series of high-ranking American visitors made clear Pakistan was expected to toe the line, not complain.

Such a hard-ball approach made short shrift of the fiction of America's former quasi-alliance with Pakistan (which somewhat unconvincingly sought to activate its traditional default position: cozying up to China.) Such was the distaste of the Pakistani public for all things American that Washington's former enthusiasm for winning hearts and minds counted for little in Obama's recessional plans. Predicting how always-complicated American relations with Afghanistan and Pakistan (and their own relations with each other) could play out is a bootless exercise. At the very least, the United States wants to prevent Pakistani nuclear weapons from falling into the hands of jihadis, a task made more perilous by the army's increasingly Islamist officer corps. As regards to Afghanistan, Washington wants to avoid repeating the error of again walking away totally—as was done after the Soviet army's withdrawal a generation ago—and somehow to prevent Al-Qaeda and associates from re-establishing a sanctuary there.

Tall orders, all, especially in the absence of a still-distant grand regional diplomatic settlement. So it is noteworthy that some Pentagon buzz after Osama's death was reduced to how to sweeten the pot and win over Afghani acceptance of a small residual American contingent capable of keeping the Pakistanis "honest," that is, limiting terrorist attacks directed outside their territory. After all, the SEAL team that nailed Osama was launched from Afghanistan and returned there. Afghanistan as a sanctuary again? Osama might be excused for chuckling. The West less so.

To be sure at the end of the Osama decade the Empire Struck Back, got its man, but do Americans get to live happily ever after? Quite apart from more possible terrorism and the parlous state of their war-impoverished economy, Americans would be wise to factor in the damage Osama and Al-Qaeda persuaded them to inflict on their hallowed institutions, on American "soft" power and the way all of us are forced to live our lives now. What happened to the America once priding itself as the world's most open society? Just read the Patriot Act and see the limitations it has imposed on rights Americans once considered natural. As part of George W. Bush's now abandoned global war on terrorism, plenty of other

OSAMA

PREFACE

Writing about terrorism naturally means dealing—or trying to deal—with terrorists and those who combat them, and at firsthand if possible. Frankly, I cannot claim to have been particularly successful in winning the confidence of major actors on either side of that great divide. Suspicion is one of several characteristics they share, especially when it comes to being asked about their respective peculiar—and by definition secret—specialties. The fact is I totally failed to meet Osama bin Laden, but not for want of trying.

For two years I boxed the compass with letters and messages dispatched from a half dozen countries explaining my bona fides. I traveled extensively in the Muslim world and elsewhere to persuade interlocutors who claimed to be in touch with Osama that I wanted to meet him and, more especially, listen to his arguments at length. With all due respect to my television colleagues, theirs is a blunt instrument and one that rarely got beyond the slogans and injunctions that Osama masterfully manipulated in largely limiting his media exposure. His infrequent in-and-out news conferences and newspaper or magazine interviews were pretty much cut from the same limited cloth.

I wanted to spend time with Osama, a lot of time, indeed as much time as he would grant me. For some reason, I convinced myself he would welcome more than a quickie interview. So did various people who questioned me at length and gave me to understand that I had passed the test and they would help me. I argued that many decades as a foreign correspondent devoted to trying to understand the Third World, and more especially Muslim societies, qualified me for such extended treatment. In retrospect, I think I was fooling myself, since Osama was the master of the television interview and had no reason to welcome the in-depth séances I was proposing.

At one point, a helpful Pakistani colleague in Islamabad agreed to pass on a photocopy of a letter in English—and its Arabic translation—that I had sent many months earlier through a friend in Central Asia who claimed he had access to Osama in Afghanistan. In that letter, I once again mentioned my many earlier efforts to reach him, restated my purpose and asked if he had received my previous entreaties and copies of my books, which I had supplied various other interlocutors who had promised to deliver them. One, *Going All the Way: Christian Warlords, Israeli Adventurers and the War in Lebanon,* chronicled the Lebanese Christians' political suicide back in the '70s and '80s. The other, *After Such Knowledge, What Forgiveness? My Encounters with Kurdistan,* dealt with repeated betrayals of the Kurds, often at Western and, more specifically, American hands. I had hoped they would establish my credentials as a Middle East hand not uncritical of the West's checkered record in the region.

In any case, my Pakistani friend instructed me to call back after four days. I did so and was told to call back in another four days. When I did, my Pakistani colleague said that yes, my message had been delivered and that Osama even had a question of his own for me. And what might that be, I asked with growing excitement, momentarily believing that it must be a good omen and that after so many attempts I finally was in an exchange of sorts with Osama. "He wants to know who translated the letter into Arabic," said my colleague. Why, I asked? "Because he says the translation is terrible." (That might indeed have been the case since a Lebanese friend in Paris had dashed off the Arabic version while a courier waited impatiently to be on his way.)

I consoled myself as best I could: at least I had established that Osama had mastered English and had a sense of humor. Even that was not 100 percent sure since my exasperated Pakistani colleague, who had a pixieish side, may simply have invented the story to get me to stop pestering him. I was still toying with other schemes to get in touch with Osama when, a week or so later, seventeen American sailors died when the USS *Cole* was blown up in a suicide operation in the Yemeni port of Aden on October 12, 2000. The attack was immediately ascribed to Osama's Al-Qaeda organization. I then concluded that whatever chances I may have had of meeting Osama were dashed. Indeed, he never again was interviewed by Westerners.

Other key characters I did get to know ended up either dead, in jail or otherwise beyond my best efforts to talk to them again. If I had learned anything in a lifetime of dealing with dodgy people pretty much the world over, it was that information was the fruit of confidence, and confidence was earned by going back to the same well over and over again. It was a time-consuming approach understood by few editors.

I spent a very, very long evening with John O'Neill, the FBI's top counterterrorism expert in New York, who was something of a racetrack character. I figured the outing might be a bonding experience that would prove useful later on. I was frankly perplexed by his categorical views of some of the more shadowy aspects of the bin Laden saga that stumped me, but he at least was on the inside. The pub crawl certainly produced a mammoth hangover as well as many a lingering doubt. In midsummer of 2001 O'Neill resigned from the bureau under a cloud and became the World Trade Center's security chief at more than twice the money. I had high hopes that out of uniform, as it were, he would prove ever more enlightening. He was last seen alive heading back into the south tower about a quarter hour after it was attacked on September 11.

Other sources disappeared or otherwise escaped my grasp. When I was in Jordan in the spring of 2000 I became intrigued by the case of Khalil al-Deek, a Palestinian born on the Israeli-occupied West Bank, who, with an older brother, had first gone to Egypt before settling in California and becoming an American citizen. He had been in Pakistan since 1993, running a computer school and an Islamic Web site as well as sharing a bank account with a major Al-Qaeda operative named Abu Zubaydah. Or so the American government said.

Despite his U.S. nationality, Deek had been arrested in Pakistan and, without benefit of extradition procedure, summarily flown to Jordan (where all West Bank Palestinians are considered citizens) in December 1999, all within days of the discovery of a plot to blow up a major hotel and tourist sites to mark the millennium. Deek was said to be a kingpin, but I suspect it was easier to squeeze him for information in Jordan than in the United States, with its cumbersome insistence on due process of law. An American diplomat in Pakistan later told me, "In the U.S., Deek would have been out of jail in about thirty seconds. We had no case against him."

For two weeks his Jordanian lawyers kept dangling an interview in jail before me, but they never delivered.

As for Deek, he was never arraigned and thus never tried. He finally staged a hunger strike and after sixteen months in various Jordanian jails he was released, in part because his California family finally came to understand his rights as an American citizen and repeatedly asked probing questions about his odd incarceration. He headed back to Pakistan and doubtless to Afghanistan, where his Syrian-born wife had taken refuge in his absence. I never fully figured out what was going on, although a highly placed American in Amman did claim that early on Deek had sung. Deek's plight was simply an early example of "rendition," Washington's self-aggrandized right to grab suspects overseas (and sometimes to move them from one Third World country to another where interrogation techniques were more robust than those allowed in the United States).

Other sources I got to know slipped out of reach behind prison bars. In Brussels I had been cultivating a Tunisian-born Islamic radical named Tareq Maaroufi. He became implicated in the assassination in Afghanistan of Ahmad Shah Massoud, the anti-Taliban leader of the Northern Alliance known as the "Lion of Panjshir," just two days before the attacks on the United States. Maaroufi was sentenced on September 30, 2003, to six years in prison.[1] In London, another talkative source, an Egyptian Islamic radical named Yasser Sirri, was arrested on similar charges in October 2001. He was ordered released seven months later by a judge who ruled he had been set up as a "fall guy," but he was immediately rearrested on the strength of an American extradition request.

Also in London, Abu Qatada, a radical Palestinian preacher I knew, suddenly disappeared on December 15, 2001, just hours before a tough new law, the Anti-Terrorism and Security Act, would have allowed his indefinite incarceration. Wanted in eight countries on three continents, Abu Qatada certainly knew what lay in store had he remained in the run-down house in Acton, in west London, where I had visited him. Several weeks later he left a voice message on an Internet site advising his followers, "I'm safe, but just don't ask too much about me."

Such are the murky highways and byways of terrorism that some European counterterrorism officials suspected their British colleagues of striking a deal with this man—sometimes said to be Osama's top European representative—perhaps because even if Abu Qatada did not turn informer he would naturally risk being so regarded by his Muslim flock if indeed he did surface again, and be given a wide berth as a consequence. It was a police technique as old as the world. Coincidentally, dozens of Islamic radicals associated with Abu Qatada across Europe were jailed, charged with plotting acts of terrorism.

Oddly, I noted, the European specialists didn't give much credence to the possibility that Abu Qatada might have gone to ground on his own, thanks to an Islamic network akin to the ratline that smuggled Nazis out to Latin America when the Third Reich collapsed in 1945. I finally asked a French counterterrorism official why. He gave me a sideways look by way of suggesting that in the terrorism game, as in so many other domains, the British were still considered the past masters for good reason. They'd invented the rules in the nineteenth century and still were writing them. Northern Ireland, the Irish Republican Army and the Protestant extremists had honed their skills. (Abu Qatada was eventually arrested in London, almost a year later, but I doubt that changed the French view of his disappearance.)

Little had changed, it seemed, since the double-dealing so tellingly described in Joseph Conrad's "The Secret Sharer" and *Under Western Eyes* and Henry James's *The Princess Casamassima*. If only what passed for present-day facts were less dubious than the tales told in those masterpieces of fiction.

BUG IN THE ELEPHANT'S EAR

FOR DAYS AFTER September 11, 2001, I wondered if Osama bin Laden, along with the rest of the world, had watched the real-time footage of those fully fueled airliners, hijacked by suicidal pilots and their henchmen, as they rammed into the Pentagon and the twin towers of Manhattan's World Trade Center. For reasons I still do not completely fathom, everything else about 9/11, as the attacks soon were called, was subordinated for me to that possibility. Perhaps it was that in years past, high up in his Afghan redoubt carved into the Hindu Kush, he had indulged a rich man's fascination with gadgetry, delighting in showing visitors his computers, satellite telephones and dishes and other high-tech paraphernalia. Did he now savor life imitating art, a pastiche of kitsch reruns of Hollywood horror movies complete with plummeting bodies, billowing flames, imploding buildings, brave firemen rushing back up the stairs to their deaths? Did he appreciate the novelty of doomed airline passengers describing their predicament on state-of-the-art cell phones while other passengers heroically rushed their captors, determined to deflect their airliner-turned-missile from yet another landmark target?

At the time I doubted ironclad answers would be forthcoming. I was indulging in pure speculation, but speculation based on more than two frustrating years trying to figure Osama out. On past form, I felt, he would approve and perhaps claim he helped inspire, but still stop short of admitting he ordered, planned, much less micromanaged this extraordinary act of violence, guaranteeing his name a lasting footnote in the annals of terrorism. Such winking indirection had become his modus operandi stretching back almost a decade. It allowed him to insinuate a kind of global reach even when by any logical yardstick no irrefutable proof linked him to some of the acts of terrorism laid at his door. And, of course, in his mind at least, it distanced him from those he had organized.

Then less than a fortnight before Christmas, a grainy, partly inaudible amateur videotape was released by a hesitant Bush administration wary of its seeming suspiciously good luck in obtaining the improbably self-incriminating "mother of all smoking guns." For the administration, the cassette's contents were literally almost too good to be true.

Entertaining some fifty to sixty dinner guests in Kandahar just days before the rapid collapse of the Taliban regime in mid-November, an almost languid Osama was shown providing chapter and verse for a hanging judge's fantasy. Right down to the occasional chuckle and laugh, the chilling tale the lanky six-foot-four Saudi told without remorse would make even a nineteenth-century melodrama villain blanch in disbelief. And indeed disbelief was how much of the Muslim world greeted the cassette, whether out of denial, because the contents seemed too pat or because the doubters could not understand why Osama would have been so arrogant, careless or plain stupid to have said what the cassette had him saying.

(If anything, the outraged accusations of fraud were somewhat subdued, perhaps reflecting the then still recent defeat of the Taliban regime and the initial disruption of Osama's Al-Qaeda organization or at least of its frontline foot soldiers. Equally off-putting to the worldwide Muslim audience he assiduously courted was his single-minded interest in Saudi Arabia to the exclusion of Kashmir, Palestine, Chechnya or other Islamic conflicts he normally championed.)

The Bush administration did not see fit to dispel the mystery of the cassette's provenance in an effort to bolster the credibility of its bona fides. For reasons elucidated neither at the time nor later, the U.S. government did no more than hint it had been found in a private house in the eastern Afghan city of Jalalabad, had been rushed to Washington in late November, had been checked and double-checked and had provoked a sharp debate about the wisdom of releasing its overly providential contents. The government's hesitation and Muslim doubts were understandable because on the tape a coldly dispassionate Osama uncharacteristically corroborates key bits of information and surmises that the Federal Bureau of Investigation, the Central Intelligence Agency and other investigators the world over had so painstakingly pieced together.

He accurately listed the nationalities and sometimes the names of the nineteen-man suicide squad, all but four his Saudi compatriots. Osama confirmed the existence of four hijacking teams, rejoiced in the tradecraft that deliberately kept each in the dark about the others' existence. He explained their division between the four witting pilots and the Saudi "muscle" who, he chuckled, learned the exact nature of their suicide mission only "just before boarding" the four airliners to cow their passengers into submission with box cutters once the plane was in the air.[1] Osama said he knew five days in advance that the operations would take place on September 11 and had a radio tuned in ready to hear the first plane hit the Trade Center's north tower.

"Be patient," he then told his "overjoyed" guests: more was to come, as it indeed did over the next hour or so. He recounted that in the planning stage his engineering training had helped him calculate the number of likely deaths from the explosive impact of a nearly fully fueled airliner on the twin towers' metal structures. He acknowledged his surprise that they collapsed completely. "All that we had hoped for," he allowed, was the destruction of "three or four floors" where the aircraft hit and those above the impact.

And, as it turned out, indeed I had been—almost—right about his watching the crashes on television. His spokesman, Sulaiman Abu Ghaith, had turned on a television set in an adjoining room and seen the first run of the constantly repeated footage of the planes hitting the twin towers before excitedly summoning Osama. "I tried to tell him about what I saw," the spokesman recounted, "but he made a gesture with his hands, meaning: 'I know, I know.'"

THE SPECIALIST LITERATURE long ago concluded that modern terrorism's objective was to inflict maximum casualties with maximum publicity. In those terms Osama had succeeded beyond his wildest dreams. For days on end television screens the world over repeatedly showed the scenes of horror that consumed nearly 3,000 lives (and initially were feared to have killed more than twice as many). Yet his very success left a string of tantalizing questions unanswered. Logically, he must have realized that the United States would react—and massively. Yet perhaps his gift for meticulous reckoning finally had gone awry or his increasingly audacious acts of violence emboldened him to the point that he felt invulnerable. He had preached that the Americans were paper tigers so long and hard that he could be excused for relishing the disarray that overtook the U.S. government and kept a humiliated President George W. Bush out of Washington for nine embarrassing hours after the fourth and final airliner crashed in Pennsylvania.

Had such cocksure reasoning now convinced him the United States dared not mount a major punitive expedition in Afghanistan, where he had come to believe his own distorted propaganda claims that his Arab volunteers all but single-handedly defeated the Soviet Red Army in the 1980s? Osama was not alone in suggesting the dangers of a new foreign intervention in Afghanistan. Russian veterans warned the United States of the horrors they had experienced there. Those tales of Afghan savagery and resentment of foreigners, reinforced by nineteenth-century massacres of British troops at Afghan hands, had played no small role in dissuading President Bill Clinton and his successor from mounting a major military operation to punish the increasingly cheeky Taliban regime and its Al-Qaeda guests. (In fact, high-tech American weaponry, combined with wads of cash and local Afghan allies, initially routed the foot soldiers of Osama's Al-Qaeda organization and its Taliban protectors with surprising ease and speed in what more properly should be called a campaign rather than a war. If there was going to be an Afghan quagmire, more likely than not it would take the form of trying to maintain a modicum of law and order on the cheap rather than investing in the "nation-building" that was so doctrinally repugnant to the administration.)

If Osama had planned his own endgame, was he resigned to his fate and even anxious to embrace the martyrdom he had so helped popularize? He may have reckoned that he and Al-Qaeda could not reasonably hope to match, much less outdo, 9/11. With his health then rumored to be undermined by an implacable kidney affliction and an often-incurable heart condition called Marfan's syndrome that threatens early death, had he decided to bow out at the top of his form, at age forty-four, rather than risk an uncertain future that might tarnish his legend? Such was the subject of endless speculation and the stuff of a myth that he and his followers were intent on creating.

But in the practical world what mattered immediately was that Osama, deliberately or by miscalculation, had acted like a Muslim Samson. He had brought the temple down on his Taliban hosts and jeopardized the peerless Afghan sanctuary that had allowed his Al-Qaeda to grow without serious challenge and to extend its operations virtually worldwide. The tantalizing mystery of his fate masked that reality. Inconclusive mountain battles and collusion with like-minded Islamic radicals in Pakistan helped maintain the illusion of intact Al-Qaeda discipline and strength. Well into 2002, Al-Qaeda and Taliban operatives found refuge in the wild and wooly tribal areas along the Afghan border in Pakistan's Northwest Frontier Province, which had scarcely changed since Kipling's day. Yet the Pakistanis caught hundreds of his operatives, many of them mere foot soldiers, and turned them over to the Americans. In April his key young lieutenant, Abu Zubaydah, was wounded and captured in a shoot-out 200 miles to the east, in Faisalabad, near the Indian frontier. In September Ramzi bin al-Shibh, a key cog in the Hamburg cell entrusted with the 9/11 operation, was captured in teeming Karachi, Pakistan's chaotic and lawless principal port.

Indeed there is a world of difference between having the free run of an entire country and the uncertainties of clandestine refuge in Pakistan and elsewhere. Whatever Al-Qaeda's long-standing connections, Pakistan now was run by a general who had stopped openly flirting with Islamist radicals and had thrown in his lot with Washington only days after September 11. Until then, ever since Osama had returned to Jalalabad in 1996, he had done pretty much what he wanted in Afghanistan and Pakistan. Money and old networks stitched together nearly twenty years earlier during the war against the Soviet occupation of Afghanistan stood him in good stead in both countries.

Osama had come so very far since the 1980s, when he had arrived in Afghanistan as an untested youth with little experience but great ambitions. He, who then had been manipulated, had become a past master of flattery, influencing, even threatening those he needed for his purposes. Over the years he had learned to cut corners while still projecting to his followers the image of an uncompromisingly pure man of action. For all his outward devotion to the details of obscurantist Islamic practice, he thought nothing of transgressing his Taliban hosts' puritanical rules. Not for him were Taliban prohibitions on such symbols of modernity as computers, television sets, audio- and videotapes, which were ritually draped by the religious police from trees as satanic works of the infidels.

Above all else, he had been careful to cultivate Mullah Mohammed Omar, the rustic one-eyed Pashtun Taliban leader who one day in Kandahar had donned the cloak that legend claimed was the Prophet's own, thus proclaiming himself the commander of the faithful. In some American circles it became popular to insist that Osama had turned Mullah Omar into his malleable creature. Initially, the record showed no more than that Osama was indeed constantly careful to keep him sweet. Osama supplied him with fancy four-wheel-drive vehicles, cash and flattery, for he knew his own precarious presence in Afghanistan depended solely on Mullah Omar's sufferance. Osama was well aware that some hardheaded Taliban leaders had sought to persuade Mullah Omar to jettison a foreigner who, for all his Islamic credentials in the war against the Red Army, increasingly represented a mortal danger to their regime.

In advertised as well as secret meetings, American emissaries constantly reminded Taliban representatives in no uncertain terms that time was running out, that Osama's next terrorist operation would at long last mean war. Such foreign warnings appeared to have a perverse effect on Mullah Omar. Already back in 1998, soon after the truck-bomb attacks on American embassies in Nairobi and Dar es Salaam that August, he had jeopardized official Saudi financing when the Kingdom's intelligence chief, Prince Turki al-Faisal, showed up in Kandahar mistakenly convinced Omar would honor an earlier pledge to hand Osama over.

Throughout 2001, telltale signs chronicled Osama's growing ascendancy over Mullah Omar. Osama openly defied the formal Taliban prohibition on his public pronouncements, staged an ostentatious wedding for a son and privately encouraged the destruction of the two giant Buddhas in Bamian and other pre-Islamic art, in keeping with the idol-smashing convictions of the puritanical Saudi Islamic faith of his upbringing.[2] But for all his careful cultivation of Mullah Omar, little if anything suggests Osama bothered to inform his host of his plans for September 11, which were a good two years in the making. To have so taken any of the Taliban into his confidence would only have encouraged dissension among those Afghan leaders who increasingly feared that Omar was allowing Osama to compromise their destiny. For years, for all the public show of solidarity with Osama—and their unconvincing claims to have him under their thumbs—Taliban leaders had argued privately among themselves about the obvious dangers of harboring a guest so patently determined to march to his own drummer. Those long-muffled dissensions were confirmed once the Taliban regime was dismantled in November 2001.

Long before, even the dimmest Afghan had an inkling of what was going on in dozens of Al-Qaeda training sites scattered around Kabul, Kandahar, Jalalabad and rural locations, many of them built into the Hindu

Kush during the war against the Soviet Union. After all, some camps simultaneously housed Al-Qaeda terrorist trainees, Taliban conscripts and cannon fodder for Pakistan's irredentist campaign in Kashmir to weaken archenemy India. The more hardheaded Taliban thought of their self-styled Islamic emirate as a state, while recognizing that the United Nations and various nongovernmental humanitarian organizations provided what passed for the few government services on offer to the population. Osama indulged Mullah Omar's hankering for renewing the caliphate to run the Sunni Muslim world that Ataturk had abolished in 1924 soon after establishing the Turkish Republic. In fact, Osama was more interested in the process of getting there—jihad and his radical methodology of spreading holy war—than in the mundane business of running a government. And so Mullah Omar and the Taliban were expendable.

IT SOON BECAME an article of faith for Americans that September 11 utterly changed their lives. Beauty, or in this case horror, was in the eye of the beholder. One of Americans' great strengths is their ability to live in the present and think in the future to such an extent that it is difficult to predict what enduring scars 9/11 will leave on the American psyche. Who before September 11 could have predicted that the Bush administration would abandon its inward-looking election platform and embark on a policy seemingly determined to reorder the Middle East, an undertaking that had brought woe to so many previous world powers? But more mundanely, what demonstrably changed was the modus operandi of terrorism; in that, 9/11 marked a radical departure.

Terrorists had hijacked planes for decades. Terrorists also had planned to blow up airliners—indeed as many as twelve simultaneously—and their passengers and crew over the Pacific in 1994. Algerian Islamic radicals took over an Air France Airbus at Algiers airport on December 24, 1994, and threatened to crash it into the Eiffel Tower, every bit as much the embodiment of France as the twin towers and Pentagon symbolized the United States. An unheeded 131-page Library of Congress study in 1999 had mentioned similar disaster scenarios using hijacked and explosives-laden aircraft to target the Pentagon, White House or CIA headquarters.[3] Novelist Tom Clancy, in his 1994 best seller *Debt of Honor,* imagined an angry pilot crashing a fully fueled airliner into the U.S. Capitol, killing the president and most of the senators and representatives gathered in joint session to hear him. But never before in the contemporary history of terrorism had so much long-range planning, money and educated manpower been involved so far away from the masterminds' terra cognita, indeed in the enemy's very heartland.

The attacks surpassed everything in terrorism's rich annals, stretching back to the Old Man of the Mountain, whose votaries so intimidated Middle Eastern contemporaries that they were dubbed Assassins, a corruption of the Arabic for "hashish," to whose steadying effects their victims incorrectly ascribed their audacious and calculated attacks. From the fastness of Alamut castle, built on a narrow rock ridge high in the Elburz mountain range of northern Iran, Hasan-i Sabbah, starting in 1090 and for the next thirty-five years, personally ran a revolutionary Shi'a splinter sect called the Ismailis dedicated to overthrowing the established mainstream Sunni Muslim order. He and his successors, all known as the Old Man of the Mountain, over the next century and a half indoctrinated their followers in the unprecedented fine art of planned, systematic and long-term use of terror as a political weapon. They thus could qualify as the first terrorists, combining fanatical zeal and cool planning. Their only murder weapon was the dagger. A point of honor held they should not seek to escape once they had fulfilled their missions. Their preferred targets were chosen from among the ruling elite. The first victim, the great vizier Nizam al-Mulk, was stabbed to death in 1092, and Hasan-i Sabbah exulted, "The killing of this devil is the beginning of bliss."

As the Assassins' modern chronicler, Bernard Lewis, noted: "It was the first of a long series of such attacks, which, in a calculated war of terror, brought death to two caliphs, sovereigns, princes, generals, governors, even divines who had condemned Ismaili doctrines and authorized the suppression of those who professed them."[4] Most victims were Sunnis. But prominent Crusader leaders also died at their hands, and Saladin, the Crusaders' great Sunni opponent, twice narrowly escaped their plots. The Assassins worked as an authoritarian secret society, with a system of oaths and initiations and a graded hierarchy of rank and knowledge, and kept an honor roll of assassinations in Alamut, complete with the names of the victims and their executioners.

The first Old Man of the Mountain extended his authority to a series of craggy mountain redoubts in Iran, and more safe-haven strongholds were later acquired farther afield. Assassin agents operated in Iraq, Syria, Egypt and beyond, insinuating themselves into their adversaries' innermost defenses with elaborate disguises, variously passing themselves off as monks, merchants or soldiers. They struck in mosques or inside a prince's tent, obliging rulers to adopt costly, often useless, security measures. One Old Man of the Mountain contemptuously brushed aside mighty Saladin's threat of reprisal by commenting, "By God, it is astonishing to find a bug in an elephant's ear or a gnat biting a statue."

Eventually the Assassins lost their sting. By 1273, Baybars, the great Mameluk sultan who drove the Crusaders from their last Outremer enclave in the Holy Land, forced the remaining Assassin castles in Syria to submit. A generation earlier the all-conquering Mongols seized the Assassin fortresses in Iran, and burned Alamut's fabled library. The lessons that Lewis, the historian, drew from the Assassins in large part apply to many other terrorist groups. They were seen as a profound threat to the existing order. They were no isolated phenomenon, but part of a "long series of messianic movements, at once popular and obscure, impelled by deeprooted anxieties, and from time to time exploding in outbreaks of revolutionary violence." They channeled "wild beliefs and aimless rage of the discontented into an ideology and an organization which, in cohesion, discipline and purposive violence, have no parallel in earlier or in later times." And in the end they failed and failed totally.

Osama did not think in terms of failure. Whatever his brand of terrorism, he was thoroughly in tune with his times, and that meant capturing, indeed terrorizing, the mass mind, not just striking down the elite. Symbolic, evocative targets are the very bedrock of any major act of modern terrorism. In those terms, short of employing a nuclear bomb or a massive biological or chemical attack, it was difficult to imagine topping thousands of victims working at the financial heart of the richest nation in history or an entire wing left in smoldering ruins at the military headquarters of the world's only superpower. By comparison, Osama's earlier terrorist exploits were rudimentary finger exercises, mere variations on standard car bombs and other explosive devices used for decades. Nonetheless, those exploits had firmly put him on the map of Third World grievance. In many Muslim eyes those operations had transformed and vaulted him into the exalted status of desert ascetic, Che Guevara, Robin Hood, Saladin and Avenging Angel of Death rolled into one and directed against the all-powerful, arrogant and infidel United States.

But then the giant had only shrugged. This time the Americans' howl of pain was heard around the world. Taking the United States down a peg—

making Americans feel the anger and pain of the rest of the world—in the age of the global, wired village also exerted an attraction far beyond the wildest limits of Islamic radicalism. Crazy, evil, call it what you will, but 9/11 represented more than mere schadenfreude, more than a new twist in the complicated love-hate pulsations that the world's paramount powers have generated since the beginning of time. As Americans grieved for their dead in New York, Washington and Pennsylvania, they could not say they had not been warned. Yet, outside the ranks of counterterrorism specialists, the ever more blatant threats were scarcely heeded. For nearly five years bin Laden had kept saying to anyone who would listen that all Americans, civilian and military without distinction, were fair game anywhere in the world. And on at least two occasions he had demonstrated he meant exactly what he said.

Only the previous June in federal court in lower Manhattan four Al-Qaeda operatives had been sentenced to life imprisonment for involvement in near-simultaneous suicide truck-bomb attacks against the U.S. embassies in Kenya and Tanzania on August 7, 1998. Twelve Americans and 212 Africans died in those blasts. And on October 12, 2000, seventeen American sailors were killed when an explosives-laden fiberglass skiff maneuvered by two suicidal Al-Qaeda members rammed the USS *Cole* during a brief refueling stop off the Yemeni port of Aden. Again bin Laden's responsibility seemed patent, albeit not yet established in court. In the summer of 2001 Osama promised the United States ever more deadly punishment in one of his increasingly frequent promotional videocassettes smuggled out of Afghanistan and eagerly lapped up by half-horrified, half-admiring Arab satellite television audiences. Interspersed between snippets of his previous television interviews and combat-training shots was Osama, reading a poem extolling the attack on the warship lulled by "the illusion of its own power" and promising Americans that "limbs will be scattered everywhere."

By then, of course, he had a proven track record that could not be ignored. But for American officials who worried about Osama, future Al-Qaeda operations were all but penciled in as the price of doing business in a nasty, distant, but crucial neighborhood involving oil. In the otherwise "no body bag" America bequeathed by the Vietnam War, oil was the one commodity worth expending lives on. Traditional symbols of national sovereignty—embassies or warships—had lost their luster in a postmodern world. Somehow it had become easier to accept losing diplomats—and even servicemen who, after all, were sent abroad to die for their country—in some back-of-beyond place ordinary Americans had never heard of.

Then the World Trade Center was reduced to rubble, vaporizing the long-complacent American sense of invulnerability. Most of the victims were civilians, and that is what Americans found so hard to accept. The victims—Salvadorean busboys, Irish cops and firemen, WASP lawyers, Jewish and Indian bank employees—were a new-century but real-life equivalent of a World War Two B movie with a corny ethnic infantry squad. Osama had warned that all Americans were fair game to be killed, and now he had done it. From his perspective, the World Trade Center was the perfect symbol for everything he hated about the United States—its wealth, its insouciant indifference to the problems of others, its master-of-the-universe self-confidence.

WHATEVER ELSE the September attacks would come to mean, they abruptly ended America's decade-long holiday from history, introduced by the Cold War's demise and a smug, neo-isolationist illusion that somehow an all-powerful United States could benefit from globalization while withdrawing into Fortress America protected by anti-missile missiles. Al-Qaeda's daring, stealth, patience, dedication, statecraft, simultaneity—and pure luck—were as breathtaking as was this most massive intelligence failure since Japan's "day of infamy" attack on Pearl Harbor on December 7, 1941, that plunged the United States into World War Two. (I was an eight-year-old then and remember Pearl Harbor as if it happened yesterday. I wonder if a boy that age today will remember September 11 as distinctly six decades hence.)

In the immediate aftermath, such was the shock that bin Laden's suddenly nervous Taliban hosts in Afghanistan, and even some Westernized Muslims, sought to question his responsibility for the attacks. They lamely insisted that the requisite savvy was beyond their Third World selves. Initially in the outer, know-nothing fringes of radical Islam, then uncritically on the Al-Jazeera satellite television broadcasts—Osama's favorite outlet and normally the Arab world's most trustworthy news source—the old defense mechanism of denial made its discredited appearance. The Israelis were blamed with the supposedly irrefutable canard that insisted no Jews had showed up for work at the World Trade Center because they knew the attack was coming. As the months went by, many Arabs came to terms with the facts and the often unflattering implications of the attacks for their own societies.[5]

Muslims were not the only conspiracy theorists. Within hours of the attacks, some senior American officials past and present—as well as Israeli generals and spymasters—found it irresistible to credit Saddam Hussein's intelligence services with providing the vital technical support required to ensure the conspiracy's success. Only Iraq, it was argued, could have trained the suicide pilots without their flight lessons arousing suspicion. (Testimony before the independent inquiry by counterterrorism coordinator Richard A. Clarke on March 24, 2004, made clear that Bush sought to establish an Iraq link with the 9/11 attacks.) What better way to settle Saddam Hussein's hash a decade after President Bush's father mistakenly left him on his Baghdad throne to spoil the "new world order" that was briefly touted to replace the Cold War. Then it quickly came to light that the suicide pilots had learned how to fly in American flight-training schools from Florida to Arizona, from Oklahoma to Minnesota. Soon elements in the Czech government, including Prime Minister Milos Zeman, insisted an Iraqi intelligence agent had indeed met Mohammad Atta, the Egyptian who allegedly masterminded the suicide hijackings, during a brief stopover in Prague the previous year; within weeks foot-leather reporters cast serious doubts on the suggestion, and before 2001 was out, cooler heads in Prague, including Czech President Vaclav Havel, elegantly backed off such claims. But in the United States, those in and out of the administration determined to tie Iraq to the September 11 attacks, kept the charges alive as a way of justifying plans to overthrow Saddam Hussein. Only in the spring did Bush administration officials reluctantly admit that, despite their best efforts, no evidence justified the accusation.[6] But opinion polls consistently showed that most Americans believed in the link. This helped justify the war to unseat Saddam.

The same "get Saddam" lobby also stoutly asserted that only Iraq, which repeatedly had used chemical weapons against its Iranian foes and its own Kurdish fellow countrymen in the 1980s, could have supplied the anthrax-laced envelopes that within weeks began showing up at American news organizations, Congress and ordinary homes and that eventually killed five men and women. Or so argued the conspiracy theorists before further investigation indicated a disgruntled American scientist in the specialized world of chemical weaponry as a more likely villain. The case remains unsolved.

Yet as disparate shards of information about 9/11 were pieced together with amazing speed, the tale they told was essentially one of systematic exploitation of the very openness of the United States that bin Laden and other Islamic radicals had come so obsessively to despise and fear. Quite apart from the chaos and panic caused by 9/11, bin Laden doubtless hoped that President Bush would overreact and thus validate his criticism of American society. For a country and administration caught so totally off guard, the United States and its then untested president initially performed with reassuring deftness bordering on sophistication. Only once, at the "Ground Zero" site of the pulverized twin towers, did Bush make the mistake of playing into Osama's hands by describing America's coming riposte as a "crusade," a word that had long since lost its religious connotations for Westerners, but not Muslims. Bush avoided statements smacking of "America versus Islam" and the "clash of civilizations" that Osama hoped to entrain. In those first few days the president reassured America's growing Muslim population, denouncing scattered acts of anti-Islamic rage and proclaiming he would not allow terrorism to curtail basic American freedoms.

But he also rallied the nation by declaring open-ended war against the "the evil one," vowing to lay hands on Osama Wild West–style, "dead or alive," and to smash Al-Qaeda and all terrorism wherever it lurked. The "us versus them" simplification of his language was excused as heady talk in parlous times, the kind of tough words expected of a former governor of Texas. He pleasantly surprised domestic and foreign critics outraged by his previous disdain for international commitments. In an impressive replay of his father's success in putting together a coalition to liberate Kuwait from Saddam's grasp in 1990, the president obtained Arab and other key international support for the U.S. expedition in Afghanistan. To win over Muslim nations, U.S. diplomats invented "terrorism with global reach." The term was concocted to exempt local groups violently opposed to Israeli occupation of Arab land, such as Hamas and Islamic Jihad in Palestine and Hezbollah in Lebanon. But once the Taliban were defeated this distinction disappeared.

The Bush doctrine soon meant an ill-defined global war against all terrorists and anyone who aided or abetted them in any way. Despite the administration's lack of a discernible exit strategy in the president's open-ended "war against terrorism," American public opinion overwhelmingly went along with Attorney General John Ashcroft's right-wing agenda. The government quickly rounded up more than a thousand foreign Muslims, held many incommunicado for long periods on visa technicalities and deprived them of access to lawyers under the provisions of a far-reaching law, the USA Patriot Act, that was rushed through Congress. Legal historians consoled themselves, recalling that previous wartime administrations had restricted civil liberties even more. Foreign governments facing their own challenges—from Israel and Algeria to Turkey, from Russia to the Philippines—leapt at the chance to gain Washington's favor by describing their opponents as terrorists. The ghost of Metternich, that nineteenth-century exponent of European reaction, was alive and well in Washington. Even before 9/11, Israeli Prime Minister Ariel Sharon compared Palestinian leader Yasser Arafat to bin Laden. In its wake the comparison took on a life of its own in traumatized America, although it was belied by the facts on the ground. Neither Islamist nor nationalist Palestinian opposition to Israeli occupation wanted anything to do with Osama.

As the panic at home gradually subsided, the administration's approach reawakened unhappy memories of legal excesses committed in the Palmer raids against suspected Communists after World War One, the preventive detention of Japanese–Americans following Pearl Harbor and Senator Joseph McCarthy's anti-Communist witch hunt in the early 1950s. Legislation restricting already curtailed rights of foreign residents and extending police powers sailed through both houses of Congress. Few Americans outside legal professionals, civil libertarians (representing both right and left) and spokesmen for the Arab and wider Muslim communities seemed upset. But an outspoken judiciary helped redress the balance. By mid-2002, in a series of forthright decisions, courts across the United States began questioning what civil libertarians denounced as star-chamber excesses of the Department of Justice.

OSAMA SHREWDLY had seen that the United States was the ideal theater for his operations. He grasped how America worked a great deal better than the United States understood Al-Qaeda. His operatives had a sixth sense for the system and its weaknesses. They realized the Immigration and Naturalization Service was a quintessentially unworkable bureaucracy unable to keep track of the some 10 million illegal foreign residents who had overstayed their visas. In the brand-new century, and to its credit, America was awash with more immigrants from the world over than at any time in the past hundred years. The United States traditionally took in smart foreigners with special talents and the unskilled willing to do the dirty work that more established Americans disdained. Osama's operatives were drawn from both categories.

In an America accustomed to the presence of foreigners, discreet and dedicated Arab plotters operating in small teams raised no eyebrows. All but four of the hijackers were from Saudi Arabia, America's single most important Arab ally. As such they entered the country with legal passports issued in their own names and valid, and easily obtained visas. They made a point of keeping out of trouble, dressing neatly and spending money. They were a self-contained unit. And they stayed clear of various native-born Americans involved in what the Department of Justice charged were Al-Qaeda sleeper cells trained in Afghanistan.

Money and the quality of key plotters made all the difference. These men were the polar opposites of bin Laden's typical low-level radical Islamic operatives. Once abroad on missions, his summarily educated operatives routinely had run afoul of the law because they often traveled on grossly doctored papers, lived in low-rent neighborhoods and were reduced to welfare and credit-card fraud or theft of car radios, cell phones and computers for survival. For some operations, a senior Al-Qaeda agent arrived on the scene to put the conspirators through their paces, then disappeared abroad before the plot was actually executed. Despite such precautions, many of these expendable agents tended to end up on police blotters.

This time the leaders and auxiliaries were well schooled and often middle class. They spoke English sufficiently well to avoid arousing suspicion among Americans long used to foreign accents among the country's large foreign-born population. In keeping with elementary tradecraft suggested in their training manuals, they eschewed Saudi-style calf-length garments called *thobes*. They sacrificed the beards many jihadis adopted as badges of Islamic honor and instead were clean-shaven and wore Western clothes. If they attended the mosque for Friday prayers, they were careful not to attract attention as radicals. Blending in was the order of the day. They knew their way around: two of them were cool enough not to panic when caught speeding in Florida's Broward County and indeed were able to drive off without hindrance after contritely accepting their tickets.

From the 1920s on, radical Islam had attracted the well educated, often those with college degrees in engineering and other sciences, as if somehow such exact disciplines could help apply the precise formulae of modern technology to the propagation of the faith. Iran's Islamic revolution in 1978–1979 had attracted many science students. So did Algeria's Islamic Salvation Front before it was banned in 1992. But this was the first time so many members of the elite were prepared to sacrifice their lives for the cause in a suicide operation.

September 11 was also the first time Al-Qaeda was willing to go first class to attain its goals. The operation was two or more years in the planning. Yet Americans were astounded by how much havoc the suicide teams wreaked with "only" the $500,000 government investigators estimated the operation cost. Americans alone would find that a small sum. In fact, 9/11 cost exponentially more than any of Osama's previous operations, but it was dwarfed by the annual U.S. counterterrorism budget of more than $10 billion that proved so spectacularly unequal to its task.

The twin towers and Pentagon attacks involved significant and repeated injections of cash, especially to train the pilots for more than a year, but also to keep the Saudi "muscle" in the United States for months on end without arousing suspicion. Osama finally had understood the limits of terrorism on the cheap and thus transformed the entire genre. For years, Western counterterrorism specialists had fantasized about urbane, well-dressed, multilingual operatives capable of obtaining visas, purchasing airline tickets, communicating via e-mail and generally fending for themselves. In retrospect, it was amazing it took Osama so long to catch on. One reason may have been his own attitude to money. For all his reputed personal wealth and funds at his disposal, Osama, like many wealthy Saudis, had a reputation as something of a skinflint. But this time in his terms he had splurged.

The overall cost arguably represented ten times more than Al-Qaeda spent on blowing up the American embassies in East Africa in 1998 or what the sustained campaign of terror bombings in the Paris metro cost in 1995. In December 1999, Ahmad Ressam, an Algerian trained in Al-Qaeda's Afghan camps, was dispatched to Canada with $12,000 in cash and left to his own devices to pick his henchmen and target. He chose the Los Angeles airport. But Ressam, who spoke little English, was arrested after an astute U.S. customs officer at the Canadian border in Washington State stopped his car and discovered explosives in its trunk.

Still, the investment in the 9/11 operations in its way was parsimonious as well as sophisticated. Most of the pilots trained just enough to learn to fly and turn airliners. (One early story that turned out to be apocryphal had Zacarias Moussaoui, the suspected "twentieth" hijacker, jailed for allegedly informing an alert Minnesota flight-school instructor that he was interested only in learning to steer, not to take off or land.) Even the weapons used to gain control of the airliners were mere box cutters, cheap even in the land of the Saturday Night special and much easier to slip past airport metal detectors.

IN TABLOID TERMS, bin Laden, the Saudi multimillionaire's son turned Islamic Goldfinger, reigned over hermetic, worldwide sleeper cells loosely linked to a nebulous, stateless enterprise guided from the quintessential failed state, the Taliban's Afghanistan. Western counterterrorism specialists could only pine for the comparative simplicities of now-extinct Cold War–era terrorism, with its predictable links to the Soviet bloc or revolving patrons for Palestinian splinter-group operatives among radical Arab regimes. Nostalgia aside, the truth was more complex, disturbing and grounded in past experience, at least for its inspiration. For starters, neither Al-Qaeda nor the Taliban turned out to be that hard to penetrate had U.S. intelligence been operating on the ground. The case of John Walker Lindh, an American convert to Islam who was captured in Afghanistan in November 2001, and later sentenced to twenty years in prison, disposed of the intelligence community's insistence that only relatives of established Al-Qaeda members need apply.

More disturbing was the U.S. intelligence community's numbing mantra that Al-Qaeda represented a brand-new breed, free-floating and thus immune from the traditional pressures that states brought to bear on their counterparts harboring terrorists for their own purposes. By the time Al-Qaeda started operating at full tilt, the Sudan and Yemen had thought better of their loose arrangements with Osama. More obvious still were the shortsighted policies of two increasingly vulnerable states—Pakistan and Saudi Arabia—and American policy-makers' failure to work out effective strategies to deal with them.

In the absence of a clear line from Washington, American foreign-policy specialists tinkered as best they could to keep periodic crises under control. But 9/11 embarrassingly exposed to public view the private contortions required to do so. The result was every diplomat's ultimate nightmare—that moment when the inevitable compromises and the practiced aversion of the eyes that lubricate relations with the outside world come under the furious gaze of outraged politicians and the general public back home, suddenly apprised of messy international realities.

More embarrassing still was the indigence of the American intelligence community. In Pakistan and Afghanistan, the United States was largely dependent on leftover agents from the anti-Soviet jihad and intelligence assets controlled by its Pakistani counterparts. And that meant being blindsided about Afghanistan. Pakistani intelligence was actively pursuing an agenda diametrically opposed to helping the United States bring pressure on the Taliban or on Al-Qaeda. Pakistani policy was dictated by the army's desire to further the interests of the Taliban in the hope of eventually controlling a friendly government exercising its writ throughout Afghanistan. For more than two decades the Pakistani army had been obsessed with dominating Afghanistan to create an illusory "strategic depth" meant to offset its bigger, richer, more populous Indian neighbor. The doctrine was inherited from the British Raj's "forward policy," which in the nineteenth and early twentieth centuries had brought disaster in three Afghan wars.

Al-Qaeda was helping the Taliban fight, so at the very least Pakistan had no interest in weakening either to please Washington. In many countries, moreover, CIA reliance on liaison with local intelligence counterparts had become ever more ingrained since the end of the Cold War. It saved money, and the U.S. government was only peripherally interested in many parts of the world. Afghanistan was at the bottom of the priorities list. U.S. efforts to learn more about the Taliban and Al-Qaeda were hobbled by other considerations. To avoid jeopardizing relations with its Pakistani partners—and Pakistan had demonstrated that it was a nuclear power in 1998—the CIA refused to do meaningful business with the Taliban's foes, principally Ahmad Shah Massoud, the ethnic Tajik leader who was the most effective single Afghan military commander. The United States viewed him with suspicion because he received desultory aid from India, Russia and especially Iran, which since the Iranian revolution a quarter century earlier consistently figured high on Washington's enemies' list.[7]

It wasn't as if the United States did not understand the Pakistani problem. Indeed within hours of 9/11, Pakistan's threadbare dance of the seven veils ended. Washington finally moved fast, demanding that Pakistan end its close relations with the Taliban and pressure the Taliban to sever their own close links with Osama. Pervez Musharraf, the general-turned-president, did not hesitate. He knew he had no choice. By extension, Washington instantaneously stopped feigning ignorance of apparently un-documented but logically cozy ties between Osama's Al-Qaeda and Pakistani intelligence.

The first concrete sign of Pakistan's reversal of alliances was the replacement of the pro-Taliban head of the Inter-Services Intelligence (ISI), the increasingly influential and pro-fundamentalist state within a state that virtually ran Afghanistan as a private fiefdom. Pakistan's shock came as a great surprise only because the army and successive governments constantly had discounted mounting warning signals about its flawed Afghan policy, gambling that just one more incremental increase in intelligence, arms and even seconded troops would ensure an elusive but definitive Taliban victory over Massoud. American spy satellites accumulated photographic evidence of Pakistani military intervention, artillery here, special forces there. Massoud happily recited for foreign visitors the names of the Pakistani military advisers, seconded army units and their commanders—and he insisted he had Pakistani prisoners to back him up.

Pakistan had all but invented the Taliban, the so-called Koranic students, but only after their initial allies, the wartime anti-Soviet mujahedeen, took to fighting each other after the Red Army's withdrawal in 1989 and stymied the dream of "strategic depth." In pursuit of ever more elusive Central Asian dreams of grandeur, an undeterred Pakistan recruited and armed Koranic students among the wretched Afghan refugees on its soil since the war against the Soviets.

For reasons of plausible deniability, the ISI found Afghanistan useful for training volunteers for Pakistan's increasingly deadly conflict with India over disputed Kashmir. The use and misuse of the Taliban was simply the latest variation in the shadowy exercise of power by the ISI, initially a modest military intelligence organization that over twenty years had come to represent ultimate authority in Pakistan. So shot through with corruption was a chronically bankrupt but nuclear-armed Pakistan—"the land of the pure"—that even the army, the supposed last bulwark, gave growing signs of falling prey to "creeping Talibanization" of its ruling officer corps. Osama's attack on New York and Washington had saved Pakistan from itself, if only temporarily.

THE SUDDEN SCRUTINY of Saudi Arabia by American politicians and media revealed what had been there all along: a duopoly of a particularly basic brand of Islam and the ever-expanding and self-indulgent royal family sitting atop the world's largest oil reserves. For a generation Saudis in and out of government had bankrolled many of the *madrasas* in Pakistan, where the Taliban and many poor Pakistani and Central Asian boys were fed, housed and taught the Koran by rote and little else, free of charge. The Kingdom helped finance the Taliban as it had the mujahedeen during the war against the Soviets. For Saudis, spreading their own peculiarly puritanical brand of Islam abroad lay at the very ideological heart of the monarchy. In all fairness, to the degree it worried about the policy at all, Saudi Arabia doubtless thought it was doing what the United States—as well, of course, as Pakistan—wanted. The policy also provided its profligate princely ruling elite with highly valued visible proof of its otherwise questionable moral credentials. Outwardly similar practices, such as the Taliban's religious police, who even borrowed Saudi terminology for their Committee to Reward Virtue and Punish Vice, helped overcome whatever real concern the Saudi royal family may have had.

Were such unpleasant foreign-policy embarrassments not enough, Americans, from the president on down, seemed at a genuine loss to understand how they could have generated so much hatred. Americans at the best of times are not good at comprehending why they should not be loved, much less singled out for such punishment. There is no built-in national predisposition for self-examination or for asking if American policies might play a role in great upheavals abroad. That is America's part curse, part blessing, the illusion of "splendid isolation" that comes from being a continent. The previous decade had lulled Americans into thinking the rest of the world could be forgotten. For most Americans the 1990s had been a period of self-absorption, encouraged by the end of the Cold War, relief at not having to worry about the wider world, and the longest economic boom in U.S. history. But much of the rest of the world was convinced that the United States was bent on running the planet.

Still, Americans reeling from 9/11 were comforted by the genuine outpouring of private and public support from around the world, especially from European allies. *Le Monde,* France's most serious newspaper and a near-constant critic over the decades of many things American, was moved to proclaim, "We all are Americans," echoing President Kennedy's "Ich bin ein Berliner," pronounced nearly forty years earlier. Relatively quickly, that foreign support became more nuanced, but few Americans noticed. The constantly proclaimed but unexamined innocence of Americans only exacerbated foreign resentment. Terrorism, after all, was nothing new to America's major European allies. Britain, France, Germany, Italy and Spain had all experienced spasms of terrorism, albeit of a less dramatic, if often more enduring kind. These older nations accepted that the fate of the most powerful states since the beginning of time was to be alternately envied and reviled.

Osama's grievances cleverly combined fact and fancy. For Al-Qaeda, by either luck or design, 9/11 took place almost a year after the Palestinians' second intifada had erupted, inflaming Muslims from Morocco to the South Seas. A half century of near-seamless U.S. support for Israel provided bin Laden with easy emotional cover among many of the world's 1.2 billion Muslims. Palestine was always a surefire cause when all else failed. And in the previous decade much about radical political Islam had failed—in Algeria, in Egypt, in Sudan. In fact, Osama was a notorious Johnny-come-lately to the Palestinian cause.[8]

As he never tired of repeating, his real focus steadfastly remained his native land, the Saudi Arabia home of Islam that he insisted was defiled by the "occupation" of American servicemen. That condemnation echoed throughout the Islamic world and beyond, indeed everywhere the United States shored up corrupt and often repressive regimes while trumpeting its devotion to democracy, "free and fair" elections and capitalism as a certain cure-all. But nothing ever matched the emotional impact of the Palestinian issue, which allowed ordinary Arabs to castigate what they viewed as Israeli excesses and to criticize their own governments' failure to take effective action to stop them.

As Americans' initial shock wore off following the September attacks, they realized they had paid only distracted attention to half-forgotten clues that terrorists had strewn like so many forgotten calling cards over most of a decade. Technical refinements abounded. American targets included a terrorist attack on the World Trade Center in 1993, in which miraculously only six people died. Its mastermind, who calls himself Ramzi Ahmad Youssef but may be someone else, was eventually caught in Pakistan two years later and brought back to the scene of his crime to stand trial. He told his American captors who flew him around the twin towers on his way to a Manhattan jail cell and eventual life imprisonment that had he had more money he would have executed a much more deadly operation.

In his computer hard drive, seized in Manila, investigators found plans to blow up a dozen American airliners virtually simultaneously over the Pacific. One of his sidekicks in Manila, Abdul Hakim Murad, had a commercial pilot's license and planned to crash a jet into CIA headquarters in Langley, Virginia. In Algeria, radicals of the Armed Islamic Group seized an Air France Airbus at the Algiers airport just before Christmas 1994, determined to crash it into the Eiffel Tower. They were thwarted by special French anti-riot police who stormed the plane during a refueling stop in Marseilles.

Such clues suggested that Al-Qaeda's suicide bombers were adept at absorbing cutting-edge tradecraft that had been experimented with elsewhere. Now Osama had proved astoundingly inventive in taking his jihad to what he considered the very heart of the beast. American officials had long been on the alert for Al-Qaeda attacks, even in the United States itself. But no one, not even veteran counterterrorism experts on both sides of the Atlantic who had been tracking jihadi radicals for years, had imagined him capable of staging quite such an extravaganza.

I ADMIT I AGAIN got Osama wrong. I figured he had minutely choreographed the last act of a life to echo through the ages, much as had the Assassins. The timing and manner of his going, I was long convinced, was to him of paramount importance. The self-advertising aspects of his character required nothing less. Arguably not since one of his favorite role models, Saladin, defeated the Crusaders had a single Muslim so personally overawed the Western world. For years Osama had honed his hero-cum-martyr image: rich man's son, ascetic to the point of instructing his wives not to iron his clothes, soft-spoken in the Arab leadership tradition of commanding respect, and eloquent practitioner of classical Arabic, which impressed those well versed in the poetic rhythms of the Koran. All seemed ready for his programmed exit from this world.

No doubt bin Laden hoped the fear and loathing he inspired so widely would outlive him and help plunge the Islamic world into a convulsive "clash of civilizations" with the West. The attacks on New York and Washington were designed not just as payback for the real and imagined grievances he felt that Muslims had suffered, but to set off just such a conflagration with the West. Osama said as much within hours of the first American air strike on October 7 in a cleverly pre-recorded video that to the Bush administration's fury was beamed around the globe by Al-Jazeera, which, alone among the world's television networks, had a correspondent and an uplink in Kabul then.[9]

Nattily dressed in camouflage field jacket and grasping a microphone, Osama gloated that America "has been filled with horror from north to south, and east to west, and thanks be to God that what America is tasting now is the copy of what we have tasted." "Every Muslim must rise to defend his religion," he said. "The winds of faith are blowing to remove evil from the Peninsula of Mohammed," meaning his native land, Saudi Arabia. He warned Americans, "I swear to God that America will not live in peace before peace reigns in Palestine and before the army of infidels departs the land of Mohammed."

It was his last carefully rehearsed televised performance. Thereafter, events moved so fast and the Taliban debacle was so total that I doubt he could call his own shots. I had expected Osama to do what he had done ever since his return to Afghanistan in 1996 (and especially since the United States fingered him for bombing its embassies in Nairobi and Dar es Salaam): keep constantly on the move. Such had become his restless modus operandi to escape the myriad eyes and ears he assumed were tracking him. He had all but abandoned his satellite telephone once he realized that the "big ears" of the National Security Agency recorded his conversations and could pinpoint his whereabouts for missiles large or small.[10] He rarely slept in the same place for more than a night or two before setting out in a convoy, and sometimes sending out decoy convoys, along Afghanistan's ruined, backbreaking roads for yet another temporary sanctuary.

In my mind's eye, I at times credited Osama with establishing some improbable impregnable secret mountain retreat that somehow he had managed to keep secret. He had built many a tunnel and fortification back in the 1980s, thanks to equipment and engineers borrowed from his family construction firm in Saudi Arabia. I also confess I probably was influenced by the example of Alamut, the Assassins' book-lined, long-inaccessible mountain headquarters in the Elburz mountains. I knew perfectly—and so did Osama—that helicopters, global positioning systems and armed drones in fact meant mountains no longer guaranteed safety for the hunted. Yet I never seriously envisaged that Osama would slink away from his embattled troops and his chosen turf rather than stand and die with his boots on. I especially never thought he would lounge around as a kind of Islamic REMF, to borrow a Vietnam War phrase for slackers ("rear echelon motherfuckers").

But what passed for evidence suggested that for many weeks after his American exploits he had pretty much stayed put in Kandahar, Mullah Omar's seat of power and the traditional Pashtun center in southern Afghanistan. That telltale grainy home movie certainly placed him there as late as early November, only days before the Taliban regime's last major bastion volatized. Such nonchalance scarcely fit my vision of an Osama determined to die guns blazing rather than undergo the humiliation of capture and trial in the United States. Ever since he had been nearly killed by Soviet troops in Afghanistan in 1986, he was on record as resigned to a violent end. He occasionally was given to expressing surprise bordering on regret that he had been denied the martyrdom he claimed he so ardently sought. Perhaps, of course, he was indeed dead and his followers now chose to maintain an aura of mystery around his whereabouts. That was a widely held view for nearly a year after U.S. intelligence last intercepted his voice giving orders to his beleaguered followers in the December 2001 battle at Tora Bora.

Indeed, when key aides, to mark 9/11's first anniversary, insisted Osama was alive, well and planning new attacks against the United States and its allies, some analysts suggested they were whistling in the dark to keep up morale.[11] Then in early November 2002, Al-Jazeera broadcast a long diatribe from Osama, and within days National Security Agency specialists confirmed the voice on the audiotape was his. Chillingly, he praised a new wave of recent terrorist operations stretching from a car-bomb attack on a tourist nightclub in Bali to an explosives-laden speedboat attack on a French oil tanker off the coast of Yemen. Al-Qaeda had been active again for many months. And now Osama was deemed alive, if not necessarily well (otherwise he would have produced a videocassette for television audiences, some analysts argued) and very much back in business.[12]

That was scarcely welcome news for the Bush administration, but not really astounding. After all, the most vivid impression that emerged from piecing together Osama's movements immediately after the Taliban defeat was not that of a would-be martyr. Rather he fell back on the trusted tools of his earliest calling as Al-Qaeda's financier—envelopes of currency (Pakistani and Iranian to ease flight to either major land border) if resistance proved too hazardous. For just such allegiance-building purposes, Osama held a late-November 2001 meeting in Jalalabad of Pashtun tribal chiefs, many of whom he knew from the anti-Soviet jihad. The envelopes were fat or thin depending on the importance of the recipient and the number of armed men each controlled. Then Osama disappeared in a convoy of vehicles heading into the mountains near the Pakistani border. It came as no great surprise to hear tales later that Afghans the Americans counted on— and paid—to block his escape route were old comrades in arms and instead had turned a blind eye to his disappearance into nearby Pakistan or even actively helped organize it.

Osama certainly was smart enough to change tactics, instructed by the destruction wrought on Al-Qaeda and Taliban ranks by American smart bombs and other high-tech weaponry. His trademark large convoys of pickups and Land Cruisers with de rigueur tinted windows soon gave way to a small group of bodyguards. Such was an elementary precaution to avoid detection by avid Afghans encouraged with banknote-crammed envelopes from the Americans, whose $25 million price on his head and missile-armed Predator drones were deployed by the CIA with great success. Some stories insisted that he moved around on horseback, as banal and undetectable a means of locomotion as the motorcycle on which the equally unlocatable Mullah Omar was rumored to have departed from Kandahar just before it fell.

Osama was reported by some Afghans to have been present in the initial stages of the early-December operation in the mountains at Tora Bora that the United States mounted with local Afghan allies (while curiously neglecting to put a blocking force in place to prevent their quarry's easy escape.)[13]

Arguably hostile stories circulated that he and his principal lieutenant, Egyptian Ayman al-Zawahiri, had harangued their followers to resist but explained the necessity for the leadership to live and fight another day. In any case, Osama was not found there or in the Americans' better-prepared follow-up, Operation Anaconda, in March 2002. Then, for all intents and purposes, Osama became a non-person. Were he not a Wahhabi, it would be tempting to compare him to the "hidden imam" who one day would return to save the world, a doctrine central to the Shi'a Islam he so despised.

President Bush abruptly stopped mentioning him at all in public. White House spin control thus hoped that Bush would not be asked about his promise to deliver Osama "dead or alive." The time for shoot-from-the-lip Texan oratory, on that score at least, was past. Defense Secretary Donald H. Rumsfeld professed ignorance about whether Osama was still alive and, if so, where. The new administration line insisted that the war against terrorism was a globe-girdling enterprise, with Osama but one of many parts of an ever-changing mosaic. To the outspoken uneasiness of its European and Arab allies, the administration shifted its attention to Somalia, Yemen, the Philippines and finally, and especially, Iraq. Saddam Hussein's regime was suddenly resuscitated in Bush's State of the Union address in January 2002 as part of the "axis of evil," alongside Iran and North Korea. No longer was this the war against terrorism America's allies had embraced in mid-September.

The administration basically sought to airbrush Osama from its official consciousness as artlessly as had Stalin's propagandists removed those fallen from grace from official photographs. As his prerecorded message on October 7 indicated, Osama was often more than one step ahead of Washington. But in a video appearance two months later it was less what he said than his altered appearance that attracted attention. His gaunt features were drawn, the ever more scraggly beard suddenly had more salt than pepper, and he did not move the left side of his body at all. Some partisans suggested it was a mistake to show Osama in such obviously diminished condition. Indeed he looked like what he was—a fugitive and, at that, a lanky one who would stand out if he sought to go to ground outside of Afghanistan and Pakistan's Pashtun tribal belt.

In light of Al-Qaeda's initial military defeat, somewhat surprisingly Osama lost little of his cult status in Afghanistan and Pakistan and beyond. After all, he had promised resistance and victory and failed to deliver either. The occasional cassettes broadcast over the next few months appeared to have been filmed in the fall; in some he remained silent, in others he spoke, but the oratory seemed dated. They may have been released to keep up Al-Qaeda spirits, but instead they fed speculation he was dead. What was sure was that hundreds of Pakistani Pashtuns, among the thousands who had rushed across the border in September to aid the Taliban and Al-Qaeda, had lost their lives in the fighting or were prisoners of grasping Afghan warlords demanding ransom on pain of handing them over to the Americans. And as the months went by, Pakistani President Pervez Musharraf seemed to have gambled and won in turning on the homegrown

ISI-backed Islamist radicals. At least briefly Osama ceased being the cynosure of Pakistani Islamists and other Asian Muslims on whom he had staked so much for the success of jihadi radicalism.

In Pakistan the temporary letdown took odd forms. For want of customers the Peshawar bazaar stopped hawking Osama posters and T-shirts. Fewer Pakistani parents named their baby boys Osama, as they had done widely in 1998 to protest American efforts then to punish him for Al-Qaeda's operations in East Africa. Such outward signs did not mean the Americans were popular in Pakistan or that Al-Qaeda and local Islamists were resigned to their setback in Afghanistan. Very soon worrying signs emerged that if Al-Qaeda certainly had been disrupted, it was still very much in business. In January 2002 *Wall Street Journal* reporter Daniel Pearl was kidnapped and then executed by Islamist radicals in Karachi. Starting in the spring, suicide bombers struck soft Western targets—a church during Sunday service in Islamabad, French naval engineers in Karachi, the street outside the U.S. consulate in the same city, a missionary school in the hill country outside the capital. In the spring Al-Qaeda was linked to the deaths of fifteen German tourists in a suicide truck-bomb attack on an ancient synagogue on the Tunisian island of Djerba.

In October, a fast-moving TNT-laden skiff rammed the *Limburg,* a French supertanker, off the Yemeni oil terminal at Mukalla in the Hadhramaut region where Osama's father was born. The incident in its modus operandi uncannily resembled Al-Qaeda's attack on the USS *Cole* almost exactly two years earlier as the warship was in the Yemeni port of Aden for a brief refueling stop. Nearly a week later a bomb killed more than 180 Western vacationers on Indonesia's island of Bali. On Thanksgiving Day, November 28, a missile fired from a shoulder-held SAM 7 ground-to-air launcher narrowly missed an Israeli airliner taking off with more than 200 vacationers and crew from Mombasa airport on Kenya's Indian Ocean coast. Minutes later three Israelis and nine Kenyans died when three suicide bombers crashed an explosives-packed jeep into the Israeli-owned Paradise Hotel fifteen minutes to the north. One man ran into the entrance and blew himself up while the two others detonated the vehicle out front. Four years and four months after Al-Qaeda's first provable attack—the simultaneous truck-bomb attacks against the U.S. embassies in Kenya and Tanzania—jihadi terrorism had come full circle in East Africa.

Nor had the war on terrorism gone according to plan. The Bush administration was embarrassed by the upset in October 2002 in Pakistan's parliamentary elections, in which an alliance of six Islamic religious parties running on an openly anti-American platform achieved their best result since the founding of the country in 1947. Never before had Islamists won more than a handful of seats in national elections. Now they were the third-largest party, in power in the Northwest Frontier Province and sharing it in Baluchistan regional assembly, free to criticize the central government's pro-American policies and block reforms that Musharraf had promised to limit their control of Koranic schools. Musharraf had no one but himself to blame for the results, which were likely to weaken his authority. He had forced through electoral rules, effectively preventing the exiled leaders of the traditional political parties, former prime ministers Benazir Bhutto and Nawaz Sharif, from running. Cynics suggested Musharraf, and especially the ISI, were not that displeased that the religious alliance filled the void. Washington would find it more difficult to press for reforms, and the ISI could resume cultivating its Islamist clientele, which 9/11 had interrupted.

EVEN WERE OSAMA still alive and eventually to go down guns blazing, a violent death risked crystallizing his myth rather than assuring future success as he defined it. Read one way, his death would consecrate the logical failure of a career frustrated in its political goal of wresting control of Saudi Arabia for himself and his followers. For despite references to the immediate and evocative issues of Palestine and Iraq, which stirred real sympathy in the Middle East, his main target remained the destruction of the ruling house of Al-Saud in his native land and with it the United States control of Middle East oil. He had taken on the United States on American soil only after despairing of overthrowing the Al-Saud at home. The odd American–Saudi alliance had withstood—just—the shock of 9/11.

The most Osama and his followers could reasonably hope for now was that the American war against terrorism would backfire on Bush. Oddly, the administration obliged, unwittingly running the risk of undercutting its own initial success in Afghanistan. Washington shied away from providing the new Afghan regime it had installed in Kabul with the military or political muscle needed to anchor its authority. Two ministers were assassinated in the capital, and Afghan president Hamid Karzai himself miraculously escaped an attempt on his life. With the Afghan mission thus far from complete, the administration abruptly shifted its attention in 2002 to "regime change" in Iraq, thereby diverting resources from its war on terrorism. Washington saw no need to intervene to stop the violence between Israel and the Palestinians, fueling further anti-American sentiment even among moderate Muslims who had little use for Saddam Hussein's regime in Baghdad. In the grand tradition of seeking to justify defeat, Al-Qaeda could take comfort in the knowledge that even those pro-Western regimes, such as Egypt, that had suppressed Islamic terrorism in much blood now dared not side openly with the United States for fear of provoking restive populations at home.

Washington's rapidly stitched together anti-terrorist coalition included Russia, Uzbekistan, China and Algeria, whose unrepentantly authoritarian regimes had smashed armed Islamic revolts at terrible human cost. Osama had no use whatsoever for democracy and scant interest in human rights as defined in the West. But radical Islam had long practice in benefiting from the resentment such often-blind repression engendered. American expediency was comprehensible in the heat of battle. The United States needed foreign bases—and fast—for the Afghan campaign. Yet deals cut to obtain overflight rights or bases in Central Asia, Russia and elsewhere sent a dangerous message to muscular regimes the world over that they could take the gloves off.

More problematic was the wisdom of the administration's ideological lurch to oversimplification. Nowhere was that bent more questionable than in the Holy Land. Immediately after 9/11, as the administration was putting together the widest possible alliance before launching its Afghan campaign, Washington expressed public displeasure at Sharon's grandstanding insinuations that the United States was sacrificing Israel in a rerun of British-French abandonment of Czechoslovakia to the Nazis in 1938. Sharon was told to pipe down and did so, temporarily, to allow Washington to woo moderate Arab states. He even swallowed the administration's distinction tolerating Islamic Jihad, Hamas and Hezbollah in the name of understandable opposition to Israeli occupation of Arab land. But with the Afghan campaign prematurely judged successful, Sharon and Israel's powerful American friends in and out of government demanded consistency in prosecuting terrorism worldwide.

Right-wing advisers in Washington cloaked their pro-Israeli preferences by insisting that the Bush doctrine meant terrorism was terrorism in absolutely all circumstances, without exception. Bush was on record early on as insisting that harboring and financing terrorism was the same as actually committing terrorist acts. To please Israel and its friends, Bush feigned ignorance of Sharon's blemished record of repeated acts of massive violence over a half century, preferring to hold Palestinian suicide bombers primarily responsible for the escalating violence in the Holy Land.[14] Bush had entered office in January 2001 determined not to get sucked into Palestinian–Israeli peacemaking, so dear to President Clinton's heart. September 11 had reinforced that belief in the face of mounting violence on both sides that cried out for American leadership.

Such had become Americans' instinctive reaction against any terrorism that the administration largely ignored Sharon's systematic destruction of Palestinian institutions, the Israeli army's indiscriminate use of force against civilians, the constant encroachment of Israeli settlements on Arab land and the desperation that fueled the Palestinian suicide bombers targeting Israeli civilians. Vice President Richard Cheney, Rumsfeld and other neoconservative true believers increasingly influential in the administration saw no contradiction in pushing ahead with removing Saddam Hussein from power in Iraq without first calming a Muslim world shaking in disbelief and anger at the dangers the administration was courting blindly in the Palestinian-Israeli conflict. Indeed, Cheney, during a spring 2002 swing through the Middle East ignored Arab governments' plea to get Palestinian-Israeli negotiations restarted. Nor did Bush endear himself to Muslims when he embraced Sharon as "a man of peace."

The ideological word from Washington was that Middle Eastern regimes were rotten, undemocratic, and no longer defensible. That meant old allies Saudi Arabia and Egypt as well as Iran and Syria, long suspect in the eyes of the Israeli lobby and their influential friends in the administration. The old saws reemerged. The Arabs only respected force. The Arab street, that unofficial thermometer for what passed for public opinion in autocratic states, no longer was important. Superpower America was so strong that by itself it could reorder the Muslim world, impose democracy and good governance and keep control of the oil. A pro-American government in Iraq would provide enough oil to end ever more gluttonous U.S. dependence on an embarrassingly medieval Saudi Arabia. In an increasingly dimming past, much-decried State Department Arabists could have made short shrift of such overblown simplifications or at least put them in context. But it had been many years since anyone with power in Washington listened to Arabists, and in the Bush administration they had become all but invisible. Oh that anyone in Washington had read and reflected on

General Charles de Gaulle's war memoirs of his own illusions while serving in Lebanon during the French League of Nations mandate in the 1920s: "I left for the complicated Orient with simple ideas!"[15]

In a way it came down to wondering if inadvertently the United States would help Osama do his work. In his Afghan camps he had trained thousands of terrorists and true believers from many lands, stretching from the South Seas to Western Europe and even the United States. He had warned time and again that others would take his place and avenge his death. Only a fool would rule out further terrorist attacks by his followers, despite the body blow Al-Qaeda received with the loss of its Afghan sanctuary. For Americans accustomed to fast solutions, the initial rapid success of their campaign in Afghanistan obscured the more sobering bedrock of transnational terrorism. The democratic age of inexpensive Internet communications favored the fleet of foot over often muscle-bound government bureaucracies. A dozen and a half dedicated Al-Qaeda operatives had wrought massive damage of a scale long monopolized by industrialized states. Throughout history, knowledge had meant power, and knowledge depended on secure communications. That dependence explained why governments so highly prized secrecy. Suddenly, the information age— supposedly the United States' own secret weapon, designed to maintain its edge far into the twenty-first century—had leveled the playing field for small groups, including those totally opposed to American values.

In such circumstances what was the real clout of the United States, with a defense budget equal to that of the world's next eight powers? What the United States lacked was knowledge (as opposed to narrow "intelligence") about much of the world. And that kind of knowledge was hard to come by for a superpower without the natural accretions of information that classic empires patiently acquired over long spans of time by administering wide swathes of the earth. How to navigate among tribes, local customs, ways of conducting business and sharing power that at first glance made no sense? Already the Americans' reliance on regional warlords in Afghanistan had resulted in a series of embarrassing errors in which rival tribal leaders or their followers were described deliberately as Al-Qaeda operatives and bombed.

No wonder the Bush administration's natural instinct was to shy away from the constraints of "nation-building." Understandable, too, was its natural repugnance for coalitions, those awkward, time-consuming alliances with troublesome foreigners all too likely to limit freedom of movement. But America's nostrum of capitalism and free elections often meant little—or indeed could be construed as the veritable enemy—in traditional societies that looked askance at more questionable aspects of globalization often summarily equated with unbridled liberty and the destabilizing cult of the individual. Osama was far from being the first man to realize that terrorism was the arm of the weak, but he perhaps was the first in the modern era to use it to privatize war. To the degree that any power, East or West, had figured out how to proceed against this thoroughly modern threat, the answer likely lay in smarter policies and better police cooperation, not the dispatch of troops from Yemen to the Philippines, "regime change" in Iraq, flashy smart bombs and sophisticated drones that so captured imaginations.

In a very real sense, it was up to the West, especially the United States, to avoid Al-Qaeda's traps and demonstrate that Osama was less dangerous dead than alive—if and when he was caught.

GROWING UP WITH
THE BUMBLEBEE

FOR MY SINS over a long career spent on and off in the Middle East, I often have lived in the shadow of what might be called ecumenical terrorism. By that I mean I have witnessed Lebanese Christian terrorism, Israeli terrorism, Islamic terrorism, Arab nationalist terrorism, Iranian and Palestinian terrorism (both with and without Soviet bloc embellishments), Western terrorism, plus some other variants I have probably forgotten or experienced often at closer quarters than I might have wished. To those who ask for a definition of terrorism, the U.S. Code, Section 2656f(d) says it means "premeditated, politically motivated violence perpetrated against noncombatant targets by subnational groups or clandestine agents, usually intended to influence an audience." To that bureaucratic mush, I can only reply that I think I know terrorism when I see it, and I have seen too much of it.

I have done enough time in the Middle East to recognize the ring of authenticity in my old maverick Israeli friend Uri Avnery's formula: "The difference between freedom fighters and terrorists is that freedom fighters are on my side and the terrorists on the other." Yet before Americans wax indignant at any suggestion of dignifying Osama bin Laden's brand, let's recall that President Ronald Reagan in the 1980s recognized as freedom fighters all those fighting the Soviet occupation of Afghanistan, and that included Osama, the Chinese, Western Europe, the Israelis, the Arab world, Muslims everywhere, but especially the Afghans themselves. At the time that was a collection of odd couples worthy of mention in the *Guinness Book of World Records.*

In my own way, I suppose I was thought of as a little odd myself. I was born in Buffalo the day President Roosevelt closed the banks in 1933, then educated at Exeter and Harvard. My entire career was spent working as a foreign correspondent for a variety of publications. I never wanted it any other way. But that was a choice with some costs. Some of those publications are no longer extant, and almost all sent me to the nastier corners of the world, much of the time in the Middle East during times of crisis.

My mother could never figure out why I had thrown away my birthright. "Jon," she once told me when I was still young enough for her to entertain hopes of channeling me into some more settled occupation, "journalists are interesting people to have to dinner, and that is all." My British colleague Nigel Ryan had the perfect rejoinder to those who question the wisdom of such a scruffy calling. "When I came down from Oxford," he once told a particularly self-important ambassador's wife, "I had to choose between boredom and vulgarity, and I chose vulgarity."

Still, during the four decades I covered Third World disorders for the *Washington Post,* I was sometimes accused of carrying around my own black cloud. Being in the right place at the right time in the most violent of situations makes good copy. The French call it *sang à la une,* front page gore—or, in American parlance, "if it bleeds, it leads." That was what I was paid for, although with every passing year I came to appreciate the lengthening odds. I don't remember ever being personally fingered by terrorists, but I was close enough to others who were, to thank my lucky stars, frequently.

Even when off duty in Paris in 1995, and again in 1996, I came within minutes of quite likely death in the express train known as the RER, the second time in the company of my wife and her daughter. Doubtless the black-cloud syndrome again. (I mention the Paris episodes because I later was told by a senior French counterterrorism expert that Osama bin Laden had a hand in financing the 1995 terror campaign in France.) For all that, I long judged terrorism, mistakenly as it turned out, a minor art form in the game of nations, often, but not always, used by the weak against the strong.

I had become familiar with many of its sick variations and would-be disguises. In Beirut in the 1970s and 1980s, specialized, too-clever-by-half operations could involve Israelis putting Shi'a Muslims up to planting car bombs against Maronite Christian targets, hoping Sunni Muslims would be blamed. The permutations seemed tiresomely endless. Indeed, my only enduring conclusion was the unsurprising, but nonetheless essential, notion that each permutation was different.

Generalizations about terrorism, especially Islamic terrorism, tend not so much to be wrongheaded as likely to induce the very errors and mindless repression by governments that would-be terrorists crave to achieve martyrdom. A one-size-fits-all approach only plays into their hands. They constantly preach that the West in general, and the United States in particular, hates Islam in all its manifestations and that moderate Muslims should wise up. If there is an answer to such an enduring phenomenon as terrorism, I suspect it lies in needlework, that time-consuming, patient, dull, but professional accumulation of detail. Jean-Louis Bruguière, the veteran French anti-terrorism judge, likes to compare permutations of Islamic terrorism to the endless mutations of the AIDS virus. I fear he may be right, with all the needlework his conceit implies.

When I became interested in bin Laden, people in all walks of life—including some involved, or pretending to be involved, with terrorism and others with counterterrorism—kept telling me to "be careful." No one had really bothered to deliver this sensible counsel during the forty years when I had put myself in harm's way as a correspondent. For once it was comforting to believe the warnings were made out of a genuine concern for my safety. Still I sometimes felt their remarks were really a signal that I should cease and desist. I didn't, but I suppose that over so many years I imperceptibly had taken on board a good dose of caution without really giving it much thought. Or maybe I was just lucky.[1]

Since I long ago decided to fly under my own colors I told all and sundry exactly what I was—a recently retired foreign correspondent. That did not stop visible nervousness on the part of many people I sought to interview, and more than once my candor bred suspicion and anal retention of the most banal facts. I recall a long, raw winter afternoon in dismal north London going over the 1982 Israeli siege of Beirut with one of the much-quoted Islamist clerics known as the "Abu Megaphones" for their trenchant defense of radical Islam on British television and in the press. We had both survived Beirut.

I hoped such a display of detailed knowledge about Lebanon would induce my interlocutor to trust me. I really wanted to learn about bin Laden's techniques in recruiting footloose young Muslims; the British capital was becoming known as "Londonistan," thanks to its centuries-old reputation for respecting dissent and/or, more recently, for sheltering Islamist radicals on the lam from less tolerant lands. "You certainly know your Beirut," he said, in ending the interview, "and that can only mean you work for the CIA." I was bemused because the agency had always kept me at many arms' length, and that had been fine by me. Perhaps it was "Abu Megaphone's" way of letting me know that for him "retired correspondent" versus "spy" was a distinction without real difference, the one being as ambiguous and suspect as the other.

I mention ambiguity because the first time I carefully studied a photograph of Osama bin Laden it struck me that his face seemed somehow divided into a feminine top half and a masculine bottom. Perhaps it was his finely chiseled brow and deep-set eyes contrasting with the full beard. Perhaps it was a recurring sense of ambivalence reflecting my inability at that time to ferret out a coherent view of his character, especially of his early formative years. It was tempting to believe that what I took to be his apparent conflicts and contradictions in fact foreshadowed the last decade, when his penchant for accelerating violence came into clearer focus.

I certainly was confronted by a series of oddities with little insight into how they might mesh together or not. I could not even decide whether his native land, Saudi Arabia, perhaps unwittingly, helped radicalize Osama, with more than a little help from the Kingdom's main protector, the United States, and some of its allies. Such was never a popular view with American officials. But it was one I never totally discarded as I traveled around the various places of interest to Osama and, in my old reporting days, to me.

From his point of view, Osama had much more to be upset about in his travels than I did. Over the years his passport was impounded, his substantial assets frozen, and his citizenship removed, and he was consigned to isolated and, it was hoped, forgotten exile in Afghanistan. I am not much given to psychologizing, but Osama's very early life had not been easy, except of course when it came to material comforts. His father had more than fifty other children, many of them considerably older and apparently cleverer than Osama. His father was also away working a great deal of the time and, in any case, had separated quickly from his mother, who did not count high in the pecking order of a life full of women. Osama was ten when his father died. His older brothers took over his father's construction firm and expanded it further. It is tempting to assume that Osama had good reasons for wanting to carve out a special place for himself. But so do a lot of people who find less deadly ways of self-fulfillment. In any event, there is a lot more to his background that defies such easy pop-shrink pigeonholing.

As for the Americans, they had tracked Osama for years, initially desultorily, then with greater persistence. In the early to mid-1990s, he was logged from all the cardinal points with such frequency that these often contradictory reports came to be known among self-deprecating counter-terrorism officials as "Elvis sightings." But only in August 1998, after he was suspected of masterminding the truck bombings of the U.S. embassies in Nairobi and Dar es Salaam—and President Clinton tried unsuccessfully to kill him with Tomahawk cruise missiles—did Osama become America's Public Enemy Number One, complete with a $5 million reward, later increased to $25 million, for information leading to his arrest.

Demonizing adversaries reflects a peculiarly American character trait repeated over more than half a century of uneasy but ever-growing U.S. involvement in the Muslim world. It was something of a tradition, stretching from Egypt's Gamal Abdel Nasser and Muammar Qaddafi of Libya to Iran's Ayatollah Ruhollah Khomeini, Saddam Hussein and, for a very long time, Yasser Arafat. Successive U.S. governments never seemed to realize what a favor they were doing in elevating their foes to such exalted status. Among aspirant adversaries the credo went something like: "If I can get Uncle Sam's goat, then I exist."

Prior to the bombing of the East African embassies, the U.S. attitude toward Osama—and much of the world's approach to terrorism of all kinds—reminded me of a story I heard many years ago in Damascus. It concerned a colonial official during France's League of Nations mandate in Syria between the two World Wars. One day in making his daily rounds he discovered that an unexplained murder had occurred in a village along the Euphrates. The body had washed up on the town's shoreline. He took the *mukhtar* (mayor) to task and said he wanted the mystery solved before he returned the next day, or else. Once the officious Frenchman was out of sight, the *mukhtar* told his men, "If this happens again, take long poles and shove the cadaver as far as possible out into the river. That way, it will be the next village's problem."

This approach meshed nicely with the thinking of many Americans, both civilian and military. "No body bags" was the mantra of a self-indulgent generation tired of a half century of Cold War responsibilities and eager to turn its sights on problems at home. Burned by its Vietnam War experience, the Pentagon feared becoming ensnared in war without massive public approval. Given America's love affair with its gas-guzzling automobiles, oil passed the "just war" test. But the ever-cautious military insisted on moving half a million men halfway round the world to end Saddam Hussein's occupation of Kuwait in 1990 (and then left the Iraqi president in power to make a mockery of that famous victory). A dozen dead American diplomats in two East Africa embassies did not tip the balance for massive retaliation in 1998. (Nor did more than three dozen American airmen and sailors who died in terrorist attacks in Saudi Arabia and Yemen between 1995 and 2000.)

Such calculations had unintended consequences abroad, especially in the Third World, and more especially still among radical Muslims. Long before the brief campaign that unseated the Taliban in Afghanistan in the fall of 2001, U.S. reliance on such state-of-the-art weaponry was not seen as manly since the Americans did not put their lives on the line in *mano a mano* combat. American soldiers with increasingly sophisticated weaponry were disdained for not "fighting fair." It was an argument that in the Muslim world could be traced back to the eruption of Napoleon's invading army in Egypt at the tail end of the eighteenth century or the slaughter of the Mahdi's men by the British at the battle of Omdurman almost exactly a hundred years later. But at least Western soldiers then still saw their foes before slaughtering them with superior firepower. Now "fire and forget" missiles were unleashed miles away from targets, and pilotless drones flying slowly overhead filmed the enemy in real time, either firing missiles themselves or directing "smart bombs" from aircraft operating well beyond antiaircraft weapons' range.

In targeting Osama in one of his Afghan training camps with Tomahawk cruise missiles in August 1998—and missing him to boot—the United States also reignited worry among Muslims that the United States is prone to overkill. Previously, Muslims had been disturbed by Osama's edict to kill all Americans. Indeed, many Koranic specialists argued that the *fatwa* was downright erroneous. With every passing day after the attacks on the embassies in Nairobi and Dar es Salaam on August 7, 1998, more and more Muslims especially had questioned the deaths of innocent black Africans, who outnumbered the American victims by almost twenty to one. Osama's propaganda insisted that the Kenyans deserved to die because of their government's long history of close relations with Israel.

That line of argument did not wash well in much of Black Africa. But as soon as the United States in retaliation fired cruise missiles on August 20 against Sudan and Afghanistan, such concerns evaporated. Leveling the El-Shifa pharmaceutical plant in Khartoum—on what soon was revealed as the palpably unprovable pretext it was making chemical weapons for part-owner Osama—proved a propaganda boon for bin Laden and the radical Islamists running the Sudan. It soon became clear that Osama had nothing to do with the plant's owners. Again a curious ambiguity took hold, especially in Pakistan, and to a lesser degree in the Arab world, and it contributed to the further glorification of the nascent myth around Osama.

Hundreds of parents took to naming their newborn sons Osama. Overnight he figured on T-shirts and posters as a latter-day Saladin on a white steed, lashing out at his infidel enemies and their tanks and jets. Unlike Saladin, for many Muslims, Robin Hood, Che Guevara and Joan of Arc were not role models that automatically suggested themselves. But although Osama would hate to admit it, he has stitched together bits and pieces from all their garments as well. His message boxed the compass: kick out the foreign armies occupying Muslim lands, defend the pure poor from the corrupt rich, upend the high and mighty, inspire youth by one's own selflessness.

For too long the Americans had been untouchable, his message insisted, while Muslims died at the hands of America and its allies. At long last, someone had hit the United States, the often envied, more often decried, superpower and inflicted death and destruction on its citizens—indeed on its officials, its diplomats—and the very symbols of sovereignty that two embassies constituted. It was the nature of the U.S. riposte that attracted dedicated young Muslims by the hundreds to Osama's cause in Afghanistan. His effrontery against the odds acted as a powerful magnet.

Such pop-art renderings could well raise an eyebrow among educated Muslim sophisticates. But the world Osama addresses and from which he emerged was not sophisticated in any real sense (and he seems to have made sure that few, if any, doubts intruded to shake his bedrock beliefs). Within a few decades in the mid-twentieth century, oil money had collided with the timeless traditions of harsh desert survival, confronting a tribal society with vast, often disrupting—and corrupting—riches. Unlike most of the Third World, and especially the Muslim world, much of what became the Kingdom of Saudi Arabia in 1932 had only peripheral experience with colonialism and then only in an attenuated form of occasional punitive raids or defensive treaties. The Kingdom was not just any other Third World country: it was the seventh-century birthplace of Islam and of Mohammed, its prophet.

Oil was discovered in Saudi Arabia in 1938 and was fully exploited by the American company Aramco (Arab American Oil Company) only after World War Two ended in 1945. In a meeting that March, just weeks before he died, President Franklin D. Roosevelt entertained King Abdulaziz bin Abdel-Rahman al-Saud aboard the U.S. cruiser *Quincy* in the Red Sea. It was the start of a very curious but enduring relationship between two countries. At face value they had little in common except a tacit agreement for the Saudis to supply oil—and the Kingdom sits on a quarter of the world's known crude reserves—in return for American military protection of the monarchy.

For years, crude was cheap and royalties to the ruling Al-Saud treasury trifling. The Kingdom in its early days sometimes barely scraped by, relying, as had past rulers for centuries, on taxes on pilgrims arriving for the *hajj* in Mecca, one of the five pillars—or obligations—of Islam. Such cheeseparing concerns disappeared abruptly with the quadrupling of crude prices as a result of the 1973 Arab–Israeli war. At long last, the producers' cartel, the Organization of Petroleum Exporting Countries (OPEC), made good its threat and used the "oil weapon" against Western nations and consumers.

Suddenly Saudi Arabia, then as now the world's largest oil exporter and swing-producer arbiter of the price of crude, was awash with petrodollars. Western businessmen out to make a quick fortune fought for couch space in overbooked hotels. During the day they courted princely sponsors to help sell everything from telephones and petrochemical plants to state-of-the-art jet fighters beyond the Kingdom's ability to fly or even maintain. In those times I remember surviving visits to theoretically teetotal Saudi Arabia as a constant effort at fending off my hosts' proffered first-thing-in-the-morning tumblers of Black Label scotch and late evenings highlighted by more booze and private projections of Western pornography.

Such passed for the high life in those heady days, a sign that Saudi Arabia was with it. For the happy few, there were weekend parties on the shore of the Red Sea near Jeddah, hosted by Saudi merchant princes or young Al-Saud boys just back from Western universities and attended by diplomats, Western businessmen, airline stewardesses, embassy secretaries, nurses and other single Western women. Smuggled booze and even drugs added a touch of living dangerously. Occasionally a Westerner had to leave the Kingdom in a hurry, amid hushed whispers of his or her misbehavior, or what was judged as such.

Much more raucous revelry was standard enough fare for Beirut or even Cairo. But Saudi Arabia was, and basically remains, different, so different that an American ambassador once compared the regime King Abdulaziz bin al-Saud created to a bumblebee. Why a bumblebee, I asked? "Because there is no aerodynamic reason for a bumblebee to fly, yet fly it does." Perhaps for the time being only, he insinuated, but it was a suspension of disbelief made possible by the oddly durable combination of Saudi oil and American protection of an Islamic theocracy. The ambassador had spoken years before many average Saudis began questioning the proliferating royal family's seemingly insatiable appetite for corruption, its questionable taste for gold faucets, its outrageous commissions on largely U.S. arms purchases and its greedy real estate deals. Only later did ordinary Saudis come to resent the Kingdom's humiliating reliance on the United States for its defense or its failure to provide for a rapidly growing population that outstripped the welfare state's ability to provide housing and make-work jobs.

Yet the bumblebee has remained aloft thanks to—or perhaps despite—a delicate, but enduring alliance forged in the eighteenth century. Mohammed bin Saud, the ruler of a desert oasis in the Nejd in the center of the country, embraced the puritanical religious doctrine of Mohammed bin Abdul Wahhab, an austere Sunni scholar, and the two set out to conquer the Arabian peninsula. In 1745 they took an oath to work together and, in the first of a series of marriages between the families, Saud's son, Abdulaziz, wed the cleric's daughter. The alliance worked only too well, capturing Mecca itself in 1803, but causing alarm for the Ottomans who exercised suzerainty in the Hijaz facing the Red Sea. A punitive Ottoman expedition dispatched from Egypt ended the early Wahhabi dream. In 1818 Saud's son was captured and transported to Istanbul where, in the Ottomans' time-honored punishment for rebels, he was executed.

The alliance's fortunes bloomed again before dissension among the heirs allowed a rival tribe, the Rashids, to triumph. The Al-Sauds' luck revived, more enduringly, when Abdulaziz bin Abdul-Rahman al-Saud captured Riyadh in 1902. Spearheading the attack were the zealous Wahhabi warriors known as the Ikhwan (Brothers), who over three decades helped consolidate his control over the peninsula. The alliance still links the temporal power of the Al-Saud, represented at present by Adbulaziz's now-elderly sons, and the spiritual authority that traces its bloodlines to the austere reformer who founded the sect.

To comprehend the system, try imagining America's Puritans and John Winthrop's vision of their pristine "city on the hill" as if they had gone unchallenged through the centuries by such forces for change as individual rights and industrialization. In Saudi Arabia, intermarriage between the regime's two pillars has solidified the system still rooted in the Kingdom's central desert heartland. Wahhabi fervor in battle helped install the Al-Saud dynasty, and the clerical clan's continuing approval provides the royal family with crucial legitimacy. To this day the partnership reposes on Wahhabism's unquestioned monopoly of religion in exchange for delivering the unswerving obedience of its followers to the temporal rulers.

But the Al-Saud dare not take the unpredictable Wahhabi for granted. The ruling dynasty invariably confers with the Wahhabi leadership and often, but not always, gets what it wants. Thus in decades past, telephones, radio and even television were approved (on the grounds of enhancing propagation of the faith). But women remain banned from driving. No other religion's place of worship is authorized, despite the presence of millions of foreign workers of other faiths. Movie houses are forbidden lest men and women mingle.

The Wahhabi insist on a stripped-down, just-the-basics, puritanical form of Sunni Islam construed as enforcing the purified faith as practiced by the Prophet Mohammed in the seventh century in their very land. They sometimes prefer to call themselves *salafi* (forefathers), in homage to the first three "pure" generations of Muslims. They are followers of ninth-century legal scholar Ahmed ibn Hanbal, who bequeathed to Islam the most restrictive of its four schools of jurisprudence, limited to the Koran itself and the Sunna, the Prophet Mohammed's sayings. Strict literal adherence to Koranic text bans dancing, music, decoration of mosques, the worship of saints and their holy places, in the name of cleansing Islam of superstition and centuries of suspect heretical accretions known as *bid'a*. Only Islam's first 220 years are considered pure. In a land of princely palaces, the royal family's cemetery is an austere collection of stones stuck in the sand. Alone of Islam's sects, the Wahhabis do not celebrate the Prophet's birthday, a major holiday for many Muslims.

Indeed when King Abdulaziz captured Mecca in 1925, the Wahhabis destroyed the tombs of the defeated Hashemite dynasty that claimed to be descended from the Prophet. Also reduced to rubble in Mecca and Medina were the tombs of the Prophet's wife, daughters, uncles, cousins and senior commanders, as well as those of many Islamic scholars who had settled in the Hijaz over the centuries. In Wahhabi eyes, only Allah was to be revered. Tombs, saints and angels, for example, were denounced as *shirk* (polytheism). Under Wahhabism's watchful gaze, corporal punishment is meted out in public: amputation of the right hand for theft, stoning for adultery, public beheading for capital crimes. The Wahhabis deny that the Shi'a minority is Muslim at all (and made sure to destroy many holy places in Mecca and Medina the Shi'a had revered, much as they had sacked the principal Shi'a shrine in the Iraqi city of Karbala in the early nineteenth century). Street patrols by religious police, known as the *mutawa'een,* rigorously enforce attendance at prayer five times a day, fasting during daylight hours in the lunar month of Ramadan and the ban on alcohol.

Xenophobic, ascetic, militant and fat with petrodollars, Wahhabism has spread abroad with the approval of the Al-Saud, ever anxious to justify King Fahd's claim as "custodian of the two holy places" in Mecca and Medina and to curry favor and forgiveness for the royal family's own excesses. Proselytism and checkbook diplomacy long have been the Al-Sauds' principal foreign-policy tools. The Saudis, both official and private, have built (or, in the case of desecrated Bosnia, rebuilt) thousands of mosques from the United States to Kenya's Swahili coast and the Muslim Central Asian lands of the former Soviet Union.[2]

These and ancillary activities have not always been welcome. In recent years reiterated protests from Western and Islamic countries, stretching from North Africa to Central Asia and the Philippines, have extracted Saudi promises to stop the official largesse that is often accused of fueling Islamic radicals bent on unseating established governments. But private Saudi fortunes still contribute generously to Wahhabism's propagation abroad. *Zakat,* the obligation to give alms, is yet another pillar of Islam.

Much of this money is funneled through Saudi and other Islamic charities. Long before September 11, 2001, its disbursement had provoked objections from abroad, often because some of the funds, it is suspected, were siphoned off for terrorism and other controversial purposes, such as subsidizing particularly virulent fundamentalist *madrasa*s in Pakistan and elsewhere. Strict accounting rarely has been forthcoming, although steady foreign pressure in recent years persuaded the government's main charity, the World Muslim League (Rabita al-Alam al-Islami), to tighten its bookkeeping.

Foreigners' complaints invariably are met with polite Saudi requests for details of suspect bank transactions. Those and other forms of proof are difficult to come by in a region where cash is still king, hundreds of thousands of dollars routinely are carried across borders in attaché cases and the informal *hawala* (transfer) money-transfer system is readily available, cheaper, faster and infinitely more discreet than formal banks.

But the Saudi bumblebee also continues to fly thanks to the exertions of the millions of foreigners who have flocked to Saudi Arabia since early in the twentieth century (and who outnumber its citizens). No group contributed more to the prosperity of the Kingdom—enriching itself handsomely in the process—than immigrants from the Hadhramaut, a desolate region in south-central Yemen, Saudi Arabia's poorer southern neighbor. And few Hadhramis achieved more in a lifetime than Osama's father, who made a fortune for his fifty-four offspring as the Kingdom's most successful building contractor.

Mohammed bin Awad bin Laden and two brothers, all humble masons, in the late 1920s walked out of Husn Bahishn, their hometown at the head of the remote valley of the Wadi Du'an. It was one of the small oasis towns of palms in the valleys cut out of the Jol tableland "like oubliettes," according to the intrepid British traveler Freya Stark, who visited the Hadhramaut in 1932.[3]

Poor Hadhramis were famous travelers, and indeed a large colony had existed for centuries in the faraway Dutch East Indies, today's Indonesia. The brothers joined a camel caravan bound for Jeddah, the Red Sea gateway to Mecca, and the pilgrims who then provided the newly triumphant Al-Saud dynasty's great revenues. Theirs was an arduous and dangerous 1,000-mile adventure that claimed the life of one brother. Even in 1999, a visit to Husn Bahishn involved a four-hour expedition from the regional capital of Seyyoun along a rocky, unpaved road in a four-wheel-drive vehicle. The only electricity in town kept soft drinks cold thanks to a diesel generator.

The older bin Ladens in the early 1960s had provided piped water to the town they'd left behind. But unlike many another local boy who made his pile abroad and endowed the town to glorify his success, there was no new mosque, school, or road due to the bin Ladens' munificence. The explanation was partly political. Rich Hadhrami émigrés did not appreciate the Marxist People's Democracy that ran the Hadhramaut for a generation following 1967, when the British abandoned the great and strategically located natural harbor at Aden—and the rest of South Yemen—after 128 years.

That held especially true for those whose fortunes were made in Saudi

Arabia. Why risk the disapproval of the Al-Saud, who looked askance at any undue interest in either Marxist South or Republican North Yemen, both poor, much more populous and warlike to a fault? By the time North and South Yemen were unified in 1990, Mohammed was long since dead, and few of his offspring had ever visited the Hadhramaut.

Mohammed was a tall, dark, wiry, ugly man with a blind right eye and pockmarked face. He never learned to read and write—indeed could not even sign his name—but was universally respected for his indomitable drive. He especially enjoyed confounding his foreign engineers by calculating the solutions of complicated problems while they were still playing with their slide rules. "He was illiterate," a Palestinian engineer said, "but he had a computer in his head."

Like many another penniless immigrant from the Hadhramaut before him, he was lodged and fed when he arrived in Jeddah by a successful Hadhrami who found him work until he could fend for himself and repay his benefactor. Once he became rich, he wore trademark gold cuff links, a gold Rolex and a silver ring on the little finger of his left hand. But he never forgot where he had come from. A family legend has it that Mohammed preserved his porter's sack as a reminder of his first lowly job in Jeddah's port. Many a Jeddah business had a Hadhrami in charge of its finances. Hadhramis were regarded as totally trustworthy, loyal to each other and to their Saudi employers, willing to shoulder responsibility, hardworking and so avaricious that vicious tongues called them *yahud al-arab*, the "Jews of the Arabs."

Soon Mohammed was exercising his talents as a bricklayer; then he worked as a general handyman in various royal palaces. He started a modest construction company in the early 1930s. His stroke of genius was to be among the first foreigners to understand the essence of early Al-Saud governance. In those days King Abdulaziz never thought it necessary to build a formal central administration. Nor did he think it fitting for princes to dirty their hands with commerce, much less manual labor. But he respected—and rewarded—those who did. And the King soon noted that bin Laden worked fast and well.

What passed for a central government in Riyadh from the 1920s to the 1940s was made up of fewer than a dozen foreign advisers—at one point two Iraqis, two Lebanese, two Syrians, a Palestinian and a Briton (in the person of Cold War superspy Kim Philby's father, St. John). The King also maintained a half dozen administrative aides, including a translator, a couple of typists and a man who cut excess verbiage out of petitions to spare the monarch boredom.

Mohammed bin Laden made it his business whenever in Riyadh to attend King Abdulaziz's *majlis,* the informal council open to all in early Al-Saud rule. In recent years the Al-Saud somewhat defensively have invoked the age-old tradition of the *majlis* to rebut both foreign and domestic criticism that they have become out of touch, secretive and autocratic. But in those simpler times, any man in then much less populous Saudi Arabia really could, and often did, participate in this form of Bedouin democracy. Abdulaziz thus kept abreast of what was on his occasionally turbulent subjects' minds. No one found anything amiss in the regular attendance at the King's *majlis* of a recent arrival from the Hadhramaut. On such occasions, Mohammed bin Laden would try to sit as near to the monarch as possible.

He had already made something of a name for himself by constructing palaces for members of the royal family, but his cleverest idea was to persuade the aging and increasingly arthritic Abdulaziz to build a palace with a car ramp leading up an outside wall straight to his first-floor bedroom. Legend has it that a cautious Abdulaziz agreed to use the ramp himself only after making bin Laden drive up and down several times in the King's heaviest vehicle. It happened to be the vehicle entrusted with gold and silver coins, a kind of mobile state treasury since no banknotes then circulated in the Kingdom. A delighted Abdulaziz announced: "The car and whatever is in it is for you!"

Mohammed "grew up with the Kingdom," a longtime employee recalled, "and the country grew very fast." Mohammed's assiduous attendance on the King paid off when he was given the contract for one of the first major roads—from Jeddah to Medina. Even more famous was the road from Jeddah to the mountain summer capital of Taif, a feat of hairpin-turn engineering that reduced the journey from three days by camel to just three hours. So trusted was bin Laden that the first two Saudi monarchs often awarded his company lucrative contracts without asking for formal competitive bids.

Gradually the bin Laden company became the biggest contractor in the Kingdom (and under his sons it has become one of the biggest in the Middle East and beyond). As a sign of the Al-Sauds' trust, bin Laden was picked to repair and enhance the mosques in Mecca, Medina and Jerusalem—the Muslim world's three holiest sites. He was especially proud of having prayed in all three mosques on the same day. But although he performed his five daily prayers, was generous with *zakat* (Islamic alms, incumbent on all Muslims, especially on the rich), and was a *hajji*, Mohammed bin Laden was neither by upbringing in Yemen, nor by inclination, a Wahhabi. Indeed early-nineteenth-century Wahhabi depredations in the Hadhramaut had destroyed the tombs of immemorially honored saints.

At one point Mohammed bin Laden served in Saudi Arabia as public works minister. Spendthrift King Saud, who succeeded Abdulaziz in 1953, was so much in debt to bin Laden in the late 1950s that he deeded over to him Riyadh's best hotel, the Yamaha. He and other wealthy Hadhramis bankrolled the monarchy through rough patches. When wealth came, he never abandoned fieldwork. His adoring workers were quite used to seeing him appear out of nowhere.

He was famous for cajoling exhausted employees to work extra hours, rhythmically chanting back and forth with "Oh, you guys, your boss is bin Laden, the contractor with one eye," until they did what he wanted—and they all burst out laughing. He was very much a hands-on boss, living with his crews on construction sites. After World War Two many of his engineers were Germans and many of his workers Italians recruited from Rome's former possessions across the Red Sea, Eritrea and Ethiopia. His company had a reputation for working quickly and well. And he took very good care of his field-workers, paying them a 25 percent monthly bonus whether or not overtime was involved.

Over the years as Mohammed bin Laden built more than 13,000 miles of roads and other public works projects all over the Kingdom, he also had copied Abdulaziz's habit of marrying local girls. The King thus cemented his dynasty, and bin Laden ensured that a tribe through whose territory his road construction crews passed would forgo troublemaking in exchange for the jobs provided by the bridegroom. In the process he sired fifty-four children by "more than 20 different mothers."[4] Osama was the seventeenth of the twenty-four boys. Three of Mohammed's permanent wives were Saudis. So, too, were most, but not all, of the other women he married; Islam allowed a man to take a fourth legal wife. He changed them frequently since a Muslim man can repudiate a wife by simply repeating "I divorce you" three times.

Whatever his roving eye, Mohammed had a reputation for generosity. Each wife was given her own comfortable home, and he took scrupulous care of his children. He delighted in roughhousing with them. Sometimes a dozen or more would jump on him, and he teased them by asking who their mothers were, as if to suggest he couldn't remember them all. Some of the children were born to black slave mothers, for the Kingdom had yet to abolish slavery. And at least one repudiated wife married a black slave, much to the chagrin of her bin Laden son, who sought unsuccessfully to have his mother divorce her new husband by offering him a bribe.

Osama's mother, Alia Ghanem, was born to a working-class family near Latakia, a Syrian port city on the Mediterranean. She was in her early twenties when her brother introduced her to Osama's father in Latakia in 1956, and they parted soon after Osama was born the following year—or at least that is what her family said in 2001 in newspaper interviews that included one falsehood and perhaps others, if Saudi friends of Mohammed bin Laden are to be trusted. A Ghanem relative was quoted as saying the family was Sunni. But Latakia is the unofficial capital of the Alawite minority, and the family is not Sunni but Alawite.[5]

Why would the Ghanems seek to pass themselves off as Sunnis? No easy answer suggests itself today, which makes the prevarication all the more curious. But to have fudged a clear answer in the 1950s would have been understandable enough. The Alawites are a heterodox sect accounting for some 12 percent of Syria's population. For five centuries under the Ottomans, the Alawites survived in the mountains of coastal present-day Syria, poor, downtrodden, and despised by the Sunni ascendancy. Under the French League of Nations mandate in Syria between the two World Wars, the Alawites briefly had their own mini-state and, along with other minorities, joined the so-called *troupes de Levant* that helped maintain law and order for France. That did not endear them to the majority Sunnis, who wanted real independence for Syria and never forgave France for carving out what they considered an artificial rump state next door in Lebanon.

Notwithstanding such considerations, throughout the Middle East and beyond, Alawite women were and are prized for their beauty. Alia Ghanem was no exception, according to her son.[6] Back then, there was also a tradition in middle-class Lebanese and Syrian families to hire comely Alawite girls as maids, and many a Beirut male friend of my generation has pleasant memories of being introduced to the delights of the flesh thanks to them.

The status of Alawites changed radically in the 1960s. They gained control of the Baath Party, with its authoritarian secular ideology (*baath* means "resurrection" or "renaissance") that appealed to the Christian,

Druze and Alawite minorities, and challenged the traditional Sunni ascendancy, which had long frozen them out of politics. Soon the Baathis seized power in Syria. The late, long-serving President Hafez Assad was an Alawite, as is Bachar, his son and successor, and so is much of the Syrian ruling elite in and out of the Baath Party, which over the decades has become an empty shell dominated by Alawites.

But in the eyes of many Sunnis in Syria and indeed some Shi'a elsewhere, the Alawites remain a heretical minority sect (so much so that Hafez Assad in the early 1970s arranged for them to be given official benediction from pliant Shi'a religious authorities in Lebanon, who traditionally shared Sunni misgivings about the Alawites' Islamic credentials). In such quarters Alawites still are viewed warily, because in addition to their own suspect habits, they share with the Shi'a the belief that Ali, the Prophet Mohammed's cousin and son-in-law, was his rightful heir but was deprived of his inheritance by the first three caliphs.

Ibn Taymiyah, a puritanical Syrian Sunni theologian who lived from 1263 to 1328, a time of great upheaval in the Muslim world (and who came to be much invoked by Osama and other Al-Qaeda adepts), condemned Alawites as more dangerous than Christians and urged Muslims to make holy war on them. In Saudi Arabia's Nejd heartland, hard-core Wahhabis refer to Shi'a as *al-Rafidha* (rejectionists) and do not think them Muslims at all, but polytheists and apostates. Alawites are accorded even less consideration.[7]

Practical as well as religious concerns help explain such views. Saudi Arabia's oil lies along or near the Persian Gulf's western shore, in what traditionally was the purely Shi'a region of Hasa. Despite the influx of Sunnis and many foreigners drawn to the oil industry, the Shi'a minority remains a source of constant concern for the Al-Saud and has been subject to on-and-off repression.[8] Theological strictures were leavened, however, by local custom and geography. A bit like American immigrants from "humbler" professions who became Episcopalians in the nineteenth and twentieth centuries as a sign of their successful integration into "society," so Wahhabi realpolitik tolerated foreign Muslims from all over the Islamic world despite inner misgivings about their Islamic purity, hoping their offspring would become good Wahhabis. This was especially true in and around Jeddah, traditionally the more open, outward-looking port of entry for Mecca (where many foreign Muslims chose to settle after performing the *hajj*).

It was to Jeddah that Osama, born in 1957 in Riyadh, moved when his mother married another Hadhrami, Mohammed al-Attas, with whom she was to have three sons and a daughter. (In the Hadhramaut and beyond, Attas is an honored name. Indeed the Attas family traditionally was more prestigious than the bin Ladens; for example, a long-serving Indonesian foreign minister was an Attas.) Just how that marriage came about reflects the way rich and powerful men in the Gulf conducted their private lives. A close Saudi friend of Osama's father recounted that Mohammed bin Laden soon tired of Alia, as he had of many other women. But he made sure she was properly married off to al-Attas, who had a steady clerical job with the bin Laden firm.

In fact, according to the same Saudi friend, Mohammed never formally married Alia. If that indeed was the case, was it because by then he had taken on the stern Wahhabi view of heterodox sects or felt he had to abide by them for the purpose of appearances in his adopted country? In any event, Osama's mother would hardly have been the only woman in Saudi Arabia so treated in the 1950s. At that time even slavery was theoretically banned but freely practiced. The Saudi friend no longer remembered what Alia's exact status had been. Other varieties of arrangements also existed, especially for rich men.[9] But his Saudi friend insisted Mohammed had done the right thing by Alia. He had found her an honorable husband, and he formally recognized Osama as his son.

Outwardly Osama was a happy child, or such at least was the impression he left with a friend with whom he grew up. Yet if a Spanish woman who claimed to have befriended fourteen-year-old Osama during a brief English-language summer school at Oxford is to be believed, he confided that his mother was "not a wife of the Koran," but a "concubine." Osama told the woman that his mother was "very beautiful and that was why she had caught the attention of his father."[10] Other tales making the rounds in Jeddah described Alia as "the slave wife" and Osama as "son of the slave." The intended slur is evident: such a child would have been born out of wedlock, with all the emotional baggage to be carried through life that such inferior status implied. Saudis tend to remain conscious of their family members' condition at birth (unlike the Ottomans, who in five centuries of imperial rule had seen many "noble" families incorporate subjects born of slaves and then manumitted.)

However wounding such stories may have been to Osama, he was—and remains—very close to his mother and Attas. But his was a strict Hadhrami upbringing. Even as a youngster, Osama went off with his father on spartan desert retreats, a deliberate toughening up reflecting both Mohammed's ethic of hard work and effort and the need to keep in touch with the realities of his hardscrabble early life. It was a regime Osama was to repeat with his own sons, who learned to ride horses and to walk in their bare feet on hot desert sand. Another Hadhrami who knew Osama as an adolescent recalled how his own father had put him to work when he was not yet nine, taking down the names of all his workers and how much they were paid. "It was the Hadhrami way of bringing up kids, and it's why Hadhramis are so successful," he said. "We were all very close to our fathers because they did it in a very loving way. Life was tough, and it was their way of saying 'don't get spoiled.'"

Then when Osama was ten, his father died. Mohammed bin Laden's Cessna crashed in the mountains near Abha, in the southwest, as the American pilot came in to land. Mohammed had been on his way to inspect yet another mountain road project. Even the oldest children were only in their early twenties. Such were Mohammed's bonds with the Al-Saud that King Faisal announced "You are all my children now" and entrusted another Hadhrami, Mohammed Ba Harith, with running the company until the older boys were deemed sufficiently experienced to manage it on their own.[11] Eventually Salem, the eldest son, took over the ever-expanding business. Outgoing, dynamic and fun-loving, he hopscotched continents in his executive jet and was equally at home at a Geneva dinner party, a Texas barbecue and a night out in London.

Salem was close enough to the Al-Saud to be entrusted with the $92 million customization of a Boeing 747 for King Fahd (complete with gold faucets and an elevator, to spare the portly monarch the rigors of climbing and descending stairs). Salem shared his father's enthusiasm for flying and, like him, died in an airplane accident. In 1988, the ultra-light he was piloting ran into a power line and crashed in San Antonio, Texas.

Osama did see some of his bin Laden half brothers and sisters, especially Salem and Bakr, who as the next-oldest brother was to replace Salem at the head of the core family business now known as the Saudi Bin Ladin Group. But there were so many children—and soon so many grandchildren—that bin Laden youngsters could go for long spells, indeed years, without seeing one another. Many siblings barely knew Osama or had not run into him for many years. For example, Scott MacLeod, who interviewed Osama for *Time* in early 1996, reported that another bin Laden brother was fascinated to find out what the family black sheep was really like since he hadn't actually seen him since the 1980s. He was not alone. In any case, many of Osama's siblings were older and already involved in the core company or other businesses established by sets of older brothers who sometimes shared the same mother. By all accounts, Osama showed little interest in the pleasures and experimentation that rich Saudi children indulge in at home and abroad. Almost all of his half brothers and even some half sisters were certainly worldlier and more Westernized than Osama. Salem, for example, was educated at Millfield, a public school in southern England where many sons of the Arab elite were formed. Indeed, "most of the boys," half brother Yeslam noted in a *Newsweek* interview, "were sent abroad to boarding schools when they were very young."[12] In the early 1970s, three bin Laden boys almost the same age as Osama spent four years at Brummana High School, an elite Quaker institution that educated rich Arab and Western boys and girls in the hills above Beirut. Many bin Laden children were sent to Harvard, the University of Southern California and other Western universities. Indeed various children have long maintained homes and routinely live in the United States, Britain, France, Switzerland, Egypt and other lands. (The "American" bin Ladens were quietly evacuated from the United States soon after 9/11.) In contrast, Osama has rarely traveled, much less lived, outside the Islamic world.

No hard evidence exists that Osama sowed his wild oats, despite persistent stories replete with chapter-and-verse quotes from purported witnesses of such alleged youthful escapades. Indeed, in what I have concluded was clumsy disinformation, various intelligence services put about the fiction that he was a skirt-chasing boozehound in Beirut's astoundingly raunchy nightclubs. The world might have been better off had these tales of barroom brawls over sexy barmaids been true. The most charitable interpretation of such fanciful accounts is that they confused Osama with his brothers or other rich Saudis out on the town.

The truth was more prosaic. Osama was only seventeen when he married for the first time. That wife was a fourteen-year-old Ghanem first cousin from Syria named Najwa; by her he has had eleven children.[13] Marriage between cousins is something of a tradition in Saudi Arabia and indeed elsewhere in the Middle East. For Saudis with sufficient means, marrying young was a classic way to remove temptation. The newlyweds moved in with his mother and stepfather for several years, although Osama could have easily afforded to set up a separate, indeed palatial, household.

His was a typically Hadhrami attitude toward money. He knew he was rich because he was a bin Laden, but he did not flaunt his wealth or hang around with the children of other rich families. If a man asked for five *rials,* he didn't get ten, a friend recalled. Wealth was to be husbanded. Osama's only known vice was driving too fast; he smashed a Chrysler as a young man. In any case, before he was eighteen, Beirut plunged into a series of little and not-so-little wars that lasted for the next decade and a half. It abruptly ceased being the happy hunting ground for rich Saudi boys and others out for a good time. Similarly apocryphal are stories of Osama hanging out in London at Annabelle's and other watering holes.[14]

In fact, in the bin Laden clan, even as a young boy Osama was known to have a deeply religious bent.[15] It was rumored that a Sudanese cleric employed to provide him private instruction in Islamic studies became sufficiently alarmed to warn the family of Osama's extremist views about implementing the *sharia,* or Islamic law. A man who knew him then insisted Osama was already a "stricter" Muslim than "most of his friends, most of his family and even his mother and her husband, who were very moderate." His half brother Yeslam put it more diplomatically. Osama, he said, "is more religious and had a different mentality from the rest of us."[16] In October 2001, on French television, Yeslam's estranged Swiss wife, Carmen, recalled with evident distaste how Osama had refused to shake her hand when he had shown up unexpectedly in their Jeddah home. She supposed his behavior reflected part shyness, part lack of manners, part disapproval of a Western woman.[17]

Khaled M. Batarfi and his brother used to play soccer with Osama when they were teenagers; they all lived on Jabal Sumayqa Street in Jeddah's Musharifah district, then a new middle-class neighborhood and now in the city center, just one street off a main thoroughfare called Palestine Street. Oum Osama ("mother of Osama," in the Arab fashion of adopting the name of the eldest child) still lives in the same comfortable white concrete-faced two-story house behind an eight-foot wall. Osama attended the Al-Thagh school with princes and other members of the Saudi elite. He impressed his professors—and indeed apparently everyone at the time—as courteous, gracious, polite and conscientious.

Batarfi described his soccer pal as a fervent but still tolerant Muslim. "Osama would chant rather than sing since for him music was *haram* [forbidden] but he did not try to enforce his views on the rest of us, who were not as strict Muslims as he was. He had a very nice way of winning over young people who did not pray, often leading them by example to become good Muslims." Even then Osama and a few equally devout friends would fast on Mondays and Thursdays. "He would encourage us to go to mosque, especially to *fajr*, or dawn prayers," Batarfi said. "I went only irregularly. He sort of hoped you would follow his example and if you did, so much the better, but if not, you were still good friends. He had a very strong, quiet, confident and effective charisma."

Osama, by then a gangling teenager, "was a very good soccer forward since he was so tall and clever at heading the ball," his friend said. "We'd play, then have a picnic breakfast. He would have fun in an Islamic way, asking such questions as when the Prophet was born, for instance, or what we knew about the *sharia*. He divided us into teams and he would announce the winners," but "even the losers got to eat the cakes he'd provided."

He struck Batarfi as somewhat "humorless." "In fact he was more serious than the rest of us about life and what was going on in the Muslim world, our role in society," his friend said. "He always knew he was a bin Laden, but did not show it, and was not embarrassed about the family fortune. He also believed all Muslims were equal, and he did not just hang out with rich kids. He had some very poor friends and in fact married poor women." Osama worried that rudderless young Saudis in those oil-boom years were "heading in the wrong way—he was concerned about sex, drugs, going abroad and doing wrong things, not attending prayer in mosques, talking dirty."[18]

Despite his outwardly proper character, he and many members of the Saudi elite shared a subversive secret: the Muslim Brotherhood. The Brotherhood, expounding a radical brand of Islamic reform, was founded in Egypt in 1928 by schoolteacher Hassan al-Banna as an underground organization. It was dedicated to removing British colonial rule and all Western influences, restoring the golden age of Islam, overthrowing the secular order and establishing an Islamic state under the caliphate abolished by Turkish reformer Mustafa Kemal Ataturk in 1924 along with the last vestiges of the Ottoman Empire. What made the Brotherhood attractive to Cold War America was its opposition to socialism and the Soviets, and their easy slogan "Islam is the solution."

By 1948 the Brotherhood had half a million members in Egypt as well as branches in many other countries in the Middle East. It is often seen as the incubator of much of the ensuing radical Islamic thought and political action (especially for the Sunnis, since the Islamic revolution in Shi'a Iran in

1979 played a major role as well). Al-Banna ran afoul of the Egyptian monarchy and was gunned down in a Cairo street in 1949.

Gamal Abdel Nasser and Anwar el-Sadat both had Brotherhood pasts. They initially sought to get on with al-Banna's successors following their Free Officers' coup in 1952 that swept away King Farouk and the monarchy and installed a nationalist regime that excited Arabs throughout the Middle East. But the Brotherhood tried and failed to assassinate Nasser, first in 1954 and again in 1965 (and its spiritual heirs in 1981 did kill Sadat, who ironically had freed many Brothers after he succeeded to power after Nasser's death in 1970). In the 1950s and 1960s Nasser's repression was pitiless. The Brotherhood was banned, and many members were tortured and imprisoned for years in desolate desert concentration camps.

Sayyid Qotb, a onetime education minister under Nasser, was executed for his part in the 1965 plot, but not before his nine years in jail inspired him to write *Signposts Along the Road*. That book remains a basic primer for radical political Islamists. Its central argument holds that jihad (struggle) was legitimate not just in the defense of Muslim lands against infidels, but against Muslim regimes such as Nasser's that were considered enemies of Islam and part of the *jahiliyya*, the period of pre-Islamic "darkness." It was an argument Osama many years later used against the Al-Saud.

From the 1950s Nasser made no secret of his disdain for the Al-Saud and their American protectors. Nor did he hide his desire to overthrow the monarchy. With tacit U.S. approval, the Al-Saud spent handsomely throughout the Middle East to counter Nasser's popular secular Arab nationalism, whose mildly socialist policies Washington equated with those of the Soviet Union. In keeping with the Middle Eastern principle that the enemy of my enemy is my friend, members of the Brotherhood were also welcomed in Saudi Arabia and other conservative pro-Western oil emirates of the Gulf. There they prospered as businessmen; their financial success was to have important consequences in future decades for furthering subversive Islamic political projects elsewhere.

Many other Brothers became teachers. As such they exercised an enormous influence on impressionable young Saudis, such as Osama, whose notions of the outside world, even of the wider Arab world, were limited. The Brotherhood's was a most delicate task. The members were political refugees in the Kingdom. As such they had to watch their step before

Nasser's death, but especially thereafter, when the threat of discredited Arab nationalism declined—and with it their usefulness to the Al-Saud.

The Brothers, of course, wanted to further their own political priorities, but Saudi Arabia in theory already was an Islamic state, and Wahhabism brooked no other form of religious expression in Islam's very heartland. At best they were tolerated, but they were always slightly suspect. By the 1970s, in its Egyptian bastion the Brotherhood had been emasculated. Its more radical children began veering into the uncharted waters of what came to be known as jihadi Islam. But in the comfortable Saudi backwater, another upper-middle-class Saudi with a Brotherhood past remarked, "Osama grew up as a Muslim Brother and did not break until he became immersed in Afghanistan in the middle-to-late 1980s."[19]

Osama was a mediocre student of business management at King Abdul Aziz University, which he chose rather than go abroad because he wanted to stay near his mother in Jeddah. About that time, in the late 1970s, an erudite and silver-tongued Palestinian Muslim Brother named Abdullah Azzam got into trouble in Jordan, where he was teaching Islamic jurisprudence. Like so many other Brothers in similar circumstances, he gravitated to Saudi Arabia, where he was given a job at King Abdul Aziz University. Only conjecture suggests that Azzam actually taught or even knew Osama, but it is entirely possible since the preacher's Algerian son-in-law swears that Azzam and his family lived in a Jeddah flat rented from bin Laden.[20]

Azzam was well known in Saudi Arabia, and his sermons circulated widely thanks to audiocassettes. He shared the Palestinian Brotherhood branch's disdain for the basically secular Palestine Liberation Organization and its armed struggle against Israeli occupation of Palestine (and is sometimes credited as a moving spirit behind its rival, the Islamic Resistance Movement, better known as Hamas). Azzam's other interests lay farther afield and soon took him from Saudi Arabia to Pakistan, where he taught in the Saudi-funded International Islamic University in Islamabad, and eventually to Afghanistan. Azzam's and Osama's paths met more durably again in Peshawar in the mid-1980s, when they worked together in the Afghan jihad.

Osama's lackluster university record—he didn't graduate—was not due to sloth. His teenage friends noticed that increasingly he was neglecting his studies to work for the family construction firm. The bin Ladens were building a road linking the Grand Mosque in Mecca to a new palace as part of gigantic construction contracts in and around Islam's two holiest sites, which were to catapult the family into even greater wealth. The road project was complicated because it went through heavily populated neighborhoods. Many buildings had to be demolished and no dynamite could be used. "We started work at 5:30 a.m. and Osama was always there before me," recalled Palestinian project manager Walid Khatib. "He worked hard and was especially effective in liaising with various government departments and smoothing over problems." Osama was also on good terms with the many Europeans and Americans who worked on the project and spoke with them in excellent English. "We were alone a lot," the engineer said, "and he could have shown he was anti-American. . . . After all, Osama knew I was a member of the Popular Front for the Liberation of Palestine," one of the most virulently anti-American—and Marxist—members of the Palestinian guerrilla galaxy. They got on well, the Palestinian said, and Osama "used to ask about his father and liked to hear us tell stories" about a parent whom he had scarcely known.[21]

In constructing his persona for the outside world, Osama likes to dwell on his early commitment to the Afghan cause. "When the invasion of Afghanistan started, I was enraged," he told a British journalist, "and went there at once. I arrived within days, before the end of 1979."[22] That would have been fast footwork since the first Soviet troops arrived on December 27 for their ill-fated decade of occupation. That initial trip was ephemeral. Osama's real, if never publicly acknowledged, interest lay elsewhere.

Indeed 1979 was an odd choice for him since it was a momentously pivotal year for Muslims and their relations with the rest of the world. The year began with Ayatollah Ruhollah Khomeini returning from a long Iraqi exile to overthrow Shah Mohammed Reza Pahlavi next door in Iran. The Iranian revolution was to galvanize not just its own Shi'a but their long-contemptuous mainstream Sunni rivals as well. On November 20, just over a month before the Soviet invasion of Afghanistan, several hundred home-grown religious fanatics seized the Grand Mosque in Mecca. Saudi urban myth has it that one of Osama's older siblings used company trucks to sneak the conspirators into the mosque.

Inspired by Khomeini's success in overthrowing the Shah, they criticized the Al-Saud for their fondness for alcohol, addiction to foreign flesh-pots and tolerance of Western influence in the Kingdom. Humiliatingly, they were dislodged only eleven days later with the help of infidels in the form of French anti-riot police. That delay focused attention on an embarrassing display of reliance on the West for the House of Saud, whose very legitimacy rested on its protection of this most sacred of Sunni holy places (to the point that King Fahd is referred to as the "custodian of the Two Holy Mosques" in Mecca and Medina). Clearly, radical political Islam was on a roll.

Yet what consumed Osama was not Afghanistan, not the Grand Mosque, not even that favorite Arab cause, Palestine. Rather what attracted him was the Muslim Brotherhood's relentless campaign of terror that nearly toppled the Alawite regime in Syria. Military cadets, government officials, soldiers on leave, army and police installations, prominent Alawite professionals—all were fair game. (The Baath regime in Syria grew sophisticated, pioneering such now standard counterterrorism techniques as giant earth-filled concrete flowerpots set back from the street to absorb blasts.)

The violent Islamist challenge began in 1976 and raged with growing intensity from 1979 to 1982. It all ended very badly. In February and March of 1982 President Assad and his ruthless brother, Rifaat, crushed the Brotherhood in the conservative Sunni city of Hama. There alone some 20,000 died, many of them innocent civilians. Much of historical interest in that ancient city was destroyed. Even by the age-old standards of Middle East violent retribution, "Hama rules" broke new ground.

The Syrian branch of the Brotherhood never recovered from that clandestine war, but more radical progeny came to the fore elsewhere. In that all but forgotten shadow war, Jordan served as the rear base. Providing the money were Saudis, rich, exiled Syrian merchants living in the Kingdom and elsewhere in the Gulf, and Brotherhood members in Germany and the Middle East. The United States had done business with the Brotherhood before and, it was widely believed, pitched in with intelligence and knowhow; in the event, Assad publicly accused Washington of involvement. Other actors included Christian warlords in Lebanon, and the rival Baath regime in Iraq smuggled arms to the Islamists.[23]

It remains unclear what was going on in the mind of young Osama, then barely in his twenties: pop psychologists have suggested that his adult life was one unresolved oedipal struggle with his powerful but neglectful father (or, in another version, reflected a desire to show his older brothers that he, too, counted). But before the final outcome, the Brotherhood appeared to come within an ace of overthrowing the Alawites, the sect of outcasts into which his mother was born. If Osama even considered this

apparent conflict of interest, he has never said so in public, and no unam-
biguous answer suggests itself.

With the blind faith of the true believer, Osama likely argued that the
Brotherhood was justified in fighting to install a Sunni government in
Syria. The enemy certainly was President Assad's regime. It was bad
enough that Syria was being run by heterodox Alawites, although he may
well have stored away that awkward link to his mother in some recess of his
mind. But the unforgivable fact was that the Alawite-dominated Baath
Party in power was secular and made no bones about it.

His exact role in the fight against the Assads also remains unclear, although, given his youth, it was almost certainly minor. But those who
claim to know insist it involved finances, probably fund-raising. Saudi
power projection beyond its borders was, and remains, all but synonymous
with the checkbook. In any case, in those early days Osama had yet to come
into a readily liquid share of his father's inheritance (which the U.S. government once estimated at $300 million, his half brother Yeslam at just
$30 million).[24]

With this curious baptism of radical Islamic political violence behind
him, Osama turned to the war in Afghanistan—with the full, but peculiarly special, blessing of the Al-Saud. It would be a fateful choice for a
world far beyond the confines of Saudi Arabia. Was he, or those who were
to entrust him with great responsibilities, even conscious of his precocious
radical agenda? In retrospect, he might have been seen as carrying a lot of
odd baggage that went far beyond his mixed parentage, with its non-Wah-
habi roots, and his Muslim Brotherhood connection.

In fact, about the only thing those who knew him before Afghanistan,
and even after, could agree on is that Osama bin Laden gave every appearance of lacking the stuff of real leadership. The Palestinian engineer who
genuinely liked Osama figured he was not tough enough to be a leader:
"When I used to talk rough to him in the field, he would look down and
smile in embarrassment." Many others didn't think he was bright enough
to get very far. "Average plus, not average minus," commented a man who
had known Osama since childhood, "but just average."

Nor for all his soft-spoken command of classical Arabic and his suspect
fatwas justifying indiscriminate killing of all Americans has Osama ever
impressed his Muslim peers with possessing the intellectual grasp of Koranic knowledge that is the mark of the religious scholar. He gradually was
to turn this to his own advantage. In fact, his magnetic appeal stemmed

from his growing ability to talk to everyday Muslims in a simple language, laced with Koranic allusions, that had little to do with the learned discourse of the official—and thus easy to influence—notables of Al-Azhar, Egypt's renowned mosque, and its lesser equivalents across the Sunni world.

After the 1998 embassy bombings in East Africa, General Hamid Gul, who ran Pakistan's Inter-Services Intelligence program that fed arms to Afghans fighting the Red Army in the late 1980s, pooh-poohed insistent American accusations of Osama's responsibility. "I know Osama," he told me airily in 1999, "and he doesn't have what it takes." But by then the general, in retirement, had become such an Islamic firebrand that this disclaimer, like a great deal else he said, was subject to caution.

Nearer the mark, arguably, was the wisdom-after-the-fact judgment of Prince Bandar, the Saudi ambassador in Washington for more than two decades. In the wake of September 11, Bandar recalled the halcyon days of international cooperation against the Soviet occupation of Afghanistan in the 1980s. He maintained Osama "came and said 'Thank you, thank you, for bringing the Americans to help us.'" "At that time," the Prince said, "I thought he couldn't lead eight ducks across the street."[25] Bandar was not alone in that view.

AFGHANISTAN:
STIRRED-UP MUSLIMS AND THE END
OF THE COLD WAR

What is most important to the history of the world? The Taliban or the collapse of the Soviet empire, some stirred-up Muslims or the liberation of Central Europe and the end of the Cold War?

—Zbigniew Brzezinski, *Nouvel Observateur*, January 15–21, 1998

The Afghanistan we loved—it wasn't the Middle Ages—it was very simply our youth. We discovered in Afghanistan the youth of the world, the essence of human destiny on this earth.

—American academic Michael Barry, 2001

I CAME LATE to the Soviets' Afghan war and incurred the wrath of my foreign editor for refusing an assignment once I got there. Foreign correspondents do not get paid to say no, and frankly it was not something I did lightly, since my very particular livelihood depended on going to places other colleagues preferred not to. The assignment made sense. In that spring of 1988 negotiations in Geneva to end the war, then in its ninth year, were in their final stages. The Kremlin clearly wanted out. U.S. officials were aglow, convinced that once Soviet troops pulled out, the Najibullah puppet regime left behind by Moscow would collapse—and much faster than had the South Vietnamese government after the United States withdrew its forces and abandoned Saigon to its fate in 1973. So much, arguably too much, of American thinking about Afghanistan was framed in terms of its still-stinging defeat in Vietnam. The *Washington Post* had its doubts, so did I, and I was to find out what was really going on.

Earlier I had refused to go into Afghanistan because of two seasoned Afghan hands, my young American-Swiss friend Edward Girardet and his British colleague Peter Jouvenal, who had covered the war since its very beginnings. I was already in my fifties. I had long since concluded that there were too few coupons left in my ration book to take silly chances above and beyond those taken as a matter of course in a precarious calling. When it came to covering a new conflict, I relied on correspondents who knew the ropes. That was a service I routinely provided newcomers covering war zones I knew firsthand. Only a week or so before I arrived in April 1988, all primed to go into Afghanistan with them, Girardet and Jouvenal had a nasty encounter with "Wahhabis," a catchall term then used to describe all Arab volunteers. Western journalists had been killed from time to time in Afghanistan, and not just by Communists. Girardet told me he and Jouvenal had survived a run-in unpleasant enough that they were not going to test their luck again soon. That was good enough for me, but I knew it wouldn't be good enough for my editor.

Frankly, I was a bit perplexed by the "Wahhabis." I couldn't remember hearing much about them in Afghanistan, although I had covered the Middle East long enough to know who they were in Saudi Arabia. Indeed only recently had the mainstream Western press even begun taking a close look at Gulbuddin Hekmatyar and questioning previously largely uncritical Western support for all Afghan mujahedeen leaders. Engineer Gulbuddin, as he styled himself, was the only one of the seven officially recognized mujahedeen leaders so anti-American that he refused to show up at the White House when President Ronald Reagan dubbed the others "freedom fighters."

At the time, such grandstanding antics were excused on grounds that Hekmatyar was the stoutest fighter of the lot, with the most Soviet scalps on his belt, and did not want to tarnish his image by kowtowing to any foreigner, even be he the president of the United States. In fact, he was merely Pakistan's favorite warlord—receiving more than half the total weapons handed out—and was responsible for the deaths of various Western correspondents and relief workers as well as more Afghan "freedom fighters" than Soviet soldiers or government troops.[1]

What Girardet and Jouvenal told me about the "Wahhabis" was chilling. By the mid-1980s Arab volunteers had become determined to root out Western humanitarian aid agencies and replace them with their own Islamic versions. Western relief workers from the early days of the conflict had worked deep inside Afghanistan at considerable risk to their lives from the Soviets and their Afghan allies. The "Wahhabis" were especially threatening to Western women doctors and nurses, many of whom "worked inside." Their reasoning was simplicity itself: Afghanistan was an Islamic country and should be helped by other Muslims, not infidels. Their principal tool was cash, lots of cash, sometimes in $100 bills still fresh in their plastic packets, more often in the local currency called *afghanis.*

"We couldn't compete," a Western aid official recalled. Years later a shamefaced Afghan mujahedeen commander living in self-exile in Paris told me "Wahhabis" from the Gulf had offered him so much money that he had sacrificed long-standing personal relations with a Western aid agency, persuading the personnel to close dispensaries and feeding stations virtually overnight. He was far from the only mujahedeen commander to have done so. Still, most Afghans didn't much like the "Wahhabis," who quickly dissipated the respect due foreign volunteers, especially those hailing from the land of the Holy Koran and speaking its sacred language. Theirs was an intolerant brand of Islam. The "Wahhabis" soon sought to put their imprint on what they considered the local adulterations of pure Islam: traditions dear to Afghan Muslims were declared *haram* (forbidden)—dancing, singing, the cult of local saints known as *pirs,* the flag-and-bottle graveyard markers that clanked so ominously in the wind.

I have put quotation marks around the word "Wahhabi" because it had become a corrupted shorthand. For the Soviets and later the Russians, "Wahhabi" was synonymous with any Muslim who took up arms against them. For the Saudis it meant their particular brand of Islam, that of the *salafi* (forefathers) of the much-revered first three generations of Muslims. But in Afghanistan and Pakistan "Wahhabi" was a blend of Saudi and other Gulf Arab money-cum-proselytism and the very much minority brand of Islam in India and Pakistan known as *Deobandism* (from the Indian city of Deoband, where it originated in the nineteenth century). Deobandism stemmed from an effort by Muslims in the British Raj to defend their faith under foreign infidel rule. At the birth of Pakistan on the ruins of the Raj in 1947, the movement, with government encouragement, made steady inroads, gradually transmogrifying into militant advocacy of revolutionary holy war, or jihadism, during the Afghan war. But Deobandism remained a distant second in Pakistani affections to the moderate mainstream Barelvi brand of Islam and, despite its noisy demonstrations and threatening rallies, had never done well in elections (until 2002).

Yet for all their harassment of Western relief workers, the "Wahhabis"—or "Afghan Arabs," as they were also called—were never considered a major fighting force in what, after all, was and remained the Afghans' war against Soviet occupation. None of the leading players—the Americans, the Pakistanis, the Afghans, the Russians and, in all truth, the Arabs themselves—regarded the foreign Muslim volunteers as more than extras. Various foreign intelligence agencies from as far afield as Algeria, Tunisia, Morocco and Egypt kept a desultory eye on them. But the volunteers were basically left to themselves. They signed up with various, often the most radical, Islamic Afghan factions in the field and can scarcely be blamed for wanting to create a place for themselves. That the Arabs and other foreign Muslims were there at all reflected the complexities of a bizarre war.

Wartime coalitions by definition bring together partners with different agendas unlikely to outlast the conflict itself. The way this coalition was put together—and predictably fell apart—gave rise to the "blowback" thesis. In recent years, blowback critics have argued that the Americans and others mindlessly created the "monster of Islamic terrorism," then walked away from the consequences until forced to launch yet another war in 2001 to lay the burgeoning threat to rest when it quite literally could no longer be ignored. In the light of Afghanistan's history of fractious politics, it was not that surprising—or the Americans' fault alone—that rival mujahedeen militias fell to fighting one another in a series of nasty little wars.

Pakistan and Afghanistan's other neighbors—India, Iran and Russia, working through its former Central Asian possessions—helped keep the fighting going after the Red Army's withdrawal. Whatever its purported merits, the blowback theory presupposed that the United States had an overall, detailed view of what was going on in the war against the Soviets. In fact, the war effort was devised deliberately to look as if the Americans would not know what was happening inside Afghanistan. The real extent of U.S. intelligence from inside Afghanistan then remains unclear.[2] In affairs of state, ignorance is rarely bliss.

The Americans' objectives in Afghanistan were specific, but limited. They wanted revenge for their comeuppance at Communist hands in Vietnam. For most of the conflict they were content to bleed the Soviets rather than risk defeating them outright. (Only in 1986, after the Soviets had clearly signaled their desire to withdraw from Afghanistan, did the United States finally supply the mujahedeen with shoulder-held Stinger missiles.

They tipped the balance against Soviet helicopter gunships that had inflicted serious casualties on the Afghans.) The more modest U.S. plan was fine by Pakistan. That way Islamabad could pursue its own agenda without persnickety Americans looking over their shoulders at the details.

And Pakistan very definitely had a private agenda. Even before the Soviets invaded Afghanistan in December 1979, President Mohammed Zia ul-Haq had dreams of using his American ally in the Cold War to help carve out a new Mogul empire extending from Pakistan all the way to the still very Soviet republics of Central Asia. Afghanistan lay at the center of that policy, with Pakistan determined to install a compliant government in Kabul in order to neutralize Afghanistan's ambition of grouping Afghan Pahstuns with their much more numerous Pakistani cousins.

Zia was a military dictator who blatantly played the Islamic political card. He was delighted when the Americans signed up to fight the Soviet troops in Afghanistan and, for reasons of "plausible deniability" so dear to intelligence agencies, agreed to funnel arms and money through the Pakistani army's hitherto minor-league Inter-Services Intelligence. That way no official Americans would set foot in Afghanistan, and there would be no American military casualties. Such was the legacy of the Vietnam War, a legacy that remained very largely intact until the attacks on the World Trade Center and the Pentagon.

The subterfuge was transparent and certainly didn't fool the Kremlin. But it meant that Zia and like-minded Islamic radicals for all intents and purposes controlled the distribution of arms, food and funds to the coalition of Afghan warlords that the ISI chose and manipulated. The United States deliberately abdicated responsibility and, with it, accurate firsthand knowledge of what was going on inside Afghanistan.

With the stage thus set, all kinds of odd actors signed up with American blessing. China was enlisted to sell arms for dollars to weaken its Communist rival in the Kremlin. So was Egypt, eager to get paid for obsolescent weapons. Israel was equally happy to sell Soviet bloc weapons captured in its various wars with the Arabs. But the prize catch was Saudi Arabia. From the very start, the royal family was brought on board by the United States. The Al-Saud did what they knew best. They paid.

For years Saudi checkbook diplomacy had spent millions to buy off predatory neighbors or on questionable causes Washington favored but found awkward to ask Congress to fund (such as financing the contras in Nicaragua or UNITA in Angola). But the Afghan cause was one they wholeheartedly endorsed for religious and geo-strategic reasons. So they happily paid, splitting the rapidly mounting official war costs right down the middle with the United States. Or as Milton Bearden, the Central Intelligence Agency's station chief in Pakistan in the climactic years of the war, put it, the Saudis matched America's own contribution "bill for bill"—to the eventual tune of about $500 million each annually.

Afghanistan was America's first experiment at franchising war, a practice employed again on a grander scale in the conflict to recover Kuwait from Iraqi occupation in 1991. (Kuwait, Saudi Arabia, Germany and Japan underwrote some two-thirds of that war's costs.) Beyond the Saudi government donations, Saudis and other rich Arabs from the Gulf's oil emirates happily kept opening their private purses to add literally untold hundreds of millions of dollars for the Afghan jihad over the years. That so-called mosque money assumed even greater importance after 1991, when Washington prevailed on the Al-Saud to cut off the official spigot. It became the only game in town and was beholden to no one. That model was to cause serious problems in the 1990s when critics accused various Saudi-based and other Islamic charities of looking the other way when bin Laden skimmed off funds.

Money was by no means the only dividend in American eyes. At long last the Saudis' puritanical brand of Islam, previously something of an embarrassment to Washington with its public beheadings, lack of democracy and other human-rights excesses, could be turned to good use. Wahhabism was unleashed against godless Communists and against Iran's Shi'a and their triumphant Islamic revolution. Washington all but licked its chops at the prospect of double payback for the most humiliating half decade in American history. Here was a chance to enlist others to get even for the fall of Saigon to the Communists in 1975 and the overthrow of Shah Mohammed Reza Pahlavi's pro-American monarchy in Iran four years later. No wonder Congress kept foisting more money on a gung-ho Reagan administration, doubling and even tripling its requested outlays.

The American calculation was Pavlovian in its simplicity. In any event, the Saudis did not require much persuading. They had been nervous for more than a decade. The British in 1971 ended a century and a half of military presence in the Persian Gulf. The modicum of British-maintained stability was replaced by a triangular power struggle involving Iran, Iraq and Saudi Arabia. The Saudis knew they were the weakest leg. They had the most oil and the smallest population and were unsure of the U.S. resolve to defend the Kingdom once Washington "abandoned" the Shah in 1979. The Saudis despised and felt threatened by the more numerous Shi'a Muslims of Iran; they had had little use for the Shah in his time.

It had been humiliating enough for the Al-Saud to have the Shah's troops bumbling around neighboring Oman in the 1970s, trying ineffectually to defeat Marxist rebels. But now Ayatollah Ruhollah Khomeini had installed a radical Islamic revolution in Tehran with wide appeal for all Muslims. No longer were Muslims automatically ready to respect the firewall that long protected the Sunni world from Iran's Shi'a influence. Indeed an essential ingredient of new radical Sunni jihad politics became a taste for martyrdom previously associated with the Shi'a.

For the Al-Saud, 1979 was an annus horribilis. It began with unease over the downfall of the Shah, the Americans' other major ally in the Gulf, and ended with the embarrassing seizure of Mecca's Grand Mosque by local Sunni firebrands—and the disconcerting Soviet invasion of Afghanistan. Radical political Islam was on a visible roll. But the Al-Saud did not appreciate competition in the Islamic purity league. Nor was Saudi Arabia comfortable with the aggressive, secular republican regime in Iraq, ever ready to squeeze its weaker neighbors.

Under increasing criticism for their profligate lifestyle, the Al-Saud rapidly saw the Afghan jihad as a way of helping restore their besmirched honor and reputation with ordinary Saudis. The embarrassing Grand Mosque violence shifted the balance of power in favor of the Wahhabis, who gradually imposed more courses on religion in schools and whittled away at the Al-Sauds' freedom of political maneuver. In such circumstances, no higher cause existed in Islam than the Afghan conflict, even if jihad as holy war (as opposed to its more commonly accepted definition as a Muslim's moral struggle—or "striving," as its Arabic root signifies—within himself) had not been practiced for some eight centuries.

Jihad also attracted a proliferating fringe of dissatisfied youths. If they died "martyred" in battle, they would rid the Kingdom and other Muslim countries providing volunteers of many troublemakers, and then would dwell forever with seventy two *houris*, the virgins promised in paradise to those who die in battle defending Islam. To deny Muslims the duty to do jihad would have, moreover, risked backfiring on Arab governments. Jihad in Afghanistan was literally a God-given chance to be on the winning side, a rare-enough phenomenon in contemporary Muslim history.

It was with all these somewhat confused thoughts in mind that Muslims from North Africa's Atlantic Coast to the South Seas were encouraged to take part in the war effort. The goal was to show the world that Islam was united in its disapproval of the Kremlin. The highest religious authorities in the Sunni world deemed jihad an absolute religious obligation binding on every Muslim, not a question of individual choice. That message was relayed in mosques everywhere. The volunteers' presence in Pakistan and Afghanistan in itself was good propaganda. Accordingly, Pakistan made visas readily available at its embassies and consulates. Saudi Arabia offered 75 percent reductions on airline tickets for Pakistan originating in the Kingdom. The United States, its Western allies and many other governments encouraged their Muslim residents and citizens to join the jihad. Radical Muslim recruiters sought out volunteers as far away as North America and the Philippines. In Egypt, President Hosni Mubarak was happy to export radical Islamists who had served their prison sentences in connection with the assassination of his predecessor Anwar el-Sadat in October 1981.

Even today, mindful of the terrible costs stemming from the unintended consequences of such a policy, Saudi officials insist they had no choice but to bankroll and promote the volunteers' travels. To have done otherwise would have been unthinkable and risked undermining the very foundations of their theocratic regime. Prince Turki al-Faisal, who ran Saudi intelligence for a quarter century, said it would have been a "grave mistake" for any Arab state to have prevented volunteers from doing their "sacred duty" in Afghanistan because "for the first time in many years many Muslims were doing something against an invader and appearing to be succeeding."[3] Thus, across some thirty countries of the Muslim world, it was Godspeed, or sometimes good riddance, or a bit of both to would-be martyrs in an authentic response to the first genuine jihad in defense of Islam since the Crusades.

Just how many foreign Muslims answered the call remains unclear, with most estimates ranging from 10,000 to 15,000 but others reaching 19,000, indeed 30,000. No one seems to have kept exact count. Or perhaps those who did—the Saudis kept track of volunteers flying cheap air tickets—found it politic not to open the records to public scrutiny. Many of these volunteers, especially the better-heeled Gulf Arabs, were students or civil servants on vacation.

Some would first visit the fleshpots of Southeast Asia before stopping for a purifying immersion in jihad on their way home. They would fly in and out in a matter of days, often staying only long enough to have a group photograph showing them just inside the Afghan border. Others drifted through the Pakistani city of Peshawar, the war's major staging area, barely more than an hour's drive down the Khyber Pass to the Afghan border.

Even less-well-heeled volunteers came and went as they pleased. No one appears to know for sure just how many Arabs actually fought alongside the Afghans, although most of those who did were absorbed in the officially anointed mujahedeen groups. Syrian reporter Ahmad Muaffaq Zaidan, who covered the war and remained in Pakistan, told me his meticulous doctoral research showed that just forty-four Arab volunteers died fighting the Soviets (although a further 198 were killed in the ill-fated offensive on Jalalabad against Najibullah's Afghan Communist regime soon after the Soviets withdrew in the spring of 1989). Such losses barely warranted a footnote compared to the million-plus Afghans who died fighting to free their country from Soviet occupation.[4]

In fact, most of the so-called Afghan Arabs rarely left Peshawar and its environs, where they were engaged in relief efforts. Many lived and worked in University Town, a leafy extension of the old British Raj garrison city that grew up around the former Indian army cantonment, itself largely unchanged since independence in 1947. So did most of the Western aid workers. But in what struck me as odd, rarely, if ever, did the twain meet. I went back twice to Peshawar in two successive years trying to understand how Muslims and Westerners engaged in the same kind of relief work in a single neighborhood of a provincial Pakistani city had practically nothing to do with each other professionally or personally. My probing prompted less ill ease than surprise.

"We were ships that passed in the night," said Anders Fange, a Swede who first came to Afghanistan as a radio journalist in 1980. He was thirty-four at the time and three years later went to work for the Swedish Committee, then as now active in providing aid to Afghans. "We were all working flat out, more than seventy hours a week," he said by way of explanation. The split became evident in 1988 when hitherto clandestine cross-border relief operations became aboveboard thanks to the Geneva Accords, which laid down a calendar for Soviet withdrawal and allowed more rational planning for bringing aid inside Afghanistan.

Suddenly, humanitarian aid operations became almost legitimate. And even more money poured in to help the Afghans. Western and Islamic relief organizations set up rival coordinating councils, with only the Sudanese sitting briefly on both. Yet, even in Peshawar relations were not easy. A French aid worker reported being threatened with a handgun by an Arab who kept following him around in a car. Western women routinely complained that Arabs in University Town spat on them in the street. These signs of tension were somehow submerged in the name of getting on with the war.

Fange, who in his youth in Sweden demonstrated against the American presence in Vietnam, saw the Afghan conflict as a case of "yet another big power jumping on a small country." In Peshawar "I felt I was part of something important and I was adamantly against the Soviet occupation." So were hundreds of other Westerners, many of them French and American, who abandoned promising careers as lawyers, investment bankers and doctors to flock to the war. "The Arabs were here to assist the Afghans, and even if we didn't like them, they were not the enemy," Fange said, casting his mind back to his early days, when he had just contracted his self-admitted lingering "Afghan virus." "We did not see the danger of these Arabs, and with hindsight it is easy to draw conclusions that they were motivated not by a desire to reestablish national independence for Afghanistan, but by radical, global jihad."[5]

Edward Girardet had Afghan–Arab hostility brought home forcefully again in 1989. He was assigned by one of his many news organizations to do a television story on the final days of the Soviet presence, which officially ended that February. Prudently he went no farther across the Afghan border than necessary. No sooner had he and his crew started working than a tall, gangling, armed Arab ordered him in excellent English to leave. Given his years of commitment to the Afghan cause, Girardet took umbrage. Speaking disdainfully and insisting his interpreter repeat every word slowly, he replied in English that he was a guest of the Afghan people and would leave only when they so instructed. The Arab and a squad of his men became increasingly menacing. "If you do not leave immediately, I will shoot you," the Arab said, "and don't ever come back because I will kill you the next time I see you for sure."

Girardet left in a foul temper. But a few days later he crossed back into Afghanistan, this time a few miles from the site of his unpleasant encounter. He had a story to finish. Fortuitously, he was accompanied by an Afghan mujahedeen commander who was a close friend. Out of nowhere the same tall Arab appeared and started screaming, "I warned you the next time I would kill you. So clear out." Girardet stood his ground. A shouting match ensued, with the now-gesticulating Arab and his men breaking cover and threatening Girardet and his crew.

These antics soon attracted the attention of Afghan government troops, who lost no time mortaring the area. Girardet's Afghan friend saved the day, not so gently pushing Girardet and his crew into a jeep that sped away as mortar rounds bracketed the path. Only after August 1998, when Osama bin Laden was blamed for the truck-bomb attacks against the U.S. embassies in Dar es Salaam and Nairobi, did Girardet realize that the man whose picture was so prominently featured on television and in the newspapers had been his tormentor in 1989.

In retrospect, Girardet's experience illustrated the Afghan war's odd side effects. How absurd it was for an Arab and a Westerner to be screaming at each other on the eve of a theoretically shared victory. In microcosm theirs was the classic story of wartime coalitions falling apart as victory looms from the fog of dubious battle. It is easy enough to look back and see why. Afghanistan long had been a weak, decentralized buffer state whose principal claim to fame throughout history was as a passageway and death trap for invading foreign armies, thanks to the formidable mountain range aptly named the Hindu Kush (literally, "Hindu killers"). When I started out in journalism, "Afghanistanism" was shorthand for a recondite, faraway and complex foreign problem of secondary interest defying easy explanation, much less solution, and guaranteed to induce boredom. Afghanistan was one of those places seemingly doomed to long periods of oblivion.

Yet in 1989, for the Americans and many of their allies, the war looked like a giant and clear-cut success, far exceeding the initial modest goal of bloodying the Russian bear. The Berlin Wall came down only nine months after the last Soviet soldier in February crossed the Amu Darya River, the Oxus of antiquity. The Cold War was about to expire, and with it the Kremlin's empire in Central Europe and in Central Asia. No wonder Zbigniew Brzezinski, who as President Jimmy Carter's national security adviser baited the Soviet trap six months before the Red Army's formal invasion, exulted.

Ten years earlier, he had masterminded clandestine military operations inside Afghanistan designed to draw the Soviets ever deeper into the quagmire. He was interested in more than just getting even for America's defeat in Vietnam. In 1998 Brzezinski told the French magazine *Nouvel Observateur* to keep things in proportion: "What is most important to the history of the world? The Taliban or the collapse of the Soviet empire, some stirred-up Muslims or the liberation of Central Europe and the end of the Cold War?"[6] You didn't need to be the son of a prewar Polish diplomat like Brzezinski to think that way.

Not all Americans officials waxed so enthusiastic. If the CIA exulted, some in the State Department were less pleased. "Just the difference between an action-oriented agency like the CIA, which left amid the cheering," an American diplomat grumbled years later, "and State, which was left to try to put the pieces back together" after the Soviets' withdrawal. Perhaps, but even that seemed a simplification.

I remembered during my 1988 visit wondering about the naïveté of the American officials' deadly certainties about the happy end they felt to be so inevitable.

My doubts reflected the two years I had spent in Iran in 1978 and 1979 chronicling the Shah's collapse and the rise of Khomeini. Street demonstrations in Tehran had dinned into my ears endlessly repeated warnings against the danger of "Westoxication" and "neither East nor West." So I kept pestering American officials in Pakistan about the dangers of awakening Islam as a political force. An otherwise friendly diplomat, fed up with my carping, one day had hissed at me, "Here we are dealing with Sunnis, not Shi'a." I did not consider his remark a clinching argument.

My doubts must have made the rounds because one day I received a telephone call from an American official asking me to come to his Peshawar office. I had no idea why, had never met the man or even heard his name. But I appeared at the appointed hour. The official kept track of the booming heroin trade along the Afghan–Pakistani border and beyond. That was one aspect of America's policy he couldn't stomach. For the next hour I couldn't stop him talking. He knew what I needed to make a strong story.

He provided the names of major Afghan and Pakistani traffickers. He also explained that the same trucks the ISI used to deliver weapons and ammunition for the Afghan fighters from depots in Islamabad and Karachi went back packed with heroin destined for Western markets and Pakistan's own city-dwellers. I reckoned he must have lost a major battle with other bureaucrats, who perhaps shared his concern but in the name of the war effort preferred to remain silent.

The Afghan Arabs had their own problems, especially after the last Soviet soldier left Afghanistan on February 15, 1989. They had persuaded themselves that the Afghan mujahedeen would sweep unopposed into Kabul to proclaim a pure Islamic state. If anything, the Arab volunteers were more crestfallen than Westerners about the chaotic course of events in post-Soviet Afghanistan. They were shaken by their defeat at the battle of Jalalabad in the spring of 1989 that they—and the cheerleading American embassy in Islamabad—had been convinced would end the war. Even earlier, the volunteers had been upset by the tensions that were to lead to unbridled fighting among rival militias.

In retrospect, the volunteers were naive. They somehow had talked themselves into believing theirs was the central conflict of the day and themselves its veritable motor. In fact, the Afghan war was in Middle East terms a sideshow and their role minor in the extreme. The Iran–Iraq War, decidedly more threatening to the Muslim heartland in the Middle East and the outside world's oil supplies, played itself out between 1980 and mid-1988, in virtually the same time frame as the Afghan conflict. (Iraq squeezed the Al-Saud for $20 billion in protection money, disguised as "loans," as their contribution for keeping revolutionary Iran at bay.) The first intifada pitting rock-throwing Palestinian boys against the Israeli occupation army began in December 1987.

But what mattered for the Afghan Arabs was that for a half dozen years or so they were left to their own devices. For Westerners like academic Michael Barry, Afghanistan meant discovering "the youth of the world, the essence of human destiny on this earth." Afghanistan represented another discovery for Muslim volunteers who had come from distant lands. Jihad was a religious obligation, but also a fortuitous chance to rub shoulders with co-religionists from the world over, to compare notes and often radicalize each other.

Years later, a Western diplomat in Peshawar was talking with Mary Anne Weaver, who had spent decades covering the Muslim world for a variety of publications, including *The New Yorker*. The diplomat remarked, "In their wildest imagination, these groups never would have met here if there had been no jihad." He ruminated on the melting-pot repercussions that flowed from bringing together a kind of Islamic version of the Comintern and concluded, "The consequences for all of us are astronomical."[7]

In fact, most of the volunteers went home and resumed normal lives. But for a tiny minority of Arab volunteers, Afghanistan was an eye-opening introduction to the extremist politics of jihad and the ways and means of freeing once-Muslim lands from foreign "infidel" domination, as well as overthrowing their Arab governments that were deemed un-Islamic.

America was as suspect as the Soviet Union for these radicals, guilty of a variety of sins, ranging from support of Israel to secularizing traditional Muslim society and "looting" the Middle East's oil. They were politic enough to hide their opinions from everyday Afghans, who still felt a debt of gratitude toward America for helping end the Soviet occupation. That was just as well since their goals and those of average Afghans were diverging even then. In the year the Russians went home, an Afghan refugee in Peshawar told a young American teaching him English, "These Arabs want to die for the cause, they seek martyrdom. We want the Russians out, but we want to live, we are not fighting to die."[8]

THE MAKING OF A LEADER

I WAS IN JEDDAH in December 1999 when a helpful Saudi colleague mentioned he was planning that evening to attend a gathering of Saudis who had participated in the Afghan jihad. The whole thrust of our conversation had clearly indicated my interest in meeting Afghan Arabs. It should have been obvious I wanted very much to attend. But no invitation was forthcoming, and I judged it unwise to mention the matter myself. I wondered why he even brought the subject up. Let's say I was disappointed rather than surprised. I'd covered enough conflicts to know that war veterans can be a breed apart. They tend to communicate in a kind of code—often lubricated by lots of alcohol in the West—and do not as a matter of course welcome outsiders, especially foreigners, in their midst.

Still, I was puzzled. Was it normal or extraordinary that in Osama bin Laden's hometown men of his generation would be meeting and, I felt certain, discussing his latest adventures along with their own wartime experiences? In the United States, Osama had become the fountainhead of international terrorism since the bomb attacks on the American embassies in Kenya and Tanzania in August 1998. He was under indictment for organizing those attacks, and the U.S. government was offering a $5 million reward for information leading to his arrest. The more the American media dwelt upon him, the more Osama basked in the reflection of the publicity and the more his own reputation grew among ordinary Muslims, not least in Saudi Arabia.

The Clinton administration had made sure of that by their choice of high-tech reprisal for the bombings. On August 20, 1998, U.S. Navy sub-marines fired more than sixty Tomahawk missiles at one of his Afghan training camps, plus another dozen and a half unleashed at the El-Shifa pharmaceutical plant near Sudan's capital, Khartoum, said to be owned by Osama and producing chemical weapons. In Afghanistan the missiles missed him. He had been in the camp near Khost, some U.S. intelligence sources said, only an hour or so earlier (although others doubted he was anywhere in the vicinity). But Western scientific experts hired by El-Shifa's proprietor, who had bought the plant only months earlier, soon embarrassed the administration by convincingly disproving its claim that the factory was producing dangerous chemical weapons and that Osama was part owner.

The very use of the Tomahawks added to Osama's aura, for they encapsulated a key ingredient of the Third World's resentment against the United States and the technological prowess needed to build such a weapon, capable of killing without risk of loss of life to its owners. Over five decades in varied locales I had watched the growing fury against the West, especially the United States, for not "fighting fair." The Third World lamented that the Americans unfairly shirked getting bloodied themselves, as if modern warfare should be a throwback to chivalrous hand-to-hand combat in which the Americans, too, could be hurt. Carried to its logical conclusion, such thinking could lead to terrorism, the traditional arm of the frustrated and weak, reduced to inflicting pain as a means of existing and being heard.

Osama repeated time and again that he wanted to make Americans taste the bitterness of defeat and humiliation that they, as latter-day Crusaders, so often had inflicted on Muslims in the past four centuries of Islamic decline and Western assertiveness. He was clever enough to harp on the massacres of Palestinian civilians in the Sabra and Chatila refugee camps in Beirut in 1982 and of Lebanese civilians in Qana in south Lebanon in 1996. Both were examples of unarmed Arabs killed either with Israeli arms or connivance. Never mind that he, like so many other Saudis, had a long record of indifference about the Palestinian cause. He knew Sabra and Chatila and Qana were names that resonated with many educated Muslims, not just the illiterate and near-illiterate masses, even if the elite knew full well that terrorism, especially his brand, was well nigh impossible to justify in Islam.

But it was so tempting to forget corrupt governments, arrogant rulers, failed institutions and everything else that didn't work at home and, of course, one's own responsibility for the endemic mess. So blame the foreigner. Blame the West. Blame the United States. Yes, especially, blame the only superpower and self-proclaimed "indispensable nation," in Madeleine Albright's unfortunate coinage, which maddeningly dominated the globe but refused to set right the festering Palestines and Kashmirs of this world.

Osama was something new, a freestanding rainmaker unencumbered with the baggage of state responsibility. Or that was the impression if you didn't look too closely at the sloppy loose ends in Pakistan and Afghanistan. For many Muslims his power and glory depended on no sovereign state backer. Instead of the ranting blowhards the Muslim world so often threw up, Osama was rich, pious and well spoken; he defied the Americans and knew how to hurt them.

In nineteenth-century America, "twisting the lion's tail" meant goading the all-powerful British, who more often than not found it judicious to look the other way. Arguably, America now dominated the world in ways even the British Empire could not have imagined at its zenith. But "no body bags," post–Vietnam War America was in no mood to unleash its terrible, swift sword for more than a quick headline or a news cycle or two. Basking in the reflected glory of its Cold War victory, the United States was an imperial power without formal colonies, pretending indifference to its pervasive influence overseas. America gave every outward sign of wanting to turn inward, in a return to classic isolationism after a half-century aberration of foreign entanglements.

That was what made Osama so fascinating. His was a schizoid view of American power as both threat and paper tiger. He belittled the prowess of the American soldier and thus logically of the U.S. military. But he was convinced that the United States was a very real threat that must be stopped before it destroyed what was left of the Muslim world. Born of ignorance of the West, and especially of the new mood in America, this was a message with great appeal far and wide. His view of his religion and the outside world was certainly rigid and limited; nonetheless, he succeeded in electrifying many Muslims who knew his was a perversion of Islam.

Thus, on June 10, 1999, Al-Jazeera, the iconoclastic satellite television station located in the Kingdom's tiny neighbor, Qatar, lived up to its growing reputation for revolutionizing television in the Arab world by airing a ninety-minute documentary on bin Laden. Since its inception in 1996, Al-Jazeera, staffed mainly by former employees of the British Broadcasting Corporation's Arabic service, regularly infuriated Arab governments by giving long-repressed opposition figures an outlet. The documentary, centered around an interview filmed in Afghanistan late in the previous December, had been delayed for months, it was whispered, by American, Saudi and even Egyptian government pressure. But Qataris took special pride in provoking the wrath of their giant Saudi neighbor. That went with the territory, a kind of background of white noise.

The documentary aired on a Thursday evening, the beginning of the Muslim weekend, to ensure a maximum audience. "The streets in Riyadh were deserted," a resident of the capital recalled. "Everyone was watching Al-Jazeera. The Al-Saud were not pleased." It wasn't so much what Osama said, since he had developed many of the themes in previous interviews with Western networks. What fascinated Saudis was hearing Osama speak directly in Arabic, rather than hearing his voice translated back into Arabic from English on foreign television programs.

That reestablished him as alive and human. Officially, he was very much a nonperson in Saudi Arabia, as Secretary of State Albright discovered when she sought to engage Crown Prince Abdullah bin Abdulaziz al-Saud about him the following autumn during a swing through the Middle East while I was visiting in the Kingdom. "I don't believe that person is a Saudi," remarked Crown Prince Abdullah, closing off her inquiry with impeccable desert logic since the Kingdom in 1994 had removed bin Laden's citizenship.

Relations had not always been so frosty. During the war against the Soviets in Afghanistan, Osama was a chosen, if initially minor, instrument in Saudi policy designed to raise funds for the Afghan jihad. Prince Salman, along with King Fahd one of the inner circle of seven sons born to King Abdulaziz's favorite wife, Hasa, was in charge of organizing humanitarian relief for the millions of Afghan refugees who had fled the war and sought asylum in Pakistan. A couple of years into the jihad, in the early 1980s, fund-raising committees were established in each of the Kingdom's regions. The local emir called on prominent families and asked them to name a family member to serve on the committee and thus encourage other donations. The bin Laden family picked Osama, apparently because he was considered the most religious sibling.

At the time Osama was working for the family construction company. The Palestinian project manager on the Mecca road extension noticed that one day Osama was absent and the next day he showed up for work only at noon. Before Osama could explain, the engineer began chewing him out,

"Dammit, you believe you are the owner of the company." Osama had a funny way of laughing to hide his shyness. The engineer exploded, "Why are you laughing? What is wrong with you?"

Osama explained his new responsibilities as the family representative on the relief committee. He disappeared and was gone a week or ten days. When he returned he was criticized again. Osama explained he'd flown to Pakistan on a Saudi Air Force C-130 with a load of blankets and canned food for the Afghans. "He disappeared a second time," the engineer recalled, "and the third time told me he was going to Afghanistan and not coming back to work."

In fact, bin Laden went to Pakistan and did not initially venture beyond the capital, Islamabad. He stayed with Abdullah Azzam, the Palestinian Muslim Brother who had left Jeddah and was teaching at the Saudi-financed International Islamic University there. Boudejema Bounoua, who arrived in 1984 from his native Algeria, remembers being introduced almost immediately to bin Laden at Azzam's house, where both were staying. Azzam announced, "This is Abu Abdullah," as Osama was known. "He is from a rich Saudi family and is not allowed to go to Peshawar and he is on his way back to Jeddah." The two men seemed to know each other although Bounoua got the strong impression this was only Osama's second visit to Pakistan under Azzam's tutelage.

His greenhorn status did not prevent Osama from telling Robert Fisk of the *Independent* in London in December 1993 that soon after what he claimed was his first visit in 1979, within days of the Soviet invasion, he began sending Arab volunteers by "not hundreds but thousands." Perhaps, but Jamal Ismail, a Palestinian university student working as a freelance reporter at the time, recalled being one of only three Arabs present in Peshawar in 1983. And a year later Bounoua discovered that just thirteen Arab volunteers had preceded him when, two days after landing in Islamabad, he traveled with Azzam to Peshawar, the old British garrison town now swollen with Afghan refugees, spies and intrigue.

Soon after arriving from Jeddah in 1981, Azzam began commuting between his teaching duties in Islamabad and the capital of the Northwest Frontier Province, with each passing year spending more time in Peshawar in order to be nearer the jihad. Such was his fervor, encouraged in regular meetings with the ISI and even Zia ul-Haq himself, that Azzam by the end of 1986 abandoned his teaching post, pulled up stakes and left Islamabad for good. He became a respected counselor to rival Afghan leaders, an eloquent preacher on the jihad's behalf and a wide-ranging raiser of funds and volunteers from Riyadh to New York.

But Azzam's real originality—and lasting influence—lay elsewhere. For the war in Afghanistan, he resurrected and gained wide acceptance for the concept of violent jihad as a tool to persuade Muslims from all over that they must join the fight. Using violence previously was restricted to small radical groups like Egypt's Islamic Jihad or Gama'a al-Islamiyya. Azzam called for Muslims "to join the caravan" in Afghanistan. He found ready financial backing, mainly in Saudi Arabia and Kuwait, for *salafi*-minded *madrasas* (Islamic religious schools), as well as military training camps in Pakistan. Backed by the prestige of studies at Sunni Islam's most respected Islamic center, Cairo's Al-Azhar University, Azzam defined two kinds of jihad.

Fard kifaya, he argued in outlining the case of an offensive attack against an infidel adversary's own territory, required participation of only a single Muslim group, not of all Muslims. But he decreed that Afghanistan was a case of *fard ayn,* involving defensive jihad to protect Muslims and their territory from infidel attack. As such, he preached, it represented an inescapable individual duty incumbent on every Muslim, much as Islam's traditional obligations, such as five daily prayers, charity, known as *zakat,* and daylight fasting during the holy month of Ramadan. First, the closest Muslim community would be required to help, then ever-expanding concentric circles, as needed to defeat the enemy.

Azzam's contribution to the success of the Afghan jihad—indeed of resurrecting jihad as an active part of Islam—can scarcely be exaggerated. Sheikh Omar Abdel Rahman, the blind spiritual guide of Egypt's Gama'a al-Islamiyya who was jailed for life in 1996 for waging a war of urban terrorism against the United States, was moved to say, "When the Afghans rose and declared a jihad—jihad had been dead for the longest time—I can't tell you how proud I was."[1]

With international backing for the jihad assured, Azzam and Osama established the Maktab al-Khidamat (Services Office). It was located in Peshawar's University Town suburb on quiet Syed Jalauddin al-Afghani street (ironically named for a nineteenth-century Muslim thinker noted for trying to modernize Islam to meet the West's challenge). Amid the bougainvillea and substantial houses of Peshawar's well-heeled elite, the office was devoted to furthering the Afghan cause by quite literally putting financial and other aid at the service of the volunteer fighters.

An associated guest house, Beit al-Ansar, provided simple room and board for new volunteers, housing a dozen to a room on hard pallets. They were brought directly by special bus from the Islamabad airport. Those returning from duty inside Afghanistan were also welcome. Funding came from all over the Muslim world, but especially from Saudi Arabia and the Gulf oil emirates. Playing a major role was Rabita al-Alam al-Islami, the World Muslim League, founded in 1962 by the Al-Saud as a means of carrying the *salafi* message abroad.

Osama initially spent his time fund-raising at home. He also persuaded his family's construction firm to send engineers and heavy equipment to build tunnels, underground hospitals, arms depots and other military fortifications near the Afghan–Pakistani border (such as the Americans bombed at Tora Bora in November and December 2001). A young Palestinian recalled that Osama in that early period would appear in Peshawar every three months or so, stay a few weeks and go back home. "As a rich man's son, he knew how to talk to rich people, how to get them to contribute to the jihad," he said. The bin Laden fortune was such that Osama enjoyed a major advantage over many another fund-raiser: "he was personally rich enough that he was considered honest and above skimming off the proceeds. In Saudi Arabia bin Laden was a household name." Few other fund-raisers came equipped with such credentials.

In Peshawar, Osama at first was remembered for assiduously visiting the wounded, handing out excellent English chocolates, taking down names and hometowns and making sure the families received both news and cash. There was something of the fop about him; his *shalwar kameez* costume (a loose tunic over pants) was tailored from the best imported English cloth, and he wore bespoke boots from London. When Prince Turki al-Faisal, the head of Saudi Intelligence, made his regular rounds to check on the progress of the jihad, Azzam and Osama were bidden occasionally to meet him in Islamabad or Peshawar.

By late 1986 Osama succeeded in adding battlefield heroism to his résumé, throughout the ages a prerequisite for many a young man's ambitious dreams of power and prestige. As he told and retold his defining moment, a much larger force of Soviet and Afghan government forces near Jaji, a mujahedeen encampment near the Pakistani border, attacked him and some forty other Arab volunteers. The Afghan fighters with them quickly and prudently withdrew, but despite Osama's orders, his men refused. "We came here to fight in the jihad, we came to die," they said, "and die we will." So, goes the story, for more than ten days they withstood Soviet air, tank and paratrooper onslaughts, accumulating a dozen or so martyrs in the process. Abdul Rassoul Sayyaf, the Arabic-speaking leader of the Ittihad-e-Islami mujahedeen group long favored by the Saudis, rushed to his Jaji camp with reinforcements to relieve Osama's beleaguered men.

Osama's own account of his baptism of fire is a masterpiece of religious faith, self-aggrandizing derring-do and inspirational fairy tale, complete with big print and a happy ending. "No, I was never afraid of death," Osama insisted in an interview seven years later with Robert Fisk that encapsulated his myth.[2] "As Muslims, we believe that when we die, we go to heaven. Before a battle, God sends us *seqina,* tranquility. Once I was only 30 meters from the Russians and they were trying to capture me. I was under bombardment but I was so peaceful in my heart that I fell asleep. This experience has been written about in our earliest books. I saw a 120 mm mortar shell land in front of me, but it did not blow up. Four more bombs were dropped from a Russian plane on our headquarters, but they did not explode. We beat the Soviet Union. The Russians fled." To this day Osama carries the assault rifle he took at Jaji from, legend has it, a dead Russian, a general at that.

Having had the misfortune of being trapped in battle, I found the account so unbelievable that I had all but written it off as over-the-top myth-making. I kept telling myself that Jaji, if it ever occurred, sounded like a minor encounter scarcely justifying the conclusion "We beat the Soviet Union" even if the Russians had abandoned the chase.

But in Yemen in 1999 I came across a man who swore he had been at Jaji with Osama. He provided chapter and verse. So at least the battle had taken place, although the Yemeni had seen a lot of much nastier combat in Afghanistan and didn't remember Jaji as much of a fight compared with the sustained violence he later survived near Kabul.[3]

In any case, my quibbling was beside the point. What mattered was Osama's view of himself as a man steeled by God, willing to die, even seeking death, but spared, much to his regret, to fight another day. He had punched his combat ticket, leading from the front. No longer was he just a fund-raiser, although that remained his main function and for all intents and purposes his combat days were largely over. Thus did he round out a persona henceforth composed of physical courage, renunciation of earthly pleasures and the privileges bestowed by great wealth, deep concern for ordinary Muslims and dedication to a very special form of radical Islam.[4]

Osama's sincerity, quiet demeanor, serenity and otherworldliness masked a relentless hankering after publicity and self-promotion. Osama became the hero of the Saudi press, only too happy to cooperate. "He was the darling of everybody," a Saudi official recalled of those years. "He was fighting the war everyone wanted to fight and he was putting his own money on the line. The Americans loved him. We loved him."[5] When back from the jihad on his frequent trips home, Osama was much in demand, speaking in mosques, schools and military academies. Audiocassettes of his utterances were churned out by the thousands. His childhood friend Khaled Batarji recalled that Osama was a "one of a kind hero of our time— indeed I can't think of any other."[6] Indeed Osama, not yet thirty, had turned himself into a something of a religious pop star in a land hungering for inspirational role models since the death of the King Abdulaziz. His irresistible ascension had begun.

Within one year of Jaji he had founded his own group, apparently the first and only time that Arab volunteers fought as a unit rather than as support for Afghan fighters. The group later was called Al-Qaeda (Arabic for "the base"). No one seems to know why, although some have suggested it was meant as a kind of database to keep track of the comings and goings of the Muslim volunteers he hoped to turn into an international legion for jihad. In fact, its initial importance was as much political as military.

The founding of Al-Qaeda marked a change in the close relationship between Azzam and bin Laden. They remained good friends and often saw each other daily when they were in Peshawar. But both were often abroad separately fund-raising, in Saudi Arabia and elsewhere, for months at a time. Osama even then was away for more than half the year. When he was back, increasingly he stayed just inside the border with Afghanistan, driving the five or six hours to Peshawar for only two or three days a month. To distinguish the two, Maktab al-Khidamat was viewed as a Muslim Brothers' operation and Al-Qaeda very much as Osama's creation and personal property. Just why Osama insisted on his own show remains obscure. In the process he had gradually shaken off his ties with the Muslim Brothers.

That made sense. In the past Saudi Arabia always had the cash, but more often than not had to hire foreign talent to run its key overseas operations. Azzam, born near Jenin on the Israeli-occupied West Bank, was thus no exception. Contemporary Saudi society was scarcely littered with pious young men of good family likely to inspire pride. Osama enjoyed the spotlight and knew how to milk his sudden fame to full advantage. Osama's name, a friend remembered, was soon "on every young Saudi boy's lips." Adolescents were not alone in succumbing to his charm. So promoting Osama made sense to the Al-Saud well.

He was chosen by the Arab volunteers as emir or prince of the Afghan Arabs, rather than Azzam, who was sixteen years his senior, a vastly more impressive Islamic scholar and a spellbinding preacher. From the jihad's very beginning, Azzam had played a vital role funneling Saudi and other Gulf funds to the Afghan fighters and welcoming and organizing the Arab volunteers. They finally began pouring into Peshawar in great numbers starting in 1986, the turning point of the war, when Washington decided to supply the Afghan resistance with Stingers and more money. Azzam's very success meant he was no longer indispensable.

To the degree doctrine played a role, Azzam followed the Muslim Brotherhood's practice of recruiting only among the elite. The jihad attracted Muslims of every possible hue and sect, ranging from Wahhabis and *salafis* to followers of much less puritanical schools and, of course, young men from one end of the Islamic world to the other. Each school and often each nationality—Yemenis, Saudis, Algerians, Sudanese and so on—tended to prefer living and eventually training and fighting together.

Al-Qaeda's inner circle from the beginning included Egyptians—key lieutenants such as Mohammed Atef, a onetime policeman better known as Abu Hafs al-Masri, and Abu Ubaidah al-Banshiri. They were not Muslim Brothers. Osama's idea was to "recruit everyone, seasonal dropouts, Wahhabis, yesterday's drunk, *salafis*, last year's adulterer, Tahrir, even Takfiris, you name it," a Saudi friend said, reeling off the names of small splinter groups of radical political Islam. Another witness from that period, Jamal Ismail, said Osama felt Al-Qaeda should get involved in the fighting "and not just make speeches" in favor of the Afghans.

This mixture of action and inclusiveness of the marginal was not without precedent in the Middle East, especially for minorities seeking to escape their long-repressed status in an overarching and all-encompassing ideology of mainstream Sunni Islam. Christian activists in the nineteenth century played a powerful role in the Arab Awakening and in the mid–twentieth century helped found political parties such as the Greater Syria Party (Parti Populaire Syrien) and the Baath, which subsumed their status as second-class citizens in an Islamic world and made them equal participants. Osama, the product of the Saudi merchant-prince class, doubtless outwardly would have rejected with horror comparison with Christians, even then decried as Crusaders.

But for a young man who was half Hadhrami and half Alawite, was Al-Qaeda a way to go beyond the confines of strict Wahhabi traditions and the Muslim Brotherhood that constituted his first deviance from the strict faith of the land of his birth? Was Osama even then mulling the transgression of another Wahhabi, indeed Sunni-wide, prohibition against the Shi'a tradition of suicidal sacrifice that was to become Al-Qaeda's trademark contribution to political terrorism?

In any case, Al-Qaeda, in Osama's mind, was to be a kind of "ready reserve," a standing Islamic legion, prepared to serve at a moment's notice not just in Afghanistan, but in still ill-defined jihads to come. For in his exaltation Osama assumed what happened in Afghanistan would happen elsewhere. His followers would go home but remain rapidly mobilizable. At that point Osama showed no outward interest in causing problems for Muslim governments, much less terrorism, although returning Afghan Arabs in Algeria, Egypt and elsewhere by the early 1990s were engaged in both forms of subversion.

Prompting the ready-reserve project were Osama's frustrations over the long delays he had experienced in recruiting volunteers for the Afghan jihad. Defeated Russian officers, as well as others, noted that generous inducements—monthly pay packets of $500 to $1,000 were rumored—played a part in motivating some jihad vocations. Running on the color green's identification with Islam, a cynic told me, "It was not Green Islam, but green dollars" that prompted many a poor boy to head for Peshawar. In any event, Osama never shied away from using money to achieve his purposes.

Azzam was devoted single-mindedly to helping the Afghans end Soviet occupation and instituting an Islamic state in Kabul. In furthering that goal, he kept to himself whatever misgivings he had about Muslim governments and his native Palestine. Osama had wider horizons. "He went to Afghanistan, not for the Afghans alone," remarked Jamal Kashoggi, the reporter whose stories from Afghanistan helped put Osama on the map in the 1980s, "but to liberate the *umma*," the Muslim community, "everywhere."[7] Less than a decade earlier, Ayatollah Khomeini, although suspect as a Shi'a, had stirred the soul of many a Sunni with the Iranian revolution's potential to sweep away the Middle East's artificial frontiers and remove the Arab world's secular rulers.

Khomeini's determination to spread his revolution throughout the Muslim world frightened the Arabs and the West—and explained the Western "tilt" in favor of Baghdad during the Iran–Iraq War. But a decade later, Osama and his followers were in no mood to call off *fard ayn* with the departure of Soviet troops from Afghanistan. There were other oppressed Muslim lands to fight for. Jihad in their eyes became a movable feast of sorts. The Philippines and Kashmir were tempting, but in 1992 the plight of Bosnia's embattled Muslims at the hands of first the Serbs, then the Croats, was more compelling.

Chechnya's war against Russia between 1994 and 1996 attracted *salafi*s and their money. Azzam's call to defend Afghan Muslims was replicated in many places. What has been dubbed "nomadic jihadism" helped spawn the international network that came to be associated with Osama and Al-Qaeda. Osama early on was specifically dreaming of "liberating" the "stans," the predominantly Muslim Central Asian republics still firmly in the orbit of the Soviet Union.[8] It was a wild scheme, but understandable for a militant Muslim increasingly under the spell of perpetual jihad.

Westerners thought of the Iron Curtain as the division of Europe in the late 1940s. For Muslims like Osama, the real Iron Curtain had fallen on the Islamic lands of Turkestan, Uzbekistan, Tajikistan, Kyrgyzstan, Chechnya and much of the Caucasus with the expansive Russification of the nineteenth century. The coming of Communism in the 1920s merely officialized the barrier separating Central Asian Muslims from their co-religionists elsewhere. So pursuing jihad there was less a question of expansionism than winning back what had been previously lost. (Similarly, Osama claimed Spain as Muslim land because eight centuries of Muslim rule ended only in 1492 with the expulsion of the Moors.)

Now the Afghan Arabs felt their hour had come. Already in 1988 they were supremely confident that Kabul would fall to their Afghan allies once the Red Army left Afghanistan the following February. Osama and like-minded Arabs proved overly optimistic about Kabul, which was captured only in 1992, but prescient about the collapse of the Soviet empire and access to the "stans."

As what they headily took for quick, certain victory in Afghanistan seemed to approach, Arab volunteers turned increasingly anti-American and anti-Western, especially after the United States and Saudi Arabia made clear they were cutting back on financing the jihad. Initially the Arab volunteers were careful not to criticize Washington and Riyadh in public, since Afghans were still thankful for the American and Saudi aid they knew had made the difference in routing the Soviets.

But in their hearts, as Osama kept insisting, they were sure the Americans, viewed as latter-day paper tigers, would fall even more effortlessly than the Russians. It became an article of faith that the age of the superpowers was ending. Reinforcing such certainties were images of the inglorious American exit from Saigon in 1975—and for Muslims, more important still—from Iran in 1979 and Lebanon five years later. In any event, "no Arab in the jihad was happy with the United States, principally because of blind American support for Israel," Jamal Ismail recalled. (Many Palestinians, to the degree they thought of Afghanistan, could only lament that the entire world—especially Arab governments—seemed more fascinated with aiding the Afghans than their own longer-established struggle.)

Osama himself was critical as well of Al-Saud rule, despite the ruling family's unstinting support for the jihad. According to Ismail, who saw Osama frequently in those early days in Peshawar, he made no bones in private about American "looting" of Saudi oil wealth, the Al-Saud's corruption and what he took as growing secularization of the "land of the two mosques." Those were themes Osama was to hammer home in years to come. But before he founded Al-Qaeda in the late 1980s, there is nothing to indicate he was actively planning to take jihad in any form to the Americans during his first stay in Afghanistan.

Once the Soviet soldiers were gone, Afghan Arabs found reasons closer at hand to criticize the United States and Saudi Arabia. Washington wanted to bring Zahir Shah, the deposed Afghan king, back into the political equation, and favored power-sharing with the despised pro-Western moderates and with Najibullah, the Soviet surrogate Moscow had left to look after their interests in Kabul.

The jihadis were in no mood to compromise. Even Azzam was upset when the Saudis and the Americans announced they were cutting their aid back because their principal war aim had been achieved with the Soviet army's withdrawal. Not just emotion was involved. The jihadis knew they held strong cards. They still could—and did—raise hundreds of millions of dollars for the Afghan cause from private backers in the Gulf and everywhere there were Muslim communities. That "mosque money" had been a precious additional source of revenue for the jihad in the 1980s. Now, with the phasing out of official Saudi–U.S. financing, it became the only readily available foreign funding.

And control of that money constituted the jihadis' first open challenge to Al-Saud policy. Such was their dedication to installing an Islamic state in Kabul that they were not inclined to give up easily. In a possibly apocryphal but widely believed incident, Azzam in a mid-1989 visit to Riyadh was said to have argued with a senior Saudi, some say Prince Turki himself, in favor of continuing the jihad until Kabul fell to their Afghan friends. Rebuffed, he threw down his Saudi identity papers, dating from his teaching period in Jeddah, and stormed off to the airport.

That quarrel also defined the doctrinal battle lines that increasingly came to pit Osama and his followers against Muslim governments. In light of Islam's explicit rejection of rebellion against Muslim rulers, jihadi radicals somehow had to prove that Arab leaders and regimes were no longer Muslim. That was no easy matter. They fell back on Ibn Taymiyah, the Syrian renowned for his writings on jihad in the late thirteenth and early fourteenth centuries, when Sunni Islam was under a double threat from the Crusaders and the Mongols.

The Mongols formally adopted Islam, and arguably jihad could not be invoked against them as fellow Muslims. But Ibn Taymiyah issued a *fatwa,* or religious ruling, inventing a loophole. Though technically Muslims, the Mongols did not qualify as such if their actions betrayed the faith. He did so as a follower of Ahmed ibn Hanbal, the founder of the most rigorous of the four schools of Islamic jurisprudence, who believed in stripping the religion of suspect accretions. Thus jihad was possible then, and modern-day radical *salafis*, ever careful to pile one religious precedent on another to justify their unusual argumentation, harked back to Ibn Taymiyah to explain opposition to their governments. Azzam's definition of jihad could be invoked against Muslim regimes deemed to be virtual playthings of the West for maintaining military links, contracting loans with international financial and monetary institutions, and accepting foreign assistance in almost any form.

Eventually despairing of changing what he considered the Al-Sauds' wayward subservience to Western imperialism, Osama was to attack the United States as the best way of wresting power away from them at home. But that lay years ahead. In Egypt's case, jihadis in the early 1990s invoked similar reasoning to fight the Mubarak government. In Algeria, *salafis* attacked the ruling military establishment as creatures of Paris still bent on stifling the country's true Islamic nature two generations after winning independence from France.

But in preferring such charges against their respective governments, these jihadis arrogated to themselves the right to declare their enemies *takfir* (apostate). Tolerance of such seeming high-handedness in Sunni Islam, especially in a relatively minor sect, may appear odd to Westerners accustomed to the authority of the Vatican or its roughly Protestant equivalent, the World Council of Churches. This decentralization in declaring spiritual and temporal rivals apostates effectively sought to wrest control from state-dominated religious courts and religious authorities. But radical *salafis* wielded the blunt instrument of *takfir* against their adversaries on the flimsiest of pretexts. In the process, they opened the door to increasingly gratuitous violence.

Indeed, it might be argued that it was only logical that the father of jihad's new doctrine would meet a violent end. In November 1989, only eight months after the last Soviet soldier left Afghanistan, Azzam and two of his sons were killed in a sophisticated, remote-controlled explosion as they drove over a bridge on their way to Friday prayers in Peshawar. Azzam's high-tech assassination was something of a novelty. In a city infamous for unexplained murders, most were carried out with cold steel by assassins recruited easily for small fees.

Boudejema Bounoua, who had become Azzam's son-in-law, remembers listening to the dozens of Afghans and Arabs who had come to the family's home to pay their last respects. "'We know who killed him,' they'd say and then blame Iran, and the next day someone would say, 'It was Gulbuddin Hekmatyar,' and two days later the villains would be Israel or the United States or KHAD, the communist regime's secret police."[9] To this day no one knows who was responsible.

The failure to elucidate Azzam's death, much less bring his killers to justice, eventually prompted insinuations that Osama was involved. (But that was years later, when anything to do with Osama grabbed the spotlight. He has insisted that he repeatedly warned Azzam to pay more heed to his own security.) The alleged motive was Osama's desire to take over as the Khidamat's boss; such rumor scandalized his followers, since by then Al-Qaeda was up and running as his own organization, quite distinct from Azzam's. At the time such a notorious murder seemingly reflected growing tensions among rival Afghan commanders just as victory seemed within grasp.

The bloodletting among erstwhile allies was a harbinger of even worse times. After a decade of upheaval throughout much of the Muslim world, radical Islamic politics no longer appeared to be the unstoppable wave of the future. Jihad for jihad's sake was not the hoped-for panacea. Full-scale fighting among onetime Afghan allies ensued. Arab volunteers were aghast. To their disgust, some were sucked into combatting one another on behalf of their Afghan commanders. Many, including Osama, tried unsuccessfully to mediate. The dream of a quick victory, of installing an Islamic state in Kabul, faded fast after the Arabs lost many men in a failed offensive against Jalalabad in the spring of 1989. Kabul was to fall only in 1992, the year official foreign funding ended.

Many Muslim volunteers drifted off, going home to resume their normal lives. They had done their religious duty and had no stomach for perpetual jihad. To be sure, fresh volunteers kept arriving even after 1989, but in ever-dwindling numbers. Iraq's invasion of Kuwait, another Arab state, in August 1990 further weakened jihadi ranks. Most of the Afghan fighters and many Arabs refused to side with the Saudis and other rich Gulf states that had so generously financed the jihad. The Saudis appealed in vain for Afghan volunteers to demonstrate solidarity.

Only a few Afghan royalist moderates answered the call. The defection of the Hekmatyars and other radical Islamist Afghan warlords who had pocketed the lion's share of Saudi, Kuwaiti and, of course, American largesse did not mean they had illusions about Saddam Hussein and his secular Baath Party dictatorship. But even in the name of delivering Muslim Kuwait from the likes of Saddam, they could not abide the presence of a half million infidel Western, mainly American, troops on Islam's sacred soil in Saudi Arabia. Islamic radicalism seemed to have reached a plateau.

For a decade the fervor generated by Iran's Islamic revolution was such that the ayatollahs seemed to have wrought a miracle: reconciling the millennial hostility between mainstream Sunnis and their own smaller Shi'a branch of Islam. But in early 1988 the fortunes of war abruptly turned against Tehran and in favor of Iraq's secular regime. The inevitability of political Islam's expanding domain collapsed and the old Sunni–Shi'a cleavages resurfaced. Six months before the Soviets quit Afghanistan, Khomeini "drank the poisoned chalice" and ended the war against Iraq that Iran could not win. All of a sudden a whole series of things were going very wrong.

Osama cut his losses in Afghanistan. By the end of 1989 he had pulled up stakes and gone back home to Jeddah. He had arrived in Afghanistan untested, a rich young man seeking to find himself in a foreign war and perchance become a leader. His time in Afghanistan had seasoned him. He returned to Saudi Arabia with a record of solid accomplishment. "What I lived in two years there," he told Robert Fisk, "I could not have lived in a hundred years elsewhere." In a way he was also describing his impatience, a desire to compress time and shoot ahead on his own. As a friend put it more mundanely, "Osama got carried away by his Afghan experience."

Indeed, he had become so convinced of his own destiny that once back home he began conducting what amounted to a personal foreign policy. It is unclear if he realized that in so doing he was deliberately challenging Al-Saud rule. In any case, as in the past, he took care not to criticize the royal family in public. Nor did the Al-Saud initially crack down on him. Quiet suasion was their favored way of dealing with the Kingdom's difficult sons, especially those of prominent families. Both his challenge and their muffled reaction were to have consequences well beyond Saudi Arabia.

FROM HERO TO TROUBLEMAKER

I N LATE 1989 Osama held a pep talk in Afghanistan for a group of young Yemenis he had handpicked and dispatched to fight in the jihad. Yemenis represented one of the largest national contingents among the foreign Muslim volunteers. But these Yemenis were especially important to Osama. They were unlike the many foreign Muslims who rarely left the relative comforts of humanitarian aid work in Peshawar or Quetta. At his own expense, Osama deliberately had recruited and sent these young men to learn the arts of war in Afghanistan. He now renewed an earlier promise and, given gnawing doubts about the jihad's swift inevitability, his reassurance was welcome. The holy war was rapidly turning sour because of tensions within and among rival Afghan mujahedeen groups and the surprisingly resilient Najibullah regime that Moscow left behind in Kabul.

Although Osama and most foreign volunteers were bitterly disappointed, he had another card up his sleeve. He told the gathering the sun was about to dawn in South Yemen, his father's birthplace. It was with South Yemen specifically in mind that these volunteers had signed up with Osama for Afghanistan in any case. Now the timing couldn't have been better. Just weeks earlier, North Yemen, nominally a never-colonized republic but in reality largely a mountainous collection of feudal baronies, and South Yemen, a former British possession originally built around the great natural harbor of Aden and since 1967 a hard-line Marxist People's Republic and terrorist haven, had announced their intention to unite the following year. The Berlin Wall had just come down, the Cold War was ending and the Kremlin was pruning expensive foreign operations.

Moscow's South Yemen satellite was broke, left with little choice but to seek salvation with its larger and more populous northern rival.

Osama's plans sounded like a dream come true for his Yemenis.[1] Almost all the young men Osama had recruited in the mid-1980s belonged to southern landowning families dispossessed by the People's Democratic Republic of Yemen. They were the lucky ones who escaped Communist jails or worse. Many such families were welcomed in Saudi Arabia, but the prudent Al-Saud took few chances. Their potentially turbulent Yemeni revanchist sons were enrolled in the aptly named Jaish Salaam (Army of Peace). The Saudis kept these South Yemenis vegetating in the north near Tabuk, not far from Israel, and a good 800 miles from their homeland.

Osama recruited them with an offer they didn't want to refuse. In addition to their religious duty to participate in the jihad, these volunteers were motivated by Osama's promise to train and help them win back the land the Marxist government had confiscated. When they left for Afghanistan, that still looked like a long shot. Arms were never a problem in Yemen, where generally accepted estimates put the number of weapons at 50 million, three times the population. Osama now promised to provide the very thing so often lacking in Yemen: cash.

So, with his help, his Yemenis went home, with an initial stopover in the north before they trickled back down south. In those early, euphoric days of the promised union, returning jihadis were welcomed, no questions asked. Indeed, of all the returning jihadis, Yemenis had the easiest time with their authorities. Yemen was so receptive it took in thousands of volunteers from other countries whose more nervous officials were already concerned about the risk of subversion from their own Afghan veterans.

Osama proved true to his word. Regularly, in 1990 and 1991, representatives of his Afghan veterans showed up in Jeddah at his unpretentious middle-class house. They left with large amounts of money that came in handy in pursuing their efforts to reclaim their family lands and destabilize the Socialists, as the hitherto Marxists now preferred to be called. Osama and his Yemenis did little to hide their transactions. One Yemeni beneficiary who regularly went to Jeddah told me years later, "No big deal, no special precautions. We put the cash in suitcases and went home. No questions asked at the border. And we came back time and again for more." It wasn't as if the emissaries benefited from some special prearranged wink and nod at the border, he intimated. That was just the way the border was.

But lax border controls did not mean the Al-Saud were without a Yemeni policy of sorts. The official Saudi view reflected a strong historical dose of innate fear of Yemen, a much poorer, more bellicose country whose hardworking population dwarfed the Kingdom's. The Al-Saud had good reason to worry about Yemen. In putting together his realm, King Abdulaziz in 1934 had seized what North Yemenis consider to be large mountainous slices of their territory. Only in the year 2000, at long last, did Saudi Arabia forgo a favorite pressure point and agree to delineate its border with Yemen. In the last third of the twentieth century, the Al-Saud were both frightened by their proximity to the South's Marxist regime and reassured because its very existence kept their troublesome North Yemeni neighbors weak and divided. Even earlier, in the early 1960s, the Al-Saud had interfered militarily in North Yemen to counter Nasser's Egypt in a deadly civil war that effectively sapped the strength from Cairo's army and helped contribute to its defeat in the Six-Day War against Israel in 1967.

Still, Saudi policy was changeable. At times the Al-Sauds' visceral anti-Communism would gain the upper hand. In 1982, for example, Saudi intelligence and CIA director William Casey teamed up in an abortive plot to blow up oil-storage tanks in the port of Aden and other targets. The Marxist government rolled up thirteen plotters, who confessed the CIA had trained them. All but three were executed.[2] One Yemeni survivor of that embarrassing disaster was my informant about the suitcase runs to Osama's house in Jeddah. But most of the time Saudi thinking mirrored French writer François Mauriac's witticism about the division of Germany after World War Two: "I like Germany so much that I am delighted there are two."

Nearly a quarter century ago, I outsmarted myself by including Mauriac's crack in a story about Yemen and was denied a Saudi visa for many years. Osama's own tactical error was to pursue his predictably single-minded goal while blithely feigning to ignore that the Al-Saud might have had second thoughts about their "two Yemens" policy. To the degree he worried about such trifles, he seems to have figured that the Al-Saud and he were both anti-Communist, and the rulers of South Yemen were Communists, so logically what he was doing was just fine.

He was wrong. The Al-Saud were not amused by Osama's freelance operation with South Yemeni tribal leaders and indeed began tracking his activities, apparently from the first wave of returning Afghan veterans in

1989.[3] (That did not stop the Al-Saud a few years later from spending several hundred million dollars trying to prop up the southerners and keep the Yemens separated. The policy backfired, and much of the money ended up in Swiss bank accounts.)

Saudi officials kept their displeasure about Osama's freebooters to themselves for more than a decade, but it was his meddling in Yemen, they later said, that first brought him under their official scrutiny and that eventually led to his estrangement, then open conflict. According to Prince Turki al-Faisal either out of naïveté or defiance Osama in fact suggested to the Al-Saud that they allow him to bring his Yemenis to the Kingdom before they jumped off for Yemen.[4]

"Of course, the Kingdom said no," on grounds of not interfering in a neighbor's internal affairs, Turki recalled, somewhat disingenuously in light of the Al-Sauds' record of manipulation in its dealings with both Yemens. Speaking in a television documentary aired less than two months after the September 11 events, Turki said Osama was praised for his work in Afghanistan but told firmly to "leave things at that." It is unclear why Turki, who had retired just twelve days before the attacks in the United States, chose to wait so long to make the disclosure.

But his extended interview, aimed principally at his domestic public, reflected deep-seated Al-Saud uneasiness following the September 11 attacks, in which fifteen of the nineteen suicide bombers embarrassingly turned out to be Saudis. With American officials repeatedly leaking their unhappiness with the Saudis to the press, the Al-Saud were clearly on the defensive. Indeed no Saudi intelligence chief had ever before written a newspaper opinion piece, much less appeared on television.

By the Saudis' own peculiar standards, Turki was downright expansive in laying out the Al-Saud case. Osama was "not pleased" at being "fobbed off," the Prince said in his television appearances in 2001. And, he explained, when Osama persisted in meddling in Yemeni affairs, even traveling to North Yemen, "the Kingdom's authorities warned him against doing such things," indeed told him to "desist from such acts," and when he did not, "he had to be stopped." That was strong language. But Osama, a scion of the Al-Sauds' close friends and business associates, the bin Ladens, was not arrested or persecuted for his misbehavior.

Instead he was grounded like an errant schoolboy. He was put on a kind of probation, and his passport was revoked. The Al-Saud thought they were handling Osama with kid gloves, but it was treatment he neither forgave nor forgot. This was the first inkling of official disquiet over Osama's stubborn insistence on deciding as he alone saw fit. Or at least it was what Turki sought to establish more than a decade later as the Al-Sauds' first indication of his behavior. As it turned out, the Al-Saud never found an effective way of dealing with Osama. Nor did anyone else.

If the Al-Saud belatedly acknowledged their upset with Osama's South Yemen adventurism, they have maintained enduring silence about a source of much more serious irritation with him. No sooner had Osama returned from Afghanistan than he was feted at a round of important social functions and began sounding off about the imminent dangers to the Kingdom represented by Saddam Hussein and his secular Baath Party regime in neighboring Iraq. Osama invoked Wahhabism against the wayward Saddam and also buttressed his argument with geopolitical analysis to justify the ready reserves of jihadis. As Prince Turki was to remark later, Osama felt Saddam was no better than an "apostate," a charge in Islam serious enough to justify capital punishment, and "not worthy of being a fellow Muslim."[5]

In the winter and spring of 1990 the Al-Saud were in no mood to have a young freelancing hero flitting from a lunch in Medina one day to another in Mecca the next day and a third in Jeddah a day later with such an explosive message. By interfering in Saudi relations with Iraq, Osama was transgressing a major red line. Anything remotely touching Iraq was deadly serious business. Yemen was a troublesome sideshow by comparison, the Afghan jihad a finger exercise to please the Wahhabis and the United States. Saudi Arabia's real problem was how to balance Iran and Iraq, its more populous, powerful and aggressive neighbors. Britain's military withdrawal from the Gulf in 1971, after a century and a half, left a tempting vacuum in a region that accounted for some two-thirds of the world's crude exports—and cascading tensions reflecting the crucial oil stakes.

The Al-Saud needed no reminding that Saddam rarely took kindly to affronts, real or imaginary. Ever since the Baathis returned to power in Baghdad in 1968, they had made a specialty of shaking down their weaker Arab neighbors in the Gulf, at times carrying out murders to get their message across. They sometimes cited alleged slights, but often they didn't even bother drumming up a pretext. The stakes had increased geometrically after Saddam declared war on Iran in 1980, obliging Saudi Arabia and the other Arab oil emirates to contribute billions of dollars to help Iraq survive the conflict he began.

Iraq barely endured that eight-year war, but Saddam remained a belli-cose, unpredictable bully of a neighbor and an oil power whose reserves were second only to the Kingdom's. The last thing the Al-Saud wanted was Osama villifying Saddam to members of the Saudi elite and exhorting them to join the jihad for the inevitable conflict between Saudia Arabia and Iraq. Now the Al-Saud had to assume that Osama's openly hostile re-marks, made in the privacy of his rich hosts' luncheons, would reach Sad-dam's ears sooner or later.

By the spring of 1990 there were signs Iraq was gearing up again for trouble. A financially ruined Saddam rebuffed politely worded but insis-tent demands for repayment of billions of dollars of wartime loans, argu-ing that the Gulf Arabs should be thankful he had saved them from certain defeat at Iranian hands. In July he accused Kuwait of siphoning off Iraqi oil and massed troops along the border. On August 2 Saddam invaded and oc-cupied Kuwait. Osama's embarrassing warnings about Saddam's designs had come true. No one else had called it right, not in Washington, London, Paris, Riyadh, Beijing, Moscow or, of course, Kuwait itself.

With Saddam's troops on the Kingdom's border, Saudi Arabia now was well and truly threatened and manifestly unable to defend itself, de-spite the billions and billions of dollars spent over the years acquiring sophisticated American war materiel and building state-of-the-art bases. The Kingdom's defenselessness came as a genuine shock to Saudis, despite long-evident signs that the armed forces were unable to fulfill their basic mission. Abruptly, the Saudis' oil wealth and cherished role as protectors of Islam's birthplace and holiest sites meant nothing. Why, they asked them-selves, would Saddam feel any compunction about grabbing the Islamic holy places, along with Saudi oil reserves that would more than double his own and make him the world's largest oil exporter by far?

Rationally, most thinking Saudis realized that U.S. arms purchases over many years were part of a tacit insurance policy linking the two countries. The United States guaranteed the Kingdom's sovereignty in exchange for the free flow of reasonably priced Saudi oil and the obligation to deflect criticism abroad of Wahhabi human rights practices. But little over a decade earlier, the United States had done nothing to prevent the downfall of the Shah next door in Iran. To Saudis who saw only an ill-concealed pro-tection racket, the Al-Saud and Washington replied that the compatible prepositioned weapons systems and U.S. Corps of Engineers–built bases worth billions of dollars were at Saudi Arabia's immediate disposal.

Fortified by his clairvoyance in predicting Saddam's move, Osama thought otherwise. What he did in the wake of Kuwait's occupation became part of his legend. Osama used his family connections and was granted an audience with Prince Sultan bin Abdulaziz al-Saud, the long-serving defense minister.[6] Boiling over with ideas inspired by his Afghan jihad experience, Osama arrived with maps and detailed diagrams. In keeping with the Prophet's injunction, he insisted that no nonbeliever army be allowed to sully the sacred land of the two holy mosques.

The Kingdom did not need to rely on the Americans to defend itself and liberate Kuwait. He, Osama, would do the job with his former comrades-in-arms. For the occasion he said they numbered 100,000 men, a vast exaggeration even if every jihadi "tourist" were counted. His Afghan veterans would train other Saudis. The Prince was suitably polite. Osama, after all, was a bin Laden and a popular hero to boot. Osama kept piling on details, explaining how his family's construction firm could dig sand traps and trenches, much as it had built mountain tunnels and defenses in the Afghan conflict.

Prince Sultan gently pointed out that Kuwait, unlike mountainous Afghanistan with its myriad caves, was mostly flat as a board, ideal terrain for the adversary's 4,000 tanks. The Defense Minister did not even mention the Al-Sauds' understandable lack of enthusiasm at the prospect of tens of thousands of armed Islamist radicals roaming around the Kingdom. Instead Prince Sultan tried to clinch the argument, according to the legend, by asking what Osama would do when confronted with Iraqi missiles and chemical and biological weapons. "We will fight him with faith," Osama said. The conversation petered out, and Osama was not satisfied with Sultan's lack of enthusiasm. As with all myths, variations abound. One version had Osama storming out with the promise that "you'll be hearing from me." Osama's family tried to reason with him, again to no avail, not to rock the boat.

The die was cast on August 6, when Secretary of Defense Dick Cheney flew to Riyadh at the head of an American delegation and read out to King Fahd bin Abdul Aziz and the senior Saudi princes a message from President George Bush. "We are prepared to deploy these forces to defend the Kingdom of Saudi Arabia," the message said. "If you ask us to come we will come. We seek no permanent bases. And when you ask us to leave, we will go home."[7]

General Norman Schwarzkopf, who commanded the U.S.–led coalition war to liberate Kuwait, summed up the King's dilemma. "If he did nothing, he risked losing his kingdom to Iraq," he wrote. "But if he invited in the Americans, even with a presidential assurance that we would respect Saudi sovereignty, Saddam and other Arab leaders would denounce him for toadying to the West. Simply put, he risked undermining the authority of his throne. There were huge risks inherent in inviting an army of foreigners into a xenophobic kingdom fiercely devoted to keeping itself religiously and culturally pure."

To the American visitors' astonishment, Fahd and his senior princes accepted the president's offer then and there, indeed within minutes. But they prudently had consulted Sheikh Abdulaziz bin Baz, the most senior Saudi cleric, who later issued a reluctant *fatwa* barely covering the decision. "Even though the Americans, in the conservative religious view," it read in part, "are equivalent to nonbelievers, as they are not Muslims, they deserve our support because they are here to defend Islam." That was not a view Osama ever shared, and he was not alone. Younger clerics also questioned the Al-Sauds' call. Uppermost in their minds were the Prophet Mohammed's dying words: "Let there be no two religions in Arabia."[8]

In the decade ahead Osama was to paint on that canvas in ever-bloodier colors. Eleven years later, Prince Turki looked back to that fateful meeting with Prince Sultan as the moment when he suddenly discovered "radical changes" in Osama's personality as he started to transform himself "from a butterfly doing good deeds to a bloody revolutionary willing to sacrifice human lives for his violent cause." That was a somewhat belated realization for the head of an intelligence operation whose agents had been instructed to keep tabs in Afghanistan on all Saudi volunteers, including Osama. "He had changed from a calm, peaceful, and gentle man interested in helping Muslims into a person who believed that he would be able to amass and command an army to liberate Kuwait," he said. "It revealed his arrogance and haughtiness.

"First, he believed he was capable of preparing an army to challenge Saddam's force," the Prince added. "Secondly, he opposed the Kingdom's decision to call in friendly forces. By doing so, he disobeyed the ruler and violated the *fatwa* of senior Islamic scholars, who had endorsed the plan as an essential move to fight injustice and aggression."

All that was true enough, up to a point. In the years to come Osama attacked the Al-Saud and the complaisant *ulema*, the authorities on Islamic law, starting with Abdulaziz bin Baz, the blind Wahhabi scholar who, with considerable misgiving, obeyed the King in approving the presence of Western troops. Possibly because he was already on probation, Osama did not speak out during the hostilities themselves. His silence was all the more curious in that many other Saudis seized the moment to push their various agendas, in an explosion of public contestation and petitions unprecedented in the Kingdom.

Saudi women demonstrated, demanding they be allowed to drive cars. Dour clerics openly defied bin Baz and the Al-Saud, denouncing submissive preachers, royal excesses and the infidels' desecration of Islam's holy land. Osama was angry, and visiting South Yemeni protégés had to persuade him to see that American sophisticated weaponry might be needed to defeat Saddam and should be tolerated at least for the duration of hostilities.[9] To old Saudi friends, Osama suggested the Americans were out to undermine the Al-Saud by encouraging their secular Saudi friends to stake out a larger role for themselves and dilute Wahhabism. He limited his protest to asking a more worldly friend for advice about how to organize a boycott of American products.

Even with the benefit of hindsight, Prince Turki's criticism of Osama was partly accurate. As he would demonstrate with increasingly devastating effect over the years, his run-in with the Al-Saud constituted a point of no return. Osama was not impressed when the United States, as promised, rapidly removed almost all the half million men it had assembled to liberate Kuwait. He had made his mind up about the Al-Saud and about the American presence. To his thinking, they were linked; to save the Kingdom, all the American military must be made to leave, and the Al-Saud then would be easy pickings without their infidel protectors. Even during the anti-Soviet jihad, he had told fellow jihadis that despite the de facto alliance, the United States even then was the enemy of Islam in his mind.[10]

What mattered was that some 5,000 American Air Force troops remained, first at al-Khobar on the Gulf, then, when nineteen servicemen were killed there in June 1996 in a terrorist bombing of their high-rise barracks, theoretically stashed out of sight at Prince Sultan Air Base at al-Kharj in the Nejd desert 55 miles southeast of Riyadh. Despite Osama's standard praise for the bombers—and some suggestions that he was indeed responsible—American and Saudi officials concluded that Iran was behind the attack. In a way, it did not matter who killed the U.S. airmen. For Osama and many other Saudis who did not share his violent bent, with every passing year the key question became what the American president had meant back in 1990 when he promised, "When you ask us to go home, we will leave." Osama became convinced he knew the answer. And he knew he had found the issue he was looking for.

Unwittingly, Washington was playing into his hands. Mistake or not, leaving Saddam in power in Iraq at the end of the Kuwait war was proving to be a messy and costly business for the United States and the Saudis as well. Given the dangerous irritant their presence constituted, why had the Al-Saud not asked the American airmen to leave? And if Al-Saud had not asked, why had they not? Under Clinton, the Pentagon and the State Department argued that continued U.S. combat missions over southern Iraq were vital to "keep Saddam in his box." Or was that just a convenient pretext for the Americans, since they now controlled an extended archipelago of bases from Kuwait, Bahrain and Qatar to Oman and Saudi Arabia?

Osama's strength was that he knew he was not alone in his suspicions about both the Al-Saud and the Americans. Casual conversations with Saudis in all walks of life quickly dispelled Americans' wishful thinking that the airmen were now hidden from sight and thus acceptable. Without exception, the dozens of Saudis I questioned in late 1999 knew they were there and wished them gone, "over the horizon," the euphemism to describe the positioning of U.S. aircraft carriers on the Indian Ocean archipelago of Diego Garcia and on Masirah Island off the coast of Oman. The message was: anywhere, but not in Saudi Arabia.

Long before Osama seized on the issue, there were good historical reasons against stationing troops in any Muslim territory, much less the birthplace of Islam. Colonial and postcolonial twentieth-century history was littered with wreckage from the disastrous presence of British, French and American forces stationed in Muslim lands from Iran to Egypt, from Morocco to Lebanon, from Algeria to Yemen. I covered the latter part of the Algerians' war of independence against France in the late 1950s and early 1960s and had gone on to chronicle the Iranian revolution and Lebanon's series of "little wars."

As often as not, terrorism and a Western military presence had played a role. Knowledge of such past humiliation should have served as a warning, especially in Saudi Arabia's case, given Koranic injunctions against the presence of infidel troops on its soil.

But the Pentagon was torn in two directions. Commissioned studies recommended the stockpiling of weapons systems, spares and ammunition on foreign bases such as Saudi Arabia's, but warned that troops should be rotated in and out only when needed, and their presence on the ground be kept to a strict minimum whenever possible. But terrorism experts seemingly wrote reports only to gather dust.

Pulling in the other direction was the American military reluctance to go back "over the horizon" for reasons of so-called efficiency mixed with issues of cost and comfort and an unspoken desire to have the basically defenseless Arab oil emirates face the reality of their dependence on American might. An American diplomat friend argued that, even if Saddam were to disappear, the bases would remain essential for the foreseeable future. "Think Iran, think Iraq," he said. "The Saudis and other smaller oil emirates live in a nasty neighborhood."

No amount of radical Islamist violence, inspired or not by Osama, could shake the Pentagon's convictions. After each fresh terrorist disaster, be it the nineteen Air Force men killed at al-Khobar in June 1996 or the seventeen sailors lost in the attack on the USS *Cole* in Aden in October 2000, the Pentagon wheeled out four-star officers to cover up and excuse culpable security breaches and warn that the world's only superpower could not be pushed out of the region. Bluster prevailed over reflection. We were number one, after all.

In the post–Vietnam, "no body bag" era, only in the Middle East (and in the rest of what Zbigniew Brzezinski a generation earlier dubbed the "arc of crisis") was the United States ready to absorb the destruction of an embassy or the crippling of a warship. In American think tanks, military analysts began postulating that Middle East oil was dictating a kind of unofficial U.S. imperial policy, with the military manning far-flung, dangerous outposts. After a half century of Cold War concern about the rest of the world, Americans wanted cheap gasoline—and to hear as little as possible about foreign problems. How odd that many foreigners thought the United States ran a global empire and intervened at will in the affairs of countries great and small.

Such American wool-gathering was tailor-made for Osama. In Saudi Arabia's case, the Prince Sultan Air Base became of questionable utility to the Americans. Saudis increasingly resented the American use of Saudi soil for U.S. combat missions that killed Iraqi civilians, but perversely did little to challenge Saddam's hold on power. It didn't take long before Arabs in and out of the Kingdom were asking whether the Americans deliberately were keeping Saddam in power in order to justify their hold on the archipelago of Saudi and other regional land bases and ensure their control of the Kingdom's oil riches. Indeed some suggested that was the real reason the United States left Saddam on his throne in 1991. Osama was scarcely original in developing these theses, but that did not stop him from repeating them endlessly.

By the time I visited the Kingdom in 1999 something of an underground debate was underway: was it useful for the Al-Saud to whisper to Saudi citizens that the heavy-handed Americans insisted on staying while the royals privately figured the U.S. Air Force presence was the dynasty's ultimate insurance policy? I decided to ask the most influential Saudi official I could meet. Thanks to a retired American general who had served in Saudi Arabia, I spent a long dinner as the guest of Sheikh Abdulaziz Tuwayyjiri, a close confidant of Crown Prince Abdullah (who himself was known to have doubts about the Kingdom's dependence on the United States).

I wasted almost the entire evening asking the sheikh, a sprightly man in his late seventies, whether the Kingdom wanted the U.S. Air Force in or out. His answers were wonderfully convoluted, beautifully expressed, courteous and imprecise, no matter how I phrased and rephrased the question. To his credit he never showed impatience or exasperation. He did his duty by receiving his friend's friend. But I was left in no doubt that only a boor would ask—and keep asking—such questions at his table. Perhaps the Al-Saud were happy with the situation, perhaps not.

As for the United States military, I never found a serving officer who voiced any doubts whatsoever. (In fairness, perhaps some did privately, but were schooled not to share them with the likes of me.) In the Clinton years the Pentagon had more money and clout than the State Department in the Middle East. I was reduced to marveling at American military hubris, a stiff-necked refusal to understand the deadly certainties of the contemporary Middle East. Not for the first time did I wish the Pentagon would create an Office of Nay-Saying devoted to poking holes in conventional wisdom. (U.S. Marine General Anthony Zinni, the leader of Central Command in the mid-1990s, was an honorable exception. He never hid his concern over how little he actually knew about his patch.)

The al-Khobar terrorist attack was never elucidated satisfactorily. Was it really the work of Iran and its agents among the Shi'a minority of the eastern oil province of Hasa, as the Al-Saud hinted, although they initially did not allow American investigators to interrogate the advertised culprits? Or was al-Khobar the work of Osama or his devotees among young mainstream Sunnis, whose handiwork was deliberately covered up?

Saudi dissidents in London pointed to the four Sunni men, three of them Afghan veterans, who in carefully rehearsed televised confessions invoked Osama's inspiration in a bomb plot in which five American servicemen working for the Saudi National Guard died in Riyadh in November 1995. Frustrated American investigators were never allowed to interrogate the four before they were beheaded. The dissidents argued that the Al-Saud could not again afford to acknowledge that Sunni radicals were responsible for the new terrorist attack. One involving Sunnis from the Nejd was embarrassment enough. So, said the dissidents, the Al-Saud invented the Shi'a culprits to conceal the real ones. The case has never come to trial. In frustration, in June 2001 FBI Director Louis Freeh did succeed in producing indictments in the United States just before he stepped down and just before the statute of limitations would have taken effect.

Such confusion reflected the opaque nature of Al-Saud governance and allowed rumor to work for Osama and others willing to think the worst of the government. At no point did the disapproving murmur of what passed for public opinion in Saudi Arabia prompt any reappraisal in the Pentagon. Signs of upset occasionally surfaced. Was the son of Zaki Yamani, the masterful oil minister during the glory days of OPEC in the 1970s, thinking of Osama's threats when he suggested in print that the U.S. Air Force might evacuate al-Kharj in favor of an aircraft carrier? The U.S. Navy had a good dozen carriers, so why not, I asked a senior American official? Surely, young Yamani was on to something, since aircraft carriers were less politically irritating. "Carriers cost much more and aren't as efficient as land bases" was the official's curt reply.

So there was to be no going back to the less comfortable, but also less vulnerable, system of "over the horizon." I recalled the tale of another American diplomat friend who, in his first foreign service post in Libya in 1969, argued that the United States would be well advised to evacuate Tripoli's Wheelus airfield in the immediate wake of Muammar Qaddafi's revolution. Qaddafi's strident Arab nationalism left no doubt that the Americans would be asked to go, he argued, so why not do so gracefully and get off on the right foot with the new regime? "Never voluntarily give up a base," grumbled the defense attaché. "Never. It would set a bad example."

Just before I left Saudi Arabia on that 1999 trip, I finally succeeded in seeing an ambassador from a European country with long experience in the Kingdom. I wanted to use him as a sounding board, and I poured out my doubts, indeed my fears. I was convinced that anti-Americanism had developed deep roots and that Osama was speaking for many more people than I had thought possible before my visit. I mentioned concerned remarks by influential members of the Kingdom's *majlis al-shura,* the consultative council, which, after decades of vague promises from various kings, finally was up and running in an impressive marble palace built especially to house its deliberations. It was not just unhappiness over the American military presence, I said. The economy was bad; the population kept growing and the standard of living dropping. Everyday Saudis were fed up with the presumptuous prerogatives of the 7,000 freeloading princes of the realm.

The ambassador listened to me, then asked if he might ask a question. "Have you been living by any chance in Europe for a long time?" I said that for forty years I had worked as a foreign correspondent all over the world. The ambassador smiled before ending the interview by saying, "The alliance between the Saudis, who govern like feudal kings, and the United States, the most powerful empire without colonies the world has ever seen, defies most tests of logic. But it is made out of titanium." Perhaps, but another ambassador years before had likened the Saudi system to a bumblebee.

In mid-1991 Osama was allowed to travel again. As with so many events in the Kingdom, there are at least two versions of his departure. Prince Turki has said Osama basically behaved properly and his probation was lifted, especially since he expressed an interest in trying to reconcile rival Afghan mujahedeen, who by then were openly fighting one another. A second version has it that at Osama's behest an influential bin Laden brother took advantage of the absence abroad of Saudi Interior Minister Prince Nayef ibn Abdul Aziz al-Saud to obtain from his son and deputy at the Interior Ministry a one-shot passport to allow Osama a business trip to Pakistan and back. He quickly left the Kingdom before Prince Nayef realized he had been granted permission.

Osama lost no time in traveling to Pakistan. He again took up residence in Peshawar. He did indeed try to reconcile the warring Afghan chieftains, but to no avail. Mindful of his mentor Abdullah Azzam's violent end, Osama kept a low profile. But Peshawar had become a backwater, Afghanistan had lost much of its luster as a Muslim cause, and the United States and the rest of the West had walked away from the country now that its "freedom fighters" had turned into cruel and ineffectual warlords.

Within months Osama was on the move again, not back to Saudi Arabia, as he promised, but to the Sudan. Indeed, he was never to return to Saudi Arabia. His brief adult period of submitting to the authority of others was over. He had found a new mission. He had identified his enemies. He had shown no scruples in manipulating his family. He still had trained men from the Afghan jihad. There was no turning back.

In light of his continuing provocations over the ensuing years, the Al-Saud showed great patience in dealing with him. Turning a deaf ear and co-option had worked wonders in the past with many a difficult customer, even with the so-called Red Prince, who in the 1950s and 1960s espoused the anti-monarchical cause of President Nasser of Egypt before rejoining the fold. But finally enough was enough. On March 5, 1994, the exasperated Saudi government took the extraordinary step of stripping Osama of his citizenship, citing in a succinct communiqué "irresponsible behavior and his refusal to obey instructions issued to him." His was a crime of lèse-majesté.

His bank accounts and other liquid assets in the Kingdom were frozen. His family the same day took its own distance from their wayward sibling. Bakr, the clan's eldest surviving brother and boss of the sprawling Saudi Bin Ladin Group, issued a two-line statement, expressing "regret, denunciation and condemnation of acts that Osama bin Laden may have committed which we do not condone and which we reject."

Both statements are extraordinary by Saudi standards. Their simultaneity was read as testimony to the close relations the clan had long maintained with the Al-Saud and to its unwillingness to sacrifice everything it had achieved over a half century for an errant sibling. In fact, the bin Ladens had little choice. Their sprawling businesses depended on the continuing goodwill of the Al-Saud, who remained Osama's favorite target, the epitome of the corruption, ineptitude, indolence, impiety and dependence on the American military and other manifestations of infidel power he so decried. The bin Laden family expressed a collective guilt for not having spent more time with Osama when he was younger, for allowing him to bring dishonor on the clan and its core business.

Yet, no other critic of the Al-Saud had ever been deprived of citizenship. Immediately, in Saudi society Osama became mere chattel, reduced to the status of a slave to be disposed of much as any other property. Other Saudi dissidents in London in the early 1990s had sent streams of inflammatory faxes attacking the Al-Sauds' policies and private lives in much more lurid detail without suffering that indignity. But they were from the Wahhabi heartland of the Nejd. The Al-Saud had fired a shot across the bow of the whole bin Laden clan and of many other Saudi citizens of mixed parentage.

What good King Abdulaziz spontaneously had given, his children abruptly could take away. In the meantime, it served the Al-Sauds' purposes to demonstrate that the Kingdom had never wavered in its faith in the clan. The firm was chosen to build the Prince Sultan Air Base, as startled American airmen discovered when they moved in after the al-Khobar bombing and read signs at the entrance bearing the family name of the very man Washington had elevated to Public Enemy Number One.

SUDAN, THE ISLAMIC HAVEN

I N JUNE 1989 army officers seized power in Sudan in a coup minutely masterminded by an Islamic theorist and politician named Hassan al-Turabi who overthrew his elected brother-in-law from the safety of a jail cell. Turabi's modus operandi represented a new twist, even in an African continent much given to political upheaval. Turabi had arranged to be incarcerated as an alibi in case the plot against Prime Minister Sadiq al-Mahdi failed; he had been imprisoned often enough to figure a jailbird could hardly be accused.[1]

His cover story didn't fool fellow prisoners arrested for loyalty to the ousted government. They mocked such excessive prudence to his face. After dark, when he mistakenly assumed their visits would go unnoticed, he regularly summoned to his cell key lieutenants of the National Islamic Front (NIF), the radical religious party that over the years he had nurtured as his instrument for seizing power. Only six months later did Turabi finally emerge from Kober prison in Khartoum North. By then the NIF, a resuscitated variation of the local Muslim Brotherhood branch that he had taken over three decades earlier, had consolidated its hold. Turabi made sure the titular head of state, General Omar Hassan Ahmad al-Bashir, and the army were both answerable to him.

Such precautions were as complicated as Turabi himself. If ever the expression "too clever by half" defined a man, it was this brilliant and ruthless intriguer who in the first half of the 1990s, defying the odds, projected himself and his peripheral, only partly Muslim land into the very forefront of radical Islamic politics. He was determined to turn his basket case of a country into a modern Islamic state, the polar opposite of the static, theologically ossified Kingdom of Saudi Arabia across the Red Sea that he so disdained—and envied—for its oil riches. His many foreign and domestic critics were convinced he was also hell-bent on spreading the radical Islamist message beyond the borders of Africa's largest country. At face value, that constituted an overreaching ambition for a failing state. Sudan was on the Arab world's geographic fringe, broke and mired for the second time in forty years in a debilitating civil war pitting the Muslim north against the largely animist and Christian south.

But the same Turabi who took no chances by plotting from the safety of a jail cell also dreamed big dreams. Now, Turabi felt, was Sudan's and his hour to stake out claims to lead radical political Islam, which elsewhere was on the wane after a wild decade of revolutionary zeal. In Iran, Ayatollah Ruhollah Khomeini had just died, and his Islamic revolution was exhausted and humiliated by its defeat in an eight-year war against neighboring Iraq. Turabi saw his main chance as a modernizer. His would be the first Islamic republic of the mainstream Sunnis, and it would outshine Iran's Shi'a revolution.

At home, his revolutionary zeal dictated uprooting the Sudanese establishment. It was an act of pure revenge for this son of a provincial notable never trusted by the grandees of the Democratic Union and Umma Parties, which had ruled, some might say misruled, Sudan for the eight years it had been spared military dictatorship since its independence from Britain in 1956. They were not impressed by his prestigious graduate degrees from England and France. A tolerant, whiskey-loving lot, they had not forgiven his crucial role under a previous military president in banning alcohol and hanging a maverick intellectual for apostasy in a futile attempt to save the regime.

Nor were they taken in by Turabi's calculations in marrying the socially prominent sister of Sadiq al-Mahdi, himself the great-grandson of the great Mahdi whose unruly troops in the late nineteenth century disobeyed his orders to spare the life of Major General Charles "Chinese" Gordon, and, by killing him on the steps of his official Nile-side residence, defied the British Empire in the name of Islam for a dozen years. Combined with his father's claim to be descended from the Mahdi, Turabi had counted on the marriage to invest him with the reflected glory of Sudan's anti-colonial struggle.

Turabi's chosen instrument for creating a new Sudan on the ruins of the old was the highly secretive National Islamic Front, which he had founded and honed. At almost sixty, he was in a hurry. But drive, ideas and an elitist political movement at his beck and call and ready to seize power went only so far. Turabi from the start realized he needed money. And it was money that made Osama bin Laden—and his reputed fortune—interesting for both the United States and Turabi. The NIF was determined that Osama was going to help achieve its goals. So, too, were hundreds of other Islamic radicals Turabi welcomed from far and wide. He was neither the first nor the last Muslim leader determined to tap into Osama's funds. (Recipients of his largesse included selected Yemenis, the Taliban leader Mullah Omar and dozens of other jihadis spread across the Muslim world.) But Turabi thought he held high cards others lacked—indeed aces—making an alliance with Osama mutually advantageous. Sudan was a perfect place, in Turabi's view, for a hundred flowers to bloom, and these radical foreigners were the very illustration of the Islamic outreach designed to put him on the map.

Turabi had flair. By the end of 1989, with the Red Army gone, the jihad in Afghanistan had turned sour as the exalted holy warriors fell to fighting among themselves. Osama and his band wanted to leave, and Sudan was located conveniently just across the Red Sea from his target, his homeland, Saudi Arabia. Ever the practical revolutionary, Turabi dispatched three NIF intelligence agents to Peshawar to sound Osama out before the year ended.[2] Osama then sent a scouting mission of his own to Khartoum. As for the money, Turabi had no real idea how much Osama was worth, and indeed his fortune was certainly well under the $300 million estimate that the U.S. government kept claiming.[3] But Turabi did not quibble. In a bankrupt country as desperate as Sudan, even a single-digit millionaire was a handsome catch.

Turabi was also a plunger. He did his best to ensure that Sudan was accommodating. Even so, his overture was not without problems. Neither side knew much about the other, and the little that was known did not make either less edgy. For many of Turabi's unsophisticated followers, Osama was suspect because of his connections with Saudi Arabia. In their eyes, that automatically meant connivance with the United States, symbolized by the joint American–Saudi financing of the anti-Soviet Afghan jihad and closer at home in the Horn of Africa. Osama's companions, noting Turabi's law studies in Britain and at the Sorbonne, argued that his Islamist credentials were open to question because of his prolonged exposure to life in the Dar al-Harb, the house of war, as the non-Muslim world was known.[4] And in the Kuwait war Osama was an early and consistent adversary of Saddam Hussein, while Khartoum backed Iraq.

Despite such reservations on both sides, by late 1990 Osama's relocation was underway, and he himself arrived from Peshawar the following year with four wives, children and dozens of Afghan Arab veterans. Taking a leaf from the Israeli practice of welcoming all Jews, Sudan had waived visas for Arabs entering Sudan. Turabi also provided those in need with authentic (and sometimes diplomatic) Sudanese passports issued under aliases and on occasion ordered airport immigration not to stamp them in and out.

Soon underground, organized movements of the radical Islamic world flocked to Khartoum. Sudan in the early 1990s acquired a reputation as a rare rest-and-recreation center for extremist Muslims under pressure elsewhere.[5] They included hundreds of Afghan Arabs rapidly becoming no longer personae gratae in Pakistan or entering wanted lists back home and indeed throughout almost all the Arab world (except in Sudan and Yemen).[6]

Some of these radical guests stayed and opened offices. Others merely used Sudan as a convenient sanctuary. Turabi initially welcomed all outcasts from the Middle East and beyond—among them Al-Qaeda's Afghan veterans, Abu Nidal's secular killers (who were as apt to assassinate fellow Palestinians as their nominal Israeli quarry), Islamic Jihad and Hamas from Palestine, Egypt's Gama'a Islamiyya and Islamic Jihad, as well as Iran's Revolutionary Guards and radicals from Algeria, Libya, Eritrea, Ethiopia, Tunisia and Uganda. With outside help from Osama and other radicals, Turabi hoped a traditional second-string player like Sudan might just elbow itself stage center and claim the elusive, ecumenical mantle of re-uniting the *umma,* the entire Muslim community, and overcoming centuries of schism between mainstream Sunni and Shi'a.

To this end Turabi even welcomed Iranian Revolutionary Guards and their fellow Shi'a of Lebanon's Hezbollah to add a zest of anti-American defiance to his otherwise solidly mainstream Sunni regime. That was essentially political theater for the NIF, a seemingly cost-free way to establish its radical credentials and put itself on the map with Washington. Turabi knew that the United States had yet to come to terms with the humiliation Tehran had inflicted on its diplomats held hostage for 444 days at the end of the Carter administration in 1979 and 1980. But the rest of the world,

Turabi calculated, realized the steam had gone out of the Iranian revolution. For Iran a token presence in Sudan was an inexpensive way to shore up its waning reputation as an exporter of Islamic zeal.[7]

Self-doubt was not Turabi's long suit. His was an in-your-face approach, often indistinguishable from intellectual arrogance, as any number of diplomats learned firsthand. He wanted them to be aware that he knew more than anyone about almost everything. Americans, official and private, steeled themselves to lectures about the minutiae of their country. He would insist to his interlocutors that he understood America and Americans much better than they did. He drew on knowledge based on infrequent, often rapid visits to America to bolster his points. In fact, he spent much of his time in the United States talking to recent Muslim immigrants, who were awed by his intellect and scarcely in a position to explain the intricacies of American life, had he bothered to listen.

Their real role, whether they realized it or not, was to showcase his growing importance in his own eyes and those of his followers back home. I had known Turabi since the mid-1970s and understood that this slim, exquisitely well-spoken man with ever so slightly protruding teeth essentially had stopped listening to everyone. An interview with Turabi was an exercise in dictation rather than the normal give-and-take of asking questions and waiting for answers. Still, over many years no visit to Khartoum was complete for me without matching wits with him.

Now in 1989 Turabi was the power behind President Bashir's throne, and the time had come for others to dance attendance on him. What he said and how he said it often dazzled audiences. At the top of his form—before an irate black-belt exile knocked him unconscious with a karate chop in Canada in 1992—Turabi possessed considerable intellect and nearly irresistible charm. Indeed, in the early 1990s he briefly succeeded in wheedling money or free oil deliveries from archenemies Iran and Iraq at the same time. Turabi's self-confidence was such that he was convinced he was on the brink of exercising near total power in Sudan and carrying out his revolution.

It was perhaps understandable a decade after the Soviet invasion of Afghanistan that Turabi gloried in playing host to a more professional, witting and dangerous version of what had begun as innocent and impromptu meetings in Peshawar and later gave new form and substance to radical jihadi Islam founded sixty years earlier. The foreign radicals were allowed to go about their business—on one condition. In keeping with the

NIF's own highly developed cult of secrecy, they were instructed to assume a low profile. Most especially, that meant avoiding mingling with ordinary Sudanese, a gregarious, curious and prying lot long expert in unraveling state secrets. Given the sub-rosa activities the NIF tolerated, that was a wise precaution. To a remarkable extent, most Sudanese had no idea what their guests were up to.

But it was not long before Sudan's neighbors knew enough to take fright. The governments next door in the Horn of Africa were the first to sound the alarm, followed by Algeria, Libya, Morocco and Tunisia, which felt threatened by their citizens who had fought in Afghanistan. Afghan veterans involved in jihadi schemes notably included key Egyptians who from Al-Qaeda's very first days had served as Osama's inner circle. By 1993 these and other governments pressured Pakistan to begin expelling Afghan Arabs still hanging around Peshawar.[8]

Such elementary caution and suspicion about the NIF safe-haven policy were essentially dictated by history and geography. Khartoum was within easy striking distance of Saudi Arabia, Yemen, the Horn of Africa, Egypt and all of North Africa. Any Muslim worth his salt knew that the great seventh-century expansion of Islam in North Africa was fashioned by armies attacking from the Sahara. And soon enough various Arab intelligence organizations across North Africa discerned an emerging pattern of money and arms smuggling and jihadi plots.

Even today it remains unclear if Turabi carefully weighed the uncontrollable spontaneous combustion that was likely to occur when Afghan veterans and experienced Middle East Islamic radicals started using Khartoum as a sanctuary to compare notes and determine how their various agendas could slot together for ad hoc violent action abroad. Chastened by their naïveté in failing to have kept tabs on Islamic radicals from the outset in the previous decade, Arab regimes and the West, especially the United States, quickly sensed the potential danger the NIF regime represented. By 1993 Sudan found itself on the State Department's list of states sponsoring terrorism.

TURABI'S PLANS eventually proved to be a massive miscalculation with ever more disastrous consequences for all concerned. Yet, with a little luck, his ambitious gamble might have at least partially paid off had it not been for the Clinton administration and for Osama. In their separate ways, these two factors first complicated, then compromised Turabi's dream. He had time to contemplate the ruin of his vision of an Islamic state. A decade after Turabi's coup, the corrupt, ruthless but secular Arab regimes he despised had faced down the challenge of radical political Islam amid much blood—more than 150,000 deaths in Algeria and some 1,500 in Egypt. Afghan Arabs, once hailed as freedom fighters, were welcome virtually nowhere.

In Sudan the threat gradually subsided without ever totally disappearing, critics insisted, since the NIF remained in power, albeit in less outwardly radical form. That was well after Turabi's machinations also had proved costly to his own revolutionary commitment, to Osama, to other foreign Islamic radicals and to the United States. Little by little, the 1990s in Sudan came into rough focus as a series of events and decisions in which the main actors on almost every occasion made the wrong choices.

On what purported to be moral as well as political grounds, the United States increasingly turned its back on the troublesome Khartoum regime it found always infuriatingly devious and finally evil, virtually consigning it to limbo. In keeping with congressional practice, major U.S. aid stopped as an immediate consequence of the NIF coup. But Turabi repeatedly used his considerable skills to appear willing to amend his ways and accommodate Washington, finding no takers after early inconclusive skirmishes. The more he tried, the more suspect he and the NIF became until Washington finally opted to isolate, destabilize and all but overthrow the regime by aiding its hostile neighbors.

Such superpower disdain contained a whiff of hubris. On more than one occasion, bad luck, bad timing and arguably bad policy dogged the Clinton administration. American officials, for example, did force Khartoum to deport Osama in May 1996, but did not follow up on NIF efforts to use his departure as a come-on to improve bilateral relations and find out more about him and other radicals. At the time the United States knew relatively little about what Osama was really doing in Sudan. But starting in 1994, France knew a lot thanks to the Carlos deal. The CIA the year before had opened a so-called virtual Osama station based in Washington, essentially to track his financial backing for other jihadi radicals. It remained little more than an administrative innovation, a left-handed way of recognizing that Osama's transnational activities were based everywhere and nowhere.

Thanks in large part to his presence, Washington kept prodding Sudan about its association with Islamists it considered terrorists. Many were Osama's close Egyptian associates who used his money to smuggle arms from Sudan and conduct a series of sensational, often bloody, but finally self-defeating terrorist operations against important ministers in Cairo. Indeed, Egypt played a central role in Osama's ouster from Sudan. The Clinton administration's successful drive was largely motivated by a near-miss assassination attempt against President Hosni Mubarak of Egypt as he drove in from the Addis Ababa airport to attend the Organization of African Unity summit in neighboring Ethiopia in June 1995. It was disturbing enough to stomach urban terrorism in Egypt itself, quite another to tolerate an attack on one of Washington's major allies while he was abroad on an official visit. Washington, Cairo and other capitals became convinced NIF agents had been involved in infiltrating the ill-fated Egyptian Islamist hit team into Addis Ababa and in exfiltrating its three known survivors.

President Bashir claimed to be horrified. So did Turabi, but, according to diplomats, less convincingly. The botched assassination attempt did prompt Khartoum to rethink its links with jihadi radicals and at least formally deem them a liability. NIF veteran Nafie Ali Nafie was eased out as the boss of the External Intelligence Department, Sudan's senior espionage organization, to signal contrition since his personal operatives were blamed for the embarrassing Mubarak operation. In typical NIF fashion, he soon was given another important post. That scarcely reassured Washington.

But soon Khartoum was willing to use Osama as a bargaining chip to achieve its larger goal of getting back into America's good graces. That became clear when for the first time the vexed question of terrorism and jihadi radicals was discussed with the United States. This was at a send-off dinner Foreign Minister Ali Osman Mohammed Taha gave for U.S. Ambassador Timothy M. Carney on February 6, 1996. The Ambassador was leaving the next day, much against his better judgment, because Washington had decided to remove all American personnel from Khartoum out of fear for their physical safety. Carney laid out in some detail what Washington required of Khartoum, and Taha listened carefully and did not demur. The dinner discussion persuaded him that a deal might be possible to improve bilateral relations. The Sudanese moved fast. By early March, Major General Elfatih Erwa, Sudan's minister of state for defense, a senior intelligence cadre and part of the NIF inner circle with a reputation as a knuckle-buster, was in Washington negotiating with CIA officials.⁹ The talks continued over three months.¹⁰

Tactically, Khartoum was several lengths ahead of Washington. Betraying Osama prompted spirited debate within the NIF, but Turabi prevailed. He justified Osama's ouster as a nearly cost-free undertaking that might just help Sudan wriggle free of its pariah status. Since August 1993 Sudan had joined the State Department list of state sponsors of terrorism alongside Iran, Iraq, Libya, Syria, Cuba and North Korea. An old Middle East diplomatic hand once told me, "It's hard to get on that list—and all but impossible to get off." The initial listing was prompted largely by what proved to be a phony intelligence report variously alleging a plot to bomb a party for U.S. embassy workers' children or to bomb an embassy school bus. Nonessential embassy staff and all families were withdrawn as a consequence. United Nations sanctions were in the offing because of the botched Mubarak assassination attempt, so Khartoum had an excellent reason to try to clean up its act. The regime weighed the consequences of sheltering Osama and his jihadi friends for its own survival. Carney, sensing Turabi was losing total sway over senior NIF cadres, was eager to press home efforts to diminish his authority.¹¹

Once the Sudanese decided that Osama was expendable, they carefully calibrated their response. The Americans had to take Khartoum seriously. Turabi already had proved that he was capable of handing over another embarrassing guest. In 1994 he arranged for France to kidnap Carlos the Jackal, the quintessential terrorist of the 1970s and 1980s, who had the misfortune of ending up in Khartoum at the end of the Cold War. In offering in the winter of 1996 to deliver Osama to the custody of the United States or, preferably, to Saudi Arabia, the Sudanese correctly calculated neither could accept.¹²

The administration simply did not have enough hard evidence against Osama to justify arresting him overseas and bringing him to trial in the United States. Washington couldn't prove in a U.S. court that he had harmed Americans or American interests.¹³ The U.S. case against him still rested on hearsay and intelligence—that is, on thin pickings from spy satellites and electronic eavesdropping rather than factual knowledge from inside sources. And as nearly always, Washington, invoking fears of being compromised, was reluctant to share the intelligence necessary to win over its allies, much less the doubters.[14]

Those were early days in the campaign against terrorism and Osama. The United States was still a stickler for respecting legal niceties. Aside from a questionable double agent named Ali A. Mohamed, an Egyptian-born naturalized American ex–Special Forces soldier who worked for the FBI and Al-Qaeda,[15] much of the little Washington knew early on about Al-Qaeda in Sudan came from Moroccan intelligence agents.[16] The Moroccans had their own reasons to please the Americans and keep an eye on their radicals, although few of their nationals were involved.

So in the spring of 1996 the negotiations about delivering Osama collapsed. The Clinton administration settled for just wanting him gone. Since his principal perceived noxiousness was his financial largesse, the U.S. goal was to reduce his influence by removing him from his Sudanese investments, which were thought to be generating most of his funds. The administration knew there were few countries willing to accept Osama and didn't much care where he went—with the notable exception of Somalia. That proviso was understandable in light of the administration's mishandled participation in a UN humanitarian relief effort there that turned into a humiliating fiasco for U.S. prestige (although it did end the famine, its nominal mission).

Washington was still smarting from the U.S. Army's comeuppance in Mogadishu in 1993. Somali warlord Mohammed Farah Aideed's tough street fighters shot down Ranger helicopters, killed the crews and dragged a dead pilot through the streets. That convinced Washington to pull out its expeditionary force. Despite Osama's self-aggrandizing claims that Al-Qaeda operatives were involved, no solid evidence was produced to substantiate such assertions. Downing helicopters by hitting their rotors had been a standard combat technique since the Vietnam War.[17]

Indeed, Aideed was viscerally anti-Islamist. His men forced senior Al-Qaeda operative Mohammed Atef, sent by Osama to reconnoiter Mogadishu, to flee for his life aboard a Cessna plane that regularly flew in the day's perishable supply of Kenya qat, the mild stimulant much in favor in the region.[18] His lieutenant's humiliating exit from Mogadishu did not stop Osama from later making much of the American retreat from the Somali capital—and a similar humiliating withdrawal from Beirut in 1984—to depict American soldiers as paper tigers. In fact, the NIF and Osama were preternaturally scared that the Americans would use the humanitarian operation as a cover, the first of several steps to overthrow the Khartoum regime. They apparently talked of creating trouble for the UN operation to thwart such a scenario. Still, anyone familiar with the Somalis knew they needed no lessons in street fighting. Smith Hempstone, the American ambassador to Kenya, drew on his experience as a journalist in Africa many years before to oppose U.S. military involvement in the UN relief operation, warning, "If you liked Beirut, you'll love Mogadishu."

As for the nervous Saudis, they were certainly upset by Osama's evershriller tirades against the monarchy. But the Sudanese correctly surmised that the last thing Saudi Arabia wanted was to deal with an Osama bound, gagged and wearing a martyr's crown.[19] Delivered dead, killed by a demonstrably non-Saudi hand, was something else. The Saudis especially resented Sudanese insistence that Osama not be punished for his wayward behavior as the price for his return. Saudi Arabia knew Osama was in no mood to sue for forgiveness. The Al-Saud resorted to a favorite tactic. With Saudi blessing, a near constant stream of bin Laden relatives crossed the Red Sea, relaying offers to unfreeze Osama's funds and restore his citizenship if he would just recant his criticism of the Al-Saud stewardship. He turned them all away, sometimes expressing regret for the embarrassment he was causing the family firm, with its traditionally close relationship with the Al-Saud. The Sudanese also knew the Al-Saud despised the NIF and deliberately added insult to injury by making their offer indirectly via the Americans.[20]

Osama was furious about his ouster, all the more so since he received little advance warning. He cursed Turabi as little better than a common thief for forcing him to abandon his major investments in Sudan virtually overnight.[21] Turabi lost no time in confiscating Osama's holdings and mocked him as a fool. "All Osama could say was jihad, jihad, jihad," Turabi told me, as if to suggest his guest was a boor incapable of discussing the finer points of Islam.[22] Behind Turabi's dismissive remark lay an exalted view of himself as a genuine reformer and modernizer of the faith. Not for him was Osama's narrow-minded salafist view, which, for example, looked with horror at what it considered the suspect role of women in the NIF. And, of course, belittling Osama after his ouster helped distance Turabi from earlier enthusiastic remarks about him.

A Sudanese acquaintance confided that early on Turabi "had needed the money and was willing to be bored by Osama." Once he was gone, Turabi had every reason to write Osama off as a religious simpleton, for it helped

diminish the NIF's own earlier role in practicing radical violence to establish its influence within and without Sudan's borders. In the months soon
after his ouster Osama tried repeatedly and unavailingly to persuade the
Sudanese to reimburse him. American officials were especially pleased at
causing a serious dent in his pocketbook, since it was his financial operations they then most feared.[23] Osama at the time claimed he had lost
$100 million.

That sum was considered an exaggeration, although he certainly was
owed millions of dollars for extensive construction work on a seventy-mile
stretch of road between Khartoum and Shendi for which Sudan never paid
him. His most prominent assets there were overage equipment that had
served in the building of tunnels and fortifications during the Afghan jihad
before being shipped to Sudan—in other words, junk. (Most of his other
fixed assets were money-losers—such as a tannery—that the NIF signed
over to him when unable to pay for his road-building.) When an angry
Osama, his family and retainers flew out of Khartoum on May 18 on a char-
tered Ariana Afghan B-727, for his third and perhaps final stay in
Afghanistan, Clinton administration policy-makers exulted. They felt they
were solving the immediate problem as best they could.

Osama was on his way to the back of beyond, or, rather, to the beleaguered eastern Afghan city of Jalalabad. Washington was convinced it had
neutralized a danger to Egypt, Saudi Arabia and allies in the Horn of Africa
and weakened and isolated the NIF in Sudan as well by depriving Osama of
his Sudanese investments, businesses and training camps. Steven Simon,
then on the National Security Council, rationalized the outcome: "It's
going to take him a while to reconstitute, and that screws him up and buys
time."[24] Such thinking betrayed a surprising ignorance of what Osama was
up to. It was rapidly shown up for the wishful thinking it was.

No sooner was he safely back in his old Afghan stomping grounds, beyond easy reach, than out of the blue the United States got lucky. A fugitive
member of Al-Qaeda talked his way into a nearby American embassy and,
when eventually he was thoroughly debriefed, the United States knew a
great deal more about Osama and his Sudanese operations, enough indeed
to question the wisdom of having forced him to leave Khartoum. Osama's
abrupt ouster only accelerated a critical mass of unstoppable rage and de-
structiveness that came to change the world in ways no one, perhaps not

even his devoted jihadis, could easily have imagined at the time. There would be no turning back for Osama. He crossed the threshold from a war of words against Saudi Arabia and the United States and planning violent operations to executing his first incontrovertible acts of terrorism.

Turabi in subsequent years never tired of recounting how he kept telling Americans—especially officials who after the Mubarak assassination attempt in 1995 insisted for the first time that Osama quit Khartoum—that they would be better off leaving him in Sudan, where he could be kept under constant surveillance. This observation was self-serving and deflected attention from the CIA's erstwhile honeymoon, but Turabi was right in thinking that Osama would prove exponentially more dangerous in his Afghan redoubt. By forcing Osama to leave Khartoum the Clinton administration lost any reasonable hope of keeping tabs on him again.

For all the post–9/11 bravado by both the Clinton and Bush administrations, aimed at buttressing their separate claims to being on top of Al-Qaeda, U.S. intelligence had no real fix on Osama after 1996 (and little knowledge of him before). Short of war, the United States was powerless to stop him. He was safe with the Taliban, and the Americans were reduced to trying to enlist their putative Pakistani allies to prevail on their Afghan friends to hand him over. That was a mug's game since the Pakistanis had heavily invested in the Taliban in pursuance of their dream of using their western neighbor as "strategic depth" against India. For the next five years Osama was to take full advantage of that American impotence, churning out thousands of jihadis in various Afghan training camps. Many ended up as cannon fodder in Al-Qaeda's 055 brigade of non-Afghan Muslim volunteers; a minority were instructed in the dark arts of terrorism and dispatched pretty much worldwide.

So, like so much else Turabi said, there was a kernel of truth to his warnings about Osama's forced removal. But the fortuitous source of American enlightenment about Osama also confirmed some of Washington's worst suspicions about Turabi and his NIF. Indeed a lack of trust in Turabi was a major reason American officials hadn't acted on his advice. Delivering the goods was a Sudanese Afghan veteran, a onetime would-be student in the United States, sworn Al-Qaeda foot soldier, self-confessed embezzler and sometime NIF informant. Jamal Ahmad Mohammed al-Fadl was on the lam. By his own eventual admission, he had stolen $110,000 from Al-Qaeda and neither could nor would reimburse the organization, as Osama demanded. Fadl was at the end of his tether when in early 1996 he walked into the American embassy in Eritrea and at long last got someone to listen seriously to his story after peddling it to half the Middle East.

Understandably, it took legitimately suspicious American intelligence professionals months, first in Eritrea, then in Europe, to establish the bona fides of this too-good-to-be-true walk-in (as unsolicited sources are called in intelligence tradecraft). Only then was he brought to the United States under the government's witness-protection program, where he pestered his FBI keepers to feed his insatiable appetite for pornographic videos. Thanks apparently in large part to information from his debriefings, a federal grand jury was convened in the Southern District of New York in 1996 that for the first time mentioned Osama by name and provided a detailed insider's understanding of Al-Qaeda and its leader.[25] But it was not until June 10, 1998, that a sealed grand jury indictment was handed up against Osama. By then, of course, he had been safely back in Afghanistan for two years.

When U.S. and Sudanese intelligence officers first seriously discussed Osama's fate over three months in early 1996, his projected departure from Sudan was meant as the first of many steps designed to improve frayed relations between Khartoum and Washington. Ambassador Carney especially favored using Osama's deportation as a lever with the NIF to chip away at Turabi's influence. In a Sudanese follow-on gesture in July 1996, Carney and a Washington-based officer with a video camera were allowed to inspect a military camp that U.S. officials suspected was training Islamic radicals. He unsurprisingly found nothing very incriminating, and other Western diplomats considered it was training young Sudanese cannon fodder dragooned into Turabi's Popular Defense Force for the civil war in the south. Obviously, the NIF had time to ensure that no foreign volunteers were around (and many, but not all, of Osama's Afghan veterans had followed him to Jalalabad). But the visit was a gesture that, if reciprocated, might have led to other steps. By that October, much to Carney's disappointment, Washington allowed the opportunity to languish, then expire for all intents and purposes.

The decision seemed odd since the Clinton administration that very year had realized that much of its considerable accumulated animus against Sudan was based on erroneous intelligence. One ill-intentioned source had convinced Washington that Sudanese hit men had targeted National Security Adviser Anthony Lake, who was an outspoken critic of the NIF. For weeks in late 1995 Lake was trundled around in a heavily armored car and forced to leave his home for the more easily guarded guest quarters at Blair House, across from the White House. At least 100 other spurious intelligence reports from another biased source finally had been run to ground and discredited in late 1995 and early 1996. No policy review was ordered there and then. The Washington bureaucrats who consigned Sudan to ultima Thule on the basis of phony information did not deign to reexamine their strategy. Unlike lesser nations, the United States felt no compunction to rethink, much less correct, its errors. Such were the prerogatives of a superpower dealing with a peripheral troublemaker.

Still, the Clinton administration's apparent abiding fear of the NIF seemed disproportionate, all the more so since the negotiations over Osama were interpreted as the first sign that Turabi's influence was waning, with key protégés questioning his aggressive stewardship. There was something vaguely unsettling about a superpower spooking itself into pulling up stakes on the basis of discredited information. Paul Quaglia, the CIA chief of station, had led the American charge out of Khartoum in December 1995, indeed forcing less-impressionable State Department diplomats, many of them women, to follow suit reluctantly that February.[26]

The Khartoum embassy was technically "suspended"—that is, left formally open and staffed by its Sudanese employees. Carney was only one of five functioning American diplomats when he flew in from his Nairobi base, 1,000 miles to the south, for a ten-to-fourteen day monthly stint. Unavailingly, he and a very small number of career diplomats, some with long experience in the Arab world and Black Africa, bucked the policy-makers, arguing that engagement and patient diplomacy represented the most practical way to influence Sudanese policies judged distasteful in Washington. Carney and those sharing his views were defeated in Washington infighting. The National Security Council (NSC) and the State Department's diplomatic security office outgunned its weak African Affairs Bureau, which was responsible bureaucratically for the predominantly Muslim Sudan and headed by nonconfrontational Assistant Secretary George Moose. That outcome effectively slammed the door on cooperation of any meaningful sort between the two countries until Al-Qaeda's attacks on New York and Washington five years later. In the intervening years Khartoum claimed it repeatedly went through the motions of trying to patch up relations with Washington, but without success.

The administration's ostracism of Khartoum soon translated into active opposition in the form of "nonlethal" military aid to the NIF's regional enemies, designed to thwart, isolate and possibly overthrow the regime. At work were domestic American political considerations. Starting in the fall of 1997, the African Affairs Bureau was headed by Susan Rice, a forceful African-American political appointee in her early thirties with unimpeachable establishment connections. She and Secretary of State Madeleine Albright's three daughters were friends at Washington's private National Cathedral School, and she became an Albright family favorite and unofficial goddaughter.

Rice previously had served as an African specialist on the NSC. Whatever her academic and insider Washington credentials, she had no previous management or field experience in Africa as a diplomat. But she did have influential friends on the NSC. She was a protégée of Samuel R. Berger, who had replaced Lake as National Security Adviser, and of White House counterterrorism coordinator Richard Clarke, a consummate bureaucratic in-fighter with a career of powerful positions in the Reagan, Clinton and two Bush administrations. "She was very young, fairly shallow and didn't know the first thing about Sudan," an official who served under Rice recalled. "She was mostly mirroring what she heard from Dick Clarke and Berger, and they never wavered from their highly personalized impressions of the really nasty NIF period in the early 1990s."[27]

Under Rice, the African Affairs Bureau wrote off the Khartoum regime as feckless liars beyond redemption, guilty of terrorism and gross human-rights violations against the southern Christians and animists. That characterization of the NIF was far from inaccurate, but arguably it was up to the much stronger power to make the first step. Carney and others in the pro-engagement camp felt that diplomacy was invented to deal with unpleasant situations, especially when backed with Washington's clout. Other unlikable regimes had been coaxed back into polite society with a mix of diplomatic sticks and carrots. But the African Affairs Bureau tired of too many unkept Sudanese promises. The NIF was never an easy bunch to trust, much less like.

Turabi and his minions had silenced a once-vibrant civil society. Khartoum abounded, especially in the early days of NIF rule, with accounts of torture, intimidation and disappearances into "ghost houses" sprinkled around the capital. Before an American-brokered peace agreement of sorts was signed in May 2004, the second Sudanese civil war in the south, which began in 1983, had swallowed some 2 million lives before and after the NIF seized power. Rice was quickly in lockstep with an odd but puissant coalition ranging from the Christian evangelical right to women's groups and antislavery militants who enlisted the support of the Black Caucus in Congress. All shared a profound aversion to the NIF. Soon the African Affairs Bureau initiated "nonlethal" military aid to Khartoum's enemies in Eritrea, Ethiopia and Uganda, including southern opposition forces.[28]

In Washington, Sudan was isolated, all but expunged from the map of terra cognita. Khartoum never gave up the appearance of trying to get back into Washington's good graces. That, at least, was its contention. The NIF insisted it kept tempting the United States with promises of intelligence about Osama and his Sudanese investments, the hundreds of Al-Qaeda operatives who had been in Sudan with him, indeed all the Islamic radicals who moved in and out, using Khartoum for their operations elsewhere. Intelligence has ever been the coin of the weak in dealing with the powerful, the opening gambit in a larger game.

By 1997 the Sudanese were claiming their dossiers came complete with photos and other detailed intelligence not easily available elsewhere. True or false, the come-ons went untested. The Sudanese found no takers in the Clinton administration until 2000. Then the FBI and CIA set up low-level operations again in Khartoum and began delving into what Turabi, Osama, Al-Qaeda and other Islamic radicals had been up to in the first half of the 1990s. Only after 9/11 did Washington take the intelligence offer seriously. And only then did the Sudanese, out of sheer fear for the regime's very existence, start cooperating meaningfully, even claiming to have handed over some thirty foreign jihadis unlucky or stupid enough to have remained in Khartoum. So late in the game, old intelligence files, although doubtless useful, must have gone somewhat stale. Most intelligence by its very nature is perishable. Who was to say if Khartoum had not painstakingly culled the most incriminating bits before offering to hand the files over to the Americans or, in a favorite Sudanese stratagem, larded them with so much extraneous data as to make deciphering them all but impossible?

Ever since Carney was disavowed in 1996 he had been tormented by Washington's repeated failure to grasp the stakes. Over the years there were initiatives to reestablish contact. Mansoor Ijaz, an American businessman of Pakistani descent who was close to the White House thanks to generous donations to the Democratic Party, traveled often to Khartoum between mid-1997 and mid-1998, but the White House rebuffed his efforts to restore dialogue between Sudan and the United States.[29] Among other initiatives was a Sudanese intelligence invitation in January 1998 to David Williams, head of the FBI Middle East and Africa Desk, to visit Khartoum, or meet in another venue, to discuss collaboration. Five months later Williams wrote back, "Unfortunately, I am not currently in a position to accept your kind invitation."

Carney still looks back at his February 1996 dinner convinced the talk that night could have provided an auspicious point of departure. In his mind he knows where the blame should be apportioned. "There was no U.S. willingness to engage with Sudan," he recalled, "to build a minimum level of trust that might—and I use the word very strongly here—might have elicited access to key Sudanese intelligence documents" in time to have prevented Osama's string of terrorist operations against American targets.[30] In light of the ensuing mayhem, it is understandable that Carney summed up his frustration by invoking, but misquoting, the well-known French aphorism, attributed to Talleyrand, *pire qu'un crime, une faute* as "worse than a crime, a fuckup."[31]

There was one brief, serious blip. In 1997 the second-term Clinton administration decided to beef up Secretary Albright's State Department. Thomas Pickering was named undersecretary, the State Department's third-ranking position. A prestigious former ambassador in important countries, including Israel and Russia, Pickering reviewed the administration's Sudan policy, found it cockeyed and had the State Department announce that the Khartoum embassy would resume normal operations with American staff in residence, rather than rotating in and out from other posts. But within days his decision was humiliatingly overturned thanks to the influence of Rice, Berger and Clarke. Pickering underestimated his adversaries inside the White House, the State Department and in Congress, where the anti-NIF lobbies held sway. "The White House, the Secretary and the Hill went batshit," remarked an official who was clearly pleased by the outcome.[32]

THERE MATTERS stood until mid-August 1998, when the Sudanese suddenly were convinced that at long last their luck had changed. They were sure they finally had what it took to persuade the Americans to talk, perhaps even to authorize reopening their embassy in Washington, a major NIF objective. The Sudanese dangled two purported suspects whose Pakistani passports somehow attracted the attention of Khartoum airport immigration officials when they landed from Nairobi on August 4. Three days later twelve Americans and 238 Africans died when the U.S. embassy in Kenya was ripped apart and in a near simultaneous, but less lethal truck-bomb, attack against the Dar es Salaam embassy in neighboring Tanzania.

Within hours the Sudanese, who said they had tailed the two suspects from Khartoum airport, arrested them in a cheap downtown hotel after noting their earlier unsuccessful effort to rent an apartment overlooking the U.S. embassy. Sudanese interrogators claimed the men confessed to involvement in planning the Nairobi attack.[33] One man admitted to staying in the Kenyan capital in what the Sudanese wrote down as the "Top Hill Hotel"—in fact, it was the Hilltop Hotel, where the Al-Qaeda plotters had assembled the lethal truck bomb. (This nugget was imbedded in a letter reprising Sudan's position that Qutbi al-Mahdi, the head of Sudan's External Intelligence Department, wrote and had hand-delivered to FBI Director Louis Freeh in January 1999.)

With these two suspects in jail, the Sudanese reasoned they were making an offer the Americans couldn't refuse. The destruction of the embassies was, after all, Topic A in Washington. The Sudanese were even willing to deliver the suspects to Nairobi, where Freeh and hundreds of agents were investigating the terrorist attacks. Surely, the Americans would swallow their pride and distaste for the NIF and agree to do business.

The NIF was wrong—or, rather, both right and wrong.

Why the administration didn't insist on questioning the two men straightaway is essentially a tale of unlucky timing compounded by the miasma, chaos, panic and arrogance that marked one of the more fraught fortnights in contemporary American history. The East African embassy bombings were destabilizing enough. But the simultaneous cruise missile reprisals against Afghanistan and Khartoum that Clinton ordered thirteen days later, on August 20, and their unintended consequences coincided with the low point of his presidency. The missiles struck with sophisticated military efficiency, but proved to be embarrassments for the administration. Osama survived the strikes, which were meant to kill him in an Afghan training camp. And the missiles launched against Sudan set off a furor when the administration was unwilling or unable to parry outraged Sudanese insistence that the target was an innocent pharmaceutical plant. The ensuing confusion added to the impression of a luckless leader at his most vulnerable. After months of self-destructive denials, a mortified Clinton was cornered and forced to confess under oath on national television that he had lied about his sexual dalliance with White House intern Monica Lewinsky.

The president had flown back from a Martha's Vineyard vacation to announce the cruise missile strikes on the very day she had resumed testifying before a grand jury. To the undisguised delight of his vengeful detractors in the Republican Party, the road to impeachment lay open. In that poisonous atmosphere, his critics disdainfully accused him of launching the missiles to steal the limelight from the Monica scandal. In their eyes he was trying to "wag the dog," the title of a recent movie in which a besieged president provokes a foreign war to distract attention from domestic woes.[34]

In retrospect, the perfervid Lewinsky affair summed up the self-indulgent 1990s, when a president's sex life titillated a nation relieved—and a bit surprised—to have emerged victorious, if nearly exhausted, from the deadly serious confrontations of a half century of Cold War. Barely more than three years after the East African bombings, Al-Qaeda's attacks on New York and Washington ended America's most carefree decade, one that began to fray in East Africa and did so with ever-greater speed. Looking back, it is tempting to speculate that the United States kept missing clue after clue before its comeuppance as much because of arrogance in Sudan as bad luck.

So why didn't the administration in August 1998 follow through completely on the Sudanese offer? Part of the answer, of course, was that it had no eyes and ears at work in Khartoum, because the embassy was closed in all but name. That meant no American diplomat or intelligence officer was on the ground to evaluate the suspects (or evaluate the controversial nature of the El-Shifa pharmaceutical plant). No working embassy also meant no fast exchange of information through diplomatic channels. Was it also a case of American quasi-imperial haughtiness, of accumulated exasperation, of justified suspicion of the Sudanese regime or of fear of looking like idiots? All these elements could apply to the Clinton administration's policy in Sudan. But a short and arguably overly charitable answer is that contacts of a sort were in the works to gain access to the dangled men, but the clock simply ran out. That may just be the best, if imperfect, explanation, but if that was the case, many questions remain.

Khartoum played its cards as well it could. Whatever else the Sudanese government stood accused of, stupidity and perseverance were never among its shortcomings. Frozen out at the State Department and the CIA, the resourceful Sudanese since 1997 had developed ties with the FBI at its Washington headquarters and in New York, where freewheeling counter-terrorism chief John P. O'Neill ran a separate satrapy. About a week after the attacks on the embassies, the Sudanese pitched roughly the same offer to both FBI offices. The Washington approach was tantalizingly vague, but the fact that it came from Qutbi al-Mahdi signaled its importance.

The message was conveyed by Janet McElligott, a onetime Bush the Elder White House employee who had become Sudan's chosen intermediary in Washington. She recalled receiving a telephone call "about August 14" from Qutbi, a smooth NIF senior operator who had acquired Canadian citizenship and once taught at the University of Massachusetts at Amherst. He simply told her that Sudan "had important information to share" and that the FBI should send a team to Khartoum posthaste.[35]

Only barebone details were provided by the Sudanese. Lucky breaks in Nairobi and Dar es Salaam had allowed the FBI investigation to make real progress and establish Al-Qaeda's responsibility beyond reasonable doubt within days of the explosions. That progress may have taken some shine off Khartoum's offer. The Sudanese did not help their case. Skimping on information was an abiding Sudanese failing, albeit consistent with NIF canons of secrecy, especially when it came to easily bugged telephone conversations. When McElligott promptly called her contact at the FBI Middle East desk after the telephone conversation with Khartoum, she told him she was sure Sudan's message involved the embassies. "You need to go now," she said, underlining her sense of urgency by stressing that Qutbi himself had telephoned her. That name rang a bell. "Holy shit," she remembered the agent saying, "he's the number one guy." "It's not like Qutbi calls me every day," she told the now-convinced FBI agent. A few days later, he called back and somewhat apologetically told her, "They won't let us go. Damn!" She said the agent had been so keen that he had wheedled his way into the FBI team dispatched to Nairobi and, once there, hoped to agitate to be sent to Khartoum to check out the two suspects.

In New York, veteran intelligence hand Elfatih Erwa, by now the Sudanese ambassador to the United Nations and as such his country's senior official in the United States, had better information and even better access. He also had an unsavory reputation with the administration; it had neither forgiven nor forgotten what U.S. officials held was his direct role in the cold-blooded murder years earlier of several Sudanese working for the U.S.

Agency for International Development in the southern city of Juba. Also starting around August 14, and with President Bashir's personal blessing, Erwa was in almost daily touch with the FBI counterterrorism unit in New York about the two suspects. But somehow not until August 19 did Erwa's message reach O'Neill himself.

O'Neill needed no prodding. He wanted approval to arrest the two suspects fast, and flew that evening to Washington to get it. He went straight to see his close friend Richard Clarke at the National Security Council. "I told John he brought me the information too late," Clarke recalled years later.[36] "Had he come five days earlier, perhaps . . . but I am not sure it would have made any difference. Something he didn't know about was going on. I told him, 'You need to talk to the Attorney General.'" Clarke was hinting that the point of no return had been reached.

What he couldn't tell O'Neill was that the Clinton administration was going to launch retaliatory cruise missiles against Afghanistan and Sudan the next day. A handful of the most senior civilian and military leaders had made a binding decision and were sworn to secrecy to prevent security leaks. The plans were too far advanced to be canceled. The final countdown was about to begin. Two iffy Al-Qaeda suspects dangled by the untrustworthy Sudanese weighed practically nothing in the balance. Who among the key senior decision-makers even knew of the two suspects until O'Neill apprised Clarke remains unclear. A man I have known for forty years who was involved in the decision later told me, "To the best of my recollection, I was aware of the offer only after the fact." Indeed, it is doubtful anything— and anybody but the president himself—could have stayed the administration's hand at that point.[37]

O'Neill did meet Attorney General Janet Reno, to no avail. He was not a man who took kindly to obstacles. He came away from the meeting predictably furious and flew back to New York empty-handed and none the wiser. Erwa's last contact with O'Neill's team was just before midnight on August 19.[38] Within hours cruise missiles struck an Al-Qaeda training camp in Afghanistan and Khartoum's El-Shifa (Arabic for "healing") pharmaceutical plant. The plant, Washington alleged, was linked to Osama and was making a chemical weapons precursor named EMPTA (whose only known use was in the production of the deadly nerve agent VX), apparently for him. The missile strikes' timing was dictated by an unusually precise intelligence report insisting that Osama and senior staff were due to arrive at a fixed time on August 20 at the targeted Afghan camp.

Such pinpoint intelligence about Osama's peripatetic movements was rare indeed. "We also knew it was a long shot," conceded a senior official who approved the missile strikes, "but we had been trying to get Osama and this was the best shot we had."³⁹ Osama's prudent security measures dictated that he never spent much time in one place. Clarke told me the report had reached the CIA just over a week after the East African attacks, thus roughly at the same time the Sudanese began trying to interest the FBI in the two suspects. And it was apparently that intelligence report alone which locked in the timing of the retaliatory strikes. That intelligence was famously wrong. Osama was not present in the targeted camp when the missiles landed—if he was there at all that day.⁴⁰

Of course, neither the Sudanese nor the FBI agents they were dealing with in New York and Washington knew the president and his advisers were going to launch reprisal attacks on August 20 (although the State Department tipped its hand in preceding days by evacuating nonessential embassy staff and families from Islamabad). Erwa, McElligott and O'Neill had done their best and succeeded in bringing the Sudanese offer, real or bogus, to the attention of the top administration policy-makers. A prudent friend then very much involved in counterterrorism at the State Department indirectly confirmed Sudan's demarche had not gotten lost in the bureaucratic shuffle. In the neutral, self-censoring language of a practiced diplomat, he said, "It was true the Sudanese offered the two men to the FBI, true also discussions about gaining access to them were going on at the working level and true these discussions were disrupted by the El-Shifa attack." "Working level" was not spelled out, and clearly it was a term of his trade meant to discourage hopes of a detailed explanation.

He thus confirmed that the United States had cut short the discussions. McElligott's FBI agent obviously was obeying orders from superiors when he cryptically complained to her, "They won't let us go. Damn." But my friend in counterterrorism would not be drawn when I asked who in the administration caused the "disruption." A Clinton official working on Sudanese policy at the time later told me that Clarke had been one of the five senior advisers "who pulled the trigger."⁴¹ My diplomat friend feigned surprise at my interest in what to him was "yet another Sudanese effort to cast themselves in a good light."⁴²

His gratuitous comment strikes me as pure hubris. Our conversation took place almost midway between the East African terrorist attacks in 1998 and the September 11 events in New York and Washington. What

bothered me then was his dismissive condescension, his built-in lack of cu-
riosity about trying to establish if perhaps just for once Sudan was on the
level. It was not as if men described as Al-Qaeda cadres were a dime a
dozen then. If the East African bombings had a message, it was that more
trouble was heading America's way; the United States was just beginning to
learn about Al-Qaeda and would be well advised to explore any and all
leads, even from the distrusted Sudanese. Khartoum's offer at best was
known about by only a handful of American officials. For example, Susan
Rice, a close Clarke associate from her NSC days, detested the NIF regime
but expressed disbelief that her African Affairs Bureau had been kept in the
dark.[43]

If Sudan's two suspects were duds and added nothing to the investigation, it shouldn't have taken long to expose the Sudanese as hoaxsters up to
their old tricks. They had offered the men on a platter, after all. Aside from
their proclaimed motivation of trying to reestablish relations with Washington, they very likely hoped the offer would more immediately blunt
American temptation to punish and destabilize the NIF regime. The Sudanese must have factored in these variables. And to prove their credentials
they held the two suspects for almost two weeks after El-Shifa was destroyed, hoping Washington would again pick up the line that Erwa and
McElligott had played out and O'Neill briefly grasped. It was a clever move,
demonstrating that Sudan was still serious about being seen contributing
to the investigations of the attacks on the embassies and about renewing
dialogue with Washington.

The more I thought about the details of the American retaliatory strikes
the more questions sprang to mind. I kept coming back to the administration's steadfast refusal to engage with Khartoum, and to the wisdom of attacking Afghan and Sudanese targets at the same time. The Afghan camp
strike was deemed time-sensitive. The same argument could scarcely be
made for the El-Shifa operation. Wouldn't it have been prudent to post-
pone the strike against the pharmaceutical plant at least until Khartoum
either delivered the two suspects or backed down? Some administration
policy-makers apparently feared that somehow the Sudanese, instructed by
a strike against the Afghan camps, would seek to remove the purportedly
telltale earth sample containing EMPTA. If the EMPTA had been in the
factory and had Osama later used it in chemical weapons, senior officials
felt not destroying it would have been unforgivable.[44]

Yet, if the suspects were handed over and provided valuable intelligence, why bother hitting Khartoum at all since the regime by its own lights would have reestablished relations of sorts with Washington and been tempted to be ever more forthcoming about Osama? Three years later, after September 11, Sudan did hand over a small mountain of documentation that remained useful but would have been much more so if available in 1998.[45] It was tempting to conclude that the administration first and foremost was interested in demonstrating that the world's only superpower could match Al-Qaeda in carrying out two simultaneous operations against two countries. In that game of asymmetric symmetry, whose tail was wagging whose dog?

WHAT HAPPENED after the August 20 missile strikes was even more curious. The administration was soon so thoroughly embarrassed that the Sudanese chose not to add to Washington's woes by making public their offer about the two suspects then and there. Indeed, no sooner was the El-Shifa plant in ruins than the missile attack turned into a public relations disaster for the administration. Khartoum moved deftly, quickly asserting El-Shifa certainly made pharmaceuticals, and especially veterinary medicines, but not the EMPTA precursor that Washington invoked to justify the attack. (*Newsday* uncovered an El-Shifa executive whose unsuccessful efforts to hide did raise questions about the plant's activities.) To bolster claims of injured innocence, Sudan, normally extremely stingy about doling out visas to foreign journalists, welcomed with open arms any reporter who flew into Khartoum.

The NIF felt it was on a roll. The Sudanese government confidently asked for an American or UN investigation of the attack. Washington was not interested. Not a word of apology was expressed by the U.S. government over the death of the plant's night watchman, the attack's only casualty. A bemused Sudanese diplomat at the United Nations pointed out the administration's double standard: the previous February "you guys bombed Iraq because it blocked UN weapons inspectors. We're begging for a UN investigation and you're blocking it."[46]

Within twenty-four hours of the missile attack the administration began an agonizing retreat, regularly scaling back its initial claims. Its handling smacked of constant improvisation; successive fallback positions unraveled in a textbook example of seemingly faulty intelligence. Washington was unable or unwilling to provide proof of EMPTA at the factory site itself, citing its fear of compromising intelligence assets.[47] Officials said the rainy season had washed away the evidence. To this day senior administration officials involved in the decision insist the intelligence was solid. Perhaps, but there were disquieting signs of sloppy homework. Officials were embarrassed when obliged to acknowledge they had not known that the plant had changed ownership five months earlier. Osama's connection, if any, was alleged to have been with the initial owner.

But that original proprietor contradicted Washington's assertion that Osama had been a part owner, further undermining the administration's claims of an Al-Qaeda connection. El-Shifa's new owner, a Sudanese named Salah Idriss, who had made a fortune working for Saudi Arabia's preeminent National Commercial Bank and picked up Saudi citizenship along the way, hired a team of senior Western scientists put together by the prominent Washington law firm Akin Gump Strauss Hauer & Feld. Within months the scientists gave the plant a clean bill of health, finding no evidence of EMPTA and rebutting the administration point by point. NBC's *Dateline* in 1999 talked to two unnamed U.S. officials who said the EMPTA soil sample was collected not at the plant, but across the street. Milton Bearden, a retired former CIA chief of station in Khartoum who retained close links with the regime, expressed his astonishment, having "never seen a single soil sample that led to an act of war with a sovereign nation with which we had diplomatic relations." Thomas Pickering explained American ignorance of the plant's change of ownership by saying, "Perhaps we are not omniscient."[48]

Rather than risk compromising what it maintained were sensitive intelligence sources by producing evidence in court, the unrepentant administration the following May grudgingly released $24 million in Idriss's U.S. bank assets it had sequestered the previous August. Detailed published accounts of dissension within the bureaucracy before the strike cast serious doubts about the wisdom of targeting the plant in the first place. Two other targets were discarded because they were judged even more iffy. It turned out the advice had been far from unanimous. The Pentagon's Defense Intelligence Agency and the State Department's Bureau of Intelligence and Research each had expressed doubts.

So, apparently, did the CIA. Critics pointed to the classic dangers of the politicized use of intelligence. But the United States neither admitted wrongdoing nor offered to reimburse Idriss for the plant's destruction. (The ever timid House of Saud, fearful of upsetting Washington, was rumored to have discouraged Idriss from suing the U.S. government, indeed even to have offered to reimburse him for the destroyed plant. This would not have been the first time the Al-Saud had bent over backward to avoid giving offense to Washington.)

The Sudanese let Washington stew while the Clinton impeachment lurched forward. Only in January 1999 did Qutbi al-Mahdi send Freeh his handwritten summary of Sudan's position. The note listed two detained suspects as Sayyid Nizar Abbass, Pakistani passport B 5534540, and Sayyid Iskander Sayyid Suliman, Pakistani passport E 061482. Both passports had suspicious Singapore, Malaysian, Tanzanian and Kenyan immigration stamps. "Our intention was to hand them over to the FBI," al-Mahdi's note read, because "most" of the preliminary interrogation established that they "could be of interest" to Washington.

When Washington initially failed to respond in the days preceding the missile attack on El-Shifa, the Sudanese were not immediately worried. Of course, they had no clue that the cruise missiles were scheduled for August 20. In the immediate wake of the attack, the NIF was furious at the destruction of the plant and understandably terrified that more dire punishment might be on its way. But the Sudanese were not dumb. Khartoum kept the door open. Qutbi's note said Sudan held the two men for twelve days after the missile attack, apparently hoping against hope that Washington would react quickly.

It didn't. The reasons were easy enough to fathom. Quite apart from its antipathy to the NIF regime, Washington was bogged down trying to sell the botched El-Shifa attack to querulous Americans. To have taken up the Sudanese offer after the attack risked prompting more embarrassing explaining about why it had not been accepted before. Only on September 2 did the Sudanese stop waiting and fly the two suspects to Karachi. There they were handed over to Pakistan's ISI, which maintained close relations with Taliban leaders, who in turn were linked to Al-Qaeda. On the face of things, the administration through sins of omission or commission, allowed two potentially important suspects to disappear.

Khartoum naturally had wanted to make the men appear as more than mere appetizers had the administration bothered to get in touch and interrogate them. By then, al-Mahdi's letter later claimed, Khartoum had extracted a great deal more information from them. For example, al-Mahdi's note said, in a telltale error the two men had given the manager of Osama's old tannery in Khartoum as a reference on their visa applications in Nairobi. A senior Sudanese official insisted to me years later that the regime had respected the rules of the game. Washington had been given a decent interval to react. Khartoum had not directly freed the two suspects and allowed them to disappear into thin air. The Sudanese intelligence agency handed them over to the ISI, their Pakistani opposite number, thus respecting formal niceties.[49]

Even if the administration found a way to talk to the men thereafter, they would have had no intrinsic interest in telling the truth. And in Pakistan neither the Sudanese nor the Americans had a way of compelling them to do so. What in fact happened to the men once in Pakistan, and whether the Americans did talk to them, remain uncertain. The counter-terrorism diplomat I saw in Washington in February 2000 insisted some-one "at the working level" indeed had seen them, logically, in Pakistan, and come up empty. He did not say when or provide any details.

There was just a hint in that odd phrase—"working level"—to suggest that perhaps no American officials had actually seen the men at all. In other words, someone else, perhaps the ISI, had obligingly questioned the men for someone in Washington who was simply going through the motions. At the U.S. embassy in Islamabad my routine inquiry about the two suspects through normal channels got nowhere. But a well-placed friend checked around for me and eventually was told vaguely the two men had been interviewed and produced no important information. He suspected that he was being brushed off and that no interview in fact had occurred. (One senior Washington official involved in approv-ing the missile strikes had a somewhat similar impression. When Sudan's offer had come to light, he asked about what had happened to the two men. He was told that the National Security Council had conducted a full investigation. The men were not interesting. No details were sup-plied.)[50]

My Islamabad friend was not the only doubter in that embassy. Years later a retired senior American intelligence officer in Islamabad at the time denied meeting the two men or even hearing of their existence. And he in-sisted he would have known if anybody else in the embassy had, meaning his FBI opposite number.[51] His doubts jibed with what a senior Sudanese intelligence officer privy to the case told me in New York: the Americans never talked to the two men at all, and he insisted he knew. He did not volunteer how he knew, but I was told he had long-standing and very good relations with the ISI.[52]

I was determined to find out what the Pakistani government had done with the men. In Pakistan in 1999 and again in 2000, I repeatedly pestered the ISI and the civilian Interior Minister who had been in office in 1998 for information about the two men, whose names and passport numbers I provided. My initial inquiries were met with promises of full and rapid response. Persistent follow-up telephone calls prompted increasingly surly runarounds from irritated subalterns. Eventually they stopped coming to the telephone when I called.

Still, I was luckier than Kamal Heyder, an enterprising Pakistani freelancer (and later a CNN correspondent). NBC assigned him to trace the two men for a *Dateline* program on U.S.–Sudanese relations. He was provided with photocopies of the suspects' passports, complete with their photographs, donated by the Sudanese. His research took him to Quetta, the capital of Pakistan's Baluchistan Province. Cooperative officials at the passport office there quickly established that the passports themselves were genuine. In the course of three weeks' digging, he also discovered both men had provided false addresses in their applications. Bribing officials to obtain even minor documents in dodgy situations is commonplace in Pakistan (and many another country).

Uncovering such subterfuge as vouching for a bogus address might just lead to further turpitude in tribal Baluchistan. Heyder thus was not really surprised when he received a threatening anonymous phone call at his Quetta hotel, advising him to get out of town fast on pain of dire consequences. He did not argue. To this day, he still does not know if the phone call was prompted by fears that his nosing around might uncover a major corruption scandal or something far more sinister—terrorism, for example. Quetta is less than an hour's drive from the border of Afghanistan, which then was controlled by Osama's Taliban friends.[53]

And thus the trail went cold and no one seemed unduly upset. The two men were rumored to have disappeared into the lawless safety of Afghanistan soon after their arrival in Pakistan and taken refuge with Al-Qaeda. At least that is what Qutbi al-Mahdi said the ISI told him.[54] Indeed, a persistent rumor suggested Pakistan's then-civilian prime minister, Nawaz Sharif, traded the two men to Osama, probably using the ISI as a conduit, to buy off increasingly hostile Islamic radicals threatening his wobbly government. If so, the trade was of little succor to Sharif. Little more than a year later, in November 1999, General Pervez Musharraf ousted him in an army coup.

AS FOR OSAMA himself, he was not in the Afghan camp when the U.S. missiles struck, killing some two dozen trainees, many of whom were Pakistanis earmarked for the struggle to wrest disputed Kashmir from Indian control. The next day, Ayman al-Zawahiri, his right-hand man and leader of the Egyptian Islamic Jihad, which the previous February had merged with Al-Qaeda, used his satellite phone to call a Pakistani reporter with a defiant message: Osama had survived. "Tell the Americans we aren't afraid of bombardments, threats and acts of aggression. We suffered and survived the Soviet bombings for ten years in Afghanistan and we are ready for more sacrifices," he added. "The war has only just begun. The Americans should now await the answer."

As Zawahiri clearly stated, that message was meant for Americans and, by extension, other Westerners. Ordinary Americans trying to make sense of the simultaneous attacks on the East African embassies had their attention drawn to a cryptic message from Zawahiri published in London's Arabic press on the very eve of those August 7 bombings. He was angry. In its war in the shadows, the United States had inflicted a serious setback on Zawahiri's operatives. Only weeks before, the CIA, with help from Albanian officials, had kidnapped and interrogated key Egyptian members of his cell in the capital, Tirana, then turned them over to Cairo for interrogation, probable torture, trial and long jail sentences for those spared the death penalty.

"We are interested in briefly telling the Americans that their message has been received and that the response, which we hope they will read carefully, is being prepared, because, with God's help, we will write in a language that they will understand." In fact, active planning for the East African attacks had begun years before, and the first practical steps were executed in the spring. But a boastful Zawahiri couldn't resist linking the warning to the Tirana arrests. Zawahiri needn't have bothered spelling out either message for young Muslim men. Soon after the American missile attacks, hundreds of volunteers were flocking to Afghanistan for training in Al-Qaeda camps from one end of the far-flung Muslim world to the other. Osama's reputation had assumed mythic proportions. The Americans, with their high-tech weapons, had missed their targets in Sudan and Afghanistan. The volunteers were convinced that Allah had intervened to spare Osama's life. They were not the only Muslims to think so.

IN THE BEST of all possible worlds things might just have turned up aces in Sudan. But in modern memory Sudan had never figured in that charmed circle. Even to entertain such a delusion was to disregard what earlier generations of politically incorrect Westerners called the wog factor. "Wogs" then was British colonial slang for "worthy oriental gentlemen," slighting shorthand to describe the many-hued peoples round the world once governed from London and long since a serious insult. By extension the wog factor was a predisposition for things to go very wrong, for reasons defying Western logic, in parts of the globe not yet described as the Third World. I preferred to think in terms of white noise, a fatal attraction for a background buzz of unhealthy troublemaking in equally unstable neighbors. White noise was all but endemic in the region, and far beyond, and grew in intensity as no longer newly independent countries unraveled after a century of corseted colonial rule.

Some basic Sudanese characteristics came with the territory and proved contagious to outsiders. Throughout the ages, Egyptians had worried about the transit of the Nile's water through Sudan since unimpeded access was deemed crucial to their very existence. The attempted assassination of President Mubarak in 1995 was vintage white noise because, had it succeeded, Egypt in revenge doubtless would have done its utmost to topple the NIF in Khartoum.[55]

White noise also was a factor in Turabi's dreams of turning Khartoum into an important center of the Muslim world. In fact, Sudan was too peripheral to the Arab heartland, too black, and its Islam was too corrupted with a very moderate African variety of Sufism (a mystical Muslim offshoot), to pretend to leadership according to the purist canons of jihadi Islamists. Sudan's extended decline helped Turabi. The accomplished British diplomats or colonial administrators who served in Sudan had long since disappeared and, with them, much of the outside world's institutional memory. Turabi and the NIF early on set about isolating themselves and the country from prying domestic and foreign eyes. Business was so bad that the once-vibrant Lebanese gave up and drifted back home, and even the ranks of the tenacious Greeks thinned. Allowing once relatively bustling Khartoum to become a backwater helped insulate NIF operations from the curious attention of the naturally inquisitive Sudanese citizenry.

I realized how much the country had changed when I got back in touch with old Sudanese friends in 2000. I hoped they would provide a detailed description of what Osama had been up to during his Khartoum period. They apologetically confessed they knew next to nothing—and not for want of trying. Yes, Osama was occasionally seen at this or that mosque for Friday prayers, always protected by bodyguards and often arriving late and leaving early in a black Toyota Land Cruiser with heavily tinted windows, routinely preceded and followed by vehicles with windows just as dark. Yes, some of his followers had arrived from Afghanistan—100, according to one source; 300, if you believed another, perhaps even 450. He liked to go to the horse races on Fridays, but as a good Wahhabi for whom music was *haram* (forbidden), he was careful to put his fingers in his ears when the trumpet announced a new race. Neighborhood men from around his compound in Riyadh remembered playing soccer with him after prayers.

Neighbors on one occasion complained of the noise from explosions at Osama's farm in Khartoum North, and indeed the police intervened. But the affair was quickly papered over with a single telephone call to higher authority. In fact, Sudanese opposition politicians I questioned in Cairo and elsewhere put on a show of knowing all about Osama and Al-Qaeda, but were not convincing. They were not alone. In late April 1995, during an assignment in Sudan, I came to the conclusion that Washington knew virtually nothing about him either. Donald Petterson, the U.S. ambassador through early 1995, later corroborated my impression in recalling that Washington instructed him to deliver a "nonpaper," as the State Department called unofficial communications, to Bashir and Turabi, warning that if suspected anti-American plotting actually took place "our reaction could result in the international isolation of Sudan, in the destruction of your economy, and in military measures that would make you pay a high price." But Petterson said his "recollection" was that Osama's name did not figure on the list of terrorists he discussed with the Sudanese because "we in Khartoum were not really concerned about him."[56]

Sudanese press visas were very hard to come by. I had one issued for the 1995 jamboree of hundreds of radicals called the Popular Arab Islamic Conference that Turabi irregularly staged starting four years earlier to put Sudan and himself on the Muslim world map (perhaps thanks, I later learned, to Osama's funding). I had no desire at the time to get stuck in the Chinese-built conference hall listening to revolutionary rhetoric. Instead I used the visa later to do a story on how Turabi the previous summer had disposed of Carlos, the self-appointed champion of Palestinian nationalism (sometimes to the intense embarrassment of many Palestinians). At the end of the Cold War he was forced out of Syria and was shunted around various radical Arab regimes before being dumped in Khartoum in 1993. His Marxist friends in power behind the Iron Curtain were no more, and radical Arab regimes dared not shelter him. He had outlived the end of the Cold War—and his usefulness.

I made a point of visiting the American embassy because I wanted to confirm a persistent rumor. The CIA was said to have first located Carlos in late 1993, soon after he landed in Khartoum with a Jordanian diplomatic passport, under an alias and accompanied by yet another young girlfriend. Washington had nothing indictable against Carlos—he had killed no Americans—and so tipped off the French. It was a gesture of thanks to the French for their cooperation during the 1991 war to free Kuwait from Iraqi occupation. France wanted the Venezuelan-born self-styled Marxist for killing two counterintelligence agents in Paris in June 1975 and for a subsequent series of deadly terrorist operations in Paris and the French provinces. In August 1994 France completed negotiations with Turabi.[57]

Carlos was abducted from a Khartoum clinic when he was still groggy from the anesthesia administered for a minor operation to correct varicoceles, enlarged veins in the spermatic cord of his right testicle. His own Sudanese bodyguards seized him. He who dreaded needles was jabbed with a tranquilizer, trussed up inside a jute sack and manacled; he had a black hood placed over his face and flown back in an executive jet to Paris where, in a legal nicety, once on French soil he was formally arrested to cover up the lack of official extradition procedure. The French snatch squad in the plane was instructed to speak English to make Carlos believe they were Mossad agents taking him to Israel. Years after he was tried and sentenced to life, I asked for permission to visit Carlos—or, rather, Illich Ramirez Sanchez, his real name—in La Santé prison in Paris. I wanted to ask him if he had known Osama in Khartoum and what he thought of the radical Islamic political violence that had displaced his Marxist brand. After many months, I received a formal letter from the director of the French penal administration turning down my request on the grounds that a meeting would "not contribute to the social or professional insertion," meaning rehabilitation of the prisoner. Still later, Carlos got a handwritten letter out to me denouncing Turabi as a "homosexual" and refusing to say if he had known Osama in Sudan. "I do not intend to facilitate U.S. judicial imperialistic tactics of amalgamation of all anti-imperialistic armed resistance forces into a ubiquitous bin Laden conspiracy network." He also praised as "admirable" Osama's willingness to forgo wealth and "fight the Red Army in Afghanistan" and with his personal fortune, "recruit, train and arm and lead in battle . . . foreign mujahedeen."

At the American embassy on my Carlos mission, instead of answering my straightforward question on the premises, two officials invited me out for lemonade at a Nile-side open-air café near the Hilton Hotel. I was unused to such special attention and supposed their choice of venue reflected fears the embassy was bugged. They readily confirmed what I had heard about Carlos's comeuppance. Then, at length, they encouraged me to interview Osama at his compound in Riyadh, a prosperous suburb also favored by Turabi and other NIF grandees. I had never heard of Osama then, but frankly I rarely took kindly to doing the U.S. government's work for it. My displeasure was a defensive reflex; American correspondents working in the Third World automatically were assumed to be CIA spies, so I tended to give U.S. embassies a wide berth. In any case, my two hosts provided so few details about Osama that I became convinced they wanted to use me for a fishing expedition.

But the day after the lemonade, I had some free time and drove out to Osama's compound. Armed guards turned me away and that was that. I later understood something simple that apparently had escaped the American embassy; arranging to see Osama, even had I persevered in Khartoum, was no easy matter. He desperately wanted publicity in mainstream Western publications, especially television exposure. But reporters did not just knock on his door and get their interviews. Osama was prudent to the point of paranoia. Even then he had his reasons.

In 1994 in Khartoum's sister city of Omdurman a would-be assassin said to belong to the extreme radical sect called Takfir wal Hijra (Expiation and Flight), which specialized in killing Muslims judged to have traduced its peculiar interpretation of Islam, started shooting at a mosque with a reputation for hostility to the NIF, but was caught before he reached Osama's compound. In 1995 a white Toyota Hilux pickup bearing four armed

Yemeni mercenaries had screeched up to his high-walled villa and opened fire on his living quarters and his office in a chocolate-colored guest house in the next block.

Osama's armed guards—Saudi, Yemeni and Palestinian—fired back from the front of the guest house, while gunshots erupted from the roof. In the shoot-out one guard was killed in the crossroads, two or three others died in the guest house and three of the four attackers also succumbed. A surviving Yemeni and a Libyan were hanged eventually by the Sudanese.[58] Thereafter, one end of the street outside his compound was sealed off, with armed guards stationed on and around the premises. Even that precaution did nothing to relieve his growing paranoia. Years later Prince Turki al-Faisal suggested the Sudanese themselves had engineered the attack to impress on their guest the advisability of hiring more protection.[59]

Both for his security and to maintain an aura of mystery Osama preferred to deal through cutouts to screen foreign visitors. In 1994 he had dispatched a trusted Saudi aide, Khalid al-Fawwaz, to London to found the grandly named Advice and Reformation Committee (ARC) located on Beethoven Street. One of its main tasks for self-advertising Osama was ensuring that Arabic language newspapers published in London picked up the growing number of his pronouncements criticizing the Al-Saud. But the ARC had another function: Fawwaz vetted the occasional journalist who wanted to interview Osama. Those who passed muster were made to cool their heels in Khartoum for days and may well have been kept under surveillance.

In subsequent years when he was back in Afghanistan, an increasingly suspicious Osama indulged in practiced tradecraft such as blindfolding visiting reporters, driving them around for hours in cars with tinted windows (or in the middle of the night), insisting that television crews use his cameras and cassettes, conducting the interviews in the dead of night and disappearing before dawn. Hamid Mir, a jovial Pakistani reporter who was the last print journalist to interview Osama after September 11, relished recounting their initial meeting in 1997. Bearded men followed Mir around for days before he was judged worthy of an interview.

For the first of several meetings in Afghanistan, Mir was stripped and obliged to undergo the indignity of an endoscopic examination, apparently to ensure that he had not somehow implanted sophisticated listening or recording devices inside his body. Osama in that interview made clear the price of betrayal by reeling off the names and ages of Mir's children, the identity and telephone number of his mistress and similar information about close friends. Before another interview, Mir said he was stripped and his testicles examined and squeezed, seemingly for fear they contained hidden electronics devices. That at least was what Mir told me and others, but perhaps he was not above spinning a tall tale.[60]

FADL, the Al-Qaeda turncoat, provided the Clinton administration with intelligence about Al-Qaeda described later in a New York court as a "gold mine." He was the star government witness in 2001 when a federal court in Manhattan tried, convicted and sentenced four men to life imprisonment without parole for their involvement in the 1998 attacks against the Nairobi and Dar es Salaam embassies. Those were the first terrorist acts unmistakably traceable to Al-Qaeda and the first tried in a U.S. court. Fadl was a one-man time line, providing a near-continuous insight into Osama's operations from the moment he joined Al-Qaeda in 1989, by pledging *bayat* (fealty), at Farouq training camp in Afghanistan, until he defected in 1995. He testified at length in court, and it is safe to assume he told the FBI in private a great deal more than was needed for the convictions.

As such, his testimony was even more precious than that of another prosecution witness named Ali A. Mohamed, a curious onetime Egyptian soldier turned Green Beret who spent a leave from the U.S. Army fighting in Afghanistan against the Soviets without the authorization or knowledge of his commander. Mohamed had a penchant for indiscriminate espionage. In 1984 he first volunteered his services to the CIA in Cairo to penetrate a Hezbollah cell in Germany. He worked on and off for Zawahiri's Islamic Jihad, even serving as his guide when Zawahiri, using an alias, made an unsuccessful fund-raising visit to California in 1995 that went undetected at the time.

Upon completing a three-year hitch in the U.S. Army in 1989, Mohamed, then in California, gave the FBI its first worm's-eye view of jihadi activism (information that might have spurred greater counterterrorism action and indeed set off a row between the FBI and the CIA after the September 11 attacks). That same year he also provided basic military instruction for Islamic radicals in Brooklyn. Four years later some of these students were involved in the first attack on the World Trade Center. In late 1993 Mohamed showed up in Nairobi as part of an Al-Qaeda surveillance team that thoroughly cased the U.S. embassy. He later showed his report and photographs to Osama in Khartoum. He told the New York court that Osama "looked at the picture of the American embassy and pointed to where a truck could go as a suicide bomber." Less than five years later an Al-Qaeda team did just that.

It is hard to exaggerate the importance of these two defectors' testimony because in previous years so little was known for sure about Osama. American officials keeping book on him in the early 1990s spoke self-deprecatingly of "Osama sightings," as if following him was like tracking fanciful "Elvis sightings," such had become the volume of unverifiable and often suspiciously hyped reports of his alleged travels and activities around the globe. (In fact, once he was an adult Osama is not known to have traveled outside the Muslim world, despite reports placing him at one time or another in the Philippines, Britain and even the United States.) Fadl's treasure trove, however, seemed to have been put to haphazard initial use. Or perhaps the FBI was plain unlucky. Acting apparently to a great extent on Fadl's information, in August 1997 the FBI and the CIA, in collaboration with the Kenyan police, raided the clandestine Al-Qaeda cell's Nairobi safe house, which was fronting as a Muslim relief organization called Mercy International Relief Agency.

American agencies had been so empowered by the New York grand jury in 1996. FBI agents seized telephone records and some of the cell's files, but missed others, and seemed generally to have failed to put two and two together. The agents did not shut the cell down. Even before that raid, Nairobi cell members became aware to the point of panic of their own vulnerability when they learned of the defection, months after the fact, of a high-ranking cadre, Osama's paymaster. For all Al-Qaeda's advertised rigor—on occasion it could order the execution of a suspected mole—Osama seemed outwardly unconcerned when foot soldiers defected or ran afoul of the law.[61] To be sure, senior Al-Qaeda cadres were instructed about how to react during interrogation.

But getting caught was a professional risk, or perhaps God's will. In his early utterances, Osama did demand the United States free Sheikh Omar Abdel Rahman, the blind Egyptian cleric serving a life sentence without parole in a maximum security prison on charges of having instigated a questionable conspiracy to blow up New York landmarks. (The cleric was basically a victim of an FBI sting operation and was convicted thanks to a rarely invoked "seditious conspiracy" law dating from the period after the

American Civil War.) Not for Osama was the systematic recourse to deadly threats and acts that Carlos, for example, indulged in to free his captured friends and colleagues. Oddly, the Americans and Al-Qaeda seemed to share a certain nonchalance. The Al-Qaeda cell in Nairobi recovered its wits after the damaging but incomplete FBI raid in 1997, and its members participated the next spring in the detailed planning for the attacks against the Nairobi and Dar es Salaam embassies. Had the FBI agents been more astute, or luckier, just possibly the embassies might have been spared destruction. A former U.S. official who worked on Sudan at the time later said that in 1998 American intelligence was intercepting telephone communications between Al-Qaeda and a "very important source" in Khartoum. In fact, the official said, the administration had toyed with the idea of killing the source in retaliation for the embassy attacks, but preferred to keep on exploiting the intelligence "take" and decided instead on hitting the pharmaceutical plant. The source apparently either knew nothing about the August 7 operations or did not mention them in the intercepted conversations.[62]

Only after the embassies were attacked did the U.S. government's luck improve. Then the change was dramatic. One plotter, who at the last second decided not to blow himself up in the truck-bomb explosion as planned, was caught within hours in a Nairobi hospital while being treated alongside other wounded. He confessed when challenged to explain why a key in his possession fit the padlock on the doomed truck. Alert Pakistani airport immigration officials in Karachi spotted the crudely doctored passport of a second suspect when he flew in from Nairobi. He was promptly shipped back to Kenya, where he was turned over to the FBI. Both those men waived their rights to a lawyer and, while in Kenya, told FBI agents enough to ensure their convictions.

A third man, a naturalized American citizen named Wadih el-Hage, had been scared into leaving Nairobi in 1997 by FBI agents and went home, as they instructed, with his large family to Texas, where he was arrested soon after the Nairobi embassy blast. The fourth defendant, involved in the Dar es Salaam explosion, was traced months later to South Africa, where he had gone to ground. He was "rendered," an American government euphemism for grabbing suspects overseas and flying them to the United States without benefit of cumbersome extradition and other legal niceties, thanks to cooperative foreign governments.

Fadl's major contribution was in providing a window into the Al-Qaeda galaxy that was crucial for understanding the past and worrying about the future. For the first time, Fadl made it clear that Osama's activities went well beyond the long-held assumption that he was just financing Islamist subversion in East Africa and farther afield. The tale he told in court made Osama into a cross between the president of the Jihad Incorporated money machine and the head of a maverick Ford Foundation dispensing seed-money grants of a very special nature.[63] Osama did make genuine business investments in Sudan. They included an aboveboard construction company, a trading firm, various farms (used at least occasionally for military training), a company to sell produce, a tannery, a freighter, a cargo plane and interests in the Al-Shamal Islamic Bank in Khartoum.[64] He also held bank accounts from London to Hong Kong to Malaysia. But Fadl also described clandestine arms shipments, several by camel train, for Zawahiri's Egyptian Islamic Jihad, another, with Sudanese army connivance, to Islamic radicals in Yemen aboard a rust-bucket freighter Osama purchased in Cyprus. The arms put aboard the ship were stored at a Sudanese army base near Port Sudan. President Bashir had provided Osama with a letter exempting Al-Qaeda from customs duties. Containers consigned to Al-Qaeda were often not opened. (Osama also owned a fishing vessel in Kenya and during his Khartoum period was said to possess others operating in the Red Sea.)

A thirty-one-man council, or *majlis al-shura,* masterminded Al-Qaeda operations in Khartoum. Specialized committees dealt with money, passports and travel or the media (headed by a man nicknamed Abu Reuter in a rare flash of humor), or military affairs or *fatwas* and other religious questions. But judging by Fadl's testimony, Al-Qaeda limited its military activity in Sudan to what he called "refresh courses" in small arms and explosives on various farm properties near Khartoum and Damazin, about 300 miles southeast of the capital. That made sense since Al-Qaeda never abandoned its training facilities in Afghanistan and the actual operatives who carried out the East African attacks were trained there, not in Sudan. (Those Afghan camps during his absence in Sudan also churned out combatants for Kashmir, Central Asia, Chechnya and Bosnia.) Osama didn't appear to be looking for a fight in Khartoum.

To be sure, Fadl said two Al-Qaeda *fatwas* were issued there against the U.S. military presence in Saudi Arabia and the Gulf, and a third against the massive arrival of American troops in Somalia as part of the UN humanitarian relief operation starting in December 1992. But they seemed meant for local Al-Qaeda members—unlike the defiant *fatwas* addressed to the entire world after Osama's ouster from Sudan. The nuance was important. Osama had vigorously denounced the U.S. Air Force operation in Saudi Arabia since its inception in 1990. Now he suspected Washington was seeking to extend its military reach. Specifically, the UN relief operation in Somalia worried the NIF and Al-Qaeda, which feared the United States was intent on using it as a pretext to establish a military presence in the Horn of Africa and threaten Sudan. "If they are successful in Somalia, the next thing could be the south of Sudan," Fadl quoted an Al-Qaeda official as saying. Worry about a U.S. military outpost in Somalia was a major reason Osama set up the Al-Qaeda cell in Nairobi, the first such operation in East Africa.

Osama at times seemed to have convinced himself that the UN operation in Somalia represented a real danger. On one occasion in 1993 Fadl recalled hearing Osama lecture an Al-Qaeda gathering on the necessity of striking "the head of the snake," meaning the United States. But soon American troops were already preparing to leave Somalia. Despite Osama's bluster and his desire to force U.S. soldiers out of Saudi Arabia, his main target then still was the Al-Saud, not the United States (although for many Arabs that was a distinction without a difference). Keeping the Americans out of Sudan meant protecting Al-Qaeda's new sanctuary, which, unlike Afghanistan, was situated in the Arab world. He had every reason to maintain a low profile. From Khartoum, Osama could count on Sudanese connivance to help dispatch his men on foreign missions.

Sudan in the early 1990s was also a place where seemingly ideologically impossible partnerships could take form and dissolve in the shadows, for pragmatic reasons that briefly made tactical sense. That did not necessarily mean they reached fruition or were reactivated in later years. Fadl, for example, told the court that three Al-Qaeda cadres had received specialized demolition training from the pro-Iranian Hezbollah in Lebanon. That raised eyebrows. Quite apart from its role in kidnapping Westerners, in October 1983 alone Hezbollah was credited with the destruction of the American embassy in Beirut as well as the attacks on the U.S. Marines and French troops, which claimed 241 and 58 lives, respectively. These acts of violence need not have bothered Al-Qaeda. But at face value, Osama's brand of narrow Sunni radicalism could have been expected to shun any relationship with its extremist Shi'a counterparts. Fadl also said that an Al-

Qaeda gathering in Khartoum had invited a Shi'a cleric to speak. And a senior Al-Qaeda cadre, he said, had argued that "now that we have one enemy, the Westerns," Sunnis and Shi'a "should unite and forget their problems and differences."

Such a call for Islamic ecumenism was strong medicine, indeed bordering on apostasy, for Wahhabis. But for all the talk of wide-ranging cooperation, even Fadl, who had every reason to persuade the New York jury that Osama and the mullahs of Tehran were in cahoots, provided few details. A Hezbollah connection of sorts did surface later when investigators established that the detonator used in the truck-bomb attack on al-Khobar in 1996 bore the hallmarks of detonators Hezbollah had perfected in the Beqaa, Lebanon's no-man's-land that was nominally under Beirut's authority but in fact existed under vague Syrian control. The Al-Saud, and eventually the FBI, concluded that al-Khobar was an Iranian operation so that such cooperation seemed to make sense. But dissenters insisted that al-Khobar was an Al-Qaeda action, which the Al-Saud were intent on hushing up by shifting blame to Tehran. Suggestions of cooperation between Al-Qaeda and Tehran surfaced again early in 2002. The administration, anxious to justify President Bush's threats against the "axis of evil," charged that Iran was sheltering Al-Qaeda cadres fleeing Afghanistan.

Fadl also vaguely mentioned Al-Qaeda links with Iraqi agents in Sudan. That, too, seemed far-fetched given Osama's well-established contempt for Saddam Hussein's secular regime, but both the Iraqi and Sudanese governments were under UN sanctions at the time. Yet nothing in the world of intelligence can be ruled out. Indeed, intelligence back channels exist to put governments discreetly in touch with unsavory regimes and movements. Such contacts can be disavowed easily if they inadvertently come to light. In any case, they do not necessarily lead to further meetings, much less cooperation on terrorism. Illustrating the point was a meeting in Kandahar in December 1998 between Osama and Farouk Hijazi, a high-ranking Iraqi intelligence officer then serving as Saddam Hussein's ambassador to Turkey.

Various sources vouch for the meeting, but who took the initiative and its outcome remain unclear and controversial. One version said Osama was looking for a sanctuary in case the Taliban caved into American pressure and forced him out of Afghanistan. Another insisted that Saddam Hussein had been impressed by Al-Qaeda's East African exploits and dispatched

Hijazi to offer Osama a base of operations. Nothing came of the Kandahar conversation until 2002, when the Bush administration sought to link Iraq and Al-Qaeda to justify "regime change" in Baghdad and eventually the war that overthrew Saddam in 2003. The problem with Fadl's titillating morsels, as with all such intelligence crumbs, was that they meant very little without a key to understanding the ever-shifting context of the times. What might have made sense in the early 1990s quite possibly did not obtain nearly a decade later. Sunni–Shi'a tensions waxed and waned, at times causing bloody communal tensions in Pakistan financed by Saudi and Iranian proxies, at another coming within a hair of provoking full-scale war between Iran and the Taliban in 1998.

Fadl was on sounder ground in describing his life as a trusted undercover operative for Al-Qaeda and the NIF. He recounted his experiences as a bag man, using phony passports—often supplied by the NIF and sometimes left deliberately unstamped by complaisant Khartoum airport officials—to rendezvous with radical Islamist leaders in Jordan, Egypt or Eritrea, dropping off as much as $100,000 at a time in $100 bills. He assumed as many as ten aliases over the years. Sometimes foreign customs agents were bribed not to open his suitcases. To fool suspicious Arab airport immigration on these missions, he used cologne, carried (but did not smoke) cigarettes, shaved off his beard, wore Western clothes, all behavioral characteristics not associated with Islamic fundamentalists. Even more useful to Al-Qaeda until his exposure and arrest was Wadih el-Hage, a Lebanese Christian by birth who converted to Islam in Kuwait, where he was brought up and acquired American citizenship and an American family. His U.S. passport and excellent English allowed him to travel virtually unnoticed. Al-Qaeda always prized Muslims with western European or American citizenship for the same reasons.

Osama then routinely moved money around through normal banking channels. But already Al-Qaeda was proving adept at skimming charitable donations and using charities as fronts both to raise money and to justify the existence of cells around the world. Fadl specifically mentioned skimming an Islamic charity in the petro-emirate of Qatar, where Osama had influential friends in high places. That practice eventually aroused Western governments' concern, as did Osama's abiding interest in procuring nuclear materials. In late 1993 or early 1994, Fadl told the court, he received a $10,000 bonus for acting as go-between for Al-Qaeda and a former Sudanese minister and a Sudanese army officer, who showed him a two- to three-foot-tall metal canister full of what they said was uranium.

The Sudanese wanted $1.5 million plus hefty commissions for themselves. Fadl's testimony did not make clear if Al-Qaeda pursued the offer or even whether it was on the level. But the account, and similar ones subsequently, smacked of a sting operation set up to fleece rich but gullible Arabs of Osama's ilk. Still, Fadl's account represented the first known instance of Osama's abiding interest in acquiring weapons of mass destruction, nuclear, biological or chemical. It also made credible U.S. suspicions of the kind that prompted the destruction of El-Shifa. As piles of documents captured in bases and safe houses in Afghanistan in 2001 demonstrated, that became a persistent and growing fascination for Al-Qaeda. In just a few years Al-Qaeda had progressed to the point that retired Pakistani nuclear scientists advised on how to make rudimentary devices and Al-Qaeda shot videos of a dog put to death in a homemade chemical weapons experiment involving cyanide.

At the New York trial, other witnesses mentioned equally curious Al-Qaeda investments. An Egyptian pilot named Essam al-Ridi testified that in 1993 Osama sent him $210,000 to buy a mothballed Saber 40 jet cargo plane in the American Southwest and fly it from Dallas–Fort Worth International Airport to Khartoum. In fact, in a transaction suggesting Al-Qaeda was an easy touch, Ridi paid considerably less for the plane and pocketed the difference. Osama wanted a plane, the court was told, to fly to Pakistan and bring back 200 shoulder-held Stinger missiles to Khartoum. The project aborted when the poorly maintained plane's hydraulic system failed before the flight to Pakistan. For years its upended carcass was a landmark at the end of the Khartoum airport runway. But the Stinger story itself was odd. American intelligence officers I talked to doubted any one person controlled that many "missing" Stingers. Contrary to legend, the CIA had managed to buy back most of them in Afghanistan after the Soviet army's withdrawal, they said, with some Afghan commanders returning theirs without payment. Indeed, specialists questioned whether that many Stingers remained unaccounted for.[65] Soviet-era shoulder-fired SA-7s were easier and cheaper to come by. Al-Qaeda used two SA-7s in a near-miss operation to shoot down a passenger jet belonging to Israel's Arkia Airlines as it took off on a homeward flight with Israeli tourists in October 2002.

When it came to money, Osama also could be as skinflint as any Hadhrami merchant and at the same time realistic about its uses for keeping his hosts happy. After he left Afghanistan for Sudan in 1991, he basically told his followers he would take them on again if they paid their own way to Khartoum.[66] His Khartoum operation seethed with discontent over pay. Like a Western office, the help was constantly complaining that some employees were better paid than others. Fadl and others somehow seemed to know the entire payroll by heart. Favored senior cadres, often Egyptians, were especially resented by the Al-Qaeda foot soldiers. Osama brought some of these headaches upon himself. Al-Qaeda staffers were paid two salaries, one for their normal jobs, a second as Al-Qaeda members. In addition, they were provided free cooking oil, tea, sugar and other scarce staples, and they also received free medical care.

The rub was that Osama's offices in town and in his compound also employed Sudanese, members of the NIF there to protect him and keep Turabi informed. They were specifically drawn from the secret police. They were paid less and received no rations, knew it and complained. But Osama realized that keeping the NIF sweet was the price of doing business, which helps explain why they were on the payroll at all. Using money in some of the poorest places in the world stood Osama in good stead when he returned to Afghanistan and eventually befriended Mullah Omar and the Taliban. If anything, Osama's ouster from Khartoum served as a constant reminder of the necessity of such precautions.

In Khartoum, Osama's approach was vaguely reminiscent of that of the Palestine Liberation Organization (PLO) back in the 1970s and 1980s in Beirut. Yasser Arafat trained volunteers from the world over—a few were men of the right, more represented the left, a few were religious, most were secular. Arafat worked on the theory that the PLO desperately needed friends anywhere and everywhere and couldn't afford to be choosy. It had plenty of money, from Palestinians' contributions and funds provided by Arab governments. Some contributed with genuine enthusiasm for the Palestinian cause, but more, especially the Arab governments, to avoid PLO threats of retribution. Someone once said Arafat in those days was so desperate he would go to the races and bet on every horse, somehow hoping a long shot would win big. But times change. In the 1990s Osama's model was more akin to a venture capitalist willing to fund selected start-ups, betting one project would prove profitable.

Among those he helped finance were his old Peshawar–era friend Zawahiri's Islamic Jihad and its rival Gama'a al-Islamiyya, Algeria's Armed Islamic Group, better known by its initials in French, GIA, as well as similar jihadi groups in Eritrea, Libya, Tunisia and Chechnya and in the former Soviet Central Asian republics. In those days, and now, Osama was not the only source of revenue. Other rich Gulf Arabs separately contributed to many of these and other Islamic causes in the Muslim world. Their reasons varied. In Central Asia it was to reintroduce Islam, albeit their narrow-gauged version and not the moderate Sufi native form, after seventy years of Soviet rule and repression. In Algeria, Gulf funds helped undermine the corrupt military regime that to many Gulf Arabs seemed to be perpetuating French rule and Western secular ways and using the French language, not Arabic, to boot. Osama, the New York court was told, financed the purchase of a printing press for Islamists in Egypt. Egyptian jihadis were so strapped that they preyed on the Coptic Christian minority, specializing in robbing and shaking down Coptic jewelers. In Algeria such foreign funding largely dried up in the early 1990s because resentful Gulf financiers did not appreciate local Islamists' backing Saddam Hussein in the Kuwait war. At the height of their jihad Algerian Islamists never hurt for want of money: they were strong enough to control major roads and extract tolls.

In Sudan Osama understood his welcome could wear out fast if he stopped paying off his hosts. It was also obvious Osama was being ripped off. Fadl said worried Al-Qaeda associates in Sudan at one point approached Osama because many of his legitimate businesses were losing money. Aside from not paying for road construction and fobbing him off with the money-losing tannery, the NIF cheated him—and the Sudanese—by constantly manipulating and depreciating the Sudanese currency and claiming to be perpetually broke. To keep Osama sweet, the NIF gave him rights to sell overseas Sudanese agricultural products as varied as sesame, corn, sunflower seeds and gum Arabic. (Under pressure from American soft drink firms, gum Arabic was specifically excluded from sanctions imposed on Khartoum since it was an essential ingredient and Sudan was the world's largest producer.)

Years later there were suggestions that tricks Osama learned in commodity trading honed his skills at squirreling funds away in dozens of countries safe from prying eyes. (Testimony in the New York trial related that defendant Hage traded various commodities for Osama in Cyprus, well known for discreet offshore banking long suspected of money laundering.) Such experience may well have put Osama on to the greater profits to be made from commodities that were easier to transport and smuggle, such as gold, diamonds, tanzanite and other gemstones. They were said to have provided a sizable proportion of his wealth in recent years. But for all his pride in having Al-Qaeda known to its employees as "the company" and in posing for visiting journalists as a businessman who encouraged other wealthy Saudis to invest in Sudan, Osama told his men they were wrong to think in traditional bookkeeping terms.

"Our agenda is bigger than business," Fadl quoted Osama as telling an Al-Qaeda meeting. "We are not going to make business here, but we need to help the government and [so] the government help our group," he said in his approximate English. "This is our purpose." So the payoff for Osama was not financial as defined by any classical yardstick. Money was for buying influence, and in any case Osama knew that his stake in Sudan was only part of his worldwide finances. But, like many another tough Saudi businessman, Osama proved persnickety with his own men over their accounting of his money.

Fadl had been exposed embezzling $110,000 from Al-Qaeda, mostly by kiting the costs of various staples and selling them on the open market. He had used the proceeds to buy a car and purchase land for himself and his sister. Osama called him into his office, kept him waiting for hours, then patiently but firmly explained that Fadl would be forgiven once he had reimbursed the full amount. At face value, Osama was playing an understanding, if firm, boss. Fadl had no intention of complying and was smart enough to realize that Osama most likely would never trust him again even if he did. "After that meeting," Fadl said, "I felt I had to leave." Taking off was the easy part, finding a soft landing proved much harder. During the months before he got lucky with the Americans, Fadl had plenty of time to rehearse his story. By his own admission, he had peddled it unsuccessfully in a half dozen countries, including Syria and Saudi Arabia (where, he told the New York court, his interlocutors had tried to enlist him to assassinate Osama).

To THE LIMITED DEGREE political careers contain morality tales, the NIF removed Turabi from power at the end of the decade. He landed in jail (or sometimes under house arrest) just as Sudan's oil came onstream with its promise of delivering Khartoum from the dangerous financial dependency of the likes of Osama. After 9/11 the United States eventually became actively involved in peace talks to end the war between Khartoum and the southern rebels, which had entered its third decade. The NIF had come full circle, and Turabi doubtless felt betrayed in his mission to revolutionize Sudan. Still, the price he made his country pay for his failed experiment had been awesome.

The more I reflect on Turabi's Sudan now, the more I wish I had been smarter back in the 1980s. So many characteristics of Al-Qaeda were visible years earlier in Sudan, albeit in more outwardly presentable form. The NIF was not then involved in terrorism akin to Osama's (although once in power its own brand of political violence was frightening enough). But they both absorbed Western technology to serve a purpose that was profoundly, and indeed by its very essence, anti-Western. The first computers I saw in Khartoum were not in the offices of the impoverished government, but in the NIF headquarters staffed by men often educated in American colleges on U.S. government scholarships.

EVEN BACK then Turabi and his young cohorts struck me as oddly out of sync with their Western experience. These often humorless NIF cadres had spent much time, indeed sometimes years on end, in the United States, Britain or Germany, often without comprehending what made these Western societies tick. Those who had studied in the United States talked a good game, right down to current slang and fascination with American sports. But culture shock or timidity had kept them from exploring the highways and byways of American life, with its contradictions and complications. Or maybe, it later dawned on me, getting to understand the West was never on their agenda. What radical Muslims like Turabi appreciated in America was the absolute freedom to develop their ideas in a society founded on the sanctity of religious freedom. Never mind that such was a luxury few Muslims enjoyed in the countries of their birth. The United States was a convenient place, convenient to acquire knowledge, convenient to raise money, convenient to move around in without being challenged or harassed, convenient to scope out what they did not want the ideal society, still the stuff of their dreams, to become.

After its coup the NIF largely succeeded in keeping itself—and its radical foreign guests—from public view. I never thought American intelligence seriously penetrated the NIF, at least in a way to understand and counteract its policies. The United States had become dependent on sophisticated electronic eavesdropping spy satellites to the exclusion of more demanding classic forms of intelligence-gathering that could not be performed in the comfort of an air-conditioned office—to wit, actually getting out and meeting people to find out what was on their minds. When a 1996 memorandum spelling out U.S. demands to Khartoum was published after 9/11, I was especially struck by its points four and five, pertaining to facilities Sudan allegedly used to train "Hamas and other terrorist elements." "Bulldoze the Mertkhiyet Military Camp located on the geographic coordinates 15–43–30N 32–24–07E," the memo demanded, "and provide evidence this camp has been torn down, such as allowing US officials to inspect the camp."[67]

Such precision in Africa's largest country! Perhaps the camp was the one Ambassador Carney visited before Washington decided to give up on the NIF and isolate Sudan in 1996. By then Madeleine Albright, still American ambassador to the United Nations, was describing Sudan as "a viper's nest of terrorism" and it was all downhill. I've since talked to other Western diplomats who at various times had visited other camps. Many of Osama's men were doubtless gone or well hidden after his ouster. In any event, the diplomats agreed that camps the Americans insisted were turning out terrorists were training young men all right. But on those very occasional guided tours, how could diplomats or even military attachés distinguish between terrorists and the People's Defense Force, often hapless students and other youngsters dragooned off the streets and given summary basic infantry training before their dispatch to the unending civil war in the south?

I am a jogger, and one of my favorite runs is along the Nile in Khartoum in the relative cool right after dawn. I recall my bemusement the first time I came across a long column of young recruits jogging in the opposite direction, all chanting, "There is no God but God and Mohammed is his Prophet." They certainly looked Sudanese to me, and I couldn't imagine terrorists being so brazen that they would chance putting their charges on public display. I confess I may have been misled by sepia memories accumulated since my first visit to Khartoum in 1964. I then had marveled at rival Sudanese politicians who called, and respected, a four-day truce in the middle of a boiling crisis rather than forgo the pomp and circumstance of an official visit by Queen Elizabeth to her former condominium.

ALGERIA: SPORT ET MUSIQUE

O N DECEMBER 14, 1999, Diana Dean, a U.S. customs officer at Port Angeles in the state of Washington, inadvertently panicked a nervous young man as he drove off the day's last ferry on his roundabout route from Vancouver in Canada to Seattle. It didn't take much to spook him. She routinely asked for his passport and instructed him to open the trunk of his rented car, a brand-new dark green Chrysler 300. Instead he bolted in the dark, tried to hide under a parked pickup, escaped again and was collared only after he failed to commandeer another car stopped at a red light. Upon examination, his car's trunk revealed that the space around the spare tire was padded out with enough RDX, a chemical cousin of nitroglycerin and other volatile explosives, fertilizer, Casio wristwatch timers and electronic circuit boards to blow up the Los Angeles airport.

That indeed was his mission for Al-Qaeda, as Ahmad Ressam acknowledged in 2001 after a jury found him guilty and he faced a 130-year jail sentence. Following his fortuitous arrest, Ressam for the next few days shared headlines with a case in far-off Jordan. There, almost simultaneously, Jordanian security forces discovered explosives hidden in a specially constructed basement cache and hauled in a ring of locally well-known Islamists who were accused of plotting to attack the Radisson Hotel, favored by American tourists, a biblical site at Mount Nebo (whence Moses inspected the Promised Land) and other targets. In Washington, an anxious Richard Clarke, the National Security Council's counterterrorism chief, was both surprised and relieved; thanks to such pure good luck New

Year's Eve passed off without the terrorist spectacular he dreaded would usher in the millennium.[1]

On the other hand, I was deeply disturbed. Ahmad Ressam was Algerian. His arrest, or more precisely his arrest in the United States, halfway around the world from home, flew in the face of everything I knew about Algeria, and I smugly thought I had accumulated a great deal of knowledge in a lifetime's acquaintance with that North African country. Algeria had occupied a special place for me ever since I broke in as a foreign correspondent in the late 1950s covering France's last colonial war, the doomed struggle to keep Algeria French. I had made it a point of trying to visit the country once a year. Now the Ressam case abruptly made me reexamine long-held assumptions about Algeria and the nature of political jihadism. I was not alone. In Washington, senior counterterrorism officials also acknowledged their surprise.

My most firmly held conviction about Algerians was that they were immutably among the most ethnocentric people on earth and had no global interests. Never in Algeria's turbulent past, which I had chronicled, did the horizons of its often larger-than-life actors—in the 1950s radical French army colonels, extremist French settlers and Algerian nationalists or in the 1990s Algerian Islamists—go much beyond Algeria itself. At the outside, the Algerians' theater of operations for fund-raising and arms-smuggling extended to France, with its large North African immigrant population, and to nearby parts of western Europe, but only as the immediate geographic prolongation of Algeria itself. Several million Algerians and French citizens of Algerian extraction lived in France. Their sentiments and their loyalties—and often their families—straddled both sides of the Mediterranean. For many Algerians, deeply marked by 132 years of French colonial rule, France remained the traditional, indeed hereditary, enemy, their national equivalent of the Great Satan. Theirs was an all-consuming, often blinding love-hate relationship that sufficed unto itself, to the amazement of outsiders.

At times that sense of never-ending wrong seemed so embedded in Algerian genes that it blotted out logic. For example, almost all the radical Arab world backed Saddam Hussein's invasion of Kuwait in 1990. In the months preceding the American-led coalition's expulsion of Iraqi troops from the small Gulf oil emirate in the winter of 1991, the United States became the butt of Arab radicals' ire everywhere except North Africa. In Algerian eyes especially, the French alone were held responsible. France was blamed because Paris claimed to be the Arabs' friend, swearing to do its utmost to prevent the war, but finally sending troops to join the coalition that ousted the Iraqis from Kuwait. That was the surface discourse.

But as I discovered when I visited Algeria just before the outbreak of the war, the grievance against France was only peripherally linked to the Kuwait conflict. In fact, to this day such is the colonial memory that the French have never been pardoned for anything in Algerian eyes. Starting in 1830 European settlers, who eventually numbered just under 1 million, had uprooted the Algerians from their land, destroyed many of their traditional values and marginalized Islam. Then suddenly all but a few thousand settlers fled within months when Algeria achieved independence in July 1962, after a brutal eight-year conflict in which Algerian propaganda insisted as many as a million of its Muslims—one in nine at the time—perished.

Yet the more I delved into Ressam's case, the more I kept losing my way. Here was a young Algerian who, like thousands of his countrymen, had left his native land soon after the army seized power in January 1992, canceling the second round of legislative elections that the Islamic Salvation Front, universally known by its French initials, FIS, was poised to win. The army coup abruptly ended three years of heady reform, much to the tacit relief of Algeria's largely French-speaking civil society, suddenly terrified at the prospect of an Iranian-style Islamic Republic in the western Mediterranean.

During those three years, for the first time since independence Algerians had dared to openly criticize their one-party state, dominated by the French-speaking military caste grown expert at skimming profits from the country's oil and natural gas riches. Visiting Algiers in that period was as exciting as visiting Moscow during *perestroika,* and for similar reasons. If the Soviet model, long revered in Algeria, could be openly questioned at home, then so could its North African equivalent by long tongue-tied Algerians.

In June 1990 ordinary Algerians surprised themselves and shocked their establishment by voting massively in local elections for the FIS, North Africa's only aboveboard Islamist party, which had been legalized the previous year, much to the horror of neighbors Morocco and Tunisia. The outcome was more a massive no-confidence vote against the corrupt, incompetent and self-satisfied secular establishment than an endorsement of an Islamic republic. The rascals were the FLN, the National Liberation Front, which had led the fight against the French, then monopolized power since independence. And the voters threw the rascals out. Such was the real meaning of the first multiparty elections in independent Algeria. The FIS worked hard for its victory, carefully organizing grassroots support. The rival secular parties hadn't made the same effort.

Over the next eighteen months Islamist rule in cities and regional governing bodies prompted widespread fear and loathing, especially among the French-speaking urban middle and upper class. But it did not persuade secular Algerian civil society to sink its differences and form broad-based secular political parties for the manifestly crucial legislative elections scheduled for December 1991. Warning signals were clearly visible. The FIS organized impressive—in fact, threatening—political rallies and marches through Algiers, sometimes right up to the gates of the presidential palace. Every Friday tens of thousands of followers listened to FIS sermons in radical mosques kept deliberately half-finished (because once completed their imams required government approval to preach).

Young Islamists, aping the recently triumphant mujahedeen warriors in Afghanistan, took to using the cosmetic kohl under their eyes in what struck those who talked to them as more radical-chic posturing than dedication to jihad. They gathered for Friday prayers in a suburban mosque nicknamed Kabul, where the relative handful of veterans from the jihad—and many more wannabe imitators—were somewhat derisively called "the Afghans." Algerian Islam, long suppressed under French colonial rule, always struck me as intrinsically rooted in Algeria. Native son Abdelhamid Ben Badis, a pre–World War Two Muslim reformer, was the reference, not Sayyid Qotb or any other Muslim Brother from the Mashrek heartland of Islam to the East. His slogan was "Islam is my religion, Arabic my language, Algeria my country."[2]

As the legislative elections approached, the FLN and its secular rivals acted as if the 1990 results were a fluke. The top FIS leaders had been arrested and safely imprisoned in late June. The secular political elite relaxed. They neglected the grassroots organizing that the FIS was so adept at. In the first round of legislative elections that December, the secular parties played into FIS hands by refusing to unite behind a single slate of compromise candidates, thus fatally splitting their own strength. The overall FIS vote was considerably down from the year before but still represented a plurality, and so many FIS candidates won outright in the first round that victory was assured in the January runoff.

In the days leading up to its coup, the army stage-managed mass rallies in Algiers with support from labor unions, women's groups and other be- latedly galvanized secular organizations. Constantly trumpeted was the counterexample of Iran's Islamic revolution in 1979—"One man, one vote, one time." Neither the generals nor the civilian politicians would entertain a risky, but potentially wiser, alternative favored by President Chadli Benje- did: let the FIS win and form the government, but under the watchful eye of the army, ready to intervene if the Islamists sought to undermine the secular constitution. That way ordinary Algerians would have judged the Islamists' excesses for themselves and been more tolerant about their even- tual removal. The generals preferred to force the president's resignation (although the alternative formula was employed years later by the Turkish army to get rid of an Islamist government in what became known as Tur- key's "first postmodern coup"). They had fatefully interrupted the election process, arguably a more explosive decision than had they invented a pre- text postponing the vote indefinitely.

Theirs was a panicky, improvised performance with terrible conse- quences. The Islamists never forgave the secular opposition for betraying its own much-ballyhooed democratic ideals. That perceived treason was invoked to justify systematic assassination in the ranks of civil society. An old French saying had it that "the Tunisians were North Africa's women, the Algerians the men and the Moroccans the lions." Soon Algeria plunged into a vicious rerun of the violence of its war of independence from France. More than 150,000 died in the new conflict's first decade, and no end is in sight (although the death toll has declined in recent years). Among the first Islamists in the maquis killed were the 200 or so Afghan vets who had come home. Within months the FIS was banned, its extensive network of local officials elected in 1990 hounded from office and tens of thousands of young suspected sympathizers arbitrarily arrested, often tor- tured and routinely dumped in detention camps in the Sahara, where many became hardened jihadis. To avoid military service in a civil war and to find work, Ressam and many another young Algerian got out while they could.

The repression played into the hands of the FIS radical minority, who somewhat abusively called themselves *salafis*. That was the name, literally meaning "ancestors" and figuratively designating the early Muslim leaders, that Saudis gave their own brand of Islam in preference to Wahhabism.

(Saudi *salafis* felt their Algerian namesakes shared little, if any, of their theological beliefs.) The homegrown North African *salafis* had never shared the moderate, so-called Algerianist wing's optimism that the FIS could achieve power through the ballot box. Now the *salafis* felt justified in doing what they had always wanted: conducting an all-out jihad to seize power and establish an Islamic republic. They granted no quarter.

My sense of foreboding was alerted when within a month of the army coup Europeans and Algerians were murdered in the Algiers' casbah, the crumbling, overcrowded old heart of the city overlooking the Mediterranean. It was a sepia throwback to the war against France, when Algerians killed fellow Algerians as well as French settlers and soldiers. Once again the macabre excesses emerged: the slit throat known as the "Kabyle smile," the hacked-off nose and breast, the severed penis shoved into the victim's mouth. I said as much to an old Algerian nationalist friend who had played a major role in that conflict. He made clear he didn't welcome being reminded by a foreigner, albeit a friend of long standing. The establishment he served soon swept away doubts about the wisdom of its chosen path and even invented a word they proudly used to describe themselves: "eradicators." At least, that spared Algerians the pussyfooting hypocrisy of "winning hearts and minds." When it came to the uses of violence there was no visible difference between the two protagonists.

Even so, for the next three years the army regime was hard put to maintain a modicum of control (and even a decade later security forces remained powerless to prevent sporadic violence). In those early years the Islamists ruled whole neighborhoods in Algiers itself, controlled vital roads to the provinces that they taxed at will and ran guerrilla operations in the maquis. Soon the conflict became so shadowy as to defy even the most accomplished local analysts' ability to draw clear lines between friend and foe. Algeria fell prey to the everyday paranoia of car bombs, ax murders, disappearances, routine torture and assassinations of journalists, pop singers and theater directors.

Islamists posing as soldiers wearing regulation army uniforms routinely assassinated travelers at phony checkpoints on major roads, or were they real soldiers in real uniforms doing the killing and claiming to be jihadis in disguise? Killers dressed as Islamist guerrillas murdered unarmed villagers within sight and sound of soldiers in nearby army bases, who failed to come to their rescue. Scores of Westerners working in Algeria were assassinated (but, significantly, no Americans were targeted). In the spring of 1994, a particularly violent period when the government was all but beaten (as it later admitted), I spent two fraught weeks reporting in Algeria. Not even the old Hotel Saint Georges, the pride of colonial-era Algeria and at one time General Eisenhower's headquarters in World War Two, was safe.

My only protection was a street-smart taxi driver whom I and other correspondents had used for years. We paid him well, and he never asked leading questions. Under our unspoken arrangement he didn't inquire where I wanted to go until I was in the cab. Unlike many other Third World cabbies, who tend to wander off when most urgently needed, he stayed in the car and was always ready to leave as soon as I walked out of my meetings. In Algiers' perpetually clogged traffic such attention to detail was important; no Westerner wanted to be out in the street any longer than necessary. I never questioned his advice. He told me when I could more or less safely visit certain neighborhoods, and I didn't argue when he judged my suggested timing inappropriate.

Most pale-skinned Westerners had long since deserted Algeria, diplomats rarely left their well-protected compounds, and journalists, especially Western reporters, were easy pickings in Algiers' notorious traffic jams or almost anywhere else in the country. The war was underreported.[3] Not every foreign correspondent wanted to take the risks, physically or professionally. The regime was not interested in foreign coverage it could not control. Visas were always hard to come by. Eventually official minders and armed escorts became mandatory "for your own safety" and for the regime's as well. Few Algerians wanted to talk under such conditions. The government became proficient in placing footage of carnage with foreign television stations, especially in France, long the only country at all seriously interested in the conflict.

As the violence continued year after year, disgusted army officers deserted and accused the high command of penetrating and radicalizing the most extremist Islamists of the Armed Islamic Group, an FIS splinter organization known as the GIA. At first such charges were dismissed as propaganda. But the defectors' accusations dovetailed with troubling word-of-mouth versions of the violence, which had become the stuff of urban legend. More and more former army officers, once safely abroad, provided chapter and verse about special units tasked with committing crimes against civilians that the government then blamed on their Islamist foes.

Army efforts to defend its honor in France backfired in 2002. General Khaled Nezzar, a former chief of the general staff and the regime's longtime éminence grise, brought a libel suit in Paris against a young dissident second lieutenant named Habib Souaidia, who in a best-selling book had accused the army of complicity in massacring civilians and blaming the Islamists. But defense witnesses repeatedly provided detailed damning evidence. The trial was closely followed in Algeria and France, thanks to full coverage in the French media. Former Colonel Mohammed Samraoui, the army's number-two counterintelligence specialist before he deserted in disgust, was the star witness. He explained to the Paris court how the army security services in the months leading up to the 1992 coup "created the GIA" before eventually losing control over the movement. The goal was to weaken and destroy the FIS. "We established a list of the most dangerous people and demanded their arrest," he said, "but in vain: they were needed [to be free] to create terrorist groups. Instead we arrested right, left and center. We were trying to radicalize the movement."[4] Samraoui said the army established a list of 1,100 "dangerous Islamists" as early as 1991. Army intelligence identified Algerian volunteers in Afghanistan and picked them up upon their return. "They all took the flight home via Tunis because it was half price," he recalled. "As soon as they landed in Algiers, we took them in hand" and recruited them.[5] It turned out many such terror techniques were carbon copies of those all too successfully employed by the French army psy-ops specialists, who had pitted Algerians against one another in the war of independence. In this new conflict, both sides sought to manipulate their fellow Algerians and foreign governments. Using terrorism to influence Western public opinion became commonplace for Algerian Islamists and army authorities alike.

The key overseas target was France. Paris awkwardly approved the army coup in 1992 and kept bailing out the regime with loans and rescheduling the ballooning Algerian debt. Keeping France on board was judged just as vital for the army as trying to force Paris to stop its aid to the government was for the Islamists. Only years later did French officials indirectly and grudgingly corroborate suspicions that the Algerian government had actively used terrorism to influence France's Algerian policy. From time to time, renegade Algerian officials provided information seeming to confirm hitherto unsubstantiated theories behind major acts of anti-French terrorism. For example, six years after the facts, Abdelkhader Tigha, a former Algerian security officer languishing in jail in Thailand, said the army was behind the murder of seven French Cistercian monks in mountains south of Algiers in 1996, an act of terrorism that profoundly shocked French public opinion. Tigha explained that army intelligence controlled overall GIA leader Djamel Zitouni and used his men to massacre civilians to turn Algerian and French public opinion against the jihadis. Zitouni, Tigha recounted, was ordered to kidnap the monks in an operation designed to expel them to France (with, he suggested, possible French acquiescence), but not kill them. The operation went wrong. The monks were beheaded when Zitouni was forced to hand them over to even more extremist GIA rivals.[6]

Error or not, the monks' barbaric fate unquestionably served the Algerian military's purposes since it created a climate of revulsion in France against the Islamists and further besmirched the GIA by adding to its well-established reputation for incomprehensible violence. (In London's Islamist circles even staunch friends from the Gulf threw up their hands about Algeria, a wild land obeying none of the tortured logic that they invoked in defense of Al-Qaeda and other jihadi groups.) Similarly opaque was the Christmas 1994 skyjacking of an Air France Airbus at Algiers airport by a GIA suicide cell in security circumstances so suspect the French government criticized what it felt was the Algerian authorities' ambiguous behavior. Only stern French insistence finally extracted Algiers' authorization to let the aircraft take off.[7] The hijackers intended to crash the plane into the Eiffel Tower in Paris, a plan that may have inspired the Al-Qaeda teams that struck the twin towers and the Pentagon almost seven years later. But French anti-riot police stormed the plane during a refueling stop in Marseilles and killed the terrorists.

Then punitive terrorism crossed the Mediterranean. From July to October 1995 ten French citizens died and more than eighty were injured in a rash of terrorist operations, mostly rudimentary bomb explosions carried out mainly in the Paris subway system. The GIA was blamed almost immediately.[8] Within four months key arrests caught the principal perpetrators.[9] A French counterterrorism specialist told me the terrorist campaign cost no more than 200,000 French francs—less than $42,000 at the time. But all was not cut and dried. At the subway terrorists' trial in the fall of 2002, defense lawyers suggested that Algeria's redoubtable *sécurité militaire*—known derisively as Sport et Musique—had manipulated Ali Touchent, the GIA mastermind ostensibly behind the attacks who then oddly vanished.[10]

But since Touchent had been interrogated by French counterintelligence as early as 1989 and kept eluding police in various European countries in the early 1990s, suspicions of police connivance ebbed and flowed. More than a year later, in May 1997, the Algerian authorities announced he had been killed in the center of Algiers in a shoot-out near one of my favorite hotels, the Albert 1er. His theoretically risky return to Algiers and the fact he was reported living in a highly protected police compound also raised questions about his real employers. Only the following February did the Algerians bother to get around to authenticating his death to the French—thanks to dental records. The delay seemed yet another not entirely friendly message to France.

These opaque details suggest the peculiar warp and woof of terrorism and counterterrorism and their various occult uses far beyond the confines of Algeria. Even before September 11, Louis Freeh, then the director of the FBI, began honoring Algiers with his presence and agreed on quiet cooperation, especially concerning Afghan veterans. But it was not until a visit to Algiers on December 13, 2002, that an American official, Assistant Secretary of State William Burns, remarked, "We have much to learn from Algeria on the way to fight terrorism." Such a public accolade was a far cry from the days when the official Algerian mantra lamented that as long as the victims were "only" Algerians, the outside world, with the notable, but rarely acknowledged exception of France, remained indifferent.

Cooperation with the United States was a long-pursued breakthrough for the regime, which in the early and mid-1990s had convinced itself that Washington was willing to live with an Islamist regime in Algiers. Intelligence files, especially on terrorism, are the coin of many a government's realm. In the past the intrigues of Sport et Musique had been of little concern to the United States. Those were problems of interest for the French. I like to think that American indifference of yore was motivated by revulsion for the wholesale manipulation, not to mention torture, long associated with the military regime.

Even were that the case, everything changed radically after September 11, when the Algerians inundated thankful American intelligence services with their files. All presents henceforth were gratefully received, and few, if any, questions were asked about how the information was gathered or its authenticity. Algerian intelligence had kept a watching brief on Algerians enrolled in the Afghan jihad in the 1980s and vastly beefed up its counterintelligence staff in Pakistan after the 1991 coup. Over the years

French counterterrorism specialists had developed something of a sixth sense for smoking out Sport et Musique's more egregious canards (and had Direction de la Surveillance du Territoire agents in Pakistan keeping tabs on Algerian and French jihadis). Nonetheless, the French experts erred on the side of caution, and that often meant systematic doubt about Islamists and other Algerians desperate to escape their country's descent into hell.

Caught between brutal "eradicators" and equally violent Islamists, many Algerians of all persuasions wanted to flee abroad, the very lucky few with visas for France, Canada and other Western countries. Emigration was an old story, even in flush times. Tens of thousands of Algerians, many of them educated, had been heading overseas since the oil-and-gas-based economy went soft in the 1980s and the police state became more repressive. Starting in 1992 Islamists on the run did likewise, seeking the protective coloration of established Algerian communities abroad. The Algerian government was happy to be rid of them. France, where many headed as their first port of call, was braced for their arrival. French security officials correctly assumed that the army coup meant radical Islamists would head their way. Some simply wanted to escape the "eradicators" at home. Others used France to collect money, arms and intelligence for the cause. France had lived through that experience in the 1954–1962 war. Paris wanted no part of a sequel.

Starting within months of the new war's outbreak, French security officials lost little time in expelling suspect Algerians, often, according to critics, with an abbreviated regard for the law. Massive arrests took place in 1992 and 1993. (A favorite trick, emulated in post–September 11 America, involved arresting suspects, holding them on flimsy charges, then condemning them to time already served when they eventually came to trial. But unlike American courts, which routinely imposed on culprits in suspected terrorist cases sentences in excess of 100 years, the French pragmatically settled for less-stringent punishment. The purpose was to keep troublemakers off the streets.) France made no secret of its expulsion policy, repeatedly warning its allies, especially its immediate neighbors, that the Islamists would attempt to set up shop on their territory.

Jean-Louis Bruguière, France's flamboyant top anti-terrorism judge, insisted to me that he had warned the United States as well, but, he lamented, initially to no avail. Housed behind remote-controlled, bulletproof glass doors in offices under the eaves of the Palais de Justice in Paris, Bruguière still glories in his sweeping powers—the most extensive in Europe—and his perks, which include two full-time bodyguards and the right to carry a .357 Magnum. He was invested with centralized muscle that could cut through the French bureaucracy, sometimes rival intelligence agencies and much of the standard penal code. He relished controversial punch lines, proclaiming that when it came to charging suspects with crimes or issuing arrest warrants, "I am the investigator, the judge and the jury." His extensive arsenal included virtually unrestricted use of wiretaps and search warrants, the right to hold suspects for ninety-six hours at a stretch (twenty-four without a lawyer), the use of police informers, monitoring of sermons in radical mosques and penetration of Islamist groups and gatherings. Bruguière had put his powers to good use in winning convictions against Carlos the Jackal, major Libyan and Iranian terrorists and minor foot soldiers.

In the United States only September 11 and the USA Patriot Act provided the Department of Justice with anything approaching the clout Bruguière and his three colleagues have enjoyed since the anti-terrorism court's inception in September 1986.[11] Their methods are rough and ready and constantly dismay civil libertarians, defense lawyers and liberal members of the bench, who note that relatively few of his arrests end up as convictions. Still, Bruguière declared he has ordered more than 400 Islamists arrested and more than 5,000 searches since the first Islamist terrorist operations on French soil in 1994.[12]

Throughout the 1990s and beyond, French and other European police forces traded intelligence and cooperated in harassing and arresting transnational jihadi networks. As early as 1993 Paris started keeping files on young French and other Muslims who traveled to Afghanistan for military training in jihadi camps. By the mid-1990s French counterintelligence estimated that between fifty and sixty young volunteers, often *beurs,* as Muslims born in France call themselves in reverse slang for "Arabs," left for Afghanistan every month. Across much of Europe, increasing importance was attached to keeping track of these volunteers' travels and activities upon their return. Such cooperation was often extremely effective. It went largely unnoticed but occasionally caught the public's fancy, as with the arrests of 250 suspects in six European countries barely a week before France staged the June 1998 World Cup.

Ressam, who came from a town just west of Algiers, near where the first French troops landed in 1830, was part of the Algerian flotsam and jetsam that washed up on France's shore. Like thousands of young Algerians, he had lost no time fleeing abroad after the army aborted the elections and began wholesale arrests. Staying put meant risking arrest, likely torture and indefinite imprisonment or obligatory military service. Ressam left Algeria in September 1992, taking the ferry to Marseilles thanks to a valid one-month French tourist visa. He drifted to Corsica, taking seasonal jobs. But he had no skills, times were hard in France, especially for untrained North African immigrants, and the French police kept a close watch on young men who survived by stealing credit cards, car radios or mobile phones. An appreciable number of uprooted young Algerian men ended up in the toils of jihadi extremism in Europe and farther afield. Ressam was arrested in Corsica for prosaic immigration violations in November 1993, was released and disappeared before his trial was scheduled the following March. Traveling on a fake French passport, on February 20 he flew to Canada. Nothing then suggested that Ressam's trajectory would lead him, at the age of thirty-two, to the fateful ferry trip from British Columbia to Washington State or to Al-Qaeda.

At the Montreal airport, an alert immigration officer immediately recognized the passport was doctored and briefly arrested Ressam. Carefully coached by an immigration lawyer, he applied for political asylum, proclaiming he was persecuted for his religious beliefs at home and indeed, for increased verisimilitude, invented a spell in jail for gun-running on trumped-up charges. That little fib buttressed his request for political asylum by providing a plausible reason for Canadian immigration officials to refuse to send him back to Algeria posthaste. Such were the tricks invoked by Algerians—and others—who wanted to start their lives anew even when their asylum requests were rejected and they were under formal deportation orders. Canada was known as a notoriously soft touch for Algerians and indeed for other French speakers, who were especially welcome to counterbalance the growing legions of English speakers. Ottawa pursued a friendly immigration policy reaching back to the aftermath of World War Two, when it asked few questions in welcoming thousands of East Europeans caught on the losing side of that conflict (and indeed sometimes involved in war crimes). Ressam's request for asylum was refused, but in light of the violence in Algeria the tolerant Canadian authorities declined to send him home. Like many another iffy immigrant in Canada, Ressam survived thanks to welfare and subterfuge. Canada's unemployment and other benefits were generous—$550 per month in his case—and as an immigrant he was not expected to get on his feet immediately.

Nothing proves that Ressam deliberately set out for Canada with international jihad on his mind. Nor does anything indicate that he knew anyone involved in radical Islamist politics in Canada before he landed. But, like all Algerians, he was aware that tens of thousands of his countrymen had preceded him to Montreal and become Canadian citizens. As evidence produced at his trial demonstrated, he settled in Montreal and soon fell in with other, already established Algerians of a special kind. Among his new friends were Fateh Kamel, who had immigrated to Canada in 1987 and acquired a Canadian wife, and Mustapha Labsi, as well as a Moroccan named Said Atmani. How and why Ressam threw in his lot with them remains unclear, but the promiscuity of immigrant life doubtless explains a great deal. For the first time, he became involved in petty crime and came to the notice of the local police. (Somewhat similarly, jihadi doctrine spread easily in prisons, where Muslims who often had little initial interest in any form of religion were won over to militant action, sometimes by prison chaplains who found willing converts among literally captive audiences.)[13]

Ressam's new friends in Montreal were jihadis whose activities in Bosnia and Afghanistan were of long-standing interest to Judge Bruguière. He became convinced Kamel, Labsi and Ressam belonged to Al-Qaeda's most important cell in Canada. He was also sure that Canada, because of its long, unpatrolled border, was the soft underbelly for future Al-Qaeda terrorist operations in the United States. No one paid him much mind. He despaired when Canadian authorities, citing legal protections afforded citizens and immigrants alike, remained largely impervious to the dangers he kept invoking. Just two months before Ressam's arrest on the West Coast, Bruguière returned, frustrated, from a mission to Montreal, unable to persuade his Canadian colleagues to round up Kamel's cell members. Still, due largely to his diligence and Canadian surveillance, eventually most members ended up in jail in Europe for terrorist activities, especially for providing stolen passports for stranded fugitive Islamists. In Canada some had cover businesses. Others survived on petty crime. Their Canadian passports allowed them to travel easily.

By March 1998 such was the influence of Ressam's Montreal friends, especially handsome, well-spoken Fateh Kamel, that he was persuaded to travel to Afghanistan for training in an Al-Qaeda camp specializing in explosives. Ressam was a good pupil. As such he came to the attention of Abu Zubaydah, a young Palestinian who acted as a kind of talent scout for Osama, selecting promising recruits for Al-Qaeda operations.[14] At the end

of Ressam's training in February 1999 he was given $12,000 and told to or-
ganize a terrorist operation against a target in the United States to mark the
millennium with maximum impact. The choice of target was left up to
Ressam. That was both a feather in his cap and an insight into Al-Qaeda's
highly decentralized modus operandi. Al-Qaeda didn't know much about
operating in North America (although it certainly had sleeper agents in the
United States, in some cases American volunteers recruited during, or in
the immediate aftermath of, the anti-Soviet jihad). And even by Osama's
niggardly pre–9/11 standards, $12,000 was not an enormous investment.

In retrospect, Ressam's comeuppance was scarcely surprising. In fact,
the sum may have reflected the risk Al-Qaeda recognized his mission entailed. Ressam was dogged by bad luck from the very start. He himself took
the precaution of returning via Korea and a stopover in Los Angeles (which
may have prompted him to choose its airport as his millennium target).
But his four confederates from the Afghan training camp were judged suspect when they transited London airport and British officials prevented
them from flying on to Canada. Ressam was on his own. Once back in
Montreal, he improvised, recruiting several impressionable Algerian ac-
quaintances as accomplices. By any reckoning, Ressam was an odd choice
for such a mission. His real papers were not in order since his request for
political asylum had been rejected, and in principle he should have left the
country. That had not fazed him. Early on in his Canadian stay, he discovered that Catholic baptismal records sufficed to establish a passport. He
usurped the identity of a recently deceased French Canadian man about
his age, purchasing the required document from the parish records.

That in turn allowed him to obtain a passport in the name of the late
Benni Antoine Noris. But dicey papers were not his only handicap. Ressam
spoke virtually no English. That meant he needed an English-speaking accomplice in the form of a Brooklyn-based Algerian who was to fly out to
meet him in Seattle and help him make his way to Los Angeles. To be sure,
Ressam did have an "exfiltration" plan: he had a ticket to fly to London.
There a flight to Peshawar and eventual safe haven next door in
Afghanistan were to be arranged by Abu Doha, an Al-Qaeda recruiter of
young Muslim citizens of western European countries.

Still, the whole plot reeked of amateur-hour tradecraft. Al-Qaeda
seemed to be in its "bet-on-every-horse" mode. If Ressam's mission succeeded, so much the better. If not, the investment was minimal. Like many
other Al-Qaeda foot soldiers caught in various climes, he neither expected

nor was provided any help by Al-Qaeda after his arrest. Over time key aides were caught or decided to come in from the cold. Ressam, the four operatives arrested in the wake of the bomb attacks on East African embassies, a senior defector with intimate knowledge of Osama's finances and other agents who ran afoul of the law were simply written off.

If Osama worried about their fate, he gave no outward signs. Nor did Al-Qaeda seem concerned by the secrets likely revealed by those who blabbed to their interrogators. In Nazi-occupied France in World War Two resistance agents subjected to torture were not expected to hide what they knew for more than twenty four hours. Other terrorists, notably Carlos the Jackal, famously went to extraordinary lengths, including placing a bomb aboard an express train in France, to free his captured operatives. Such flamboyance was not for Osama. Even senior aides were expendable, possibly because he knew their sacrifice would prompt others to join Al-Qaeda and take their place. Martyrdom was part and parcel of Osama's recruiting program.

When he met worthy recruits, he often came straight out and told them he was looking for candidates for "martyrdom operations" and asked if they were prepared to accept suicide missions. Like Mafia stand-up hoods, the four men convicted in New York in 2001 did not seek to plea-bargain and were sentenced to life imprisonment without parole. But Ressam was something of an exception. Once the likely 130-year prison term sank in, he began to sing. His testimony sufficiently implicated his immediate accomplices to ensure their convictions at a later trial—and eventually a reduced prison term for himself. But as of late 2003 he was kept dangling in solitary confinement since the Justice Department was in no hurry to formally sentence him before his usefulness as a prosecution witness was exhausted.[15] Ressam's betrayal and the fate of the men he fingered elicited no public comment from Al-Qaeda.

JUDGE BRUGUIÈRE likes to compare Al-Qaeda and other radical Islamist organizations to the AIDS virus. By that he meant they constantly change form but become ever more virulent and tantalizingly beyond the grasp of those determined to stamp them out. It is a striking metaphor illustrating the amorphous nature of loosely linked transnational terrorism (in counterterrorist jargon). But it might also be argued that Islamist organizations, like many revolutionary movements before them, are prone to quarrels, splintering and new groupings. Ressam's case is as good an illustration as any. His was the odyssey of a small-time Algerian reaching manhood at the very moment radical religious revival abruptly thrust his stultified country into the radicalizing crucible of upheaval, violent repression, threatened incarceration and finally exile. His loose-ends existence in France was miraculously transformed by the born-again possibilities of a fresh start in the new world of Canada.

Reinventing himself was his for the taking. Instead of embracing his barely believable good luck, he turned to his fellow countrymen who had preceded him to Montreal and had years of jihadi fieldwork under their belts in Afghanistan or Bosnia or both. It is easy enough to say he missed an extraordinary opportunity when he landed in Canada. But how and why did he cross that fatal line between Algeria-centric Islam and the world-wide universalism of the *umma*, the nation of Islam constantly invoked by the jihadis? I suspect he came under Fateh Kamel's influence more by chance than design. Or, more likely, he chose the line of least resistance. Striking out for himself, embracing the challenges of an open society is the stuff of legend and myth, and what myth is stronger than the American— or, in his case, the Canadian—dream? The facts of immigrant life are often more prosaic and less heroic. Living in a foreign country can prove trying for men better educated and more self-assured than Ressam.

MY PERFORCE unscientific observations over many decades suggest that recently arrived Muslims often find adjusting to life in the West particularly difficult. (But so, too, do most other first-generation immigrants.) Ressam's hometown was by Algerian standards sophisticated, but still light-years away from the dynamics of a modern Western city like Montreal. The nature of relations between men and women, the lack of familiar family ties, learning to live among many different ethnic groups, the great disparities of wealth, these and other factors can prove frightening and encourage a headlong retreat to the like-minded certainties of one's own kind. Ressam's sense of difference was sharpened by a past he would just as soon forget, but could not. He was under deportation orders stayed only by Canada's realization that to send him back to Algeria was tantamount to renewed imprisonment and might even cost him his life.

Many Afghan Arabs became radicalized when they could not return to their native lands and had to settle for precarious refuge in Sudan, Yemen, Bosnia or Chechnya. The Algerians and the French wanted no part of the Ressams and were only too happy to push them back into the middle of the river, hoping they would end up elsewhere. After all, Ressam did not head directly off to Afghanistan for training in an Al-Qaeda camp. He very likely had never heard of Osama before he landed in Canada. Yet, he was Osama's first chosen instrument in bringing terrorism to the United States.

Ressam arrived in Afghanistan in March 1998. That was more than four years after he landed in Canada, but a mere month after Osama unveiled the International Islamic Front for Jihad against the Jews and Crusaders, his new vehicle designed to signal that henceforth his principal target no longer was Saudi Arabia or other suspect Arab governments, but the United States itself. By then, of course, that alliance—with Ayman al-Zawahiri's Egyptian Islamic Jihad, a leader of a minority wing of Gama'a al-Islamiyya as well as lesser Afghan, Pakistani and Bangladeshi jihadis—already was actively planning the complex simultaneous attacks on the American embassies in East Africa the following August.

While Ressam was growing up he was certainly exposed to a very Algerian strain of Islamist violence. Even in the heyday of FLN rule in the early and mid-1980s a Robin Hood jihadi figure named Mustapha Bouyali led Algerian security forces on a merry chase not far from the capital itself. His Armed Islamic Movement was determined to establish an Islamic Republic and impose *sharia* law on Algeria. The group was finally crushed, but it remained an inspiration a decade later. With the state's successful penetration of the FIS and, later, the GIA in the middle 1990s, a hardcore jihadi rump founded a new movement, the Salafist Group for Preaching and Combat (SGPC).

Its members were horrified by the GIA's record of unsparingly butchering civilians and soldiers alike and hoped to preserve themselves from Sport et Musique machinations. Bouyali, the FIS, the GIA and their descendants were quintessentially Algerian groups, but partly financed by rich Gulf Arabs happy to undermine what they took for a Westernized regime. Osama helped the GIA and then the SGPC. But the record indicates that these radical groups became useful for transnational jihad only after they failed to achieve their goals in Algeria itself.

I once talked to a GIA emir who had weighed life on the run in the maquis and bailed out of the fight in favor of a marginal but safe existence in Paris. Life expectancy for Algerian maquisards, especially the emirs, was not good. As we chatted in a bar on the Champs-Élysées, I asked him about Osama's influence in Algeria. He thought for a while, then recalled that he had commanded a jihadi trained in an Al-Qaeda camp in the Sudan. No big deal, just another field hand, the former emir said. The Algerians had enough homegrown jihadis and didn't need Al-Qaeda ringers.

In Algiers I asked the same question when Colonel Ali Tounsi, the country's very tough top cop, who gave jihadis no quarter, agreed to receive me in the spring of 2001. As a teenager the wiry colonel had fought in the war of independence; put out to pasture in 1988, he was recalled to active service in the fall of 1994 when the regime was on its knees. To my surprise, he basically agreed with the emir. "I'd rather neutralize one little terrorist here than collar Osama," he told me in the immense office near the Admiralty that I had last visited when its occupant was an equally self-assured French colonel. I must have looked skeptical. Osama, after all, was on a rampage. He had the East African embassies and the holing of the USS *Cole* in Yemen under his belt, and his next terrorist attack was presumed to be only a question of timing. "Our terrorists don't even know who Osama bin Laden is," the colonel boasted.

I knew better than to contradict him. Maybe they didn't know who Osama was, but the Algerian newspapers sure did. He was blamed for practically every bloody incident in the country. I asked the colonel about Ressam and about a fellow Algerian accomplice named Abdelmajid Dahoumane, who had barely eluded arrest in Canada despite an impressive $5 million U.S. bounty on his head and curiously resurfaced in Algeria, where he eventually was jailed, apparently to please the United States. (A Ressam brother I questioned in Algiers about Dahoumane remarked it was "a bit odd this guy coming home when every other Algerian is desperately scheming to get out of the country.") For the paranoid—and Algeria, in my experience, had never lacked for conspiracy theorists—Dahoumane's return and arrest in August 2000 suggested that he perhaps was an agent provocateur or at least manipulated by Sport et Musique (which indeed was rumored to have discovered him in Pakistan or Afghanistan and coaxed him into coming home).[16] The colonel disagreed about Ressam and Dahoumane. "Both are illustrious nonentities," the colonel bellowed. "Our terrorists are not brilliant," he insisted. "My men are in the field deal every day with terrorists who are much more dangerous than Ressam."

When I mentioned Osama, outside financing, the support rings in Europe providing money and arms for the Islamists in the maquis, the colonel sputtered contemptuously. "The money raised outside is nothing compared to the funds they extort under our noses here," he said. "Same goes for the handful of weapons they've managed to smuggle in. The maquisards we're fighting now are down to sawed-off shotguns, in any event." The colonel certainly was aware of, but did not mention, the police and counterterrorism efforts deployed in France and western Europe to smash clandestine rings tasked with providing the maquis with arms and money. Of course the French resistance and other underground operations throughout history often took terrible risks, thinking they were achieving great results when in fact they caused their pursuers relatively little disruption. Nor did Tounsi let on that his statements deliberately contradicted Algerian government propaganda. I didn't bother to ask how his worm's-eye view squared with "eradicator" Algerian politicians who ceaselessly carped at "advanced Western democracies," and especially Britain, for not collaborating on counterterrorism—that is, not hounding their critics who succeeded in finding refuge abroad.

I think I knew the answer. He said he was pleased he had helped reduce the terrorist death toll to 2,200 the previous year (although human rights campaigners estimated more than four times that number had died). He had no use for the Islamists—"many don't know the five pillars of Islam or where Mecca is." I didn't have to like the colonel to believe him. He was fighting the fight. The rest of the government was, among other things, justifying what he was doing and the way he was doing it. His methods were not always pretty. Human-rights abuses year after year filled volumes of reports from Amnesty International, Human Rights Watch and the International Federation of the Rights of Man, as well as getting regular mention in the annual State Department worldwide human rights roundup. In his own way, the colonel was claiming back the struggle for Algeria. The Ressams of this world were not his concern. They had disappeared from his radar. If they now frightened the United States, which once took a detached view of Algerian events, then so be it.

And they obviously had. Only days before my visit, the FBI's Freeh, nearing the end of his tenure as director in the spring of 2001, had stopped off for high-level counterterrorism discussions with Algerian officials. The American embassy was visibly upset when I asked about the visit. I suspected at the time that Freeh wanted at least access to Dahoumane and would have been delighted if the Algerians handed him over in time for the Ressam trial then under way in Los Angeles.[17]

September 11 accelerated the nascent cooperation, and soon the United States was providing Algeria with military equipment and training so prudently refused in the past. The Algerian regime was delighted. President Abdulaziz Bouteflika was received in the White House, a clear signal that counterterrorism—and Algeria's gas and oil concessions—trumped scruples about human rights. (The Algerian justice minister made a breakthrough visit to London to discuss counterterrorism cooperation with British officials, who previously had ignored hectoring from Algiers.) America felt it needed all the help it could get. The days of letting France deal solely with the Algerian hot potato were over. The United States was in the front lines fighting terrorism worldwide. Cooperation with repressive regimes from Central Asia to Latin America was the order of the day. How this squared with Washington's policy of actively advocating, indeed sometimes seemingly threatening to foist, democracy on Muslim lands was never spelled out. If the United States understood the apparent contradiction in riding such disparate chargers, the White House rarely let on. (Even in Bush's excellent speech during his November 2003 visit to London advocating greater democracy in the Muslim world, he was obliged to contrast his noble sentiments with past American moral corner-cutting in its bilateral dealings with Islamic countries.) Human rights activists could only rue the high-water mark of their influence in the preceding decade.

What was true for Algeria also held for other authoritarian regimes, most especially Russia. In the failing months of Boris Yeltsin's disintegrating rule in the autumn of 1999, the career of his handpicked successor, Vladimir Putin, was mightily advanced by a series of still-mysterious explosions in and around Moscow. They were blamed on the Chechens and indeed served to justify launching the second war against that famously restive Caucasian republic.[18] By happenstance, shortly after the explosions I was in the office of a Washington counterterrorism expert asking him about rumors that Osama was financing the Chechens, training their young men in Afghanistan and sending in volunteers to help their cause.

"Funny," my Washington expert said, "just the other day I received a phone call from a Russian think tank asking me if anyone in the United States intelligence community had anything on that. I knew nothing, and I don't think anyone in Washington knew very much either at that point. I figured my Russian counterpart was out to put a bug in my ear." Putin jumped on the Bush bandwagon soon after September 11 out of realpolitik, setting aside his nationalist displeasure at the American military bases in Uzbekistan, Tajikistan and Kyrgizstan that had been established to prosecute the war against the Taliban. Soon the Bush administration was spouting the Russian line on Osama's links with the Chechens and soft-pedaling massive human-rights abuses there.

IN THE LATE 1980s, and early 1990s, certain bookshops, certain mosques, certain cities in western Europe were known recruiting grounds for radical Islamists, particularly among second-generation Muslims born in Britain, France, Belgium or elsewhere on the Continent who were tempted to renew vestigial ties with Islam that their immigrant parents had often allowed to lapse. Jihadis also prized Westernized converts. Obtaining visas, passports, checkbooks, credit cards, airline tickets—the basic ingredients of modern living that allowed easy and anonymous passage through the global village—was second nature for both categories. The European converts attracted even less attention and were thus deemed even more useful.

Some of these second-generation immigrants were easy to recruit because they felt alienated, convinced they were second-class citizens in the countries of their birth, yet unconnected to their parents' homelands to the point they did not speak the language. Some were ashamed and contemptuous of their parents, who had been recruited in the 1960s and 1970s from North Africa or Pakistan or Turkey as cheap labor in the textile plants, mines, steel plants or other labor-intensive industries that no longer needed their strong backs. The parents were not particularly religious. Some of their children turned to Islam to show their difference, to establish their own identity in European societies they felt were intent on keeping them pigeonholed in unskilled jobs, when jobs there were. Assimilation in many European societies had rarely been easy for immigrants but proved particularly laborious for Muslims, especially those from illiterate, rural backgrounds. For the second generation, humiliation, real or imagined, began at home. It did not rely on such mythic models as the Afghan jihad, Israeli repression of the Palestinians, Serb and Croat misbehavior toward Bosnia's Muslims or Russian excesses in Chechnya. But such foreign examples did give a sense of purpose—holding out the possibility of righting the wrongs done Muslims over the centuries—that transcended the perceived limits of their own lives in Europe.

Often, exemplary Muslims attracted the young. In high-crime immigrant neighborhoods Muslim activists were credited with working with footloose adolescents, dissuading them from committing the acts of violence that landed so many of them in trouble. And in much of Europe the Tabligh, a quietist order of Islamic missionaries headquartered in Pakistan, had a long history of reclaiming lost souls in countries outside the Muslim world but was not involved in jihadi politics. In the 1990s that did not prevent the Tablighis from being denounced as unwitting recruiting agents, enticing young Muslims in Europe to travel for religious instruction to Pakistan and Afghanistan, where they were taken in hand by much more radical groups, often those involved in terrorism.

All these snapshot views had the virtue of simplicity. None was more persistent than the role of radical jihadi preachers operating openly in London mosques. I got an inkling while trying to understand an odd group, mostly made up of second-generation Algerians and their convert friends, and its connections with Ressam and his Montreal acolytes. A young French convert named Lionel Dumont, in a heartfelt letter to Judge Bruguière written in 1996 from a Bosnian prison, blamed a well-known radical London preacher named Abu Hamza al-Masri for leading him and another French convert, Christophe Caze, astray. Dumont's purpose was transparent: he hoped his denunciation would persuade the judge to arrange his transfer to a French jail, preferably close to home.[19]

I was never totally convinced. Dumont had been visited in his Bosnian jail by Judge Bruguière, who lectured on the evils of Abu Hamza. So Dumont's letter was playing back the judge's own conviction that Abu Hamza, along with two or three other like-minded London preachers, was running a latter-day Islamic version of Fagin's infamous school instructing the young in a life of crime. In fact, Abu Hamza was so public in his outrageous jihadi pronouncements that he and his fellow preachers were derisively nicknamed "Abu Megaphones," written off at least at the time as hyped television news sound-bite favorites who were too outspoken to escape police notice or be taken seriously by real jihadis. But in late May 2004, the U.S. government paid him a backhanded compliment by requesting his extradition from Britain in order to indict him for alleged terrorist activities committed in Yemen more than a decade ago.[20]

Some sort of relations did exist. Dumont and Caze had fought for the Muslims in Bosnia in the 900-man Seventh Mujahedeen Brigade commanded by an Algerian Afghan veteran known as Abu Maali. Often trained by Afghan war veterans, the 7th was a volunteer unit comprised mostly of Bosnian Muslims displaced in the fighting, but with foreigners accounting for a third of its strength. The young Frenchmen also had met Abu Hamza, who had briefly visited Zenica, the central Bosnian industrial city that served as brigade headquarters. Caze, a last-year medical student in France, operated on Muslim war casualties in Zenica. One of his patients was Fateh Kamel, who suffered leg injuries in fighting during one of his periodic visits to Bosnia.

Still, foreign volunteers were never highly valued as soldiers, although their brutality did frighten the Serbs and Croats on occasion. The more devout among the foreign Muslim volunteers often did not stay long; they were put off by Bosnian Muslims' fondness for plum brandy and the Westernized ways of Bosnian girls. Bosnian Muslims generally didn't appreciate the foreigners' disapproval of their integration into Marshal Tito's secular Yugoslav state. Accepting the volunteers was the price the embattled Bosnian state paid for obtaining desperately needed outside money and arms from Saudi and Gulf donors. For all their comings and goings, the number of these volunteers never exceeded the high hundreds. But just as the Sudan and Yemen had provided Afghan Arabs with a refuge and meeting place, so Bosnia fulfilled that role for the new jihadis in the Balkans.

When the Dayton Accords ended the fighting in November 1995, most of the foreign volunteers simply went home, their duty done. Some, naturally, formed lasting friendships; such are the bonds of war. Several hundred, among them men fearing arrest back home, stayed, and much to American displeasure, acquired Bosnian citizenship by marrying local girls. For all that, the would-be terrorist cell that Dumont, Caze and other Bosnian veterans established in late 1995, upon their return to the depressed northern French industrial city of Roubaix, seemed relentlessly local in its focus. Dumont's Roubaix gang staged a series of violent operations, many of them senseless small-time stickup robberies using assault rifles and even rocket-propelled grenades. Their haphazard and violent ways attracted attention and seemed odd for men claiming to raise money for the clandestine Islamist cause.

Their last operation, typically ineffective, brought about their downfall. An amateur car bomb they'd prepared was discovered on March 28, 1996, by alert police just outside police headquarters in the neighboring city of Lille, only two days before the G7 heads of government were scheduled to meet there. Had the bomb exploded, it would have been lethal in a 200-yard radius, police specialists said. The RAID, a unit of specially trained counterterrorism police, was called in. In a dawn shoot-out on March 29, its operatives killed four defiant Algerian gang members holed up in a two-story redbrick hideout on the rue Henri-Carette in nearby Roubaix that burned down, as did a similar house next door. The Islamists refused to surrender, firing back with Sten guns, Uzis and Kalashnikovs until consumed by the flames.

Years later I visited the neighborhood. In rue Archimède, sullen young men lounging near a neighborhood mosque advertised their radical faith by wearing thigh-length *thobe*s they imagined approximated the dress of the Prophet Mohammed and his followers. Evidence from the Roubaix case led Bruguière to Ressam's Montreal associates clustered around Kamel. The giveaway was Caze's electronic address book. It was found when he was killed in a skirmish with Belgian police as he and a colleague sought to flee Roubaix by car. The Belgians, alerted by French colleagues just across the nearby border, had set up a roadblock. Once decoded, Caze's address book revealed the telephone numbers of Kamel, Said Atmani and Abu Hamza, as well as other Islamists in Britain, Germany, Italy and the United States. Arrests took time. Kamel was collared and extradited, at Bruguière's request, in only mid-1999 from Jordan, and it was not until April 2001 that he was sentenced in Paris to ten years in jail.

Over the years European police kept the usual haunts under surveillance, and Islamist recruiters were obliged to take greater care. Belgium was conveniently located next to France and Germany. Unlike in France, there was no specific counterterrorism legislation in Belgium. That made it harder to arrest and convict Islamist suspects, but not to identify them, perhaps because they thought they were relatively safe there.[21] In the company of a Belgian counterterrorism official who is a respected specialist on Islam, I spent a morning driving and walking around Brussels, an unusual European city since neighborhoods mix immigrant and long-established residents. My friend had a sixth sense for identifying new storefront mosques that to my untrained eye seemed perfectly innocuous. He duly noted each discovery.

In France the various police and counterterrorism authorities of the Direction de la Surveillance du Territoire (DST) had their own effective methods. They were on good terms with the preachers, who needed little prompting to report worshipers in their mosques tempted by jihadi thinking. So efficient were the French and so tough the counterterrorism legislation that most jihadis preferred generally to give France a wide berth. In Italy the DIGOS counterterrorism police so regularly arrested jihadis involved with the Islamic Cultural Center in Milan that outside observers could only wonder why the Islamists failed to learn from their errors.

The two softest landings for Islamists were the Netherlands and Britain, at least until 2001, when tough British counterterrorism legislation was enacted that in many ways went beyond the greater police powers on the books on most of the Continent.[22] Immigrants from all over Britain's once far-flung former empire and beyond felt comfortable there. Londonistan, as various Muslim refugees mockingly described the British capital, was made up of various inexpensive neighborhoods with such names as Dollis Hill, Wood Green and Ealing Common and key mosques in Finsbury Park, Brixton and Regent's Park. Algerian Islamists in trouble with their own authorities could count on alighting in Britain, getting a job (or picking up decent unemployment allowances) and generally getting on with their lives. The same, of course, was true for secular Algerians who simply wanted to flee the violence at home.

The governments of Algeria and France, for example, regularly complained about British laxity. Rightly or not, British intelligence was still credited with being the world's best. But the governments of Egypt, Jordan and Algeria gnashed their teeth at what they took as British hypocrisy in not linking up the police and the courts in bringing suspects from their countries to book. Foreigners, including Americans, at times had trouble fathoming the sanctity of the law in Britain. England boasted a long and distinguished record for welcoming victims of foreign persecution. The common law offered its proud protection to citizens and foreign residents alike. Prosecuting citizens or foreign residents for what they might be about to do was not British. In any case, the British authorities for much of the 1980s and 1990s also had their hands too full with Irish terrorism to worry about Islamist varieties. It was left to the Special Branch and MI5 to keep a discreet eye cocked for jihadi activity.

But the British seemed torn between the policeman's age-old choice: arrest suspected lawbreakers early on or keep string on their activities to better understand what they were up to. In the eyes of their detractors the

British stood accused of tolerating plotting on their soil for terrorist operations carried out abroad. (French critics were ill-placed to snipe since in the 1970s and 1980s France had tolerated the same thing.) In Britain it was the edifice of the law that provided protection, either because statutes did not prohibit various activities or because, as in the case of extradition, the common law provided tortuous procedures that often took years in the courts.[23]

One spring morning in 2001 before Friday prayers, I showed up at the Finsbury Park mosque for an interview with Abu Hamza. I was kept waiting and killed time by inspecting the wooden collection boxes for Chechyna, Bosnia and Palestine, as well as three or four other conflicts dear to Islamist hearts. Equally interested was a slight, very young man with whom I struck up a conversation. He seemed somewhat lost and homesick and was eager to talk. He had arrived from the eastern Algerian city of Constantine months earlier to learn English and study engineering. From what I could judge he seemed to have done neither with much application. So, much to his relief, we spoke in French. He said his father, who owned a garage, had paid for his ticket.

I turned over in my mind what really might have brought him to London. Perhaps his family, worried about the boy's likely military service in the continuing strife in Algeria, had shipped him out of harm's way. Fewer questions were asked about young Algerians arriving in England with questionable travel documents than those who tried the same thing in France. Many Algerian families had lingering reservations about France, and the desirability of learning English was a useful justification. How did he manage to stay in Britain? As we talked idly, I admit I wondered if the young man was the kind of easy mark for the hard men bent on recruiting for the Afghan camps. Even if recruiters were too savvy to operate at Finsbury Park itself anymore, they doubtless knew where to find the young and impressionable. The candidate jihadis were advised to fly to Pakistan from London, where such travel was less scrutinized than in France or Germany.

Shortly after September 11 a friend in Paris introduced me to a thirty-something son of Algerian immigrants who a decade earlier had left France for England and eventually ended up in jihadi training camps in Afghanistan. Malik, as he called himself, cast himself a bit too easily in the role of the *beur* who, just in time, had seen the light and drawn back from jihadi violence. Aside from that questionable flourish, Malik made no attempt at self-promotion. His tale was less cautionary than banal, in the way so many young men through the ages have been attracted to adventure. He grew up in the *banlieue,* the drab Paris suburbs where many Muslim immigrant families lived in the French equivalent of American inner-city ghettos. At home only his immigrant father prayed. But France's "hypocritical" attitude toward the war to liberate Kuwait from Iraqi occupation in 1991 infuriated him and drew him to Islam. First Paris tried its best to prevent the conflict, then joined in. The new conflict in Algeria demonstrating the West's "hatred of Islam "also radicalized him.

When he began to frequent mosques in and around Paris, he was picked out by Tabligh missionaries, many of them Pakistanis. "They were very clever pilot fish and never talked about jihad, just a call for peace and prayer," he said. "They would invite you for a meal, then propose you spend two or three days with them praying and studying the Koran. Then it was a week, then a month or two and finally a suggestion you fly to India or Pakistan." Other favored destinations for would-be jihadis were Indonesia and Thailand. Leaving France behind sounded all the more attractive since Malik suspected that Algerian, Moroccan, Tunisian and, of course, French police had penetrated many mosques.

His first stop was London, where he developed a lasting admiration for the English, especially for the tolerance he felt he found there, which he contrasted with the vexations he felt as a *beur* in France. Compared with the limited horizons he saw as the *beurs'* lot in France, he discovered that the English basically asked few questions and provided greater opportunities for Muslim immigrants. "I was able to accomplish there in three months," he recalled, "what would have taken me fifty years in France." He was amazed to find a large Algerian community, with people working even without proper documents, making good money, dressing well, sending money back to their families in North Africa. He was especially struck by a friendly young Algerian woman who had joined the police. Such interest in a professional woman, and a bobby at that, was not something a traditional jihadi would have remarked, or at least not favorably. But jihad was very much on his mind and London the best place to pursue his new passion.

Back in 1992 and 1993, Malik recounted, "You'd go to Finsbury Park mosque and sign up with FIS and be gone the next day" to Pakistan or India. For lonely Algerian immigrants the mosque was a place to meet where there was much talk of jihad, sometimes with veterans of the anti-

Soviet jihad in Afghanistan. "In those days we didn't care about Kabul or Afghanistan," Malik recalled, "but Afghanistan was a good place to train," as far from prying eyes of European governments increasingly concerned with Islamist terrorism. Candidates were told to ask for person X and mosque Y, and in Pakistan or Afghanistan they were placed with a sheikh who enjoyed tribal protection. Even before Osama returned from the Sudan, those camps were often joint ventures, training volunteers for Kashmir and for Pakistan's ISI in one corner, Al-Qaeda devotees in another.

Once recruits were trained, Azerbaijan, Chechnya, Uzbekistan and Kashmir were popular destinations, as was the war in Bosnia, which began in April 1992, shortly after the new violence erupted in Algeria. For those who went back to France, "you could choose Algeria or go back to a sleeper cell in France." As time went by, the needs in the field changed and volunteers had less choice. By the late 1990s the Taliban were fighting for control of all Afghanistan, and many foreign volunteers, especially the less educated, were assigned to front-line duty against Ahmad Shah Massoud's Northern Alliance forces.

The old easy ways were over. Muslim and Western governments began trying to pay serious attention to the flow of recruits heading for the training camps. With time, Malik said, FIS agents became more suspicious. "They wanted to know who you were, to be sure you weren't working for the French services or Sport et Musique." Fear of counterterrorism penetration was such that by the time Malik arrived in Afghanistan in 1996 for a basic training and explosives course, entire fake training camps were set up to fool American spy satellites. With Osama's return, the camps turned into an archipelago stretching over much of the east and south of Afghanistan, as well as Kabul itself.

A RARE PERSONAL insight into the thinking that led Muslims to Al-Qaeda was provided by a *beur* named Kemal Daoudi, who was arrested, at age twenty-seven, as an accomplice of Djamel Beghal, the ringleader of an alleged plot, personally blessed by Osama, to blow up the American embassy in Paris. Daoudi barely avoided capture in France in September 2001 and escaped to Leicester, an old industrial city in the English Midlands, where he was soon traced and arrested and quickly extradited to France. Such was the electric shock caused by September 11. An engineering university graduate, he at one point ran a government-subsidized computer café in the Paris suburb of Athis-Mons. It was no great shakes of a job for a man of his education and once-vaulting ambition. But before he was fired for absenteeism by the town authorities, French counterterrorism specialists charged he used the café as a cover to communicate via e-mail with Al-Qaeda in Afghanistan.

Al-Qaeda, of course, maintained a permanent interest in recruiting Westernized Muslims pretty much the world over. That was obvious well before September 11. Years earlier, a companion of Osama's in Peshawar tantalizingly told me American veterans of the anti-Soviet jihad were already established in the United States in the late 1980s. No amount of pleading produced even a hint of their identities. Native-born American citizens were arrested for having traveled to Afghanistan for training with Al-Qaeda even in the spring of 2001, in places as geographically separated as Seattle and the old Lake Erie steel town of Lackawanna, New York. And, most famously, Mohammed Atta, Ramzi bin al-Shibh and several of the other key Arab plotters involved in the September 11 operation had lived for years in the German port of Hamburg, some as students.

Daoudi was one of few Al-Qaeda operatives who willingly bared his soul in public, explaining, indeed justifying his once middle-class aspirations, his turning to jihadi Islam and the radicalization that led him to Afghanistan and eventually jail. He called himself a terrorist while denying involvement in the Beghal network.[24]

Daoudi was born in a small town called Sediata in eastern Algeria, but for all his formative years lived in Paris at 22 boulevard de l'Hôpital, at the edge of the middle class fifth arrondissement in the Latin Quarter. There he discovered "the heart of Paris with real Parisians," a welcome change after life across town in the racially mixed eleventh arrondissement, where he attended an inferior "United Nations school," a veritable "tower of Babel," meaning one with students drawn from many countries. His words betrayed the condescending superiority of the poor immigrant who had seized the main chance and escaped the fate of most *beur* children. By his own account he became a "brilliant" student. He was frequently the only Arab in his class but regularly had the best grades, although often he was two years younger than most of his classmates. They teased him because of his name and his modesty. He felt his classmates were jealous, but he befriended slower and lazier students by doing their homework.

Daoudi gobbled up languages—Latin, Greek, English and Spanish as well as Arabic, the language of his parents, which he had neglected when he moved from Algeria to Paris when he was five. He also excelled at mathematics and science, the high road to the so-called *grandes écoles,* the famously selective summit of French higher education. He was something of a hothouse flower, relentlessly driven by his semiliterate father to excel at school. The lowly hospital employee told his son, "You must work twice as hard because you are a foreigner," and he applied a wooden ruler when the marks faltered. Evenings and weekends were devoted to study. Kemal pointed out that his name in Arabic means "perfection." His was a classic tale of immigrant success through education, or so it seemed.

His daydreaming escape from such pressures was the nearby Jardin des Plantes, facing the river Seine, with the Museum of Natural History at the far end. There he created his own universe, drawing inspiration from the museum's dinosaur skeletons and greenhouses to go on imaginary safaris in what he conjured up as tropical forests. Influenced by the Indiana Jones movies, through much of high school he was fascinated by paleontology and anthropology. In his next-to-last high school year he decided he must be useful to Algeria and turned to the sciences, hoping to become a doctor, an engineer and perhaps even a fighter pilot, despite his poor eyesight. He ended up studying science and engineering at the University of Paris, moving on to aeronautical engineering and earning a degree in 1993.

He embarked on a graduate degree at an elite engineering school and was proud of his design for a simplified version of the landing gear for France's new fighter jet called the Rafale. But he dropped out, preferring to help a friend with his thesis on the history of Islamic civilization under the Ottoman Sultans. In fact, Daoudi, the hitherto well-programmed student, was coming unhinged. At work were political events, plus what he described as an "adolescent crisis" that distracted him to the point "I could no longer study serenely." "All the pressure on me during my school years so I could succeed at any price," he wrote, "suddenly transformed itself into the energy to challenge my environment and my father." He traced his oedipal revolt to the street violence in Algiers in 1988, when he identified with the Islamist demonstrators against his father's preference for the regime.

He already had resented his father as a "tourist"—a distant, once-a-year summer visitor from France—when he was a child in Algeria and later pitied because of his subaltern status. But such was the fate of most of those first-generation Algerian immigrants. A part of Kemal's pleasant

Paris world fell apart when the family fortunes soured and he and his three siblings and parents were obliged to leave the capital for an inglorious suburb. "That's where I became aware of the abominable treatment meted out to all the potential 'myselves' who had been conditioned to become subcitizens good only to keep working to pay for the retirements of the 'real' French when the French age pyramid gets thin at the base."

This bitter language of disillusionment reflected the depressed French economy of the early 1990s, heady times for many young Muslims in France confronted with bleak job prospects and tumultuous political events at home and especially abroad. The American-led war expelling Iraq from Kuwait in 1991 stirred anti-Western resentment among many Muslims. So did the rise of the FIS in Algeria. A year later, the army coup there was followed within months by the outbreak of the war in Bosnia, where the predominantly Muslim "legal" government had to fight off both the breakaway Bosnian Serbs and its sometime allies among the Croats. But for Daoudi the point of no return was reached in October 1995, when French security police at the end of a giant manhunt gunned down in cold blood Khalid Kelkal, a young *beur* from a Lyons suburb who had become a convinced jihadi in prison and emerged to participate in the GIA's campaign of terrorism in France that summer. Kelkal's death convinced him that "the West was openly at war against me, and I had to fight back."

"I then began to hate France, the United States and the West in general," Daoudi wrote, because he became convinced that the West hated all Arabs and all Muslims. He recognized that he was deliberately rejecting his chance to succeed as an assimilated Frenchman and indeed scoffed at the "Uncle Tom" existence he knew was well within his grasp. Not for him the prestige and popularity of "de-cultured" French Algerian role models such as soccer star Zinedine Zidane or Cheb Khaled, the king of *rai* music, popular on both banks of the Mediterranean. "I want to be the worthy successor of glorious ancestors," he insisted, mentioning members of his own family whom he admired as courageous nationalists who since the nineteenth century had fought to the death to oppose French colonialism in Algeria.

Daoudi became increasingly agitated by the French financial and other assistance that was propping up the Algerian government and thwarting an Islamic state, by the plight of the Palestinians, by the fate of Iraqi children subjected to the UN embargo and by the Dayton Accords of November 1995 ending the Bosnian war just when he felt the Bosnian troops and foreign volunteers were beginning to hurt their foes. All these themes were ji-hadi favorites, of course. In keeping with his studious habits, he set out to acquire the political tools he felt necessary to know his enemy and fight back. He plunged into the great writers of twentieth-century radical polit-ical Islam, Maulana Abul a'la Maududi and especially Sayyid Qotb and Hassan al-Banna, whom he studied in French or English translation be-cause his Arabic was not good enough to read them in the original.

Soon he took to speaking in rote jihadi jargon, stringing together real and imaginary slights to Muslims in Afghanistan, Bosnia, Kosovo, Pales-tine, the Gulf, Lebanon and, of course, Algeria. The West was never cred-ited with intervening, belatedly, but decisively, to end the Bosnian conflict, in which Muslims were by far the most numerous victims, or with con-ducting a war against the Christian Serbs to protect the Muslim Kosovars in 1999. Rather these distant battlefields "strengthened my conviction that the Judeo-Christian community was influenced by atheism and harbored a visceral hatred for Mohammed." Daoudi traveled in Algeria for four months in the summer 1995, when the worst of the war was over. He toyed with the idea of joining Islamists in the maquis, but rejected it on grounds that Sport et Musique had infiltrated GIA and the FIS ranks. His lack of de-cisiveness in Algeria was mirrored by similar hesitation concerning his per-sonal life.

Daoudi had married in Hungary a Hungarian woman he had met in an American Internet chat room, thinking his interlocutor was a man. Given those beginnings—and his inner turmoil—the marriage, not surprisingly, did not last. He acknowledged his error in thinking that it would "regener-ate and make me more stable." Instead it "did not live up to my dreams" and became a "social trap." Despite his wife's "many qualities," he lamented that she lacked his "gene for strong sensations and adventure." That stimu-lation, he now intimated, he found in the "concrete jungle" suburbs he had disdained when younger. Thus began the final chapter of his adventure, the one that led to an Al-Qaeda training camp in Afghanistan with Abu Zubay-dah and the plot against the American embassy in Paris. "I had to get reli-gious and military training in Afghanistan," he wrote, "which is a mythical country and the best destination" because it coincided with his view of a perfect Islamic state. He said Afghanistan proved that victory of Islam over the West was possible.

Summing up the personal, religious and political influences that had brought him to this pass, he wrote, somewhat melodramatically: "For all these reasons and all these events, I went over to the forces of the dark side." He knew he was cribbing a line from *Star Wars* for effect. But his prose at other times could be chillingly authentic. He felt he had two choices—to "sink into depression," as he had for six months at the end of his second year at university, or "to react by taking part in the universal struggle against this overwhelming iniquitous cynicism" he found in the West. In reviewing his life, he wrote, "everything became clear to me and I understood why Abraham went into exile, why Moses rebelled against the Pharoah and why Jesus was spat on and why Mohammed said, 'I came with the sword. My battle was and will be to eradicate all those who are opposed to the law of Allah.'" Laws inspired by men—and not the *sharia*—were worthless, he noted. "This glorious battle will not stop until the law of Allah has been reestablished and applied by a just and honest caliph" heading an Islamist state, he wrote, parroting impeccable jihadi doctrine.

"My ideological commitment is total, and the reward of glory for this relentless battle is to be called a terrorist," he concluded. "I accept the name of terrorist if it is used to mean that I terrorize a system of iniquitous power and perversity that comes in many forms." So he admitted that indeed he was a terrorist as charged. But Daoudi could not eschew his taste for self-dramatization, proclaiming he had never "terrorized the innocent." "But I will fight any form of injustice and those who support it," he wrote. In an epitaph to his once-promising life, he predicted, "My fight will only end in my death or in my madness."

Hundreds, indeed thousands of other young Muslim men, some equally well educated and once bound for mainstream lives, trod the same path to Afghanistan from all over the Muslim world and beyond. Compared with Daoudi, Mohammed Atta and his friends from Hamburg who spearheaded the September 11 attacks were even better educated, often in the sciences. They were also better read in Islam and came from even more comfortable homes. What really distinguished Daoudi was his gift of rhetoric to memorialize himself and so many others who were less articulate. It was his revenge for failure, a gift carefully honed in jail while awaiting trial. The Hamburg plotters needed no such props.

FLOOS

M Y INTRODUCTION to Arabs and money was a tale recounted by an older correspondent more than half a lifetime ago for me—and light-years ago for the people of the Gulf, whose existence was even then being irredeemably changed by oil riches. The British, the story went, had recently felt compelled to depose the autocratic ruler of an emirate in the Trucial States, so-called because Her Majesty's Government in the mid-nineteenth century had forced a truce, really protection, on the warring sheikhdoms dotting a good slice of the Arab side of the Persian Gulf then known as the Pirate Coast. Despite much jawboning from the British political agent (read proconsul), Sheikh Shakhbut bin Zayyid al-Nahayyan of Abu Dhabi could not be persuaded to put his treasury to work in a bank. Legend had it he preferred to stuff the banknotes he received as oil royalties in cookie tins and other nonproductive hiding places around his fort in Abu Dhabi, including in the growing number of mattresses he slept on.

Oil in the emirates had begun to flow in the early 1960s, the storyteller recalled. The British soon were increasingly insistent the oil money be invested in schools, roads, hospitals—in other words, the standard panoply of improvements they planned for the suddenly wealthy citizens of what they eventually renamed the United Arab Emirates. An adamant Shakhbut refused, instinctively preferring to have his subjects scrape by on traditional pearl fishing and the sale of exotic postage stamps. He had heard tell of the near-instant modernization of Kuwait, Bahrain and even Saudi Arabia and wanted none of it. The British finally replaced him with his pliant younger brother in 1966, maliciously spreading the word that mice had chewed through much of the Shakhbut's treasury. Five years later London relinquished vestigial control in the Gulf, ushering in an era distinguished within thirty years by three major wars and seemingly endless buffeting. But when I first heard of Shakhbut's comeuppance, it was still just a good story.

Less than a decade later a French friend with a major American bank in Geneva regaled me with tales of Gulf Arabs showing up unannounced with big suitcases crammed with large-denomination dollar bills.[1] His visitors' command of English, my friend reported, was not perfect, but their design was clear. They wanted their money to work for them in a less turbulent neighborhood than their own and figured a big American bank, especially one located in Switzerland's temple of bank secrecy, was just the place. They had learned the lesson of Shakhbut's downfall. It hadn't taken the Arabs long to understand the virtues of investing their *floos,* that most wonderfully evocative Arabic word for money. I cannot now remember if my friend said his Arab callers were Saudis.

But had they been, their perspicacity was remarkable since the first purely Saudi bank in the Kingdom, the National Commerce Bank, opened for business only in 1950. (Elsewhere, in the Gulf, British banks dominated in those days.) What Gulf Arabs then lacked in financial sophistication, the Muslim Brothers promptly provided. Driven out of Egypt and other Middle Eastern lands because of their opposition to then-ascendant Arab nationalism and given asylum by conservative Gulf rulers, the Brothers insinuated themselves into local banking with ever-greater success. So-called Islamic banks, often created with Muslim Brothers' assistance by Saudi princes and other wealthy men in the 1970s, eschewed *riba,* or interest, in keeping with the Koranic law, *sharia.* Thanks to the quadrupling of oil prices in the early 1970s, the Gulf was awash with petrodollars, and Islamic banks were judged just another way of recycling the windfall income. The great gusher prompted neither departure from traditional casual attitudes about moving cash across borders nor enthusiasm for regulation. For the Muslim Brothers, Islamic banking was part revenge for political repression and past setbacks, part promise of renewed and enduring influence.[2] Soon Brothers' offshore banks were dotted around the globe, from the Bahamas to the Channel Islands and Lugano, a Swiss financial center located conveniently close to Milan for rich Italians—and others—to put cash beyond the taxman's grasp. From time to time in the 1980s, Islamic banks came in for unwanted, if fleeting, scrutiny for cornering Sudan's cereals market during a major famine and indulging in Ponzi schemes in Egypt.

Islamic banks long aroused little interest in the West.[3] Certainly, American and other Western officials gradually became aware of their sometimes questionable practices, but it was not until the mid-1990s that concern grew about their suspected role in jihadi extremism. For a long time Islamic banks were seen as an Arab world peculiarity. Eventually, Western bankers sought to compete by creating interest-free investment portfolios in keeping with that key requirement of Islamic banking. But for many Gulf Arabs, sudden prosperity only deepened an abiding fondness for cash, often big bundles of banknotes kept in pockets or desk drawers. Shakhbut was not alone.[4]

I came to appreciate the virtues of banknotes in the Third World, especially $100 bills, which I carefully folded four times to fit into money belts, making sure never to accept banknotes with the slightest suspect tear or disfiguring mark for fear they be rejected in some crucial transaction. I was honoring ancient local mores just as emerging Arab financiers from the Gulf were learning the ropes of the City in London and Wall Street. I did so because I was moving around in cash-and-carry country, often places in the throes of upheaval. I never knew when I would need cash to pay for a taxi to the border and safety or other emergencies that were a war correspondent's lot. Pristine, if creased, dollar bills were my generation's equivalent of the gold coins that Cyrus Sulzberger, chief foreign correspondent and columnist of the *New York Times*, always kept on his person when traveling through his beloved Balkans in the 1930s. Just the thing, he told me, to ensure strong arms would pull your car out of the mud.[5] Credit cards and ATMs eventually appeared even in much of my patch, and, alas, some Third World bad guys cottoned on to money belts.

But for most Arabs an attachment to folding money persisted. During the anti-Soviet jihad in Afghanistan, young Saudis routinely arrived with suitcases of freshly printed dollars in plastic packages for their favorite Afghan mujahedeen commanders. Such displays of wealth represented immediately recognizable clout. When I began pondering Osama's success in moving funds around, I tentatively concluded that any effort to track his financial dealings was going to be difficult, if not impossible, because of the cultural fixation with cash. Eventually a frustrated banker likened the endeavor to "looking for a needle in a needlestack."[6] A key government witness in the trial of four men convicted for their role in the 1998 car-bomb attacks in East Africa told a New York court three years later of his duties as an Al-Qaeda bag man, dropping off up to $100,000 in cash to like-minded Islamist radicals in Egypt, Jordan and Eritrea, among other places.[7] Customs officers at airports could be easily bribed, he said, not to open bags.

A onetime South Yemeni ally of Osama's confided to me that he regularly traveled to Jeddah in 1990 to pick up suitcases full of banknotes designed to further bin Laden's Islamist projects in Yemen. (The list of tasks over the next few years included, I knew, assassinating more than 100 leaders of the newly minted Socialist Party who, in the eyes of Osama and his friends as well as the North Yemenis, were still godless Communists, even if their Stalinist state in South Yemen had ceased to exist formally with official reunification in 1990.)[8] The context of our conversation about money was such that my Yemeni interlocutor clearly meant he was not confiding anything exceptional, much less secret. Cash was cash, and cash was the way business, sub rosa and aboveboard, was done. Formal borders were lines on maps, not realities, and often were not even demarcated. In any event, the same tribes existed on either side of much of the Saudi–Yemeni border (as was also the case with Pashtuns along the Afghan–Pakistani frontier, another artificial boundary Osama has frequented since the early 1980s).[9] Indeed the 1,800-mile-long frontier between Saudi Arabia and Yemen was notoriously porous when it came to not just money, but arms, explosives and men on the run.[10] And that border was just one of dozens such in the Third World.

It was easy enough to understand why borders meant so little to ordinary people. In addition to often arbitrary frontiers, many governments delighted in absurdly impractical mandatory currency declarations, requiring a statement upon arrival and departure and listing cash (but not necessarily traveler's checks) exchanged at authorized hotels or banks, often at outrageously skewed rates. In fact, immigration and customs officials often checked the declarations only when they wanted to intimidate foreigners (since locals in iffy circumstances knew how to routinely skirt immigration and customs formalities).[11]

In fact, when I started covering the Third World I took to using money belts because as a Westerner, and an American at that, I fully expected to be inspected with special thoroughness. But there were odd conventions. Actually obliging Westerners to empty their pockets, much less undo their belts (as opposed to going through suitcases), curiously remained taboo in most of the Third World. Still, you never knew when you would be searched. So my money belt's real function was to keep large amounts of cash neatly out of sight in a reliable and handy place. Maybe I was just lucky. The only time I came a cropper was with a busybody Greek customs official at Athens airport, and it was my fault because I forgot to wear the belt and he found it in my carry-on bag. But latter-day highwaymen operating in trains in Armenia and Azerbaijan, a smarter lot, soon after the Soviet Union's collapse regularly checked Westerners' belts and sometimes made off with the proceeds.

SINCE OSAMA first came to the attention of American intelligence agents, law-enforcement officials and diplomats as a financier of terrorism, I tried to learn how much was actually known about his financial modus operandi. In February 2000 I came away from a meeting with Richard A. Clarke, the hard-driving American counterterrorism expert, with the worrisome impression that the answer was not much or, perhaps more accurately, not much even that a consummate Beltway bureaucrat could act on. The encounter took place in room 303 of the Old Executive Office Building overlooking the Mall, and in a way I nonetheless was relieved as I walked back to the exit. Clarke could have fed me a line, bragging that he knew plenty, but I should understand he was not at liberty to share his knowledge with me. Instead, he left me with the distinct impression that his quandary was every bit as profound as mine (despite U.S. government computers chock-full of data).[12]

I was not really surprised. In fact, in a way I was testing Clarke. Barely three months after the East African embassies were car-bombed on August 7, 1998, an old friend intimately acquainted with counterterrorism described trying to figure out Osama's finances as "an exercise in frustration." To prove his point he said, "Where Osama keeps his money, how he moves his funds around, what their origin is, whom he pays—all that remains murky." "The National Security Council, State, Treasury, the FBI, the CIA," he added, "everyone has approached the problem intensely. But we have advanced exactly nowhere, and we lack enough hard information to approach a foreign government." Leads petered out largely because Osama had had fifteen years to salt away and invest his money.

Bank accounts were not in his name, and it was proving hard to uncover his cutouts.[13] Many months later I got the same message from a foreign-service friend in Pakistan who had served an earlier hitch during the anti-Soviet jihad. "We have only the haziest idea" how Al-Qaeda's finances are organized, he said. To illustrate American frustration, the diplomat cited the Al-Rashid trust, a Saudi-financed charity ostensibly involved in distributing humanitarian aid in Afghanistan and Pakistan. Wa'el Jelaidan, a Saudi active in the anti-Soviet jihad while working for the Saudi Red Crescent in the 1980s and then on good terms with Osama, was suspected, despite his denials, of using Al-Rashid for less-wholesome purposes in the 1990s. "We get no further than Al-Rashid's nominal boss, a somewhat vague Pakistani in his eighties," the diplomat said. Later, a complicating factor turned out to be President Pervez Musharraf's ex-officio presence on Al-Rashid's board. God knows, what passed for chapter and verse on the subject was there for the reading. Books around for years were full of detailed, if sometimes fanciful, information about Islamist bankers and businessmen, and their alleged links with Islamic terrorism, including Hezbollah and sundry Palestinian organizations, as well as favorite recipients stretching from Algeria to Chechnya and Central Asia.

Many were in the Gulf, especially Saudi Arabia and Dubai, others in Switzerland or offshore havens often on exotic islands. And they and their institutions generally stood accused of helping finance extremist Islamist organizations, including, of course, Al-Qaeda and its associates, directly or indirectly, to the tune of hundreds of millions of dollars. The events of September 11, 2001, durably froze American attention on the Kingdom for the inescapable reason that Osama and fifteen of the nineteen members of the suicide teams were from Saudi Arabia. The focus never moved far afield, and indeed narrowed after teams of Saudi jihadis targeted the capital, Riyadh, in suicide attacks that killed twenty-nine Saudis and foreigners, nine of them Americans, on May 12, 2003.[14]

Quite apart from complicated shell companies and banks, rich Gulf merchants, businessmen or princes (sometimes the same people) used Islamic charities to funnel funds to radical jihadis, including Al-Qaeda. Motivating them was a jumbled, and sometimes seemingly contradictory, mixture of protection money, genuine religious conviction in favor of jihadi Islam (or just plain, homegrown Wahhabism), resentment in Saudi Arabia against the Al-Saud and a desire to vent anti-Western feelings. None of that hodgepodge particularly surprised old Arab hands, at least not in general outline. Still, not all Saudi revenue was wasted on gold water taps or gambled away in Western casinos. Indeed, it was scarcely a secret that over the decades the Saudi regime made generous use of its checkbooks to please—and often keep at bay—the more powerful, whether the black-mailers were Iraqi thugs or even insistent Washington bureaucrats intent on selling a surfeit of warplanes or Boeing airliners to a Kingdom that lacked the capacity to put them to practical use.[15] Saudis were not the only Gulf Arabs to spend freely, either by choice or perceived necessity. The an-cient art of the shakedown, for instance, was evident in documents sal-vaged from a computer hard drive seized by police in Manila as early as 1995. A draft letter to a rich, recalcitrant Arab donor, apparently first ap-proached at a mosque in the Gulf, read: "Fear Allah, Mr. Siddiqi, there is a day of judgment."[16]

Doubtless, some Islamic charitable donations were skimmed for terror-ism, and clearly some rich Islamists deliberately made contributions to charities with a pretty good idea the money was quite likely to end up with Osama, probably, it was thought, by favoring terrorist front organizations. But how exactly was it done, how much was involved and how witting, if at all, were the donors? The Gulf Arabs were extremely reluctant to do much explaining, although their stonewalling played into their detractors' hands. Much of the public information seemed inspired by Western—and Is-raeli—intelligence agencies eager to influence a larger audience without having to stand up and authenticate their findings with ironclad evidence. Insinuation had its limits. Despite years of persistent efforts, for example, only after 9/11 did Israel and its friends persuade the United States to move against American-based Islamic charities helping Palestinian organiza-tions such as Islamic Jihad and Hamas, the prolonged inaction explained partly on grounds that some of the funds were spent on genuine humani-tarian aid, partly because no Americans or American interests had been targeted.

At times the details were suspect because of some telling, palpably erro-neous claim. Numbers tended to be biblical, or rather Koranic, a bit like the quintessentially uncheckable (and probably vastly exaggerated) $300 mil-lion the State Department claimed in 1999 was Osama's share of his father's heritage.[17] More reasoned estimates of his inheritance are in the $25 to $30 million range.

The problem, which Clarke and the other officials indirectly confirmed, was that it was often all but impossible to be sure or rather sure enough. Such were the limitations imposed by the rule of law in the United States before September 11, 2001. Very occasionally there were tantalizing clues. In

1997, Madani al-Tayeb, a Saudi citizen and Al-Qaeda's senior finance official, went through a major crisis of conscience and defected. Also known as Abu Fadl al-Makki, al-Tayeb had lost a leg fighting in Afghanistan and was believed to be married to a bin Laden relative. In 1995 and again 1996 he spent some time in London, according to several accounts, discussing his doubts about Al-Qaeda with radical Islamist exiles from Saudi Arabia. One such sympathetic Saudi told me al-Tayeb said he wanted to learn English, to live in the countryside, to remove himself from his life with Osama. Thus, the Saudi was not surprised when al-Tayeb decided, apparently without Kingdom pressure, to go back to Riyadh and recant the error of his ways. His two conditions—no prison and no torture—were accepted, my interlocutor said.

As far as I could ascertain when I was later in Saudi Arabia, the authorities kept their word, although my repeated efforts to find al-Tayeb there were unavailing. It stands to reason he told the authorities about Osama's worldwide finances in the minutest detail. But it is not clear how much they actually passed on to Washington and London. Still, a top-secret NSA report by early May 1997 had informed Clinton administration officials that, thanks to an intercept, "an unspecified country" had arrested a senior Al-Qaeda financial cadre who became a valuable intelligence source.[18] An apparently deliberate leak three months later seemed designed to panic Al-Qaeda. American officials never publicly mentioned al-Tayeb as a source of intelligence. Sharing the take on suspect Saudi citizens such as al-Tayeb would have marked an important departure from traditional Kingdom practice in those years.

Indeed, much to the accelerating fury of suspicious American officials, the Saudis, starting with Prince Nayef ibn Abdul Aziz, the interior minister, consistently refused to share potentially embarrassing intelligence even after September 11, 2001. Such was demonstrably the case in the November 13, 1995, terrorist operation against the Riyadh office of the Saudi Arabian National Guard program manager, in which five Americans died, and again in the car-bomb attack that killed nineteen American airmen in al-Khobar on June 25, 1996.

The Saudis carefully cultivated their secret garden and had no desire to let the FBI or any other foreign agency poke around digging up their weeds. The Al-Saud had never done so before and saw no reason for making an exception. In fairness, no government would welcome a foreign power delving into its inner workings. But not until the May 2003 attacks in Riyadh did the House of Saud take seriously Al-Qaeda's designs on the Kingdom and accept heightened cooperation with Washington.[19] In no way did this stance necessarily signal criminal coddling of anti-Western terrorism, although American officials long suspected the Al-Saud had much to hide, if only in their ever-delicate relations with the Wahhabi establishment and its proselytizing missions at home and abroad. But those acquainted with the vagaries of Saudi bookkeeping were quite prepared to believe that even with the best of intentions the authorities would have trouble figuring out how funds were disbursed. Foreign governments were angered by Saudi unwillingness, or inability, to understand the need to ensure that charitable contributions were effectively spent for their intended and aboveboard purposes. Part of the problem may have been due to the heavy-handed FBI, entrusted with Washington's lead responsibility in foreign investigations. As their rivals in the CIA and State Department never tired of pointing out, whatever the FBI's virtues, diplomacy and schmoozing with foreign governments were not, initially at least, its agents' forte.

The al-Tayeb case illustrated some tradecraft oddities in Al-Qaeda operations suggesting nonchalance bordering on sloppiness. Al-Tayeb was said to have returned to Saudi Arabia in May 1997 (even before the NSA report corroborated the date). But that news and other details, if accurate, were printed in London only that August in the *Daily Telegraph*, rightly or wrongly often seen as the British intelligence community's chosen instrument for disseminating such tidbits, and subsequently relayed on the BBC World Service radio's Africa Service. As court documents in the New York terrorism trial demonstrated, the BBC broadcast panicked the Al-Qaeda cell in Nairobi in which al-Tayeb had been intimately involved.[20] Curiously, nobody inside Al-Qaeda apparently had noticed al-Tayeb's disappearance, or if they had, no one bothered to warn the cell in Nairobi. Its members religiously listened to the BBC, heard the report and then read the story in the *Telegraph*. They suddenly felt they were in "100 percent danger." Frightened and cash-strapped members—down to their last $500—desperately sent off messages ever so deferentially asking the leadership for information and instructions. They became convinced—correctly, it turned out—that they were under American and Kenyan surveillance.[21] They specifically worried that al-Tayeb had compromised Al-Qaeda's financial links with supporters in Brooklyn, Jersey City and Detroit.[22]

When the Al-Qaeda subcell in Mombasa, Kenya's main port on the Swahili Coast, innocently called up, the Nairobi operatives told them never to use that telephone again because they were convinced it was bugged. When the Mombasa crowd did so anyway, they were barked at. Compounding the Nairobi cell's anguish was the fear that Osama and his top cadres still were unaware of al-Tayeb's defection. They sent off messages to Al-Qaeda leaders but received no answers. That prolonged silence only added to their paranoia. How could Osama not have noted al-Tayeb's absence? Why were they not informed promptly? On this occasion Al-Qaeda tradecraft seemed uncharacteristically offhand. If indeed Osama had not realized al-Tayeb's betrayal and failed to take fast remedial action, how much damage had his inconstant lieutenant's defection inflicted on Osama's financial—and other—operations? Did the Saudis act on the information quickly? Or did they simply store it because, in keeping with past form, taking action might implicate important Saudis, perhaps within the upper reaches of the royal family, and risk complicating the Kingdom's fraught relations with Washington?

After the Al-Qaeda leadership learned of the defection, how long did it take Osama to switch gears and set up alternative networks? Given their inherent suspicion of the outside world, the Saudis had no obvious interest in trumpeting their success in enticing Madani al-Tayeb to come home. It is, of course, always dangerous to extrapolate too much from court documents. But arguably the potential damage al-Tayeb's defection caused would have gravely impaired a more hierarchical organization. That was evidently not the case for Al-Qaeda or, if it was, then Osama is not known to have let on. He was never given to lamenting the arrest, defection or confessions of Al-Qaeda members in public. After all, much of Al-Qaeda's success depended on the very looseness and ambiguity of the connections linking its amoeba-like parts to other like-minded jihadis. In this particular case, Al-Qaeda's leadership demonstrated impressive powers of recuperation. Or perhaps Al-Qaeda was just lucky. After all, the same cell in Kenya carried out the attacks on the two American embassies (with, according to insiders, money, key bits of equipment and the master bomb artificer himself skip-jumped into place in professional, just-in-time manufacturing fashion, starting in Afghanistan, then skimming across the Red Sea from Yemen to Somalia, and thence across the border into Kenya).

American counterterrorism's initial ignorance of Al-Qaeda's financial inner workings was depressing enough. U.S officials also felt constrained by their own rules. I ran into an odd example while trying to help a friend. Aware that I was planning a trip to Washington in late December 2000, a

British colleague asked me to find out about an Islamist charity called the Muwafaq (Blessed Relief) Foundation, which had scuttled itself sometime in the late 1990s. Its onetime board members were suing my colleague's employer, a respected political newsletter in London called *Africa Confidential,* for linking the charity with a man involved in the nearly successful attempt by Egyptian jihadists to assassinate President Hosni Mubarak in Addis Ababa in June 1995. British libel laws are draconian and place the burden of proof on the defendant. It would be helpful, I thought, if the U.S. government would say what it knew about Muwafaq. So when I was talking again with Richard Clarke, I brought up the matter, and one of his assistants obligingly checked. Indeed, the charity was on an informal blacklist of the Treasury Department's watchdog Office of Foreign Assets Control.[23] But, no, was the answer, at that point going public was not on the cards. No explanation was offered. *Africa Confidential* was forced to make an expensive settlement.[24]

The administration's stance struck me as odd. To be sure, the charity had not financed a direct attack on U.S. interests. But Mubarak was a pro-American leader and the abortive attack had Sudanese fingerprints on it that further soured Washington's strained relations with Khartoum and resulted in UN sanctions against Sudan. Cracking down on terrorists' misuse of charities and other nongovernmental organizations seemed at face value to fit neatly into the remit of the international counterterrorism arsenal that grew out of drug-related money-laundering measures first endorsed at the 1989 summit of the world's major industrial powers, known then as the G7. Specific counterterrorism provisions were added in October 2001 after the September 11 attacks. Despite their increasingly stiff provisions, the hitch always seemed to be producing the evidence in court—or at least to the satisfaction of other countries, whose cooperation was vital for the United States if terrorist financing was to be blunted, much less stopped.

MANY COUNTRIES suspected of being soft on terrorist financing in fact ignored various other sleight-of-hand operations without obvious links with terrorism. A prime example was the *hawala* (transfer) system, which had much in common with the exchange methods of the Lombards in medieval Europe and flourished as far back as China's Tang Dynasty (A.D. 618–906). Its contemporary avatar took on enormous proportions when, with the oil boom of the 1970s, millions of poor people in the Third

World began flocking to jobs in the Gulf states and regularly sent money home to keep their families afloat. In Saudi Arabia, for example, foreign workers accounted for most of the estimated $15 billion the Kingdom sent abroad every year.[25]

Banks were slow, expensive and needlessly complicated for these often illiterate workers. *Hawalas* (called *hundis* in India and Pakistan) had agents in the smallest villages who seamlessly delivered the funds thanks to a network based on extended families and friends. No nosy bureaucracy was involved. At first glance, it was scarcely a secure system, yet in the final analysis the *hawala* system worked because any monkey business was punished harshly, less by violence than by loss of reputation. It worked as well because governments tried to enforce absurd, self-defeating regulations for official transactions. *Hawalas* also proved useful to the well heeled. Throughout much of the 1990s Pakistan went through a steady downward spiral. The rich and the middle class lost faith in the country and, disregarding laws against exporting capital, transferred billions of dollars abroad thanks to the *hawala* system. A notable spike in such transactions followed Pakistan's first nuclear tests in May 1998 and the immediate U.S. economic sanctions imposed for disregarding Washington's advice not to do so.

A Pakistani banker told me, "Hundreds of millions of dollars were sent out of the country via *hundis* within days." High-ranking politicians in government and the opposition found it convenient to use *hawalas* for their own corrupt purposes because such transfers were among the most difficult to trace in accounting terms. *Hawalas* traditionally also helped pay for the gold illegally smuggled from Dubai to India and Pakistan, where it was prized as a hedge against adversity. My Pakistani banker estimated that as much as half the region's transactions were "undocumented," a euphemism for *hawala* transfers used to pay for drugs, weapons, kickbacks and whatever else would not bear close scrutiny. For both straight and crooked, *hawalas* long remained under the intelligence and law-enforcement radar.

An otherwise scrupulously honest Pakistani friend justified the *hawala* system to me. His family had come from India when the British Raj ended in 1947, and recently an old aunt wanted to sell an apartment in Delhi. But India and Pakistan had no legal banking relations. So he went to a *hawala* dealer working out of a cubicle just big enough for a telephone, a fax, a kettle, a tea service and a few cushions. Over a cup of tea, he recalled, the dealer arranged the transaction and informed him, "Have your aunt go to the flower market near Delhi's central mosque and tell my agent the following number." Such deals were carried out by a coded fax or telephone call, through a third country if necessary. Typically, transactions often were recorded in a cheap notebook; when one was completed, a page was torn out and destroyed. The system was totally anonymous. No names and no addresses were required. There was no paper trail. Overhead was minimal. At regular intervals *hawala* dealers would tidy up their accounts. For just that purpose, enormous amounts of dollars and other currencies regularly arrived by courier or air freight in Dubai, host to most *hawala* dealings and the biggest banking center between Europe and Hong Kong.

Hawalas, of course, were just as ideal for terrorists as they were for remittances or tax-dodging fat cats. Terrorists' relatively modest needs could be hidden away in the great flow of "innocent" *hawala* transactions, which in normal times went unnoticed because all such transfers were tolerated. In one important way, money-laundering for purposes of terrorism was even easier than its more usual employment in legitimizing ill-gotten gains. As its name implies, money-laundering turns dirty money, generated by all kinds of lucrative illegal activities such as drugs, gambling and prostitution, into acceptable, bankable assets. But terrorists almost exclusively deal in money that started out clean as revenue from legitimate businesses, donations or *zakat,* usually the 2.5 percent tithe on wealth that good Muslims are enjoined to contribute to the poor. Only the use to which terrorists put these funds is dirty.

No one has succeeded in producing an accurate figure of how much money is laundered, much less the percentage involving terrorism. The International Monetary Fund has estimated that between $500 billion and $1.5 trillion is laundered every year, a spread equal to as much as 5 percent of gross world product and so glaringly imprecise and enormous as to suggest suspect guesswork.[26] Specialists believe that by far the biggest slice is generated by drugs, with terrorism's share relatively unimportant. Experts at the Financial Action Task Force based at the Organization for Economic Cooperation and Development in Paris have tracked money-laundering since 1989 in hopes of choking off illegal transfers. Since 2000 they have reviewed dozens of countries—large, small and often flyspeck—and used persistent suasion to get them to tighten up their banking legislation. Through the implicit threat to expose noncompliance, the experts have achieved some notable results.[27]

In recent years the Task Force has paid increasing attention to transactions with suspected links to terrorism, and in 2003 zeroed in on Islamic charities, applying the tools initially designed for laundering drug-trafficking profits and other criminal proceeds deposited in offshore havens. And for years I have regularly called or visited the same senior official and bothered him with the same question about terrorist finance. Just as regularly, he tells me which countries are on and off the black list of compliance with money-laundering rules, monotonously cautioning that the volume of laundering remains impossible to pin down. The degree of cooperation, especially in the Gulf, another specialist notes, is subject to serious interpretation. (One wag suggested a good start would be investigating Arab countries starting from the end of the alphabet, meaning Yemen, the U.A.E and Saudi Arabia.) My senior official always adds he is convinced now, as in the past, that terrorism finances account for just a tiny sliver of money laundered worldwide.[28]

He deliberately may have been playing down his own merit. Such modesty contrasted with the general U.S. theme, constantly repeated since 1996, that Osama was dangerous because of his financial mastery. Describing Osama as an Islamic Goldfinger was crucial in ousting him from Sudan. President Clinton articulated that theme even after the embassies in Kenya and Tanzania were car-bombed, labeling Osama as "the preeminent organizer and financier of international terrorism in the world today." In fact, those operations were the first acts of terrorism clearly traceable to Osama and, as such, proved he was much more than just that. Only very gradually did the United States learn much of anything about Osama's finances and other aspects of his modus operandi.

An early breakthrough came in 1996 in the form of a turncoat Sudanese Al-Qaeda member named Jamal Ahmad Mohammed al-Fadl. Unannounced, he walked into the American embassy in the Eritrean capital of Asmara and provided, among other things, a detailed insider's account of Osama's finances and organization, rivalries within Al-Qaeda, investments and extensive business investments in Sudan. Long known only as CS (for confidential source) 1, Fadl in the New York trial in 2001 became the key government witness whose testimony helped convict four men for their part in the attacks against the two embassies in East Africa. And in a stroke of luck three of those men, arrested soon after the attacks, talked freely to their American captors and filled in further financial details. That became public knowledge only during the trial, which ended with four life sentences.

The government's desire to keep key information secret until the trial itself was understandable. Still, every once in a while a slipup provided an intriguing insight into its problems in shutting down Osama's finances, a consistently embarrassing failing it had no interest in advertising. While I was in Pakistan in the summer of 1999, I read a short newspaper story. A high-powered U.S. government delegation from the State Department, the Treasury and other agencies was visiting Dubai, Saudi Arabia and Bahrain to follow up reports that $50 million had been transferred by rich Saudis to the Dubai Islamic Bank for Osama. That struck me as a great deal of money, especially to be so obviously transferred in one go. I was due in Dubai in any case and prevailed upon an influential retired State Department Arabist to provide an introduction. That proved a wise precaution and got me an appointment to see a wary American diplomat in Dubai a few months later.

He was reluctant to provide any details, much less reveal how Washington came to discover the suspect bank transfer in the first place. He made clear he was upset that news of the visit had leaked to the press. I nonetheless asked him why he thought Osama's purported benefactors had sent the funds by a classic bank transfer to the Dubai Islamic Bank, an institution specializing, like other Islamic banks, in highly speculative commodity trading with iffy countries, including Afghanistan under the Taliban. (The bank was founded in 1972 and was long owned by the Lootah family, known for its vast real estate holdings in Dubai. It had been involved in various scandals, including one in which an African scam artist recently had bilked it of millions of dollars. When I was there the bank was in the hands of an upright former central bank governor.)[29]

I failed to understand why Osama's would-be benefactors used such an obviously traceable procedure, since all foreign transactions of more than $10,000—reduced to $3,000 after 9/11—automatically went through the New York branch of the Federal Reserve for scrutiny and had done so for a long time. The Treasury over the years devised sophisticated software capable of sniffing out suspect bank accounts and distinguishing Arab names, despite their often baffling transliterated multiple variations. I asked the diplomat, "Wouldn't it have been smarter for them to have divided the funds into a series of transfers of under $1 million and sent the money via *hawala*?" I'd been told that $1 million was about the normal maximum for a *hawala* transaction and indeed most amounted to $5,000 or even less. He looked at me with astonishment. "Funny," he replied, "that is exactly what they asked" when the earnest American delegation had come calling during the summer. Who, I asked, were "they"? "The Maktoums," the ruling family in Dubai, he replied. The diplomat was not amused when I smiled. "Don't they realize," he all but hissed, "that the U.S. Fifth Fleet in the Gulf ultimately protects them from all kinds of predators, including Al-Qaeda?"

I REPRESSED the temptation to repeat what an Iraqi friend once described as the paradox of the Gulf Arabs. Of all the Arabs, he maintained, they can be the most anti-American. They know, he said, they are the most dependent on the United States for protection against larger, more populous and stronger neighbors, specifically Iran and Iraq. And they just hate it. Financing jihadi Islam might seem self-defeating, the Iraqi argued for what it was worth, but did constitute an emotional safety valve to alleviate a predicament they could not otherwise remedy. Nor did I tell the American diplomat the obvious. To my mind, yes and no were both correct answers to the question he had asked. If the rich were careless enough not to use a *hawala* to cover their tracks, then, Arab or not, they deserved to get into hot water with the United States. And if Americans were dumb enough to challenge frontally the ways of Gulf merchant princes, they, too, warranted no more than gracious promises and sugary words, used since time immemorial to calm the irascible, powerful, but ultimately transient foreigner.

With the Arabs, the United States long passed as a country without a colonial past—somehow Cuba, the Philippines and Central America in the early twentieth century didn't count. Such oversight had its advantages, and indeed Arabs had preferred the United States to Britain and France right after World War One, when asked their choice of Western mandatory powers in the former Ottoman lands in the early days of the League of Nations. The Arabs had believed Woodrow Wilson's catchy promise of "open covenants, openly arrived at." Those days are a distant memory. Now the United States was the undisputed superpower, and any superpower was always suspect in itself. America was also a busybody superpower seen by almost all Arabs as increasingly doing the bidding of their archenemy, Israel.

This self-indulgent thinking was arguably the most pernicious of illusions. It suggested that the Arabs, and especially the Saudis, thought of themselves as merely kibitzing spectators who need not take sides in a dangerous game. Just as jihadi Islam abruptly ended America's self-image as an untouchable sanctuary on September 11, 2001, so Al-Qaeda's attack on Riyadh in May 2003 shattered Saudi Arabia's much more limited reservoir of self-confidence. Osama had never made a secret of his desire for regime change in Saudi Arabia. That lethal three-pronged attack in Riyadh by suicide teams on three residential compounds largely reserved for foreigners brought home to every Saudi that this time they were not to be spared.

Henceforth, a reasonable citizen could not play down the thrust of terrorism directed against the Kingdom, as had been the case in 1995 and 1996. Then American servicemen died in attacks, and many Saudis brushed aside the implications by reassuring themselves that only Americans were killed. This time within days the Al-Saud gave the impression of realizing the error of clinging to such distinctions. Even after September 11, the royal family time and again had resisted Americans ever more insistent on full cooperation, especially on financial matters. No longer, it seemed.

One explanation for why Gulf money kept flowing Osama's way was that he knew he was pleasing the Arabs—and indeed many other Muslims—when he characterized American soldiers as paper tigers and pointed for proof to abrupt U.S. military withdrawals from Beirut and Mogadishu. But the real U.S. weakness was not military in any narrow sense of the word. Rather the Americans' failing was that without colonial experience they didn't have the trained manpower, the generations of friendships, the easy economic ties, the institutional knowledge, the police files, indeed everything that spelled inspired flair and intuition. The British mostly ruled with a light hand in easier times and did not seek to regulate what was beyond their needs or power (and even so their armies, like the French, were driven out of the Middle East or chose to leave because of the financial burden). Muddling through, they called it. It was not an American management technique. The dhows of Dubai had been trading with the rest of the Gulf and far beyond in Africa and the subcontinent for centuries before they were fitted out with powerful marine engines in recent decades.

Ship captains along Dubai's fabled Creek were expert in trading everything from gold for India and Pakistan (where such commerce was outlawed), to bootleg oil from Saddam Hussein's Iraq, beset by UN sanctions, and any other lucrative and often questionable commerce, including American goods U.S. legislation wanted the Islamic Republic of Iran deprived of. Helping grease the wheels of commerce—and enrich the emirates' 3 million inhabitants—were forty-seven banks and more than 100 money changers. Many of these institutions' employees were Indians, Pakistanis or other foreigners. They were guest workers happy to have their jobs and not inclined to risk them by confronting potentially dicey Arab customers and demanding more than summary identification, much less the detailed information Washington required.

During the Taliban period in Afghanistan, Dubai did brisk business with Kabul. The U.A.E. was one of the three countries that recognized the Afghan regime (along with Pakistan and Saudi Arabia). Osama was credited with having purchased in Dubai hundreds of secondhand Toyota pickups, which the Taliban used as modern-day cavalry in their war against the Northern Alliance of Ahmed Shah Massoud. Such an outlay represented a very major investment for parsimonious Osama, who until September 11 carefully husbanded his funds. The pickups were designed to keep Mullah Omar happy. They added punch to the non-Afghan volunteers of Al-Qaeda's 055 brigade, who provided zeal and backbone to the Taliban's own often less motivated fighters. Osama knew all about the soothing influence of gifts in foreign lands not adverse to the rewards of betrayal. "Betrayal is certainly not unknown in those mountains," said Milton Bearden, the CIA station chief who ran the final stage of the not-so-secret war against the Red Army in Afghanistan. "I always found a million dollars here and a million dollars there would work wonders."[30]

Osama, of course, was aware that the United States advertised far and wide a reward of $5 million, later raised to $25 million, for information leading to his arrest. Selling out foreign guests often is said to be forbidden in *pushtunwali*, the body of tribal law governing relationships among Pashtuns.[31] Still, Osama had lived long enough in Pakistan and Afghanistan to know that Arabs, especially jihadi Arabs, were not loved by everyday Afghans, who felt, with some reason, that Wahhabi Arabs looked down on them as backward bumpkins whose corrupted notion of Islam required strict Wahhabi remedial measures. Osama doled out cash to his hosts even while constantly flattering Mullah Omar and praising the Taliban as the beau ideal of Islamic governance.

Osama was only indulging in a habit that had stood him in good stead since his initial stint in Afghanistan in the 1980s. To smooth his arrival in Khartoum, Osama gave Turabi several million dollars cash upon first setting up shop and built a segment of road basically for free.[32] When he came back to Afghanistan from Sudan in May 1996, he spread money around in Jalalabad, a thriving smuggling center then run by former Afghan commanders in rapidly waning control of three eastern provinces bordering Pakistan. When the Taliban defeated the so-called Eastern Shura that September, Osama smoothly switched his allegiance to Mullah Omar, building him a pastel-colored palace in Kandahar and repairing stretches here and there of Afghanistan's wretched roads. Money—and Pakistani military advice and support—had helped the Taliban secure the loyalties of wavering warlords during their rapid advance. But money first and foremost represented a vital form of insurance. Cash helped guarantee Al-Qaeda recruits and officials virtually unimpeded passage in and out of Afghanistan and Pakistan and what amounted to sovereign immunity from Taliban interference in the archipelago of camps and offices Osama established or expanded upon his return. It was this money that allowed him to use Afghanistan for his peculiar purposes without having to bear the responsibility of formal government. In any event, the Taliban grew so dependent on Al-Qaeda's volunteer infantry that they learned not to ask questions about his training camps.

Still, gifts to key Pakistani officials Osama had cultivated for years kept them aware of his constant need to know about American plans against him. Even with minor officials, his operatives knew whom and how much to "sweeten," say at Peshawar airport, to ensure incoming volunteers for jihadi training trouble-free passage through customs and immigration and then across the nearby border into Afghanistan by bus.[33] In fact, Western intelligence analysts were convinced, very few bribes were needed since Pakistan's powerful ISI encouraged the arrival of jihadis. Still, money played an indirect part for Osama in the negotiations the United States conducted on and off with the Taliban. Washington dangled the international recognition the Taliban so dearly desired in exchange for handing over the Al-Qaeda leader.

And when the going got nasty, when the Taliban collapsed, money stayed the hand of would-be traitors. In the twilight of Taliban rule in December 2001, Osama personally distributed envelopes brimming with cash to tribal chieftains in Jalalabad before heading off for the mountains of Tora Bora near the Afghan–Pakistani border. Thoughtfully, some envelopes contained the banknotes of Iran and Pakistan, just in case the recipients decided to seek refuge in those two neighboring states.

Al-Qaeda extracted protection money, according to Osama's Western critics. But aside from what remained of his own personal fortune, almost all of his funding came from witting donations in the Gulf and was spent freely in Afghanistan and Pakistan. Westerners could well find that abhorrent, but there were plenty of Arabs willing to give generously to propagate Wahhabism and fund the Taliban, Pakistan jihadi leaders, their *madrasas* and indeed Osama. Despite persistent rumors, no solid evidence has established that Osama sought to make money in Afghanistan (or anywhere else he had field operations, for that matter). It was clear enough where his money went. His biggest outlays were spent on the training camps in Afghanistan, which he kept going even during his Sudan period. The output of volunteers increased enormously once he gained Mullah Omar's confidence and did not waver until September 11, 2001. Those camps churned out foot soldiers wholesale—some American estimates ran as high as 30,000 over a decade—and a much smaller and selective group of better trained terrorists, some of whom were given a small grub stake and instructed to carry out operations in their home countries or the West. U.S. government accusations that Osama was making money in the opium trade have never been verified and seem based more on deductive reasoning than on hard fact. Frankly, he was likely far too busy running Al-Qaeda. But European intelligence analysts are convinced he had discussions with key traffickers and reached an understanding with them on sensible coexistence.

To have horned in on Afghanistan's lucrative opium trade, moreover, would have been risky. Such interference would have been all too likely to arouse the ire of the well-placed and powerful Afghans and Pakistanis involved in the traffic since the 1980s. It also would have angered his Taliban hosts, who derived a good slice of their revenue from taxing peasant opium-poppy growers.[34] The 2003 crop was estimated at 4,000 metric tons. Narcotics experts are convinced that at most Osama's involvement was limited to providing contacts abroad, key people who might prove helpful to the unworldly Taliban. Since the Taliban in many instances retained the local commanders they persuaded to come over to the cause, these warlords already were well versed in the intricacies of the traffic. The experts' professional doubts did not stop Osama's enemies—including the Indians, the Saudi-owned press and Western governments—from accusing him of trafficking in drugs. They reasoned that he backed Islamic insurgencies in

Central Asia and Chechnya and had agents in many countries, so it seemed logical that he would have done what the French and Americans, among many others, had done before him: used narcotics to pay for operations. Western governments out to blacken his reputation were sparing in hard facts, but not blunderbuss accusations. One example among many was the claim in the British government dossier issued on October 4, 2001, to justify the coming American-led campaign against the Taliban and Al-Qaeda, that "they jointly exploit the Afghan drugs trade." No corroborating details were provided despite major expenditures designed to produce ironclad evidence. (Western intelligence analysts privately argue that as time went by the Taliban, who did levy a 10 percent tax on traffickers, and Al-Qaeda became virtually indistinguishable, and indeed Osama effectively came to control his hosts.) In any event, many of the same warlords involved in the trade in the past survived the 2001 fighting and are again trafficking in drugs. The main difference is that increasingly the Afghans have raised the value added of their opium by transforming much of it into heroin instead of primarily exporting raw, dried poppy as in the past.[35] The International Monetary Fund believes "the export of opium and its derivatives, which yielded about $2.5 billion last year, now accounts for half of Afghanistan's Gross Domestic Product."[36]

As Osama's reputed purchase of used Japanese pickups demonstrated, Dubai was the tolerant, everything-goes hub so vital for all manner of intolerant regimes, such as the ayatollahs' Iran, Saddam's Iraq and the Taliban. Above everything, Dubai was a trading center with excellent banking and communications and few rules. Goods of all descriptions, but especially refrigerators, television sets and household electronics, were dispatched as part of Dubai's multimillion-dollar trade, sent first by dhow across the Gulf, then trucked across Iran or Pakistan and into Afghanistan.[37] The truckers had helped finance the Taliban's rise to power, preferring to pay them a single tax rather than having to deal with troublesome roadblocks manned by greedy warlords every few miles. The Taliban and the powerful Afghan trucking cartel earned considerable revenue by smuggling these goods into Pakistan. It was a perversion of the half-century-old arrangement between Pakistan and Afghanistan allowing Kabul to use the Pakistani port of Karachi for goods to be sold in Central Asia. And the Taliban punished their Pakistani allies by depriving them of badly needed customs revenue. That was a price the Pakistani establishment willingly paid in fulfillment of its will-o'-the-wisp dream of using Afghanistan for strategic depth against its hereditary enemy India. Osama was welcomed because he was useful to the Taliban who were useful to Pakistan.

SEPTEMBER 11, 2001, radically changed Washington's approach to terrorist finances. Within weeks Congress rushed through the USA Patriot Act. The new law vastly and controversially restricted civil liberties, expanded the government's ability to snoop at home and abroad and authorized the seizure of funds practically whenever and wherever it saw fit. Suddenly American banks were effectively banned from operating offshore shell banks, and other loopholes tolerated by the Bush administration were closed. For example, its earlier defense of tax havens—one of its trademark challenges to multilateral international cooperation in its initial months— was buried quietly and without ceremony. Despite the intelligence community's failings, and the crippling rivalries between the CIA, the FBI and other agencies that came to light, a great deal of information was rapidly made public, especially about money. Within days it was apparent that much of the September 11 suicide teams' success stemmed from a major departure from what Western intelligence thought had become Al-Qaeda's standard modus operandi.

Instead of scrounging for money to keep going in the targeted country, this time the terrorists were wired generous funds from abroad in their own names or brought in large amounts of cash that they legally declared to U.S. customs officers. By Al-Qaeda standards, Osama had bet the bank. But Americans who had not yet grasped the cheapness of other terrorist operations were astonished by how little these attacks cost. More than a year after 9/11, the U.S. government estimated the operations cost between $500,000 and $600,000, amounts that were later drastically scaled back to $175,000 to $250,000 by the FBI.[38] The larger sum was initially viewed by many Americans as a pittance, but in fact even the reduced estimate represented a fortune in historical terrorist terms. The campaign of terror in France in the summer of 1995 cost little more than $40,000, according to French counterterrorism officials, who suspect that Osama may have provided some of the financing dispatched via Western Union from London.[39] No more extravagant were operations involving truck and car bombs, a time-honored terror technique employed against the East African embassies in 1998, the American airmen's barracks in al-Khobar in 1996 and the Bali nightclub in 2002.[40]

Similarly, terrorist operations—in Tunisia, Indonesia, Morocco, Pakistan, Saudi Arabia, Spain, Turkey and again Kenya, even the 2000 attack on the USS *Cole* in Aden harbor and a later attack against a French supertanker off the Yemeni coast—all fell into the same classic budget-priced category. In the past, jihadi terrorists on short rations had come to grief when caught for petty crimes committed to keep themselves going as they prepared their operations (although with thefts sometimes amounting to no more than $50 a go, the police often took some time to catch on). Even for major undertakings Osama had rarely wagered much. When he approved plans, he generally preferred to encourage operatives with a smallish sum they were left to supplement by themselves once their operations took shape on the ground. No wonder Al-Qaeda was sometimes called the "Ford Foundation of terrorism" because of its seed-money approach. (Ahmad Ressam, for example, was entrusted with just $12,000 when he left Al-Qaeda bomb-making training in Afghanistan in 1999, with orders to dream up and execute a spectacular operation in the United States to mark the millennium.)

Radical jihadis had learned the hard way that sooner or later the dumbest police catch on to classic petty money-making dodges. Jihadis in Egypt robbed Coptic Christian jewelry shops. Their Indonesian counterparts held up gold merchants. In western Europe and North America, jihadis took full advantage of government welfare. Other standard favorites involved the theft of cell phones or credit and debit cards. In Europe jihadis acquired secondhand cars and resold them in Africa or the Middle East. They also acquired legitimate businesses to provide employment and cover for their operatives—gas stations and pizza parlors in Britain, automobile tire shops in Nairobi and Dar es Salaam, a fishing boat on Kenya's coast. Some of these tricks were eventually rolled up, but most continued and probably always will.

For September 11 Osama changed tactics and shelled out. All the financial dealings were aboveboard and aroused no suspicions. His teams spent money rather than scammed for funds. The meticulously planned American operation was the brainchild of Khaled Sheikh Mohammed, an ethnic Baluch and Pakistani citizen who was born and brought up in Kuwait and educated as an engineer in North Carolina in the mid-1980s. The apparent prototype operation for the attack was carried out by his nephew Ramzi

Youssef. He had staged the first bombing against the World Trade Center in 1993 and escaped, and later, when living in Manila, was thwarted in his plans to destroy American airliners. Other jihadi terrorists had digested his advice. When Youssef was captured in Pakistan and flown back to New York in 1996 to face charges in the first World Trade Center case, he told his interrogators that had he had more money he would have "made a more efficient bomb."[41]

From the very start of the September 11 plot, which began taking form in early 1999, Mohammed delegated financial details to Mustafa Ahmed Hawsawi, a Saudi Al-Qaeda specialist based in the United Arab Emirates. He was the paymaster who wired the money from the emirate of Sharjah to various American banks, effortlessly setting up some thirty-five separate accounts with little fuss, thanks to bankers who obligingly entered random digits to meet the requirement for Social Security numbers that the hijackers did not possess.[42] In the single biggest blow to Al-Qaeda since its inception, Mohammed and Hawsawi were arrested together in March 2003 at the home of a radical Pakistani Islamist in Rawalpindi, the old British garrison town and latterly a major Pakistani army headquarters.

An American government executive jet flew back to Washington with a trove of seized mobile telephones, paper documents and computers, all of which provided further information about Al-Qaeda financial operations. But until then Al-Qaeda had proven amazingly resilient in recovering from admittedly less-telling setbacks. Hawsawi had taken the precaution of not using his own name in making legitimate transfers via banks and money-changers to keep the suicide teams in cash (with an occasional additional transfer from Germany). Since the Al-Qaeda teams in the United States knew they were going to die—and were proud of their martyrdom mission—they used their own names to open bank accounts, obtain drivers' licenses and pay rent. Still they were incredibly lucky, for had it not been for bureaucratic error, the plot could well have been uncovered.[43] In fact. they left so many clues—either inadvertently or on purpose—that after September 11 law-enforcement officials quickly traced bank and credit-card transactions and ATM withdrawals for everything from airline tickets and rent to flight-school fees and car rentals.

The suicide teams even allowed themselves a nice final touch. Just days before the attacks, some $25,000 they no longer needed was wired back to Hawsawi via a Sharjah money-changer. It remains unclear if that transfer was dictated by thrift, derision or, as seems likely, a basically honest return of surplus operational funds. It certainly helped confirm U.S. suspicions that the recipient, Hawsawi, was not just the same man who had wired more than $100,000 to the suicide teams in the United States. He clearly was a key Al-Qaeda financial officer.[44] His eventual comeuppance, it has been suggested, was perhaps due to this bit of derring-do, which left telltale clues in Sharjah. Still, even if the return of those funds bore the mark of ever-penny-pinching Osama, the transfers also served as a galling reminder that the 9/11 operators were sure enough of themselves to risk providing a clue for American investigators.

ONCE THE ADMINISTRATION recovered from the initial shock of the September 11 attacks, Washington moved quickly to put long-suspect organizations, banks, charities and individuals on terrorist watch lists, freezing their American and overseas assets and asking friendly governments to do likewise. The immediate focus was on Saudi Arabia, which was home to all but four of the nineteen hijackers. Ordinary Americans and politicians were furious that a longtime ally somehow had not nipped the plot in the bud. The administration went through muscular motions in a kind of virtual "perp walk," a favorite law-enforcement tactic involving deliberately shaming high-profile defendants by exposing them to the full glare of publicity. In fact, none of those frozen funds were directly linked to financing the attacks in New York and Washington. But in the first few months updated lists of individuals, corporations and foundations at home and abroad kept spewing out of Washington. The Europeans rapidly agreed to a degree of hitherto unimaginable cooperation. Britain, Canada and Ireland, which had resisted American efforts to extradite suspects in the name of their exacting standards of evidence, began cooperating to some extent. An English court in early 2002 refused the U.S. request to extradite an Algerian pilot named Lotfi Raissi for lack of evidence. He was released and sued the U.S. Department of Justice and the FBI for falsely accusing him of having trained the September 11 suicide pilots in Arizona.[45] For similar reasons, another English court the same year would not extradite Yasser Sirri, accused of helping in the assassination of Ahmad Shah Massoud. He, too, was released. And Khalid al-Fawwaz, Osama's man in London, is still in England, if in jail, more than five years after his extradition was requested following the attacks on the two U.S. embassies in East Africa. For many Americans distressed by the unmistakable intelligence debacle, the administration at least seemed fast off the mark in following the money trail. Specialists were less impressed. They realized Washington had accumulated a backlog of detailed information that legal constraints had kept officials from acting on. It no longer mattered that the available evidence would not have secured convictions before September 11. At long last the gloves were off.

In the months immediately after the attacks, the United States and its allies, often at American request, seized or froze $112 million in assets belonging to some 240 often long-suspected members or supporters of Al-Qaeda and other terrorist organizations.[46] According to a UN report, roughly half the frozen money was said to be linked with Al-Qaeda or the Taliban although the evidence was rarely made public.[47] Funds seized in the United States and Saudi Arabia amounted, respectively, to just $36 million and $5.5 million of that total.[48] Much of the money frozen domestically belonged to the Taliban. Occasionally the administration departed from its fixation with secrecy to explain the whys and wherefores of its actions. For example, in November, Al-Barakaat, a Dubai-based *hawala* dealer, with offices in more than forty countries, was shut down in the United States, much to the consternation of hundreds of thousands of Somalis resident abroad—including some 25,000 to 30,000 living in Minnesota and elsewhere in the United States—who regularly used it to send money back home to their families. U.S. officials were unmoved by the hardship visited on these remittances, the country's biggest source of revenue, and by arguments that shutting down Al-Barakaat was likely to swell pro-Osama feelings there.

Since Somalia no longer had a formal banking system, Al-Barakaat clearly provided useful services. President Bush himself accused Al-Barakaat of raising, investing and distributing funds for Al-Qaeda's benefit but did not link its operation specifically to the September 11 attacks. U.S. officials insisted, without producing any evidence, that Osama was creaming off the remittances handled by Al-Barakaat, one of many scams that they estimated raked in between $20 and $30 million a year for Al-Qaeda. They also accused Al-Barakaat of providing Osama with a secure near-worldwide communications system.[49] Since Somalia had ceased to exist as a viable state, Al-Barakaat's operations there were easy pickings. Still, not everyone was convinced by the U.S. case or Attorney General John Ashcroft's fondness for a shotgun approach. In Sweden the government took up the cudgels for three Somali-born Swedish citizens employed by

Al-Barakaat whose assets had been frozen. And Luxembourg released frozen assets allegedly connected to Al-Barakaat because authorities there felt they did not have sufficient access to reliable intelligence information related to the case.

In Saudi Arabia, Yassin Abdullah al-Qadi, a well-known businessman with Islamist leanings, was one of the first Saudis to have his assets frozen in the Kingdom and abroad. He noisily protested his innocence and sued, so far unavailingly, in London to have his holdings in Britain unfrozen. Zeroing in on Qadi and a handful of the wealthy Saudis was the administration's way of saying that this time it meant business. Washington was signaling it was no longer willing to be fobbed off with Saudis' protestations of innocence and professions of renewed willingness to improve cooperation. For many years the United States and other Western governments had made representations to Saudi authorities, imploring them to monitor funds sent overseas for charitable purposes. To no avail.

Treasury Department officials specifically said they acted against Qadi in October 2001 because he and other prominent Saudis had transferred millions of dollars to Osama using charities, including the Muwafaq Foundation, the very Islamic nongovernmental organization that had caused *Africa Confidential* legal grief in London. Qadi had served as chairman of Muwafaq's board of trustees. Also on the board were Abderrahman bin Mahfouz, the son of Khalid bin Mahfouz (the founder of the National Commercial Bank), and another member of that most senior Hadhrami family, long the Al-Saud's favorite bankers.[50] Qadi was on record as protesting that Muwafaq only built schools and mosques and paid for educational programs in Afghanistan and Sudan. Ironically, in view of the Bush administration's post–September 11 moves against Qadi and Muwafaq, just months before the attacks against New York and Washington the charity's former trustees won their libel case in London, but curiously the court decision did not request *Africa Confidential* to publish a retraction.

Still, in 2000 I questioned a senior representative of the World Muslim League, an official Saudi charity that annually dispensed hundreds of millions of dollars abroad through various entities, including the International Islamic Relief Organization.[51] Why did foreign governments, especially the United States, keep insisting that the Kingdom failed to keep accounting records justifying outlays for charity? The response was heartfelt, mechanical and tantalizingly uninformative. "Government funds are monitored scrupulously," my interlocutor insisted, "but we have no right to supervise donations for private charity, which is an Islamic duty." Senior Saudi cadres earnestly asked for details when foreign officials asked them to turn off a suspicious spigot. Saudis noted that many fortunes long since had migrated to banks overseas and thus beyond their reach. The rub, of course, was that Saudi society was so opaque that it was, for all intents and purposes, impossible to discern where public funding ended and private contributions began. Thanks to their control of oil revenue, the Al-Saud were believed to have an interest in practically every major business in the Kingdom. In many they did, but not all.

Of course, that did not mean the royal family deliberately was encouraging Islamic jihadi terrorism. But much of Saudi domestic affairs involved tolerating seemingly unhealthy arrangements in everything from the narrow Wahhabi version of Islam dispensed in schools to sloppy controls of overseas aid that ended up propagating and financing that very same view of Islam in hundreds, indeed thousands, of *madrasas* from Pakistan to Central Asia and Black Africa. No Saudi official wanted any foreigner, much less the Kingdom's all-powerful, but infidel American protector, uncovering any manner of potentially embarrassing private arrangements.

Well before 9/11, many Saudis understood that the Al-Sauds' covenant with the Wahhabi establishment was coming in for increasing domestic and especially foreign scrutiny, even if in their own minds they felt they had nothing to hide. Any hint of foreign intrusion in the Kingdom caused them to recoil. Since the quadrupling of oil prices in 1973, petrodollars had propelled Wahhabism abroad in well-financed programs to build thousands of mosques and pay for religious instruction and imams' salaries, not just in the Muslim world but as far afield as the United States. Proselytism traditionally is part and parcel of many religions, as the history of Christian missionaries demonstrates. The difference was that the Saudis were ready to disburse their fabulous riches to propagate their faith. Such Saudi largesse made sense in local terms: Saudi Arabia hosts Islam's two holiest sites, and by encouraging Wahhabism abroad the Al-Saud tried to preempt homegrown Islamist opposition. Still, such lavish expenditures were sure to raise hackles overseas.

But it was all rooted in a compromise worked out in the aftermath of the 1979 occupation of Mecca's Grand Mosque: the royal family basically gave the Wahhabi elders a free hand and the necessary funds to proselytize abroad in return for silence about the family's notorious personal excesses. Two other timely reasons were involved. Ayatollah Ruhollah Khomeini's

Islamic revolution earlier in the year had seized power in Iran, projecting a Shi'a threat to the Kingdom's claims to mainstream (Sunni) Islamic purity. And in preparation for mounting the throne, Crown Prince Fahd wanted to shed his reputation as a playboy wastrel and turned loose the *mutawa'een* religious police.[52] American enthusiasm for Saudi bankrolling of the anti-Soviet Afghan jihad obscured the arrangement until the Red Army withdrew from Afghanistan in 1989. Saudi money in one form or another had helped Afghan refugees in Pakistan, educating them—and poor Muslims from Pakistan and Central Asia—in the narrow, exclusively religious curriculum in thousands of Deobandi-rite, boarding-school *madrasa*s there. These schools, in which the Taliban was created in Pakistan, later churned out leaders and cannon fodder for the Taliban jihad. Saudi money was also held responsible for the sporadic violence pitting Pakistan's Sunni mainstream against the Shi'a minority, sometimes explained away as a prolongation of that other conflict pitting Saudi Arabia against Iran (but in fact a reflection of long-standing sectarianism). Rightly or wrongly, the Saudis supposed that financing such tensions, in which hundreds of Pakistanis were killed, caused few qualms in Washington.

American interest in ferreting out Saudi financing for such Islamic charities had accelerated after the destruction of the East African embassies in August 1998 and the attack that nearly sank the USS *Cole* in Aden. Occasionally Washington flexed its muscles, especially when Al-Qaeda was under suspicion. Before the new year, U.S. pressure persuaded Kenya to close down local chapters of suspect Islamic charities, including Al-Haramain, the International Islamic Relief Organization (IIRO) and the Mercy International Relief Agency. (Kenya since has authorized them to resume some programs.) Clamping down on the IIRO, an official Saudi charity over which the World Muslim League exercised operational control, was a clear signal to the Al-Saud.

U.S. intelligence was sufficiently solid half a year before the September 11 attacks to bring about the revocation of the charter of the bank Al-Taqwa in Nassau in the Bahamas, an offshore tax haven much favored by American and other businesses. Al-Taqwa, for years under surveillance from Egyptian and Western intelligence organizations, occasionally was mentioned in the media and books, albeit it was often referred to only by the initials A.T. to avoid libel action. Egyptian, U.S. and other Western specialists had long suspected this well-known Muslim Brothers bank had ties to Al-Qaeda as well as to radical Algerian, Egyptian and Palestinian Islamist groups. (One persistent rumor suggested Osama had been bugged telephoning the bank in Nassau in 1996 to discuss rearranging his finances at the time of his departure from Khartoum.) Al-Taqwa representatives insisted the Nassau bank closed voluntarily because of trading losses, and steadfastly denied any involvement in funding terror. The Bahamian authorities turned over to Washington the record of its operations in November 2001.

That same year Al-Taqwa's Italian–Swiss branch was wound up, and the name plate in the Lugano, Switzerland, office building that once housed the bank was changed to read Nada Management. Muslim Brother Youssef Nada had left his native Egypt under a cloud in 1959 and made a fortune in the Gulf before helping found Al-Taqwa in 1987. The septuagenarian banker protested he had done nothing wrong in terms of Swiss regulations. Swiss police questioned Nada, then released him. Indeed the Swiss Banking Commission gave him and the establishment a clean bill of health that October. But in the immediate wake of September 11, such was U.S. pressure that Swiss police raided Nada Management in November, just before Washington named it as a sponsor of terrorism.

Senior American officials insisted Al-Taqwa and Al-Barakaat raised, invested and managed funds for Al-Qaeda. Nada's detractors suggested a keen knowledge of local loopholes had helped him fend off threatened closure for years. Thanks to his acquired Italian nationality, Nada was allowed to live in the town of Campione d'Italia, an Italian enclave on Lake Lugano surrounded by Swiss territory. He was legally entitled to reside, but not work, in Italy. Swiss law allowed him to work in the city of Lugano, but not to live in Switzerland. By the end of 2002 Nada Management was forced to close, but a year later Nada companies were reported back in business in real estate and investment funds in Liechtenstein and Switzerland.[53] The persistent inability to neutralize Nada illustrated Attorney General Ashcroft's abiding difficulty in his overseas endeavors. To stamp out the likes of Nada for good, international assistance was required. That meant sharing intelligence and maintaining good relations with foreign governments, not notable Bush administration attributes.

In the United States Ashcroft, anxious to be seen cracking down fast and hard on terrorists, went for low-hanging fruit. Throwing the book at a handful of Americans of Yemeni descent in Lackawanna, New York, who had been foolish enough to have trained briefly at an Al-Qaeda camp in Afghanistan, brought headlines and convictions for his Department of Justice. So did other easy-pickings cases dotted around the country. Additionally, once the Taliban were defeated and the administration no longer felt the need to humor the Muslim world, out went the immediate post–9/11 tolerance of terrorism as long as it was not deemed to possess "global reach." Much to Israel's pleasure, henceforth all terrorism was lumped together and condemned. Thus the Department of Justice in December 2001 seized assets belonging to well-known Islamic charities in the United States long suspected of financing Palestinian Islamists opposed to Israel's occupation of Arab land. Suddenly in trouble were the Holy Land Foundation for Relief and Development, based in Richardson, Texas and considered the largest in the country, the Benevolence International Foundation of Peoria, Illinois, the Quranic Literary Institute and another Illinois-based charity called the Global Relief Foundation.

American Zionists and the Israeli government for years had sought in vain the closure of these foundations on grounds they were raising money for Hamas and other Palestinian causes and specifically providing funds for the families of suicide bombers. (In fact, it turned out, Benevolence International had little interest in Palestine but was involved in Al-Qaeda ventures in Chechnya and in postwar Bosnia.) Successive administrations had demurred partly because the pro-Palestinian charities had not targeted Americans or American interests, partly because Hamas and the others, whatever else they did, also provided legitimate humanitarian aid and in any case were not breaking U.S. laws.[54]

Of the initial list of Islamic charities whose resources were frozen in 2001, only Benevolence International and Global Relief turned out to have links with Al-Qaeda. Even so the Department of Justice preferred not to spell out these connections in prosecuting them. Indeed, the Department eventually had to back down in its case against Global Relief and its Lebanese co-founder, Rabih Haddad. He spent seventeen months after 9/11 in a Michigan jail, accused of funneling money to Al-Qaeda. But neither he nor his charity was charged with the offense. Instead, he was deported to his homeland in mid-July 2003 for having overstayed his visa. Global Relief filed a defamation suit in February 2002. Similarly, Enaam Arnaout of Benevolence International pled guilty to charges not linked to Al-Qaeda.[55] The crackdown on these organizations' funds was made possible only by the Patriot Act's vastly widened powers—and the president's decision to seek and destroy (almost) all terrorism. Swept away were long-sacrosanct firewalls limiting the use of intelligence files in bringing prosecutions. A

controversial exception was the Mujahedeen Khalq (MK), an Iranian opposition organization on the State Department terrorist list. The MK over
the years changed its political coloration from extreme left to extreme right
and for fifteen years had repaid Saddam Hussein's hospitality on Iraqi soil
by doing his dirty work, notably in helping Saddam brutally put down
the uprising of Iraqi Kurds in 1991. The MK's opposition to Iran's Islamic
republic won it considerable support from principally right-wing congressmen despite its terrorist organization status. Accordingly, its brigade-
strength forces were surrounded but not totally disarmed or dissolved in
April 2003 when American troops overthrew Saddam's army. That curious
favor reflected influential neoconservatives' hopes of refashioning the
Middle East by using the MK against the regime in Tehran. Such notions
ignored the fact that the organization's alliance with archenemy Iraq long
since had forfeited virtually all support in Iran. Significantly, in July 2003
the Bush administration demanded that Tehran hand over key Al-Qaeda
leaders it insisted were sheltered in Iran, and later refused an Iranian coun-
teroffer to exchange them for senior MK officials in Iraq.[56]

The most intriguing U.S.–based Islamic charity suspected of links to
Al-Qaeda turned out to be, or rather had been, SAAR—sometimes known
as the Safa Group Foundation—based in the Washington suburb of Hern-
don, Virginia. (Wafa, another Islamic charity, but located in Saudi Arabia,
also was suspected of having ties to Al-Qaeda.) SAAR's inventive mix of
profit and nonprofit entities distinguished it from simpler charities. Its
maze of apparently interlocking foundations, companies, and financial institutions had belonged to the family of Suleiman Abdulaziz al-Rajhi, one
of Saudi Arabia's wealthiest dynasties, before the foundation itself was liquidated in December 2000.[57] The Department of Justice tracked SAAR's
interests in eighteen countries ranging from the United States and Saudia
Arabia to Turkey, Malaysia, Switzerland and Morocco. (Significantly, SAAR
had shared offices with the Al-Taqwa in the Bahamas, further adding to
suspicions of financial connections to Al-Qaeda.)

In March 2002 SAAR's various offices were raided and truckloads of
records and computers seized. But the administration at the time acknowledged that no evidence connected SAAR to specific acts of Al-Qaeda terrorism.[58] Because of bureaucratic turf battles, the seized documents had
led to no charges whatsoever more than eighteen months later while some
of the scuttled foundation's various entities remained operational.[59] A 101-
page affidavit, released in October 2003, reflected a frustrated law enforce-

ment agent's evidence-shy conclusion: "There appears to be no innocent explanation for the use of layers and layers of transactions between Safa Group companies and charities other than to throw law enforcement authorities off the trail."[60] Also under suspicion of financing Al-Qaeda was the Muwafaq Foundation, which the Department of the Treasury in November 2001 finally had described as an Al-Qaeda front organization.

After that initial spasm of freezing suspect assets soon after the September 11 attacks, a lull ensued. A UN report noted that in the first eight months of 2002, only $10 million more had been neutralized.[61] (Treasury Department statistics listed a grand total of $137 million as frozen by the United States and its allies in the two years following 9/11. Involved were 321 individuals and organizations.)[62] The report estimated that Al-Qaeda money managers in North Africa, the Middle East and Asia had at least $30 million invested. Annual donations, it suggested, were in the $16 million range and were continuing to flow without significant obstruction. Following the East African bombings, Al-Qaeda had adjusted to Washington's heightened interest in stemming the more obvious transfers of funds.

The UN report noted a gradual shift from traditional investments into gold and other precious metals and gemstones such as diamonds, lapis lazuli, tanzanite—the kind of largely untraceable riches as easy to transport as they were to turn into cash. Al-Qaeda involvement with tanzanite mining in East Africa dated from Osama's Sudan period. An important switch into gemstones had begun in the late 1990s. Many of the diamonds were purchased in Liberia and Sierra Leone, quintessential failed states in West Africa years before Al-Qaeda discovered their utility. Both countries were victims of long-standing civil war that had reduced them to a textbook state of savagery and indigence, bereft of electricity, running water, indeed any form of administration. In 1995 I spent two days in the alluvial diamond-mining town of Kenema in Sierra Leone, then temporarily protected by South African and Namibian mercenaries who had recently kicked out Liberian-backed rebels.

The mercenaries made sure the government got a share of the diamonds and they got theirs. Kenema and other diamond towns were notorious for trafficking with Lebanese—and sometimes Israeli—dealers in these illegal, so-called blood or conflict diamonds. Sharing the lucrative spoils were Charles Taylor, the rebel-turned-president of Liberia, and his ally Foday Sankoh, the sanguinary leader in neighboring Sierra Leone of the Revolutionary United Front (RUF). In the months before its attacks on New York and Washington, Al-Qaeda transferred millions of dollars of potentially vulnerable funds from Switzerland and elsewhere to Taylor, who paid Osama back in diamonds.[63] Taylor's links with Pat Robertson and other influential members of the Christian Right apparently accounted for FBI and CIA reluctance to seriously investigate his involvement with Al-Qaeda. Taylor was indicted in March 2003, for crimes against humanity by the United Nations–backed Special Court for Sierra Leone, with evidence on the diamond trafficking provided by special court prosecutor David Crane and chief investigator Alan White, both former Pentagon officials. Foday Sankoh, whose troops specialized in amputating limbs, died in August 2003 in custody in Sierra Leone, where he was standing trial.[64] Taylor that same month gave up his last foothold in Monrovia, the Liberian capital surrounded by rebels, and negotiated asylum in Nigeria, thus dodging his indictment. Senior RUF and Liberian officials are said to have corroborated the links with Al-Qaeda officials stationed in Afghanistan. Lebanese diamond merchant Sami Osailly, on trial in September 2003 in Belgium, telephoned Al-Qaeda operatives in Afghanistan, according to Belgian documents that also are said to establish bank transfers.[65]

THE PROBLEM of terrorist finances is of enormous magnitude," James Gurule, the outgoing Treasury undersecretary for enforcement, told the Senate Finance Committee in Washington. "We have more than a year after Al-Qaeda's operations in New York and Washington made a dent, but we have a long way to go."[66] A year later, David Aufhauser, the Treasury's general counsel, who inherited Gurule's mission, in a valedictory statement of his own boasted that the global crackdown on terrorist financing had cut the flow of terrorist money to Al-Qaeda and related organizations by two-thirds.[67] Both Gurule and Aufhauser might have spoken more humbly of the enormous complexity of terrorist financing. A congressional report by the General Accounting Office (GAO) in December 2003 was closer to the mark. The GAO castigated rival federal agencies for failing to cooperate with one another and lamented that the United States still had no clear idea how terrorists moved their financial assets or how to thwart the flow of funds to terrorist groups.[68] The truth was that despite the fanfare given the crackdown on terrorist financing, only fragmentary evidence had surfaced to suggest that Al-Qaeda and other Islamist terrorist organizations either needed enormous sums or were wanting for rich Saudi and other sympathizers willing to pony up several million dollars at a go.

Some Western intelligence analysts argued that Al-Qaeda needed more cash than ever before to fund the covert existence of key leaders who had scattered after the loss of the Afghan sanctuary. Others argued that Al-Qaeda now required less money. Once Osama was forced out of Afghanistan, he no longer had access to an unchallenged fallback safe haven where he could welcome thousands of volunteers (even if small-scale training was said to continue in the southern Philippines and Chechnya). Recruiting, transporting, training, housing and feeding volunteers accounted for his biggest expenditures, and they hadn't come cheap, even if the real estate and instructors cost nothing and some jihadis paid their own room and board (with their welfare payments, in the case of those from western Europe). Since the early 1990s, American intelligence was convinced perhaps as many as 30,000 volunteers had passed through Al-Qaeda camps in Afghanistan.[69]

Still, there was anecdotal evidence that Al-Qaeda finances were under strain. Contributing to that unease were the loss of the Afghan sanctuary, with its attendant disruption, the death or capture of key cadres, the exploitation of intelligence from Al-Qaeda prisoner interrogations, documents retrieved from computer hard drives and others seized in safe houses in Kabul, Kandahar and elsewhere, as well as the tribulations of being subjected to the new century's most serious manhunt. In June 2002 a star Al-Jazeera reporter, for example, was stunned when senior Al-Qaeda cadres Ramzi bin al-Shibh and Khaled Sheikh Mohammed asked him for a $1 million fee—later scaled back to a paltry $17,000—for twin interviews for a program broadcast just before the first anniversary of Al-Qaeda's operations in New York and Washington. Yosri Fouda, Al-Jazeera's London bureau chief, was taken aback. These men had masterminded those attacks with an attention to detail worthy of a Rommel or an Eisenhower. "This seemed to me a symptom that something was wrong, there was some breakdown. These people don't ask for money."[70]

Yes and no. Jihadi leaders had been short of cash in the past. But they always found new sources of finance. Ayman al-Zawahiri, before he submerged his wing of Egypt's Islamic Jihad group into Al-Qaeda in 1998, had been hard up enough to risk traveling to the United States in 1995 for what proved a disappointing fund-raising tour of California mosques.[71] Still, coming from Khaled Sheikh Mohammed, such a pitch for money seemed particularly revealing. Years before throwing in his lot with Osama in Afghanistan in late 1996, Mohammed had proved something of a financial genius as well as a man of some twenty bewildering disguises, varying from rich playboy sheikh to importer of holy *zamzam* water from Mecca.

Unlike Osama's businesses in Sudan, whose main purpose was to provide employment, training and cover for fellow Afghan veterans, his actually made money. Mohammed's profits in Karachi in the mid-1990s financed his nephew Ramzi Youssef in the January 1993 attack on the World Trade Center and subsequent terrorist projects. Central to Mohammed's finances was the Konsojaya company, an outwardly innocent import-export firm incorporated in Kuala Lumpur, the capital of Malaysia, on June 2, 1994, and specializing in commodity trading, such as selling Malaysian palm oil to Pakistan.[72] The firm conveniently had trading ties with like-minded Islamist radicals elsewhere in Southeast Asia.

A key figure in Konsojaya's operations was an Indonesian known as Hambali who eluded arrest until tracked down and caught in Thailand in August 2003. Also called Riduan Issamuddin, Hambali was the elusive kingpin of Jemaah Islamiyah, eventually Al-Qaeda's regional partner, which maintained operational units in Indonesia, Singapore, Malaysia, the Philippines and Australia dedicated to imposing a caliphate in Southeast Asia. After 9/11 he disappeared from sight, but for U.S. officials he remained Al-Qaeda's chief of operations in Southeast Asia until he was arrested. Konsojaya had links with Osama's brother-in-law Mohammed Jamal Khalifa. In the early 1990s Khalifa provided long-restive Filipino Muslims with humanitarian aid in Mindanao and other southern islands. Embarrassed officials in Manila, ever unable to negotiate a political settlement with their Islamic minority, insisted he was really financing terrorism.

By 2003 Al-Qaeda clearly gave signs of hurting financially, but the damage did not seem life-threatening. The United States had succeeded in shutting down some financial spigots. The arrests of Khaled Sheikh Mohammed and Mustafa Ahmed Hawsawi deprived Al-Qaeda of very experienced financial operators who would have been hard for any organization to replace. Moreover, counterterrorism officials were beginning to dismantle Al-Qaeda networks thanks to intelligence gleaned as a result of the war against the Taliban in 2001. An elaborate FBI sting operation in January 2003, for example, lured a senior Yemeni cleric named Mohammed Ali Hassan al-Moayad to Frankfurt for medical treatment. German police bugged his conversations with an undercover agent for three days in a Frankfurt airport hotel, then arrested Moayad and a younger assistant on charges of helping finance Al-Qaeda and Hamas. (They were extradited to the United States and arraigned in Brooklyn in November 2003 after American officials promised Germany they would be tried in a civil court and not be subject to the death penalty.)

The sting operation was made possible thanks to documents discovered in Afghanistan after the Taliban's collapse—and the collaboration of an old Yemeni acquaintance working for the CIA. In conversations with the informant, the skeikh bragged he had met Osama and prior to 9/11 given him more than $20 million, raised mostly by the Al-Farouq mosque in Brooklyn.[73] Sheikh Moayad was the imam of a mosque in Sanaa, Yemen, and a senior figure in the opposition Islah (Reform) party; he described himself in court documents as Osama's spiritual adviser. No wonder U.S. officials preferred to lure him abroad rather than risk serious strain with the Yemeni government by requesting extradition or a shortcut rendering of so respected a religious leader. An FBI informant baited the hook by getting the Imam's agreement to pass $25 million to Al-Qaeda as part of Moayad's role in providing arms and money to jihadi radicals worldwide.

In Pakistan a tough-minded finance minister with distinguished International Monetary Fund service was credited with tightening up some of the more obvious loopholes that had encouraged corruption, uncontrolled foreign capital flows and other anomalies. Under heightened American scrutiny authorized by the USA Patriot Act, *hawalas*, at least in Pakistan, went into steep decline by early 2003.[74] Pakistani banks helped, shaving near-usurious rates, improving their efficiency to become competitive and capturing much of the business they had abandoned to the *hawalas* over the previous thirty years.[75]

But U.S. officials and ordinary Americans remained focused on Saudi Arabia as the likely main source of Osama's finances. September 11 also had irrevocably identified the Kingdom as the homeland of Osama and most of his hijackers. Steady application of U.S. pressure on the Al-Saud, mostly in private, gradually brought changes. Saudi foundations and charities began cooperating with measures often long on the books but infrequently implemented. Or so it was claimed in official U.S. statements. In private, the administration repeatedly said Saudi Arabia was not doing enough. The Saudis appeared genuinely incapable of coming to terms with their own predicament despite Crown Prince Abdullah's determined efforts to introduce drastic reforms. They seemed unwilling to comprehend that for the first time their six-decade-long odd-couple relationship with Washington had changed. Americans demanded concrete action, not carefully couched answers to embarrassing questions. It was tempting to think that perhaps the Saudis were as responsible as everyday Americans believed, and perhaps the perfidy reached right up into princely ranks.

Those well disposed to the Kingdom suspected that skullduggery was less at work than sloppiness and paranoia, but admitted that doubters are entitled to their dark thoughts suggesting that deliberate, large-scale obfuscation was at work. Despite expensive advice from the best American image-makers, for too long the Al-Saud failed to understand the U.S. conviction that promptly making a clean breast of even the worst news was the best way to proceed. In American eyes, the Al-Saud were indulging in denial, bluster and cover-up, this was preferred to the truth, which was judged too hurtful to acknowledge. But for the Al-Saud, prompt punishment of irresponsible citizens, no matter who they were, acknowledging that Saudis were sometimes subject to blackmail and facing up to the damaging aspects of Wahhabi proselytism certainly would have been embarrassing. After September 11, arguably nothing the Saudis could have done was likely to have helped much with Americans. In all fairness, Saudis were not the only people to fall into the denial trap, but their predicament was real. Many Saudis had oddly prided themselves on understanding the American psyche. Aside from a few oilmen, diplomats, academics and intelligence officers, Americans generally had not the slightest clue about what made Saudi society tick.

When the Al-Saud finally saw the wisdom of accepting total exposure, it was Washington that dragged its feet. It took Al-Qaeda's suicide attacks on foreigners' compounds in Riyadh in May 2003 to convince the Kingdom that its only salvation was relentless repression of jihadis in its ranks and rooting out Osama's financing network.[76] That was the very approach the United States had been urging for years. But, as the incident of the twenty-eight blacked-out pages demonstrated (see note 14 in this chapter), the Saudis were thwarted in efforts to clear their name. Before the Al-Qaeda attacks in Riyadh, whatever the Al-Saud grudgingly did to stanch suspect financing had been largely discounted by many Americans, if not the Treasury and other U.S. officials who had persuaded their Saudi counterparts to cooperate. Charities and foundations with foreign operations long had been required to register with the Foreign Ministry, which now was entrusted with monitoring overseas donations regularly to ensure the money was actually spent for its official purposes.[77] Now an oversight body was established.

In Washington, the Treasury Department recorded other signs of progress, but kept muttering privately that the Kingdom could and should do more, and faster. Given the Saudi record of passive resistance over more than a decade, the constant pressure was understandable, and the stakes greatly changed. Al-Qaeda's shock tactics in bringing terrorism home to the Kingdom helped clear the air of much long officially tolerated cant.[78] For the first time American and Saudi counterterrorism officials began cooperation in earnest. It was tempting, but probably rash, to suppose that the Saudi rich would suddenly stop financing Osama, but it was equally likely they now weighed the increased dangers to their narrow interests and to the Kingdom if they continued. Less than three months after the Riyadh attacks, in a good-faith effort to stop the money flow to Al-Qaeda, the Al-Saud agreed to ban cash donations in mosques and the removal of donation boxes for charities from shopping malls. (One can only wonder whether Christian denominations in the United States would stand still for such trifling with the Sunday collection box.) The Al-Saud also approved the permanent presence of more than a dozen FBI and Internal Revenue Service agents to work alongside Saudi counterparts.[79]

Still, judging by the number and geographical dispersion of post–September 11 attacks on soft targets—Indonesia, Kenya, Tunisia, Pakistan, Morocco, Saudi Arabia, Spain and Turkey—jihadi terrorists proved adept at moving money around much of the globe to pay for terrorist operations. In fact, cash was the best, and often the only, instrument at their disposal. The key to their success: the operations once again were relatively simple and the amounts required small enough not to arouse automatic suspicion. In the summer of 2001 in Pakistan, Khaled Sheikh Mohammed had entrusted a Canadian citizen named Mohammed Mansour Jabarah with $50,000 in cash for Jemaah Islamiyah operations in Southeast Asia, with the recommendation he should be on his way before September 11. Nearly three years later, Moroccan officials said local jihadis received $50,000 to $70,000 in foreign financing for a series of operations. The first attack, in Casablanca, Morocco's economic capital, cost the lives of eleven jihadis and thirty-three local and foreign civilians in June 2003. Other jihadi terrorist attacks in 2002 alone targeted an Israeli airliner and tourists in Kenya, a

French supertanker off the coast of Yemen, a Tunisian synagogue, a bar and nightclub favored by Australian and other Western tourists in the Indonesian resort of Bali, French naval engineers and the U.S. consulate in Karachi. Whatever other distinguishing characteristics these attacks had in common, they were all low cost. And as a terror finance specialist at the Justice Department acknowledged, "Tracing money in the best of circumstances is very, very difficult, and when you're talking about terrorist operations that can be carried out for $50,000 or $75,000, it's almost impossible."[80]

In late May 2003 international civil servants in Paris tracking money-laundering still doubted *hawalas* had ceased being prime instruments for terrorist financing.[81] Indeed, within three months a *hawala* transaction was mentioned as the means of payment in a complicated international sting operation involving U.S and Soviet cooperation. A British arms dealer of Indian descent and two New York–based accomplices were arrested and charged with importing a Soviet-made shoulder-fired SA-18 antiaircraft missile into the United States aboard a Russian ship.[82] Not content with writing anti-*hawala* language into the Patriot Act, American counterterrorism specialists followed up with suggestions designed to close what they considered another fatal loophole: cash letters, sometimes known as "international pouch." Basically they are checks (or cash instruments such as cashier checks or money orders) that foreign banks present for payment in the United States. They arrive via pouch or international bag in such quantity—5 to 7 million a day—that terrorists and other money-launderers use them because the odds of getting caught remain slim. Sifting manually through so many checks looking for the bad guys is a daunting and expensive task for banks. Favorite dodges were pre-dated checks and checks whose beneficiaries were conveniently left unnamed. The suggested riposte was requiring U.S. banks to keep close tabs on overseas banks, singling out egregious offenders, punishing them with fines and sanctions and eventually cutting off access to the U.S. banking system.[83]

Experience indicated such legislation might be considered necessary but would not prove sufficient (and there is no evidence that Al-Qaeda resorted to this dodge in any event). The record suggested terrorists were endlessly inventive. No sooner had counterintelligence and police officials stumbled on a new jihadi source of income than their quarry was on to something else. Trade in honey, a much-touted traditional pre-Viagra

aphrodisiac for elderly Muslim gentlemen, provided funds for Al-Qaeda jihadis in Sudan, Yemen and Southeast Asia until counterterrorism officials
caught on soon after September 11. Then gemstones and gold enjoyed a
vogue.

Al-Qaeda also appeared adept at keeping its assets liquid. In March
2003 the United States broke up a complicated plot to use a Pakistani textile
importer in New York to impersonate a once-resident Al-Qaeda operative
in the hope of obtaining immigration reentry papers for him. Court documents released in the summer maintained the Al-Qaeda cadre said he
wanted to invest $200,000 in a Karachi business for which the importer
had worked previously. The Al-Qaeda agent gave the importer to understand he "wanted to keep the funds liquid and to be able to retrieve them
on short notice."[84]

By mid-2003 Ronald K. Noble, the secretary general of Interpol, which
coordinates law-enforcement information from 181 countries, said his organization was "sounding the alarm that intellectual property crime is becoming the preferred method of funding for a number of terrorist groups."
Selling fake look-alike running shoes, knock-off copies of designer jeans
and pirated Japanese electronics guaranteed handsome profits. It also
avoided the harsh legal penalties for actually making the counterfeit goods
and thus entailed little downside danger. Noble's testimony to the House
Committee on International Relations noted that convicted culprits got off
with relatively low fines and light prison sentences.[85]

Could an organization as devoted to violence change its ways and lower
its money-generating profile? Not really an organization, Al-Qaeda de-
pends on its often pickup members—as peculiarly different as rival Algerian jihadis and Egyptian and Asian operatives, legitimate businessmen,
petty criminals and smugglers. Would time, sensible political reforms or
repression erode Al-Qaeda's hold? A possible clue, albeit within a group
with a totally different worldview, was provided by the November 17 terrorists in Greece. A member of the N17 on trial in Athens for a long string
of killings told the court in the summer of 2003 that he and others had become bored with the clandestine life despite their unrivaled success over
three decades. So bored, he said, that they had discussed dropping everything and opening a fast-food restaurant in Athens. But Al-Qaeda, less an
organization than an amorphous grouping, showed no signs of succumbing to such temptations anytime soon.

"The Behinder We Get"

The safest place for me is Afghanistan.

—Osama bin Laden

Is our present situation such that "the harder we work, the behinder we get"?

—Secretary of Defense Donald Rumsfeld

ONCE BACK FROM SUDAN in May 1996, Osama lost no time in transforming a backwater of a failed state beset by interminable civil war into a sanctuary. He landed in eastern Afghanistan, a messy place to be sure, but where he had cut his teeth as a young man a decade earlier. He had retained many useful friends in the Pashtun borderlands overlapping Afghanistan and Pakistan. At its peril the Clinton administration had overlooked, or at least underestimated, those ties, preferring to believe his return to turbulent Afghanistan would, in Washington's jargon of the times, box him in. In fact, Osama, through luck, money and diplomacy, soon had an entirely free hand to train jihadi volunteers by the thousands to wreak havoc when and where he wanted. And, angrier than ever, he was determined to do so. Still rankling from his ouster from Khartoum, for the first time he made no secret of his desire to resort to violence. Well before the year was out, he made clear his intentions in a *fatwa* declaring open season for killing all Americans—men, women, children, military or civilian—for his jihad.

Still, initially all was not clear sailing for Osama. When he landed in Jalalabad, the great eastern city was administered by old mujahedeen who ran what they grandly called the "Eastern Shura" council. Barely four months later, the rival Taliban captured that virtual extension of Pakistan as well as the Afghan capital, Kabul. At first glance, that was not a pleasing prospect for Osama. He was almost certainly bluffing when he said in an interview, just as power was about to shift abruptly in the Taliban's favor, that "the safest place for me is Afghanistan."[1] Osama was obliged to establish, then cement ties with Mullah Omar, the Taliban leader. During the anti-Soviet jihad, he likely did, as he claimed, meet Mullah Omar, then a minor holy warrior who in the mid-1990s emerged as the Taliban leader thanks largely to Pakistani help and Saudi financing. But there is no record that theirs had been the kind of close, sustained friendship that bound Osama and the now-defeated Eastern Shura leaders in Jalalabad.

Indeed, Mullah Omar might well have taken umbrage at Osama's friendship with the Jalalabad warlords. Instead he invited Osama to his headquarters in Kandahar, the Pashtun stronghold in the south. Over the next five years, theirs was to prove an odd, but durable partnership virtually immune from U.S. threats, episodic bouts of often ambivalent Pakistani advice and even occasional significant protest within Taliban ranks. Osama constantly flattered the Taliban leader, building him a palace and going along with his rudimentarily educated host's pretensions as commander of the faithful (which were formalized in a public ceremony in which he donned what was purported to be the Prophet's cloak, piously preserved in Kandahar). Osama never lost an opportunity to publicly praise Taliban rule as the sole paragon of a genuinely Islamic state, the very model of the caliphate whose abolition by Ataturk in 1924 had cast the *umma* into a new period of *jahiliyah*, the pre-Islamic era of ignorance and darkness.

Osama's tactics worked, and he came to exercise increasing influence, then something approaching full sway over his host, indeed to the point that some Taliban leaders resented and feared his domination.[2] Over the years, Osama persuaded Mullah Omar to approve his hegemony over a variety of foreign Islamist organizations and finally, in 2001, to subordinate all non-Afghan jihadis to Al-Qaeda (albeit in the formal name of serving the Taliban). A host of little signs demonstrated Osama's growing power and confirmed both him and Omar in their belief that the United States was a much-overestimated paper tiger unwilling to sacrifice its soldiers in a land renowned through the centuries for humiliating invaders. Judging by the Clinton administration's behavior, they could scarcely be blamed.

The United States held Osama responsible for the attacks against its embassies in Kenya and Tanzania in 1998. But its riposte, when it came, was fired from U.S. Navy ships 1,000 miles away and was ineffective to boot. The Navy's cruise missiles that hit Osama's training camps on August 20 did not kill Osama and indeed served principally to magnify his reputation to near-mythic proportions. The episode only encouraged even more Muslim volunteers to flock to his Afghan training camps. It was a classic case of cultural cross-purposes. An American diplomat who repeatedly met the Taliban insisted, "They were out to lunch and didn't take notice one way or another, but never believed we would do anything to punish them, no matter how much we said they would be held responsible for the next Al-Qaeda attack."[3] Their view was not far from Osama's own.

The Americans were not the only ones to be wrong-footed. Only weeks later, in September, Prince Turki al-Faisal, the Saudi Intelligence boss, returned to Afghanistan hoping the bloody events in East Africa would convince Omar to make good on a promise to hand over Osama, which the Prince thought he had negotiated in June. Instead, Turki was upbraided and informed he should be backing Osama, not opposing him. The Prince stalked out of the meeting and flew home. By way of a slap on the wrist, the House of Saud, which had contributed many millions of dollars to the Taliban cause over the years, withdrew its ambassador. But private Saudis and Saudi charities kept funding the Taliban. Despite the histrionic encounter with Turki, the Taliban for a while did seek to lower tensions. Osama was instructed to lie low. But in late December 1998 he conducted two long television interviews, to the apparent embarrassment of his Taliban hosts, who had promised the United States that he would not be allowed access to the media.

At one point the Taliban claimed that he had disappeared, a clumsy stratagem that fooled no one since they earlier had stated he was guarded by their men in order to keep track of his movements. In January 2001, in a public ceremony aired on Al-Jazeera, Osama married off a son to a daughter of one of his chief lieutenants, Mohammed Atef. And the following spring, it was under the influence of Osama's Wahhabi strictures that Mullah Omar disregarded worldwide supplication and protests and destroyed two giant rock statues of Buddha in Bamian. Osama's ascendancy over Omar reached its zenith in September 2001. Al-Qaeda's masterstroke in assassinating Ahmad Shah Massoud just two days before the September 11 operation certainly was a calculated maneuver to curry favor with Omar.

Massoud's death removed the last major impediment to Omar's total control of Afghanistan, which, in turn, would further Taliban claims for

formal international recognition. It remains unclear if Omar was informed
in advance of the plot. Indeed, the plan succeeded only through daring and
luck. On the spur of the moment, Massoud agreed to meet two bogus Arab
journalists from a nonexistent Arab television network who had been
hanging around his headquarters and, having all but given up hope of obtaining an interview, were about to leave his territory. Massoud died when
the cameraman ignited explosives hidden in his camera. That assassination
helped mask what appears to have been Osama's calculated failure to inform his host of Al-Qaeda's plans for striking New York and Washington,
which soon unseated Omar and deprived Osama of his Afghan sanctuary.

IF THE CONNECTIONS between Osama and the Taliban—and those between the Taliban and Pakistan's Inter-Services Intelligence (ISI) directorate—became unmistakable by 1997, the exact nature of the relations
between Osama and the ISI for the most part still remains obscure. At least
in the beginning, those links were dictated by Pakistan's overweening interest in dominating Afghanistan, an idée fixe since Islamabad became a vital
player in the anti-Soviet jihad in the 1980s. Indeed, Pakistan's interference
in Afghan affairs pre-dated the Red Army's invasion by five years. Pakistan
had bankrolled Afghan Islamists since 1974 and calculated that its crucial
role in the anti-Soviet jihad was a worthwhile risk to protect its western
flank and provide strategic depth against India.

At the very least, a future Afghanistan under the Taliban was likely to
depend on Pakistan, thereby depriving godless and long-expansionist
Moscow, suspect Shi'a Tehran and hostile Hindu Delhi of their prewar influence in Kabul. (Until his mysterious death in a plane crash in 1988, President Zia ul-Haq of Pakistan dreamed of creating something akin to a new
Mogul empire stretching through Afghanistan and Central Asia, and indeed that fantasy constituted a major reason for his agreeing to team up
with the United States to oppose the Soviet occupation.) Afghan territory
also proved useful for training Pakistani volunteers for the disputed Indian
state of Kashmir, a front against India the ISI opened in 1989 just as the last
Soviet soldiers were leaving. Training men next door to liberate the Muslim
majority state provided plausible deniability in the face of inevitable Indian accusations of Pakistani involvement, or so the ISI reasoned. The
United States disengaged rapidly once Moscow's humiliation was complete. But in the early 1990s the Afghan warlords fell to fighting one an-

other, thus frustrating the Pakistanis, who had hoped to pacify them and Afghanistan with Gulf money and American-supplied arms left over from the anti-Soviet jihad.

Undeterred, the ISI did not cut its losses and drop the Afghan option. Instead, it all but invented the Taliban as the new way to protect its stake in Afghanistan. They were a byproduct of the war against the Soviets—for the most part, sons of wretchedly poor Afghan refugees who were educated gratis in jihadi Islam (and little else) in first hundreds, then thousands of *madrasa*s in Pakistan paid for by Saudi and other Arab benefactors. For the ISI the Taliban seemed sure winners. Whatever their shortcomings, they were not likely to play footsy with the Russians, Iranians or Indians. But the ISI got sloppy. Before and after the emergence of the Taliban in the mid-1990s, the ISI trained volunteers in the same camps where Osama put his own recruits from around the Muslim world through their paces. The rationale was easy enough to understand. Osama was rich, the ISI was not, so why not piggyback on him? Whatever the supposed virtues of such an arrangement, it left telltale traces linking the ISI and Osama and suggesting the relationship went well beyond such mundane sharing of real estate.[4]

Indeed, Pakistani recruits for Kashmir embarrassingly accounted for most of the casualties in the shared Afghan training camps targeted by the 1998 U.S. cruise missiles. The missiles famously missed Osama (who had left the camp either an hour earlier or immediately after the embassy bombings on August 7, depending on which of several versions is to be believed). Pakistan's killing of ISI recruits angered the Clinton administration. "Aware, displeased, but paralyzed" pretty much sums up Washington's predicament in dealing with Pakistan, which in the spring of 1998 had entered the world's nuclear club by conducting a series of explosions in outright defiance of American pleas not to do so.

To the outside world, Pakistan may have combined all the horrors of a rogue state with nuclear weapons and a civil society threatening to spin out of control at almost any moment. But in the game of nations, being dangerous has ever had its attractions. Pakistan was all but broke, its political system and armed forces vulnerable to the inroads of militant jihadi Islam, its army outnumbered and outspent by its more populous and prosperous Indian adversary. But it was capable of causing major headaches and thus was a player whose problems and desires had to be dealt with. Arguably, Kashmir was more important in the Pakistani scheme of things because it directly challenged India and had caused two wars in the past. But Pakistan's forward policy in Afghanistan reinforced its trouble-making potential and kept the Americans and others constantly engaged—and worrying.

Inside the shared Afghan camps was a telltale fact, indeed one of the few that American intelligence could produce. ISI officers, including senior colonels, were reported in those camps on and off, liaising with senior Al-Qaeda officials. Those joint ventures remained a logical way to exchange information between Al-Qaeda and the ISI.[5] But so far little else has come to public light about the exact nature of the ISI–Al-Qaeda relationship. (It is logical to assume that Washington now knows somewhat more, thanks to many documents and prisoners seized during and after the rapid unraveling of the combined Al-Qaeda and Taliban forces by the United States and its Northern Alliance allies in late 2001. And it is also logical to assume the United States has its own good reasons for not divulging what it learned.)

Curiously, Pakistani officials could be disarmingly frank about some aspects of their role in helping the Taliban in Afghanistan. To my surprise, the Pakistani ambassador in Kabul, who received me in the fall of 2000, made no mystery of the presence of ISI agents across the length and breadth of Taliban-controlled territory, which then amounted to about 95 percent of Afghanistan. The same Pakistani candor did not extend to acknowledging the existence of Pakistani military aid for the Taliban forces, including staff officers for command and control, artillery specialists and special forces. The Pakistani government was also rumored to have allowed Taliban forces to enter its territory in a flanking movement that helped capture Ahmad Shah Massoud's strategic base at Taloqan in September 2000. Such were Massoud's constantly repeated accusations. But his distrust of all things Pakistani—and Pakistan's own suspicions about his Northern Alliance—had long since reached the point where neither's insinuations and invectives were taken at face value by outsiders.

Pakistan officially always insisted none of its soldiers was in Afghanistan, much less fighting against Massoud's forces, who were clinging tenaciously to ever-shrinking positions in northeastern Afghanistan. Pakistani protests of injured innocence masked the country's more obviously traceable support for the Taliban in materiel and petroleum products (which were partly balanced by Iranian, Russian and Indian help for the Northern

Alliance). Washington was not taken in—"we knew their denials were ab-solute bullshit," in the words of an American diplomat in the Islamabad embassy. But the United States preferred to keep its steady pressure private rather than pick a public fight with Pakistan. The Pakistanis just hunkered down.

American support for Massoud, starting in late 1997 and early 1998 and continuing through 2000, amounted to $600,000 to $700,000—"pocket change," in the words of a former senior U.S. intelligence officer conversant with the region.[6] To bolster his case against Pakistan, Massoud as a matter of course encouraged visitors to interview his Pakistani prisoners, who were described as soldiers or former soldiers. According to the Northern Alliance, Pakistani soldiers in Afghanistan were formally retired from ac-tive Pakistani service, then seconded to the Taliban.

Massoud also insisted that Pakistani professional staff officers played a growing role in Taliban battlefield successes and his own setbacks. How many Pakistani military ringers were needed is open to question. Not many, according to American intelligence specialists. Many Afghans fight-ing for the Taliban, particularly specialists in armor, artillery and even the air force, had been trained by the Soviets and then fought for the Naji-bullah regime before eventually throwing in their lot with the Taliban. They were very much at home with the Northern Alliance's Soviet weapons systems. Still, the CIA had its doubts, or rather kept pleading in vain with Massoud in the late 1990s to produce incontrovertible proof of the pres-ence of Pakistani professional soldiers, which it intimated would prove crucial in enlisting support from doubting Thomases in Washington.[7]

When the Taliban collapsed in November 2001, Pakistani pretenses became demonstrably threadbare. Despite the detailed testimony of wit-nesses, Pakistan kept denying that its Air Force C-130s flew into the be-sieged northeastern city of Kunduz for at least two nights to ferry out Pakistanis whose capture along with Taliban and Al-Qaeda forces might raise awkward questions. Whether these men were just ISI operatives, whose presence in Afghanistan was never disputed, or more embarrass-ingly, seconded soldiers, including field-grade officers—indeed even a gen-eral, as was rumored—remains unclear. The multiple flights suggest that more than ISI operatives were involved. Passenger manifests were said to have been subject to U.S. scrutiny. The U.S. Air Force, which operated AWACS electronics-warfare aircraft over Afghanistan, obviously tolerated the flights and kept mum in return for American use of Pakistani bases and other favors needed to prosecute the overall campaign against the Taliban and Al-Qaeda. Pakistan, even that considerable part of the ISI long devoted to the Taliban cause, had, officially at least, changed sides. That did not discourage rumors that the Pakistanis used these flights to evacuate high-ranking Taliban and even Al-Qaeda personnel.[8]

Aside from the oddly indiscreet joint use of Afghan training camps, the ISI relationship with Osama was of a subtler nature. There was, to be sure, a hint of connivance in the specific mention of Osama and "the state, the government and the people" of Pakistan in the dedication of the six-volume so-called Al-Qaeda encyclopedia of terrorism, which became a regular exhibit in major terrorism trials (but strangely came to Washington's attention only after the Jordanians provided a copy in 1999).[9] Much of the encyclopedia was culled from American and other Western army manuals that were dumbed down and translated into Arabic with simplified diagrams. The encyclopedia, which was said to be readily available on CD-ROMs in the Peshawar bazaar in the late 1990s, was published by the Services Office, with the final volume dated 1993—during Osama's Sudan period. A Jordanian lawyer specializing in cyber law in Amman told me in April 2000 that the "encyclopedia was no big deal." In preparing the defense of a client, he said, he had found hundreds of sites on the Internet providing detailed "how-to" instructions for making explosives. A different and shorter manual, introduced in the 2001 New York trial of the four men eventually sentenced to life imprisonment for their part in the East African bombings, ran to 180 pages, divided into eighteen chapters. It dispensed in Arabic such advice as how to lie low in the West (shave beards and don't be chatty), how to commit assassinations (using bombs, clubs and a lethal stew of spoiled meat, green beans and corn), how to forge documents, set up safe houses, use code and cipher, survive interrogation and make booby traps. Seized in Manchester, England, at the home of Al-Qaeda cadre Anas al-Liby in May 2000, it also provided religious scholars' justification for the torture of hostages.

Responding to my abiding puzzlement about the ISI links with Osama, in October 2000 a knowledgeable Pakistani journalist spent an afternoon in Lahore doping out for me the never officially explicated understanding. Each side has good reason to fudge the relationship. Osama had no interest in advertising his long-standing friendship with various ISI officers he had known since the anti-Soviet jihad or others he had met since his return from Sudan. He was far too wary to be in touch with the ISI on a direct, hierarchical basis. He understood that the ISI was not a monolith and that not all its officers looked kindly on links with Al-Qaeda or even with the Taliban, for that matter. For Osama, it sufficed to have well-placed friends inside the ISI. Having long honed the fine art of using money to get his way, he was careful to keep his relations informal. He, of course, realized the United States had a price on his head.

In essence, Osama's dependence on the ISI was real, but limited. His most pressing need at that stage was for free passage and cover for his agents moving in and out of Pakistan. He doubtless also counted on being tipped off about anything his contacts in the ISI picked up about American plans against Al-Qaeda. Such friends squirreled away inside the ISI at face value made a mockery of a Pakistan-based joint American–ISI snatch team, tasked with capturing Osama, that the Clinton administration put together after the bombing of the East African embassies. U.S. cynics wrote the team off from the start, convinced it would never work. Actually, the venture collapsed only because a very anti-Osama ISI general lost out in the fast-moving events in October 1999 that unseated civilian Prime Minister Nawaz Sharif, put General Pervez Musharraf, then the army chief of staff, in power and consigned the unit to limbo.

In fact, as an institution the ISI had every reason to keep Osama at arm's length, knowing full well that any fingerprints connecting them would bring the heavens down on Pakistan and land it on the State Department's list of state sponsors of terrorism. There had been close calls in the past (notably after a lethal Egyptian jihadi car-bomb attack against the Egyptian embassy in Islamabad in November 1995). Whatever the costs of its fascination with Afghanistan, the ISI was less a rogue organization than a military outfit carrying out government policy. The trick for the ISI was to transform Osama into a kind of wild card for the Taliban, but not directly for Pakistan itself. For the ISI his principal use increasingly was helping the Taliban, providing them with trained and highly motivated non-Afghan volunteers from around the Muslim world for the 055 brigade at a time when Afghans were exhausted by two decades of war and far from enthusiastic about having their sons press-ganged into the ranks.[10]

Thus, Pakistani officials argued, it was left to the Taliban leadership to know where Osama was and more or less what he was up to. That didn't stop the Taliban from repeatedly trying to persuade a skeptical world that Osama somehow had gone missing. The ISI, above all, had no interest in knowing what foreign operations Osama was planning and indeed had every reason to want to stay clear and to be seen doing so. When the United States kept pressing the Pakistani government to cooperate in persuading the Taliban to deal with Osama, the civilian power structure demurred. This was a hallowed Pakistani tradition (shared by many another army-dominated Third World regime). Since Pakistan's creation in 1947 the military as a matter of principle had kept civilian governments in the dark about defense matters. Their advice, for civilian leaders under the gun from Washington about Osama, was to have the Americans told that Pakistan knew nothing, nothing at all, but would sound out the Taliban. The Pakistani military's realm was writ large, and the country's occasional civilian leaders in notional command learned not to inquire into such matters.

For example, after Osama's return to Afghanistan, Nawaz Sharif told American officials who asked him to intervene with the Taliban to collar bin Laden that as prime minister he could deliver almost anyone else, but not him. He insisted he knew nothing about Osama and would rather not intervene. Of course, that was a convenient excuse for fending off ever more insistent Americans determined to make the Taliban disgorge Osama. But it was not necessarily as hollow an excuse as might appear. If there is a constant in Afghan politics through the ages it is a certain bloody-mindedness toward all comers, including the Pakistanis. More Pashtuns indeed lived in Pakistan than in Afghanistan. But the millions of Afghan refugees in Pakistan during and after the anti-Soviet jihad never really forgave their hosts for persecuting them, especially restricting their access to jobs. For all the help provided the Taliban, Pakistan proved curiously powerless in getting its way, even on seemingly open-and-shut matters.

For instance, the Taliban steadfastly refused to hand over the would-be Pakistani assassins who had tried to kill Nawaz Sharif and then took refuge in Afghanistan. So Pakistan could legitimately plead that the United States was not the only government subject to an Afghani runaround. But such was the ISI's obsession with Afghanistan that few Pakistani officials clearly faced up to the contradictions in its strategic-depth fixation. Those who did grasp the implications involving Osama were apt to be diplomats, and the Foreign Ministry wielded little power. To offset Pakistani stonewalling about Osama, officials in Islamabad would try to prove their good faith in other litigious bilateral matters. From time to time, the Pakistanis would deliver in cases where the American brief was cast-iron and the culprits notorious. Before September 11, much to Washington's annoyance, the Pakistanis only occasionally cracked down on Al-Qaeda members moving in and out of their country, usually sparing the big fish and arresting small fry.

They also cooperated with Washington, helping arrest Ramzi Youssef, who carried out the 1993 World Trade Center bombing, and Mir Aimal Kansi, a fellow Baluchi, who had indulged in a fatal shooting spree outside CIA headquarters a month earlier.[11] That was a policy Pakistan maintained after the September 11 attacks. Whatever else it did not do thereafter, Pakistan did cooperate in arresting major and minor Al-Qaeda members. Abu Zubaydah, Khaled Sheikh Mohammed and Ramzi bin al-Shibh were among the more prominent of 500 cadres captured by Pakistan by mid-2004, with considerable loss of life among its security forces.

Still, before September 11 Pakistani civilian governments in the 1990s tended to pussyfoot rather than confront the rising influence of homegrown jihadis. In a country long dominated by the military such caution was understandable. In furtherance of its fight for Kashmir, the ISI encouraged and indirectly financed almost all these Islamist radicals. Some indeed came to be associated in one way or another with Al-Qaeda. These Pakistan Islamists took advantage of the popular discontent that followed the end of the anti-Soviet jihad. The United States, long Pakistan's unquestioned champion during the Cold War, after 1989 increasingly was seen as an ingrate dropping a loyal ally. Pakistan's burgeoning nuclear program, deliberately overlooked by Washington in the 1980s to further the jihad next door, reemerged as a major irritant once the last Soviet troops evacuated Afghanistan. Congress passed the Pressler amendment in a futile effort to force Pakistan to shut down its nuclear program's suspected military aspects. Far from exacting compliance, the amendment instead provoked anti-Americanism by freezing delivery of prepaid F-16s and refusing to return the money to boot. Many ordinary Pakistanis were also outraged by the repression of two Palestinian uprisings by America's ally, Israel.

Westernized, secular Pakistanis increasingly worried about the "creeping Talibanization" of their country. They wondered if theirs was, if not a failed state, at least a society coming precipitously close to becoming unmanageable. The undercover designs of the ISI were never far from such concerns. Thanks to its support for homegrown jihadi militias dedicated to the struggle for Kashmir, ISI power and influence now extended further into initially off-limits domestic affairs, threatening the ever-shaky secular foundations and civil society itself. The ISI deliberately entertained an aura of mystery. Secular Pakistanis never succeeded in pinning down where it found the money for its Kashmir and Afghan adventures. They were left to guess that their political adversaries were financed by a mix of drug trafficking and Saudi and other Gulf funds extending well beyond the bounty lavished on the Taliban and the more than 10,000 religious boarding schools in Pakistan. Year in and year out, those *madrasas* produced thousands of highly motivated graduates (including scholarship boys from Central Asia and China's oppressed Uighur minority), whose principal intellectual baggage was rote memorization of the Koran and devotion to jihadi Islam. Thousands were willing to fight and die for the Taliban next door in Afghanistan long before new volunteers poured across from Pakistan in a futile bid to thwart American military might in 2001.

WITH PAKISTAN in such a parlous state, jihadi theorists predicted that the brightest future for their vision of Islam lay not in the old Arab heartland, but in South and Southeast Asia.

Demography lent some credence to this thinking. The majority of Muslims resided in an arc from Afghanistan through the subcontinent and into Malaysia, the Philippines and Indonesia (where 180 million Muslims constituted the world's largest single community). After September 11, this new hinterland accounted for a number of terrorist operations in sympathy with Osama and demonstrated that jihadis were still capable of striking, despite the setback in Afghanistan. The terrorist operation in Bali, which on October 12, 2002, claimed 202 lives, most of them Australian, was only the most spectacular of the series, combining tried-and-true car-bomb techniques with a soft target in the form of a well-known Western holiday resort. But losing the Afghan sanctuary in the long run deprived Al-Qaeda of a free hand in welcoming and training foreign volunteers, even if fresh jihadis were still formed in Chechnya, the Philippines and even Saudi Arabia itself.

If the fulcrum for future success, from a jihadi perspective, now lay in Afghanistan and Pakistan, Osama never lost sight of Saudi Arabia and of his abiding desire to drive the Al-Saud from the land of the two holy mosques, by force if necessary. On the other hand, Ayman al-Zawahiri of Egypt's Gama'a al-Islamiyya, Osama's formal partner after 1998 and long a major influence on his thinking, kept insisting that the main jihadi thrust should be against his homeland, the most populated Arab country. Osama and Zawahiri argued back and forth. Unable to agree and unwilling to compromise, they decided to strike on both fronts and eventually confront the United States head-on.

That at least was the despairing analysis of Montassir Zayat, a lawyer close to Zawahiri, whom I visited in his Cairo office in 1999. Zayat felt his friend and Osama thus committed a fatal error. Zayat had served time (and been tortured) for his own radical Islamist beliefs before gradually concluding that jihadi politics were doomed. But Osama had other strings to his bow. The conflicts in Bosnia in the mid-1990s and in Chechnya, first at virtually the same time and then in the second war starting in late 1999, provided Al-Qaeda with tailor-made battlefields for a post–Cold War: Muslim countries resisting infidel armies. Jihad was a forceful recruiting tool, but in fact the volunteers played a minor role in the actual fighting despite their efforts, and those of their adversaries, to exaggerate their importance.

Al-Qaeda's loose arrangements with jihadis in South and Southeast Asia had their foundations in the flood of Muslim volunteers from those lands who had joined the anti-Soviet jihad. By the time Osama felt confident enough to strike from his Afghan base, in August 1998, he had made a point of associating radical Muslims from Afghanistan, Pakistan and Bangladesh, as well as Egypt, with his *fatwa* authorizing the killing of all Americans anywhere.[12] Oddly, at the time Osama made no mention of Indonesian jihadis who were to play a vital role in terrorist cells in a span of Southeast Asia including Thailand, Malaysia and Singapore.

There were residual Muslim separatists in the southern Philippines and Indonesia itself. Indonesia was just then shaking off four decades of authoritarian military rule under President Suharto. Whatever his other failings, Suharto had been as ruthlessly efficient in suppressing radical Islam in the 1980s as he had been in liquidating hundreds of thousands of local Communists a generation earlier. His fall from power in 1998 prompted Indonesian jihadis to return from their overseas sanctuaries and take advantage of the relative freedom and chaos that ensued. They soon were at work exacerbating Christian–Muslim violence. Even by Osama's demanding standards, these jihadis proved especially talented.

Only many years later did it come to light that early Indonesian volunteers who joined the anti-Soviet jihad in Pakistan and Afghanistan in the mid-1980s were especially highly educated and motivated. They earned high marks from Al-Qaeda leaders. Well into the 1990s, successive yearly intakes of co-opted Indonesians, joined later by a smattering of Malaysians and Singaporeans, arrived in Afghanistan and stayed for three-year hitches in intensive jihadi indoctrination, military training and the dark arts of terrorism.[13] No Arab group put in such a grueling Afghan apprenticeship. When the internecine fighting in Afghanistan spun out of control in the mid-1990s, seasoned Indonesian jihadis struck deals with Filipino Muslims in the Moro Islamic Liberation Front to set up training camps in Muslim island strongholds such as Mindanao, Jolo and Basilan in the southern Philippines. More than 100 volunteers trained in Afghanistan, perhaps twice as many in Mindanao starting in 1996. In 2000 the Philippine army shut down the Mindanao training site of what became formally known as Jemaah Islamiyah only in the late 1990s. (In 2003, much to the Philippines' embarrassment, yet another clandestine camp was discovered in Mindanao.)

Southeast Asian jihadis received some funds from Osama. But with their own string of religious boarding schools and mosques, they had an agenda quite independent of Al-Qaeda. They dreamed of setting up a caliphate comprising all of Southeast Asia's Muslims, but did not share Osama's view of worldwide jihad. Nor was Muslim insurgency in the southern Philippines new and attributable to Osama. A civil war against the government in Manila had dragged on for decades (and at times had been financed by Libya's Muammar Qaddafi, who, whatever his other adventures with terrorism, was no friend of the jihadis).[14] As for the United States, American troops first had encountered Muslim insurgents in Mindanao following the Spanish-American War of 1898. Indeed the still standard U.S. Army–issue Colt .45 was invented with enough punch to stop even the most determined Moros, as the Americans called the Filipino Muslims they had so much trouble subduing.

LAWYER ZAYAT's view of the relations between Osama and Zawahiri, the nature of Indonesian Islamic radicals and other subtleties of the jihadi movement seem to have been largely unknown to Western governments even after the embassy attacks in East Africa. Indeed little apparently had changed since an unvarnished report the CIA issued July 1, 1996, soon after he left Khartoum. "We have no unilateral sources close to bin Laden, nor any reliable way of intercepting his communications," it lamented. "We must rely on foreign intelligence services to confirm his movement and activities. We have no sources who have supplied reporting on Saudi opposition cells inside Saudi Arabia, and little information about those cells' location, size, composition, or activities."[15]

An old CIA acquaintance in Washington expressed awe at the constantly cascading government funding earmarked for counterterrorism and how disproportionately little intelligence it was producing. A year after the East African attacks he was particularly dumbstruck by the recent purchase of executive jets that, if I understood correctly, were on permanent standby, ready to whisk counterterrorism specialists to the scene of the next terrorist operation. His former employers, he intimated, were very proud of this example of their forward thinking. He decidedly was not. Waiting for the next terrorist attack summed up for him what was wrong with the ballyhooed counterterrorism program.

Some younger ex-CIA hands had drawn similar conclusions with the end of the Cold War and left government employment. One such was Reuel Marc Gerecht, who grew so disenchanted with the agency's lack of imagination in the early 1990s that he had quit—and spat in the soup to boot. In op-ed and magazine pieces well before September 11 Gerecht laid much of the blame on intellectual sloth and operational mindlessness. He had studied Farsi and Arabic as a Princeton undergraduate with Professor Bernard Lewis and joined the CIA's Directorate of Operations, honing his knowledge of Iran thanks to years spent in the Istanbul consulate interviewing hundreds of would-be Iranian applicants for U.S. visas and trying to recruit agents. He finally snapped when he realized that no one in Langley shared his fascination with things Iranian or indeed cared enough to open, much less read, the Iranian newspapers to which the agency subscribed.[16]

By the end of the Cold War the CIA was so low on language-savvy agents that it resorted to recruiting Mormons on the theory that they learned difficult tongues for their obligatory missionary work abroad. No one apparently saw the irony, much less the pitfalls, of employing clean-cut Mormons to infiltrate down-and-dirty foreigners in general, much less an Islamist movement that prided itself on carefully vetting its recruits. "The CIA probably doesn't have a single qualified Arabic speaker of Middle Eastern background who can play a believable Muslim fundamentalist, who would volunteer to spend years of his life with shitty food and no women in the mountains of Afghanistan," Gerecht noted. "We didn't do that kind of thing."[17] Still, the sense of the ridiculous lived on in the agency. The CIA official responsible for the "stans," as the Muslim lands of the former Soviet Union were called in Washington officialese, is said to have entertained staff meetings by monotonously announcing, "Yesterday, I had no agents, today I have no agents, tomorrow I will have no agents." In the wake of the Cold War, why bother about Central Asia, this march of an extinct enemy's former empire?

Why pay attention to the Russians, who were seriously worried about Islamist inroads in the southern reaches of Moscow's "near abroad" and hoped to enlist Washington's aid in shutting down Pakistani and Saudi encouragement to these jihadis?[18] Only the joint congressional investigation of the September 11 intelligence failures prompted the State Department and the various intelligence agencies to start recruiting first- and second-generation Arab-Americans who had maintained proficiency in their families' mother tongue.[19] Without enough language specialists, the often-rival American intelligence agencies—the CIA, the Defense Intelligence Agency (DIA), the eavesdropping National Security Agency and the National Reconnaissance Office, responsible for satellite photos—simply could not winnow the increasing telephone and e-mail intercepts accumulated by Washington's electronic harvest.

In such circumstances, the more efficient the electronic intelligence "take," the more information was left unanalyzed.[20] These were not the only bottlenecks crippling the counterterrorism effort. The congressional investigation and various books written by Clinton administration insiders pinpointed shortcoming after shortcoming, ranging from traditional turf battles among branches of government (especially the deep-rooted FBI–CIA antagonism) to the Pentagon's reluctance to do much of anything without committing enough troops to conduct a minor war.[21]

I was ensconced in an elegant waiting room at the Taliban Foreign Ministry, one of the few largely undamaged buildings in the much-fought-over capital of Kabul, on October 12, 2000, wondering if just such a minor war was about to begin then and there. After the East African embassies were hit in 1998, the Clinton administration geared up for conflict, at least verbally, repeatedly warning the Taliban that they would be held responsible for any new Al-Qaeda terrorist outrage. The president issued a new intelligence finding authorizing the use of force to bring the Taliban and Al-Qaeda to heel and, if necessary, to kill Osama. Only minutes before, while still in my hotel, I had listened to the BBC World Service radio account of the near-sinking of the USS *Cole*, a billion-dollar missile destroyer, in a terrorist attack during a refueling stopover in Aden, Yemen's premier port.

Piloted by two kamikazes, a speeding fiberglass skiff loaded with high explosives, arranged in a shaped charge to maximize damage, blew an enormous hole in the destroyer's side at the water line, killing nineteen sailors and requiring $250 million in repairs.[22] Even the BBC's initial report was enough for me to comprehend that the attack bore the hallmark of Al-Qaeda—long preparation, careful planning and daring execution. Despite the East African attacks twenty-six months earlier and Yemen's well-established reputation for lawlessness and Islamist activism, the *Cole*'s crew had failed to observe standing Navy regulations requiring marksmen be posted during the Aden stopovers.[23]

I was in the waiting room because I had been promised an interview with the Foreign Minister, who on the spur of the moment had decided to travel to Kandahar instead. I had wanted to meet the minister, a man credited with a modicum of independent thinking who passed for a moderate in Taliban circles. Since he didn't show up, I was entitled to leave. I wondered briefly if the ministry constituted a legitimate military target and recalled reading that six hours were needed to set a cruise missile's gyroscope prior to firing. So I stayed and in the minister's stead was received by a high-strung man in his thirties. I decided not to tell him about the USS *Cole* since he seemed nervous enough answering—or, as it turned out, not answering—my questions about the Taliban, Pakistan, Osama and the United States. Indeed, even for this functionary in the ministry, tasked to reflect the Taliban's sunniest countenance to the world, reeling off the double-talk answers to questions asked by many another visitor reduced him to bouts of perspiration on what was a pleasantly cool autumn day. I rather enjoyed his discomfort and noted his obvious relief and delight when I took my leave and two smiling *mullah* friends were ushered in.

I kept thinking of the afternoon, a few days earlier, spent in Jalalabad's Amanullah Gardens (named for an unwisely Westernizing ruler who was overthrown in the 1920s). Amir Shah, the resourceful Associated Press stringer in Kabul, had driven down to the Torkam post on the border with Pakistan to pick me up and take me to the capital. As he expected, the gardens were happily free of the Taliban's religious police and full of everyday citizens quite prepared to talk. A young girl tried to sell me her goat and a rug salesman complained about the lack of tourists and diplomats, but I learned the most from a half dozen young grease monkeys. We had met them earlier at an open-air garage when they repaired some minor ailment afflicting the AP vehicle. They came to the gardens every afternoon to escape mandatory attendance at the mosque, enforced fitfully by the Committee to Punish Vice and Promote Virtue. The boys had grown up in refugee camps near Peshawar during the Soviet occupation.

Playing hooky from afternoon prayers certainly showed they had little use for the Taliban. They knew Osama's men all right, because their garage often repaired the Arabs' vehicles, mostly four-wheel drives with tinted windows. They didn't much care for the Arabs and sensed the Arabs felt the same way about them. If anything, they seemed to like the Pakistanis even less, a reflection on their ill treatment in the camps, from which they recently had returned. Their dream was somehow to get to the city of Dubai and find work in that wide-open Gulf port. But when I asked what would happen if the Taliban and Osama's men were to be hunted down by a foreign, specifically a Western, army, without exception they rallied to the jihadi cause.

They expressed their opinion without passion, indeed as if it were self-evident and not in contradiction to their earlier remarks critical of Arabs and the Taliban. Although the boys did not mention *pushtunwali,* their reaction reflected automatic deference to that ancient code regulating much of Pashtun tribal life on both sides of the border. It was something of a default position.[24] So the United States learned when the largely Pashtun Taliban shook off their rapid collapse in the fall of 2001 in little more than a year and began mounting increasingly disruptive attacks inside Afghanistan from positions in Pakistani tribal lands, where many Pashtuns lived in any case.

RARELY HAS AN AMERICAN military undertaking rallied a nation as thoroughly as the campaign routing the Taliban. Those nearly 3,000 American dead in New York, Washington and Pennsylvania were invoked to justify the long-delayed punishment of the much-warned Taliban and Al-Qaeda. America's major allies approved without demur. Yet the whirlwind initial success of the campaign was quickly tarnished. In what was described as its greatest military error in its war against Al-Qaeda, the United States failed to commit American ground troops immediately to the battle of Tora Bora, Osama's mountain retreat close to the Pakistani border, which he had used since the anti-Soviet jihad.[25]

But the ill-equipped and possibly venal Afghan militiamen that the United States entrusted with engaging several hundred of Osama's fighters failed to press home the attack and were suspected of having been paid off handsomely to collude in Al-Qaeda's escape. The militia commanders, it was said, were Pashtuns who had known Osama since the 1980s and shared their Pakistani tribal cousins' affection for him. The presence of Osama himself in Tora Bora was reported in the first half of December among some 1,000 estimated fighters: Al-Qaeda prisoners told their captors he had issued orders there on December 3, and a radio or satellite telephone message of Osama haranguing his troops was intercepted more than a week later.[26] But he slipped away, most likely following goat tracks to cross into Pakistan with most of his men. After-battle reports established that only a relative handful of Al-Qaeda combatants were killed and twenty-three captured.[27]

Why the Pentagon failed to put the Tenth Mountain Division's "boots on the ground" from the start remains unclear and was known to have infuriated nearby British elite troops—sixty men of the elite Special Boat Service. They were convinced they had located Osama and wanted to trap or kill him, but were told not to.[28] The Pentagon has avoided explaining its reasoning. But time-consuming dithering, a desire to avoid American casualties and the habit of micromanaging even the smallest deployments from Washington apparently counted heavily in the decision-making. So no American soldiers, not even the specially trained Delta Force, were committed to block the retreating Al-Qaeda units on their way to sanctuary in nearby Pakistan. If no American ground troops were to be committed, the generals in overall charge didn't want the British involved either.[29] "Within weeks high-ranking British officers were saying privately that American commanders had vetoed a proposal to guard the high-altitude trails, arguing that the risks of a firefight in deep snow, gusty winds and low-slung clouds were too high."[30] Clearly, the British were intimating that those were risks their men weighed and were ready to assume. That version gave birth to another. The British force was "eager to move in," but the American high command didn't want the embarrassment of having even its closest ally "claim the war's great prize."[31] Without such a blocking force, Pakistan could not be compelled to man its side of the border and kill or capture Al-Qaeda fugitives after their six-hour slog from Tora Bora.

A possible explanation lay in Defense Secretary Donald H. Rumsfeld's new military doctrine. He used the Afghan campaign to demonstrate his conviction that U.S. military thinking was still mired in the big divisions arrayed against a defunct Soviet Union of the defunct Cold War. The army especially badly needed a revolutionary shaking up. Rumsfeld's reliance on lightly armed Special Forces units working with Northern Alliance militiamen and air power was meant as a lesson for the tradition-bound American army.[32] Be that as it may, the failure to kill Osama allowed him to harp on his favorite theme—the alleged cowardice of American soldiers unwilling to duke it out on the battlefield with his own dedicated troops.[33]

Such reasoning at the time struck Americans as ludicrous in light of their speedy victory over the Taliban. Jihadis, and many members of the wider Muslim public, did not see it that way. Osama's presence in Tora Bora and his "miraculous escape" from American firepower only added to his stature. That was not all. Soon Osama and Ayman al-Zawahiri were back with taped audio messages aired over Al-Jazeera and other Arab satellite stations. Pakistan, which abruptly had chosen the American camp after September 11, showed signs of wavering. President Musharraf was reported to have fired some 20 percent of ISI's 12,000 officers as unreliable, but Western intelligence doubted he had removed all the pro-Taliban sympathizers. In any event, Musharraf had his own balancing act to pursue, and his sudden conversion to American demands was unpopular enough at home for critics to dub him "Busharraf."[34]

Soon after Tora Bora, President Bush's interest shifted elsewhere. By early 2002 he conspicuously stopped referring to bin Laden by name and dropped the "dead or alive" rhetoric of the immediate post–September 11 period. Bush's favorite "evildoer" was perhaps dead, perhaps alive, but in any case inaccessible somewhere along the rugged Afghan–Pakistani border. It was only a matter of months before Americans began joking that "Osama bin forgotten." The president himself contributed to that impression by seeking to play down Osama.[35] As became clear later, Bush was already gunning for Iraq much earlier. Indeed, if his former Secretary of the Treasury Paul H. O'Neill was to be believed, Bush privately articulated his desire to overthrow Saddam Hussein as early as his first meeting with the National Security Council barely a week after taking office in January 2001.[36] That was more than eight months before the events of September 11 abruptly focused his attention on terrorism for the first time and changed his presidency.

In his State of the Union speech on January 29, 2002, Bush played down the elusive Osama and sought to widen his sights. The president's focus swung to the "axis of evil," as he termed Iran, Iraq and North Korea. In June he spelled out his "doctrine of preemption" at the West Point graduation ceremonies. By early summer it became clear that he had decided to over-throw Saddam Hussein's Iraq, a somewhat toothless tiger, but an adversary requiring serious military planning and a long, staged buildup of forces in the Gulf. Bush was convinced that his "war on terrorism," which had made him immensely popular with Americans, would be furthered by toppling Saddam, the man, he pointed out, who had tried to assassinate "my dad" in Kuwait in 1993.

Within days of the attacks on New York and Washington, the influential neoconservatives inside the administration had seized on war against Iraq as a means to alter the face of the Middle East. To their minds only root-and-branch changes would bring about democracy, cleanse corrupt allies from Egypt to Saudi Arabia and Pakistan, and impose a new order on ad-versaries such as Syria and Iran. Removing Saddam and downsizing and defanging the Iraqi armed forces lay at the heart of the game plan. A future Saddam-less Iraq would keep its oil riches, but no longer constitute the Arab world's premier armed forces to threaten its neighbors and, of course, Israel. Many of the ideologues pushing such a radical course—such as Richard Perle, initially chairman of the Defense Policy Board, Deputy De-fense Secretary Paul Wolfowitz and the aides they sprinkled throughout the Pentagon and Vice President Dick Cheney's office—had long-standing ties with Israel, especially the Israeli right. Perle and Douglas Feith, number three at the Defense Department, had helped write a paper in 1996 for then newly elected right-wing Israeli prime minister Benjamin Netanyahu, ad-vocating ousting Saddam as "an important Israeli strategic objective" be-cause "Iraq's future could affect the strategic balance in the Middle East profoundly."[37] No wonder Bush's policy struck many in the Arab world and well beyond as a formula for empire, or rather a regional American–Israeli condominium.

Bush's logic escaped all but Britain among Washington's major allies, notably setting off a durable transatlantic disaffection. Bringing to heel Al-Qaeda and other jihadi terrorist groups was one thing, reordering the Middle East quite another. Indeed, critics in the Middle East, Europe and far beyond argued such an approach was calculated to add to the jihadis' luster, not contain it. By deliberately refusing to follow the Clinton lead in promoting an Israeli–Palestinian settlement, the Bush administration thumbed its nose at its predecessor and virtually gave the Israeli govern-ment a free hand to repress the Palestinians. Bush's stand offended Muslims everywhere and especially Arab governments, who were fearful such tactics would only radicalize their citizens and make Osama more popular and powerful. Bush's views also split an American establishment wary of ideological commitment, which many held responsible for the disastrous U.S. involvement in the Vietnam War of an earlier generation. The United States was doubtless the world's only military superpower. But planning—and prosecuting—the Iraq war siphoned off its intelligence community's already badly strained assets among Arabic linguists and area specialists.

Ground troops were diverted to the Iraq war who might have helped secure Afghanistan and extract strict compliance from a Pakistani regime subject to jihadi influences inside and outside its ruling military. Instead of conducting the war against Al-Qaeda to its ever-difficult conclusion with the approval of much of the world, Bush's rush to topple the Iraqi regime prompted outright resistance in the United Nations, led by France, Germany and Russia. Just before the fighting in Iraq began in March 2003, a poll registered a sudden and precipitate drop in worldwide support for the United States in countries ranging from unsurprisingly critical Muslim nations to NATO allies (including Britain, Spain and Poland, whose governments backed the war).[38]

In what struck Afghanistan watchers as a sad rerun of the mistakes that had helped bring the Taliban to power, the Bush administration contritely proclaimed that the United States had learned from the costly errors of walking away after the withdrawal of Soviet forces in 1989. Despite high-sounding protestations of support for the new Afghan government of Hamid Karzai that Washington had handpicked in Kabul, the Bush administration earmarked just one infantry division for Afghanistan's Pashtun belt. The United States initially refused to dispatch the essentially NATO–staffed international force entrusted with protecting Kabul to secure the provinces. Instead it relied on its warlord allies who had helped topple the Taliban regime.

These powerful (and often corrupt) local rulers had little interest in a strong central government, which Washington repeatedly, if halfheartedly, insisted was the best way to ensure Afghanistan's security and reconstruction. So taken with the preparations for the Iraq war was official Washington that little heed was given to the danger signals pointing to resurgent Taliban activity in southern and southeastern Afghanistan. By early 2003 ISI officers were reported helping Taliban infiltrators from Pakistan's Pashtun tribal areas cross the Afghan border. Their presence prompted official American as well as Afghan complaints, which did result in the arrest of an undisclosed number of Pakistani army officers linked to Al-Qaeda.

Pakistan's behavior was, as ever, ambivalent. In the months following September 11, Pakistan collaborated with Americans tracking Al-Qaeda cadres. Osama's operatives by the hundreds were arrested worldwide, but principally in Pakistan—as Musharraf, in his defense, kept pointing out. Most of the top captured Al-Qaeda cadres were arrested in Pakistan. (A notable exception was Mohammed Atef, the first major Al-Qaeda leader who was killed in Afghanistan, by a newfangled Predator drone equipped with a Hellfire missile, in 2001.) Starting in early 2002, hundreds of detained small-fry operatives were flown to the legal limbo of Guantanamo Bay, a U.S. naval base that Cuba at the turn of the twentieth century had agreed to rent in virtual perpetuity to Washington. There they were held as "enemy combatants," a category the administration conjured up to deny them prisoner of war status and access to counsel.

Bigger fish were held incommunicado at "undisclosed locations" said to include Thailand, friendly Arab countries, the Bagram Air Base north of Kabul and even Diego Garcia, the flyspeck archipelago in the Indian Ocean that its British colonial rulers decades before had emptied of its indigenous residents to allow the United States to stockpile materiel and build an air base. "Rendition" took on new meaning. Initially it was a legal euphemism that entered the American counterterrorism lexicon in the mid-1980s to designate sending wanted foreign suspects to the United States without benefit of the legal niceties of extradition treaties (when such agreements obtained). But, increasingly, the United States preferred to "render" terrorist suspects to Third World countries, especially those in the Arab world with a reputation for muscularly extracting information without reading them their Miranda rights. After September 11, American intelligence operatives contrived to persuade a veteran jihadi named Mohammed Haydar Zammar, a Syrian-born German citizen allegedly involved with kamikaze leader Mohammed Atta, to fly from Germany to Morocco, where cooperative authorities put him on a plane for Damascus. Germany was not informed. The Syrians turned over (at least some of) the interrogation "take" to the Americans.

A Syrian-born Canadian citizen named Maher Arar was luckier. Because the United States believed him to be an Al-Qaeda member, he was apprehended in September 2002 by officials while transiting New York's

Kennedy Airport on his way home to Canada after a holiday in Tunisia. He was held incommunicado in New York for thirteen days, then flown to Jordan and driven to Syria, where he was jailed, interrogated and incarcerated for 374 days. Unlike Zammar, he eventually was allowed to go home—thanks to an irate Canadian government, which demanded his return. On January 22, 2004, Arar, who claimed he was savagely tortured in Syria, sued the U.S. government in New York for unlawful arrest and deportation, as well as damages, in what his lawyers said was the first challenge to "extraordinary renditions." His lawsuit said the United States deliberately dispatched him to Damascus "precisely because Syria could use methods to obtain information . . . that would not be legally or morally acceptable in this country or other democracies." Despite Syria's well-documented history of human rights violations, the Department of Justice oddly argued that it was "provided with reliable assurance that Mr. Arar would be treated humanely."[39]

U.S. officials insisted they themselves inflicted no torture on their captives. But subjecting prisoners to sleep deprivation, solitary confinement, painful cramped positions and extremes of heat and cold were deemed acceptable. So, too, was the use of mind-altering drugs, such as sodium pentathol.[40] Interrogators alternatively provided and then withheld short-term pain killers from Abu Zubaydah, who was shot in the groin during his arrest in March 2002 in the eastern Pakistani city of Faisalabad. (It was perhaps no surprise that he provided information that led to the arrest of Joseph Padilla upon landing at Chicago's O'Hare airport after a flight from Zurich on May 8, 2002. (Padilla, a Puerto Rican from Chicago who converted to Islam while serving an American prison sentence, was accused of embarking on a reconnaissance mission for an eventual "dirty bomb" operation and, although a U.S. citizen, was jailed in a Navy brig in South Carolina as an "enemy combatant" and denied access to counsel.)

After September 11, as the months, then years went by, arrests, interrogations, analysis of captured documents on paper and on computer hard drives paid off. So did the fastidious work of compiling hundreds, indeed thousands of interrogations and confronting prisoners with the testimony of fellow inmates. The USA Patriot Act gave the administration much wider powers of arrest, and in any case few countries wanted to defy the United States, especially not weak Muslim states accused of harboring terrorists. On paper there was cause for optimism, if the rosy statistics were believed and recklessly projected to their linear extremes. Al-Qaeda formally was in disarray, deprived of its Afghan sanctuary, between two-thirds and 75 percent of its senior leadership killed or captured, some 3,000 operatives in jail or dead, its surviving foot soldiers and cadres dispersed.[41]

Thanks to meticulous domestic and international police work, enhanced by high-tech listening devices and other electronic means, the United States learned a great deal about its quarry and came to realize how little it had understood before. The Taliban and Al-Qaeda were preternaturally suspicious of outsiders, and that meant anyone who had not been carefully vetted by their own security people. (As for John Walker Lindh, the Taliban had watched him sufficiently over the months before 9/11 to gauge his commitment, and in any case, his foot-soldier status had not made him privy to the Al-Qaeda inner circle or its structures.) When Al-Qaeda agents communicated by telephone or e-mail, American "Big Ears" detection equipment regularly picked up what intelligence officers called "chatter," but it was often in the code of everyday language that proved all but impossible to comprehend. When word-of-mouth communications became garbled, Al-Qaeda came to rely on messengers, including women, who were less suspect than men.

In the words of a CIA station chief with long service in the region, before September 11 "we had spies in Afghanistan dating from the war against the Soviets and we reactivated them, but we had no one under the tent" with Osama or Mullah Omar. That helped explain why it sometimes took so long to connect the dots to what then seemed obvious. Nothing better illustrated the surge in American comprehension than the case of Khaled Sheikh Mohammed (or KSM, as he became known to U.S. counterterrorism officials). Only eight months after September 11 did American intelligence realize that he was at the very center of the attacks against New York and Washington and indeed those against the East African embassies and the USS *Cole* as well.[42] Curiously, a great deal about KSM had been known for years. Indeed a $2 million FBI reward for his capture had long existed, but even so only in December 2001 did his name appear on the list of the twenty-two most-wanted Al-Qaeda cadres (and the reward money upped to $25 million, the same price offered for Osama). His gift for meticulous planning was well established when he worked with his nephew Ramzi Youssef, who had masterminded the 1993 attack on the World Trade Center and fled abroad, eventually to Manila, where he teamed up with KSM.

There they devised a sophisticated plan, known as Project Bojinka (a made-up word, supposedly Serbo-Croat for "loud bang"), to blow up a dozen U.S. commercial airliners virtually simultaneously over the Pacific in the winter of 1995. The plot was discovered when an accidental explosion in Youssef's rented Manila flat led to the seizure of his computer, which, when decoded, yielded a mother lode of intelligence. Youssef himself escaped but was arrested in Islamabad a year later. Enough was known about KSM, including a photograph found on Youssef's hard drive, to get him indicted by a New York grand jury on terrorism charges in 1995. Thanks to luck and surpassing tradecraft, he kept eluding his would-be captors in two dozen countries. He used some fifty aliases, and his name appeared on a hundred watch lists even before the September 11 operations.[43]

KSM was a master of disguise, no small feat for a squat, overweight man with thinning hair. He regularly changed his routine, at times canceling scheduled meetings to confuse pursuers. When he was in Qatar he was said to possess some twenty passports and was at home passing himself off as a Gulf oil sheikh or a humble peddler of holy water from Mecca. He spoke four languages—his native Baluchi, English, Urdu and Arabic—with a strong Kuwaiti accent, since he and Youssef had grown up in the Gulf emirate before, at age seventeen, he began studying mechanical engineering in two small colleges in North Carolina in 1982. He was born in the working-class oil town of Fahaheel, south of Kuwait City, which was full of alienated Palestinians and Muslims who flocked to the refinery for work but were denied Kuwaiti citizenship. KSM, Youssef and Wadih el-Hage were among Fahaheel residents recruited into jihadi terrorism.

For a while in 1995 and early 1996 KSM lived under virtual official protection in the Gulf emirate of Qatar, thanks to a member of the ruling family who provided refuge for veterans of the anti-Soviet jihad in Afghanistan. Such are the vagaries of the Gulf that, at the same time, the small, natural gas–rich country was busy ingratiating itself with Washington. Qatar agreed to an energy deal with Israel and entered into a de facto military alliance providing the United States a giant air base, materiel depot and forward headquarters for Central Command, which was used in the wars against the Taliban in 2001 and against Iraq in 2003. Much to American fury, early in 1996 jihadi insiders in Qatar tipped off KSM that Washington had discovered his clandestine job as an engineer in the water department and had sent an FBI team to arrest him. Then FBI Director Louis Freeh in 1996 wrote Qatar's foreign minister, "I have received disturbing information suggesting that Mohammed has again escaped the surveillance of your security services and that he appears to be aware of FBI interest in him." Freeh prophetically noted that failure to apprehend KSM "would allow him and other associates to continue to conduct terrorist operations."

He fled, and in retrospect, American intelligence officers concluded the United States lost its best chance of heading off the September 11 attacks.[44] KSM was then variously traced to Brazil, Germany and other European countries. But the heat was on. And some time in 1996 or more likely early 1997 he traveled to Afghanistan, the fabled bolt-hole for jihadis on the run. There he met Osama. Whether their meeting in Kandahar was their initial encounter is open to dispute; it is sometimes advanced that he first served Osama as a bodyguard. Both men certainly had been in Pakistan in the 1980s during the anti-Soviet jihad. But so had thousands of other foreign jihadis. Senior American counterterrorism officials claimed that during a Philippine sojourn in the early 1990s Youssef and KSM were funded by Osama (along with the Moro Islamist Liberation Front and the Abu Sayyaf Group, which later degenerated into a glorified kidnapping ring). Osama consistently denied knowing Youssef. Youssef, in turn, did not volunteer KSM's name when he talked freely to FBI agents in the mistaken belief his remarks, made aboard a jet flying him back from his arrest in Pakistan to New York, could not be used against him in court. Rohan Gunaratna, a Sri Lankan expert on Al-Qaeda, is convinced Osama deliberately denied knowing Youssef as a way to protect KSM, but offers no supporting evidence. In Manila, in any case, both Baluchis developed a decidedly un-Islamic taste for cocktail lounges, bar girls and the good life and were not known to have set foot in a mosque.[45]

But KSM was no lowlife dependent on petty theft. His Konsojaya company generated quite enough revenue to keep him going at the head of an independent organization. In fact, his real importance lay elsewhere—in his uncanny ability to operate without outside help. Like Carlos the Jackal and the Lebanese Shi'a Imad Mugniyah, he had a gift for conceiving terrorist operations and plotting their minutest detail. He was the consummate operator, the hands-on practitioner whose inspired devotion to detail made Osama's other operatives look like amateurs. He and Youssef and their gang had given every sign of working their own corner without easily discernible dependence on Al-Qaeda. Theirs was one of the parallel organizations Osama was to team up with in various parts of the world.

But in KSM's case there was a crucial difference. Osama knew quality when he saw it. And much like the owner of an American professional basketball, baseball or football team determined to recruit the best talent, Osama was willing to shell out to persuade him to join his team. KSM had a proven track record, so Osama was not taking much of a risk. His new operations chief's commitment was to minutely planned and increasingly sophisticated terrorist undertakings that required recruiting dedicated personnel, daring and, for September 11 at least, lots of money by Osama's usual standards. What American counterterrorism specialists at long last came to realize well into 2002 was that all the major Al-Qaeda operations starting with the East African embassies were KSM's handiwork.

They all bore his meticulous hallmark: his natural talent for conceptualizing long-range projects, choosing the right candidates for his jihadi teams and putting them in place undetected. He had an innate sense for the careful sequence of planning, be it the lead time for purchasing trucks or a skiff (in the case of the USS *Cole*) used to deliver the explosive charge or the right moment to dispatch pilots to American flight schools, the just-in-time arrival of a master bomb-maker for the East African embassies job or of the "muscle" for September 11 or the niceties of banking and money transfers in the United Arab Emirates and the United States. When American investigators started unraveling the September 11 attacks they could only marvel at the combination of stealth and openness KSM demonstrated in keeping nineteen plotters below the radar screens of U.S. intelligence and law enforcement. And the plot had ramifications not just in the United States but in Germany, where Mohammed Atta's Hamburg friends provided the pilots and key handlers, as well as in Afghanistan, Britain, Pakistan, the Philippines, Spain and the United Arab Emirates.

He knew exactly how much money at a go he could order transferred without arousing the suspicions of American banking regulators. Neither Osama himself nor his principal lieutenants had that kind of practical knowledge of how the West worked. KSM had spent more than three years studying in the United States, somehow acquiring a touch and appreciation for the smallest details that have ever been the mark of an inspired engineer and a perfectionist plotter. Yet the fine meshing of plans and men that accounted for September 11's success was curiously devoid of artifice. Indeed, it owed its success to its openness. Since the operations against the World Trade Center and the Pentagon were "martyrdom" (that is, suicide) missions, there was no need for aliases or covering tracks. Thus telltale clues were left in rental cars, along with the last will and testament of operation leader Atta, with its detailed instructions for his funeral.

Obviously, KSM and his teams had the advantage of surprise in reconnoitering their targets (and video footage was seized in Afghanistan of various stalking missions to the United States). Even when his charges made mistakes or were plagued with bad luck, it was after they accomplished their missions, not before. Neither he nor Osama attached any visible importance, for example, to the four men who were caught, tried and condemned to life sentences for their parts in the East African bombings. They were expendable.[46] Their trials and the information they disgorged beforehand certainly added to the knowledge American intelligence agencies developed about Al-Qaeda, but in no way compromised the ensuing implementation of the USS *Cole* operation, much less the New York and Washington spectaculars. All these operations were years in the planning.

KSM's luck finally ran out on March 1, 2003. American and Pakistani agents tracked him down in a section of the old Raj cantonment city of Rawalpindi, favored by serving and retired Pakistani generals. He was captured in a private house without a fight, sleepy and disheveled in a white T-shirt. U.S. officials were jubilant, understandably so after months and months of mediocre results. Taking KSM was far more important than the previous arrests and the occasional killing of senior Al-Qaeda cadres. His arrest dwarfed the killing the previous November in Yemen of Qaed Saneyan al-Harthi, a key figure in the USS *Cole* attack, by a Hellfire missile aboard a Predator drone. It outshone the more conventional arrest in Oman of Abdal Rahim Nashiri, Osama's operations chief in the Gulf.

And his arrest even eclipsed the capture of his sidekick Ramzi bin al-Shibh, with whom KSM had bragged about the September 11 attacks in an Al-Jazeera documentary that aired on the first anniversary of the New York and Washington operations. The Bush administration obviously hoped that no one half as capable would replace KSM. That would be solace of a sort, even if he was masterminding terrorist operations in the pipeline at the time of his capture. KSM's stature was such that Nizar Nasrawi, a Tunisian sometime travel agent, called him by satellite telephone for personal approval before blowing up himself and a truck packed with explosives just outside a synagogue on the Tunisian holiday island of Djerba. That attack, in April 2002, was the first Al-Qaeda operation after New York and Washington. It claimed the lives of fourteen German and a few other

European tourists and proved that Al-Qaeda was still very much in business, albeit against a soft target. KSM's computers and other documents were promptly flown by executive jet to the United States, where they were analyzed by the FBI, the CIA, the DIA and other intelligence agencies. He himself was spirited out of Pakistan to an undisclosed destination where American intelligence specialists began a long process to squeeze everything they could out of him.

Even before KSM's undoing, the CIA and other American intelligence agencies began making known their growing confidence in GWOT, Beltway-speak for the administration's Global War on Terrorism. But in the immediate aftermath of his arrest, counterterrorism officials in Washington went as public as intelligence organizations go. Senior administration officials in and out of intelligence began boasting for the first time since September 11 had tarnished their reputation and exposed their bureaucratic infighting and general incompetence. The timing of KSM's capture was extremely serendipitous for the administration. It helped undercut a phalanx of worried, mostly retired generals, intelligence officials and senior members of past administrations (including that of the president's father). They doubted the wisdom of what they considered a reckless rush to invade Iraq on the basis of iffy intelligence, even if France shared what turned out to be the erroneous view that Iraq still possessed weapons of mass destruction. Their message: better to allow Hans Blix's inspection teams the time to complete their investigations for the United Nations and avoid a split in the Security Council.

These critics wanted no distractions from the struggle against Osama. But despite a drumbeat of public warnings from often retired, anonymous or foreign counterterrorism specialists who felt they could talk freely, distractions were what they got. Gunaratna, the Sri Lankan analyst, put the case succinctly. "I feel that if they had not gone to Iraq they would have found Osama by now," he said. "The best people were moved away from this operation. The best minds were moved to Iraq. It's a great shame and the biggest military failure in the war on terrorism so far. The Americans need more resources, and more high-level people exclusively assigned to this task."[47]

Compounding the critics' upset with the dispersion of assets was their suspicion that the administration was fabricating intelligence to fit its "regime change" needs. To be sure, the end users of intelligence in democracies were politicians. But the vexed intelligence veterans insisted that never before had they come under such pressure to read often wispy indications as rock-solid evidence to please their civilian masters. In the months before the Iraq war began, critics were openly contemptuous of the questionable intelligence they felt the Defense Department's neo-conservative civilians at Douglas Feith's Office of Special Plans tweaked, hyped and fabricated to justify overthrowing Saddam Hussein. The critics worried—correctly, as it turned out—about postwar political uncertainties. They were especially concerned about the open-ended expenditure inherent in such a war. They warned the United States would likely have to foot the bill virtually alone (unlike the first Gulf war in 1991, which cost Washington virtually nothing). Among more dubious—and telling—administration claims were the repeatedly trumpeted purported ties between Saddam Hussein's Iraq and Al-Qaeda, indeed their alleged but never-proven collusion and collaboration in the September 11 attacks themselves.[48]

Administration officials were also accused of having suppressed widely circulated debriefing reports from Abu Zubaydah and KSM in which they said Al-Qaeda cadres had discussed possible collaboration with Saddam Hussein, but rejected it at Osama's direction.[49] Thanks to the administration's repeated allegations of Al-Qaeda involvement with Baghdad—and the enduring near-panic Al-Qaeda produced—opinion polls in the United States before and after the American invasion of Iraq showed overwhelming belief that Baghdad was involved in the attacks in New York and Washington. Only in January 2004 did Secretary of State Colin L. Powell, long the only member of the Bush cabinet to enjoy the trust of foreign governments, finally acknowledge that he had "not seen smoking gun, concrete evidence" backing up administration assertions and insinuations that Saddam had ties to Al-Qaeda.[50]

But by then the damage was done, again proving the validity of Joseph Goebbels's dictum that the "big lie" works with gullible citizens. More than the hyped insistence that Iraq retained weapons of mass destruction, the alleged Al-Qaeda links exposed the administration's approximations when it came to telling the truth. But the hype worked, and opinion polls before the hostilities showed that more than half of Americans questioned—but virtually no one outside the United States—were convinced the connection existed. Critics were reduced to worrying about the damage such falsified intelligence could provoke in the exemplary everyday collaboration among the intelligence agencies of allies after the September 11 attacks. In their view, the Bush doctrine of preemption—that is, of making war on any adversary, singly or with allies of America's choice without United Nations approval—weakened the likelihood of future political cooperation among longtime allies and eventually even of intelligence exchanges. (Remarkably, intelligence collaboration on counterterrorism was maintained to a degree despite the grave transatlantic crisis engendered by the Iraq war, reflecting a shared fear of jihadi terrorism more than faith in American policy.)

By early 2004 Kenneth M. Pollack, a former Clinton-era National Security Council staffer who had written a best-selling book favoring invading Iraq, felt compelled to admit the error of his—and the Bush administration's—ways. (He argued, somewhat disingenuously, that the errors were innocent and even shared by the French, who also had thought Saddam was hiding weapons of mass destruction but, of course, did not approve of the administration's exaggerations buttressing its rush into controversial preemptive war.)

In what approximated a mea culpa, the onetime CIA analyst allowed: "When the U.S. confronts future challenges, the exaggerated estimates of Iraqi weapons of mass destruction will loom like an ugly shadow over the diplomatic discussions." His admission of error did not explicitly mention the seemingly always bogus Al-Qaeda–Iraq links, but his blanket conclusion covered that particular charge, which no ally except Britain had ever believed. "Fairly or not, no foreigners trust U.S. intelligence to get it right anymore or the Bush administration to tell the truth. The only way we can regain the world's trust is to demonstrate we understand our mistakes and have changed our ways."[51]

Since the Bush administration demonstrated a marked aversion to admitting errors and gracefully accepting responsibility for their consequences, such redemption did not seem to be an immediate prospect. Indeed, even after David Kay resigned on January 24, 2004, as the chief U.S. weapons inspector in Iraq and acknowledged "we were almost all wrong" in assuming Saddam possessed weapons of mass destruction, the president played for time. Forced by public opinion, the opposition Democrats and even Republicans, Bush finally agreed in early February to an independent investigation regarding the weapons of mass destruction fiasco, but made sure any report would be published well after the November elections.

Such timing made sense in terms of domestic politics, but it was unlikely to persuade the rest of the world watching the Bush administration sink deeper into the quagmire of its preemptive war in Iraq.

Thus, the next time the United States seeks international support in a time of tension, it is doubtful major allies would react as General de Gaulle did during the Cuban missile crisis in 1962, when Washington and Moscow came close to war. The French President then was certainly regarded as every bit as much a thorn in Washington's side as the Bush administration considered his successor, Jacques Chirac. President Kennedy had chosen the perfect emissary to send to Paris. Dean Acheson, the distinguished former secretary of state, arrived at the Élysée Palace with reconnaissance photographs said to show long-range missiles aboard Soviet ships steaming toward Havana. When Acheson offered to lay them out to his host, de Gaulle waved him off: "The word of the President of the United States is good enough for me."[52]

IN THE TENSE WEEKS before the long-telegraphed Iraq war actually began in March 2003, the administration understandably sought to extract the most from KSM's capture. His comeuppance was admirably suited to remind Americans of a favorite theme: dethroning Saddam Hussein was essential to GWOT. "It's a big deal," said CIA Director George Tenet. "We've got them nailed and are close to dismantling them" was how one senior U.S. intelligence official described the war against Al-Qaeda two weeks after KSM's arrest. The prisoner was reported to be "cooperating" with his interrogators.[53] "I believe the tide has turned," said Republican Congressman Porter J. Goss, a onetime CIA case officer who chaired the House Intelligence Committee. "We're at the top of the hill." A senior intelligence official felt confident enough to taunt Al-Qaeda. "If they don't pull off something big soon," he said, "some of their financial backers are going to ask whether it makes sense to give them a lot more money. Soon their viability is going to be questioned around the world. They are probably under pressure to show they are still valid."

Those proved to be provocatively unwise words. No sooner had the president's famous victory in Iraq begun to turn sour and his advisers come to regret his May 1 stunt of landing a Navy jet on an aircraft carrier decorated with a "Mission Accomplished" sign than Al-Qaeda resumed its operations with a vengeance. The big attacks were no longer in Bali or

Kenya, as in the fall of the previous year. Nor did Osama immediately make good his threats, contained in a cassette broadcast by Al-Jazeera in February, to cause trouble in Iraq itself. That did not stop the administration from seizing on his statement as proof of his collusion with Saddam, despite Osama's clear distinction between his support for the Iraqi people and his deep-seated distrust of the secular Baathist regime. (Saddam returned the compliment. He consistently refused operational cooperation with Osama before he fell and went into hiding in April. In written instructions seized when he was at last captured in December 2003—and deemed authentic by the CIA—Saddam warned his Baath Party followers against joining forces with foreign Arab jihadis entering Iraq to fight the Americans.)[54]

Instead Al-Qaeda struck inside Saudi Arabia, first on May 12, and again on November 9, killing thirty-four, including nine Americans in the first operation, then eighteen, mostly non-Saudi Arabs from places like Lebanon and Egypt, in the second. In both cases the targets in the capital of Riyadh were soft—gated and guarded—residential areas for foreigners. The targets were fateful choices. After thirteen years on Saudi soil the U.S. Air Force had just announced its withdrawal from the Kingdom, and indeed by early September the last planes and personnel disappeared from Prince Sultan Air Base. Right to the end, the Al-Saud tried to have it both ways, but obviously hoped that the Americans' departure would deprive Osama of his favorite argument against the regime now that the land of the two mosques was no longer besmirched with infidel soldiers.[55] Of course, neither Osama nor the boiling anti-American sentiment in the Kingdom was mentioned. The officially invoked reason for the withdrawal was that Saddam no longer constituted a threat to the country. That was true enough. But neither the Saudi regime nor the United States derived popular approval for the move. It was simply too late to expect such a lift from a decision that, if taken only a few years earlier, might have avoided much grief.

Saudis thought they had plenty of other grievances against both their government and the superpower whose policies contributed so much to the disaffection of average citizens. Jobs were scarce for the young, the standard of living stagnant at best, the heavily religious education ill designed for the Kingdom's needs and the Al-Sauds' 7,000 princes a greedy lot indifferent to their countrymen's growing frustration. In the age of satellite television, Saudis of all walks of life thought they had plenty of reasons to rage: American indifference to the plight of the Palestinians; an American war in Afghanistan against a fellow fundamentalist Sunni regime; and another American war, this one an ideological conflict of Washington's choice, in Iraq, where the hated and dreaded Shi'a majority seemed poised to gain power and encourage trouble with the Kingdom's own repressed Shi'a minority sitting atop the oil fields.

A local wit said that "half the Saudis are anti-American and the other half are pro-Osama." There was more than a kernel of truth to the joke, and certainly never before in his long struggle against the royal family had Osama won over more followers in his native land. Such was the perverse effect of the September 11 attacks in Saudi Arabia and many another Muslim land.

The mood was only marginally less volatile in the United States. Ordinary Americans who previously would have been hard pressed to locate Saudi Arabia on a map were furious at a supposedly friendly country that produced all but four of the nineteen September 11 hijackers. An always-complicated alliance born of America's growing oil thirst suddenly was subjected to minute scrutiny. What ordinary Americans saw did not please them, and no amount of high-priced public relations in Washington could contain their anger. The Bush administration carefully refrained from criticizing Saudi Arabia in public. But neoconservative Richard Perle's Defense Policy Board made sure that Saudi Arabia was considered a virtual enemy. Frenchman Laurent Murawiec, a pro-Israeli analyst for the RAND Corporation who, curiously, once worked for right-wing radical Lyndon LaRouche, on July 10, 2002, briefed board members, including former Secretary of State Henry Kissinger, that "the Saudis are active at every level of the terror chain, from planners to financiers, from cadre to foot-soldier, from ideologist to cheer leader." Murawiec's briefing stated that "Saudi Arabia supports our enemies and attacks our allies." A talking point attached to the last of twenty-four slides claimed the Kingdom was "the kernel of evil, the prime mover, the most dangerous opponent" in the Middle East.[56] But private leaks from senior officials made clear their anger at a lack of cooperation by Prince Nayef's Interior Ministry (and secret police) and frustration with obstacles thrown up in tracking suspected financing for Al-Qaeda in the Kingdom. The Al-Sauds' virtually official outlays on Wahhabi proselytism abroad was no longer glossed over. Egregiously anti-Christian and anti-Jewish passages in schoolbooks were quoted at length.

Long-standing Western criticism of the sorry state of women's rights and other human rights in the Kingdom resurfaced. Saudi Arabia always had been a delicate—indeed, at times an embarrassing—foreign policy-problem best handled by experts and a deft and well-connected lobby in Washington. The lobby's much-vaunted clout evaporated overnight after September 11. Senator Richard Shelby, the Republican from Alabama who became chairman of the Intelligence Committee, summed up a general feeling in Congress. "I wouldn't look on Saudi Arabia as an ally," he said. While acknowledging America's growing dependence on Saudi oil, he maintained, "They've got a lot of answering to do in my judgment."[57] Anguished Saudi protests of having helped America in many crises over the decades barely registered. Suddenly Saudi Arabia was transformed into grist for more or less well-meaning newspaper columnists, grandstanding congressmen and rabid radio and television talk shows. In other words, the relationship was out of control.

The events of May 12 demonstrated that the royal family's efforts to contain Osama's jihadis were ineffectual—like so much else of their governance. After the Grand Mosque embarrassment in 1979, the Al-Saud had felt obliged to grant greater power to the Wahhabi clergy. Now a generation later, the royal family, for all intents and purposes, was split over how, indeed if, to redress the balance. And it found itself under growing pressure from an increasingly radical clergy, some of whose more popular preachers were spouting a line virtually indistinguishable from Osama's (save for demanding the Al-Sauds' overthrow, which he so devoutly desired). In a country where Crown Prince Abdullah was over eighty and his immediate hierarchical successors only a year or so younger, the seemingly perpetual interior minister, Prince Nayef, had marked the first anniversary of the attacks on New York and Washington by insisting that the Zionists were behind them. Such talk infuriated American officials but fascinated Saudis, who understood its domestic political intent.

In fact, the two princes were protagonists in an unresolved struggle for the succession to King Fahd, who since a stroke in 1995 was barely compos mentis. Along with the small, educated pro-Western elite, Abdullah saw the necessity of reforms to clean up the Saudi act after September 11, including removing hate themes from textbooks, modernizing curricula and coming to an accommodation with the outside world, both Muslim and infidel. Prince Nayef relied on the Al-Sauds' ancient alliance with the back-to-basics Wahhabis, who imagined or genuinely felt under threat from local and Iraqi Shi'a, the "Zionist-American conspiracy" dear to Osama and homegrown Sunni reformers wittingly or unwittingly playing their game. Nayef did nothing to rein in radical Islamists clustered around preachers such as Safar al-Hawali and Salman al-Awada who, after several years in jail for anti-American exhortations in the mid-1990s, were back publicly propagating the line that long endeared them to Osama.

Nayef's manipulations, of course, mirrored the remarks by Muslim hoi polloi that had gained instantaneous currency in the Muslim world in the immediate aftermath of the attacks. Such talk then was charitably seen as a threadbare defense mechanism (along with claims that only the Israelis or Americans, or both, were clever enough to stage such accomplished operations, deemed far beyond the powers of mere Arabs). But Nayef's motives later on were political. That helped explain why, two months after the attacks in the United States, he insisted, "so far we've received no evidence or documents from the U.S. authorities that justify the suspicion or accusation" that Saudis were involved.[58] Similarly, he knew what he was doing in reiterating his denial in his anniversary utterance: "I still cannot believe that 19 youths, including [15] Saudis carried out the September 11 attacks with the support of bin Laden. That's impossible."[59]

Seen in the light of this power struggle, the Al-Qaeda terrorist operation in May 2003 initially succeeded temporarily in stopping Abdullah's reforms just as they began gathering steam thanks to the "national dialogue" he launched in March. (A major battleground was the reformers' suggested purge of the most intolerant passages in schoolbooks dear to the Wahhabi clerics and Osama.) Deflecting reforms was enough to satisfy Nayef, who, despite his earlier remarks, played both good cop and bad cop and after May 12 began hunting down Al-Qaeda cells with a vengeance. The unstable status quo was maintained, but the gut issue remained unresolved: Could the Al-Saud reduce the power of the religious establishment—that is, gain back the ground conceded since 1979—without breaking the 150-year-old compact between themselves as rulers and Wahhabism? Some specialists argued that Al-Qaeda knew it was not yet strong enough to seize power and thus "objectively," as the Soviets used to say, was content to have "turned a terrorist attack against Americans into a political coup against the Americanizers" in the Crown Prince's camp.[60] But Prince Abdullah and his partisans cautiously kept probing, looking for step-by-step ways to further his reforms.

The Americans especially favored his efforts to moderate the Wahhabi school curriculum and hold elections. To the degree that they ever really believed in the reforms' chances the terrorist attacks revealed a jihadi network far more lethal and ramified than even Saudi pessimists had suspected. Striking at soft targets such as foreigners' housing complexes couldn't hold a candle to September 11 or attacks on the East African embassies. But nonetheless such tactics succeeded in making foreign workers think hard about the wisdom of staying in a land where foreigners were essential to tasks as varied as running banks or driving taxis.

In a lifetime as a foreign correspondent, I developed something of a sixth sense for recognizing the tipping point when the hired hands first packed off their families, then left themselves. In 1960 in the early days after the Belgian Congo became independent and the capital, now Kinshasa, but then still Leopoldville, was subject to looting, rape and (relatively little) murder, the Belgians and other foreign residents left the keys in their big American cars at the "beach," as they called the landing of the ferry that traversed the river Congo to the still-orderly other Congo recently under French rule. In Algeria, settler violence and Muslim reprisal stampeded all but a few tens of thousands of French onto ships and planes for metropolitan France in a few months on either side of independence in July 1962. (General de Gaulle, in fact, was not that unhappy, since he wanted France to be finished with its colonial experience and wished to leave no hostages to fortune.)

Again, in 1975, I watched as repeated bouts of murderous violence in Beirut quickly emptied the Levant's most sophisticated city of all the foreign Arab movers and shakers who had migrated to Lebanon to escape the political turmoil and chaos of their own countries. Europeans and Americans who used Beirut as a base for their Middle East operations followed suit. Eventually many educated and uneducated Lebanese left as well. Covering the Iranian revolution in Tehran in 1979, I was amazed that a few well-publicized murders panicked thousands of Americans and other Westerners into fleeing.

If these various events had any common thread, it was that violence, mindless or organized by terrorists, quite often worked and seemingly invariably left those countries affected poorer for the departure of their homegrown or foreign elites, and for far longer than anyone imagined at the time. I kept thinking back to my visit to Saudi Arabia in 1999. I wondered which of my diplomats would prove right, the European convinced the de facto alliance with America was made of titanium or the American worried about the Al-Saud and the aerodynamics of the bumblebee. By this time I was far from alone in asking the question. Certainly, the two terrorist operations in 2003 had reminded ordinary Saudis of the price of disorder. So, too, did America's messy involvement in Iraq, which discouraged once-active fears that Saudi Arabia would be next on the administration's list of targets. Were there, as so often, other alternatives? Osama had done much to frame the stark choices. What role he would be assigned in either eventuality (or another outcome) remained unclear. But through willful application of American wealth and power, the Bush administration's GWOT in all its facets was likely to be held responsible for accelerating the outcome.

As UNSETTLING as they were, the Saudi attacks were far from constituting the jihadis' only operations in 2003. New fronts were opened in Morocco and Turkey, and Indonesia was revisited. Four days after the first Riyadh attack, twelve young Moroccans recruited in the Sidi Moumen slum of Casablanca went on a five-pronged suicide attack rampage under the local banner of *salifiya jihadiya*. They ended up killing themselves and thirty-one others, including five Spaniards and Frenchmen, in attacks against a prominent hotel, a fashionable restaurant, the Spanish Club, the Jewish cemetery and a Jewish club. But they were an ignorant and ill-trained lot, for instance, planting explosives in the dwindling Jewish community's social club on a Friday night when it was closed for the Sabbath.

The government initially charged that jihadis had received between $50,000 and $70,000 from overseas backers for those and other undisclosed operations. At the time, blaming Al-Qaeda for financing the attacks distracted attention from a serious intelligence failure. But no evidence was produced in public or in court. The money, according to government sources, was linked to Abu Musab Zarqawi, the Jordanian-born leader of the jihadi *tawhid* organization that the United States has equated with Al-Qaeda. A year later, Moroccan officials acknowledged that Al-Qaeda was not involved in the financing.[61] Western and Arab intelligence sources said Zarqawi escaped in November 2001 from Afghanistan to Iran, where he was detained before being released from house arrest and allowed to travel to Iraq. Washington held Zarqawi responsible for the assassination of

American diplomat Lawrence M. Foley in Jordan in 2002 and for planning the abortive millennium operations in Jordan two years earlier.[62] Various Al-Qaeda pronouncements had declared that Morocco was on the punishment list. Still, the shock was considerable in the still royal-directed parliamentary democracy where King Mohammed VI was officially the commander of the faithful (the same title Mullah Omar delighted in) and Islamists for years had been under close scrutiny and often house arrest. The repression was massive, with several thousand suspected jihadis reported arrested for questioning and hundreds brought to trial and condemned in short order. The no-nonsense justice was partly aimed at reassuring European and Arab visitors, since tourism accounts for a sizable slice of Morocco's foreign-exchange earnings.

More than a dozen death sentences were meted out, in addition to jail terms running from one to thirty years and life imprisonment. In the past Morocco somewhat miraculously had escaped the kind of wholesale jihadist violence that next door in Algeria had claimed more than 150,000 lives since 1992. Why Morocco was targeted remains unclear, and Moroccans from all walks of life reacted to the attacks by asking, "Why us?" Ten days after the attacks, 2 million Moroccans marched in Casablanca to demonstrate their condemnation of the terrorism. Still, for those looking for motives, some noted the kingdom's long history of close relations with Israel (partly as a means of endearing itself to Washington), as well as with its European neighbors and the United States. If the jihadis had hoped to deter the monarch from enacting reforms, they were disappointed. At his instigation, and to the delight of Moroccan feminists, in January 2004 the obedient parliament unanimously voted far-reaching reforms basically ending traditional Islamic male control over many aspects of women's lives. In all the Muslim world, only the republic of Tunisia, under its founder-president, the late Habib Bourguiba, had dared go so far, half a century earlier.

A more unmistakable Al-Qaeda trademark was discernible in two separate days of double suicide truck bombings five days apart in the heart of Istanbul in November 2003, in which sixty-two people died and hundreds were wounded. The first attacks, against two synagogues on November 15, claimed six Jewish and seventeen Muslim lives in addition to those of the two bombers. In the second, British Consul-General Roger Short was blown up in his consulate and the London-based HSBC Bank, with roots in the old Hong Kong Shanghai Bank, had almost all its twenty-story façade stripped clean when pickup trucks exploded within minutes of each other. (The imposing consulate, which housed the British embassy in the Ottoman era, was around the corner from a similarly imposing pile abandoned by the Americans for security reasons a few months earlier, and from the Pera Palace, Agatha Christie's favorite haunt when in town.) The timing could not have been more embarrassing for the government of Tony Blair or his guest.

Britain's prime minister was receiving President Bush on a long-planned, minutely choreographed state visit to London designed to showcase the Anglo-American alliance, celebrate their military cooperation in Iraq and provide colorful footage for the president's reelection campaign. The terrorist attacks on NATO's only Muslim member state stole the media spotlight away from the London celebrations. The modus operandi pointed to Al-Qaeda: the use of suicide bombers, near-simultaneous explosions and the sense of timing, all designed to expose the vanity of British and American claims they were getting a handle on terrorism. In addition, the targeting of the synagogues focused attention on Turkey's de facto military alliance with Israel. The targets also underlined the jihadis' hatred of the Turkish Republic, its secular parliamentary democracy and its dogged desire to join the European Union.

In various pronouncements over the years Osama had made clear his deep resentment against the Turkish Republic. Various anonymous telephoned messages claimed Al-Qaeda's responsibility for all four attacks, a view that the Turkish interior minister eventually endorsed. Even with a convenient foreign hand to blame, the Turkish establishment was seriously embarrassed, and not just the moderate Islamist government of Prime Minister Recep Tayyip Erdogan, but also the army, the gendarmerie and the principal intelligence agency. Among the terrorists who died in the attacks—or were associated in its planning—were former members of the banned Hezbollah, initially an underground militant group of radical local Sunni Islamists with no known major links to their better-known Shi'a namesakes in Iran and Lebanon.[63]

As a Turkish parliamentary report and private investigations had already noted, the local Hezbollah for more than a decade were allowed to kidnap, kill and extort with impunity. Covered by the local authorities in Turkish Kurdistan, Hezbollah gunmen who were Kurds acted as death squads in the dirty war the state waged against other Kurds suspected, rightly or wrongly, of sympathy for the Kurdistan Workers Party, better known as the PKK. From 1984 to 1999, the Marxist PKK had led a rebellion in Turkey's southeastern Kurdish heartland that reawakened the sense of identity for Turkey's large and repressed Kurdish minority at the cost of some 35,000 lives, largely Kurdish. When the rebellion petered out, in a technique perfected centuries earlier by the Ottomans, the Turkish state turned on the Hezbollah. The government suddenly made mass arrests and discovered hundreds of missing government arms in the group's possession, as well as graves of Hezbollah victims. Almost 500 long-unexplained murders were eventually laid at Hezbollah's door. In the crackdown, security forces liquidated Hezbollah's top leader and senior cadres, but largely ignored its estimated 20,000 foot soldiers. Some escaped abroad—

principally to Iraq, Chechnya and Afghanistan, where they underwent military training by like-minded jihadis. Turkish officials who had covered up Hezbollah excesses essentially escaped punishment.

Embarrassingly for the state, especially the Turkish intelligence agency (MIT), at least two of the Istanbul suicide bombers were former members of Hezbollah, and all four hailed from the impoverished Kurdish city of Bingol. (Their favored meeting places were Internet cafés, and no longer mosques or Islamist bookshops, which they knew were kept under police surveillance.) The danger of such leftover loose ends reminded many Turks of America's own oversight in walking away from the Arab Afghans after the Red Army departed Afghanistan in 1989. Instructed by the dangers of involvement in the Middle East's political quarrels, known popularly as "Arab hair" for their complexity, Turks needed little reminding that they lived in a tough neighborhood. Fears about entanglement in America's war in Iraq helped explain why in March 2003 Turkey's parliament, mirroring overwhelming anti-American public opinion, had preferred to incur Washington's ire rather than authorize the transit of American troops through Turkey on their way to overthrow Saddam Hussein.

For the first time in recent Turkish memory, a reform-minded party, Erdogan's Justice and Development Party, had won an outright majority of parliamentary seats—and exercised its democratic prerogatives, despite a superpower's arm twisting. For all Bush's elegant prose about the virtues of democracy in the Middle East (notably during his London visit), the administration was not amused. So when an angry Washington came in the fall with offers of badly needed financial aid in exchange for a troop commitment in Iraq, the same parliament in Ankara voted in favor of sending 10,000 Turkish soldiers to its southern neighbor. The Pentagon finally backed off after stout opposition from the Kurds and other members of the Iraqi Governing Council, who for once dared stand up to the Americans who had named them. It was against this background of Turkey's complex relations with the United States and the Arab world that the attacks in Istanbul took place. And in the aftermath of those terrorist operations, Al-Qaeda could take satisfaction from the widespread view, including in Turkey's mainstream press, that the CIA and Mossad were the real instigators of the carnage.

Nonetheless, a message claiming to emanate from Al-Qaeda accepted responsibility for the suicide bombings and warned: "We tell the criminal Bush and his Arab and Western tails—especially Britain, Italy, Australia and Japan—that the cars of death will not stop in Baghdad, Riyadh, Istanbul, Nasiriyah [where a suicide bomber killed nineteen Italian troops on November 12] and Jakarta—until you see them with your own eyes in the middle of the capital of the tyrant of this era, America."[64] The message was signed by the Abu Hafs al-Masri Brigades, named after Osama's military chief who was killed by a missile in November 2001 in Afghanistan. The same organization had claimed responsibility for the suicide truck-bomb attack on the curiously unguarded UN headquarters in Baghdad in August in which the UN head of mission, Sergio Vieira de Mello, and twenty-one others were killed. Vieira de Mello was partly to blame. He deliberately wanted to keep UN security to a minimum. Intent on demonstrating the United Nations' independence from the still all-conquering United States—which had insisted on retaining all the levers of power for itself—he had turned down proffered American troop protection. Moreover, the United Nations had a long record of cooperation with the Baathist regime and thus was not without enemies in Iraq.

But if jihadis since September 11 had demonstrated an uncanny ability to make good on public threats to punish an impressive list of countries on their enemies' list, it was in Pakistan where they came closest to bringing down the established order. Twice within eleven days in December 2003 they came literally within seconds of assassinating President Musharraf. As the Istanbul communiqué predicted, motor vehicles and explosives were featured in these attempts on his life. Al-Qaeda had made no secret it was gunning for the Pakistani leader. In an audiotape broadcast in September 2003 by Al-Jazeera, Osama's number two, Ayman al-Zawahiri, had called on "our brother Muslims in Pakistan" to carry out their "Islamic duty" and overthrow the "traitor" president, who also was the chief of staff of Pakistan's armed forces and an ally of the United States.

Had the jihadis succeeded in killing the leader of the only Muslim power possessing operational nuclear weapons, they would have scored a rough Third World equivalent of the attacks on New York and Washington. The jihadis were not shy about their desire to create instability capable of catapulting themselves into power. The chaos, disruption and violence they hoped would ensue in a state rarely far from collapsing of its own contradictions could well have put the American operations to shame even if conventional wisdom predicted another general automatically would replace Musharraf.

The circumstances surrounding both attempts on his life—on December 14 and again on Christmas Day—stank of treachery. They took place as he was being driven back along a four-lane highway to his residence in Rawalpindi. His itinerary was never publicly disclosed, and his security specialists routinely deployed decoy cars and planes. Both these operations involved insider knowledge of the timing and route taken by his heavily armed motorcade. The first operation failed, it was said, thanks to an American-provided high-tech jamming gadget called a VIP2 Bomb Ranger. It delayed for a few vital seconds the remote-controlled electronic triggering device that set off 450 pounds of C-4 explosive hidden in five charges under a bridge supposedly closely guarded by police and regularly swept by security specialists. Debris fell over a half-mile radius.

In the second, two suicide bombers rammed explosive-laden Suzuki pickup trucks into the presidential motorcade. Only the sacrifice of a member of the police bodyguard who jumped in front of one of the kamikaze trucks spared Musharraf's life. A memory chip recovered by investigators from a bomber's cell phone revealed that he had been alerted when to expect the motorcade by a call from a Special Branch police officer who saw the president leave a meeting in Islamabad some twenty miles away. These were the third and fourth attempts on Musharraf's life since September 11, 2001, when he threw in his lot with the Americans. No life-insurance actuary was needed to conclude, in the words of Talat Masood, a retired general turned commentator, that the president was "a marked man" and that his enemies were "determined, organized and well-informed."

Nor was much imagination required to finger jihadis as the culprits. Indeed, an identity card quickly identified one suicide driver as a militant from the Pakistani part of disputed Kashmir named Mohammed Jamil. He had been captured with the Taliban in 2001 and recently judged "white," meaning harmless, and released by his Afghan jailers.[65] Officials identified the other suicide bomber as an Afghan named Walid Sultan. More telling still, they said, was Jamil's involvement initially with Harkat ul-Ansar and later with a faction of Jaish-e-Muhammad. Both were prominent jihadi groups trained and encouraged by ISI to join the struggle for Kashmir. Long before September 11, both Harkat and Jaish had figured on the State Department's list of terrorist organizations, and Jaish's leader, Masood Azhar, was known to entertain particularly close links with ISI.

Under American and Indian pressure, Musharraf formally banned them and three other jihadi groups in January 2002. But members of these groups soon resumed their activities unmolested, often by simply changing their names. Azhar was ordered released by a Pakistani court and went back to his fund-raising and political activities. Musharraf's ringing promises to vet the curriculum for some 600,000 students in 4,000 *madrasas*, 65 percent of which were in the radical Deobandi tradition, were never carried out. Such was the virulently anti-American mood in Pakistan that Musharraf in the past had not dared tackle the jihadi organizations head-on, especially in light of Islamist complaints about FBI agents working alongside Pakistani colleagues to neutralize Al-Qaeda agents.

Still, the two attempts on his life in December were judged sufficiently serious for Musharraf to subject Jaish to something smacking of public scrutiny, and its leader was reported under heavy surveillance in his hometown. Specifically, the government transferred the most embarrassing Jaish convict from a provincial prison to Islamabad, where he could be questioned about the new assassination attempts and links to Al-Qaeda. Thus moved was British-born Ahmed Omar Sheikh, a leading member of Jaish serving a sentence of death for masterminding the kidnapping and killing of *Wall Street Journal* correspondent Daniel Pearl in Karachi in 2002.[66] Sheikh had already caused Musharraf much grief in the past. Karachi police, who had little time for the ISI, leaked Sheikh's past links with the intelligence organization. Further embarrassment was caused by the revelation that Sheikh had been in the protective custody of a senior security official in the Punjab for a week before his formal arrest was made public. All these oddities encouraged rumors that a panicky Sheikh had turned Pearl over to

Al-Qaeda operatives, who did the actual killing. The bridge explosion was reminiscent of an unsuccessful 2002 attempt to kill Musharraf using a parked car bomb in Karachi. That operation was the work of three members of Harkat-ul-Mujahidin al-Almi, an offshoot of banned Harkat-ul-Mujahidin that reportedly trained some of its fighters for Kashmir in Al-Qaeda camps in Afghanistan in the Taliban era.[67]

Clearly the would-be assassins' motive was revenge against Musharraf who, in the words of Zawahiri's audiotape, had "sold out the blood of the Muslims in Afghanistan." More accurately, the would-be assassins in December were principally exercised about Musharraf's renewed interest in finding a compromise solution with India to the vexed Kashmir problem, which had helped trigger three wars between the neighbors since their independence in 1947. But Musharraf had become suspect in jihadi eyes in the immediate wake of Osama's attacks on Washington and New York in 2001, when he abruptly ended the ISI's "forward policy" of supporting the Taliban in Afghanistan. Pakistan's turn as the victim of blowback had arrived.

The Bush administration then had left him little choice. Dropping the Taliban openly and cooperating in the hunt for Al-Qaeda agents saved Musharraf and curiously ended the virtual pariah status that had been Pakistan's lot for stubbornly pursuing those relationships and building, then exploding five nuclear devices in May 1998. Musharraf himself had been basically in quarantine with the Commonwealth and the United States—a general who had seized power in a bloodless coup from a corrupt, but elected civilian government, prorogued parliament and banished overseas the leaders of the two traditional secular political parties.

In return for Musharraf's cooperation against Al-Qaeda, Washington rewarded Pakistan handsomely. All economic and military sanctions imposed in 1990 for acquiring nuclear know-how and in 1998 for exploding Pakistan's nuclear bombs were removed. Washington proved generous as well. Enormous debts to Western countries—$12.5 billion—were rescheduled by the IMF and the World Bank, and the United States provided a $1 billion soft loan, wrote off $1 billion in bilateral debt and promised a $3 billion bilateral loan over five years. Washington looked past Musharraf's gradual and iffy transformation from military dictator to (just) constitutionally proper civilian president in January 2004. All it took along the way was a referendum in 2002 prolonging his rule for five years, and then national and regional elections that international monitors and domestic opposition insisted were rigged. In Pakistan's seemingly constant penchant for contradictions, he weakened the traditional secular parties by encouraging militant Islamist groups dedicated in the final analysis to his elimination.

As a six-party coalition called the Muttahida Majlis-e-Amal, the jihadis won 20 percent of the seats in the national parliament, gained control of the Northwest Frontier Province's regional assembly and shared control in Baluchistan's. They thus were free to protect their Taliban friends, who in 2003 staged ever more frequent cross-border raids into Afghanistan, to the fury of the Afghan and American governments and the embarrassment of Musharraf. The Islamist politicians also knew when to compromise. They were wise enough to go along with Musharraf's presidential subterfuge. No one in their ranks, or Musharraf's, had the bad taste to note that their barely more radical friends in the jihadi militias twice had tried to kill him less than a month earlier. The Islamist parties also received an additional payoff: a concession requiring Musharraf to relinquish his army post in a year's time. That did not stop them from ostentatiously walking out of parliament rather than hear him denounce jihadi excesses.

Small wonder that Donald Rumsfeld in a leaked Defense Department memorandum dated October 16, 2003, asked, "Is our present situation such that 'the harder we work, the behinder we get'?"

EPILOGUE

"All right," said the [Cheshire] Cat; and this time it vanished quite
slowly, beginning with the end of the tail, and ending with the grin,
which remained some time after the rest of it had gone.

—Alice's Adventures in Wonderland

E VERY DAY AFTER September 11, 2001, that Osama eluded death or humiliating capture at the hands of the American military he so despised added another touch to the legend he had carefully created over the
years. Dodging his pursuers and staying alive were extra dividends for a
man who had become a household name in every corner of the earth. It
was with that knowledge that he and other jihadis persevered in their war
against the United States, the West and Muslim regimes deemed unworthy
of their dream of restoring the caliphate. Time and again Osama embroi-
dered on the theme that "the survival of this slave of Allah" was of no importance.[1] What counted for him was his place in Islamic history, more
especially in reawakening jihad after centuries of somnolence. For friend
and foe, his reputation was secure thanks to the daring, surprise and universal impact of the attacks against New York and Washington.

Still, the endgame was important. The American onslaught in Afghanistan, massive arrests and his followers' violent excesses in such key states as
Pakistan and Saudi Arabia certainly had weakened Al-Qaeda. Even so, periodic alerts in Europe and especially the United States kept Westerners on
edge. At Washington's insistence, specific transatlantic flights were canceled without detailed explanation. The administration repeatedly issued
warnings, at times producing the directors of the FBI, the CIA and the Defense Intelligence Agency for televised congressional testimony to ensure
that Americans got the message that Al-Qaeda was down but not out. With

so many Al-Qaeda senior cadres either dead or captured, it was largely left to loosely associated regional jihadi organizations to keep the cause alive by striking at soft targets from Morocco and Turkey to Indonesia. The administration claimed its vigilance had thwarted repeated terrorist attacks on American soil.

But in jihadi eyes, that Osama and his right-hand man, Ayman al-Zawahiri, had avoided detection so long bordered on the miraculous (although Western observers suspected Pakistani intelligence had deliberately ignored their whereabouts). After all, Osama and Zawahiri simply had disappeared following the defeat of the Taliban in late 2001 and had not been heard from for months. For the better part of a year after 9/11 Osama was thought to be seriously wounded, ill or even dead by officials in Washington, London and Islamabad, as well as by many ordinary Muslims.

Almost immediately upon his return to Afghanistan in 1996, unsubstantiated stories kept insisting Osama was sickly. A senior British official dealing with security in 2000 told me that Osama would be dead of natural causes in a few years. A Palestinian engineer said that as a young man Osama worked for him on a bin Laden family construction site and "didn't have much energy." The engineer surmised Osama had low blood pressure. Later, in the anti-Soviet jihad, he reportedly contracted malaria, and his admirers accepted as an article of faith that he had been gassed by Russian troops. In the late 1990s Osama affected a cane in several interviews, but it was never clear whether he thought the walking stick lent gravitas to his persona or he was genuinely ailing. His putative major ailments ranged from serious kidney disease to Marfan's syndrome, a form of cardiovascular and optical degeneration associated with tall, thin patients. If indeed Osama was living in the rough in the primitive tribal areas of Pakistan and Afghanistan and constantly moving to elude arrest, doctors doubted he could survive with a serious kidney ailment. Portable dialysis machines weighing less than forty pounds were on the market, but doctors reasoned that he would also need a water-purifying apparatus and a generator to power them. In other words, the gear could only be transported in a four-wheel-drive vehicle or by donkey. Rebutting the "sickly Osama" stories, a Pakistani doctor who examined Osama in Afghanistan during the Taliban's comeuppance in November 2001 told FBI and ISI officers (who detained and interrogated the doctor for a month) that the Al-Qaeda leader was in excellent health.[2] Healthy or ailing, Osama was deemed alive in late 2002 by the CIA. Its experts authenticated a series of audiotapes from him or

Zawahiri that precluded prerecording. By 2003 they referred to specific recent terrorist attacks, mentioned timely events such as Saddam Hussein's capture and predicted other attacks would follow. All too often, they did.

Still the tone of his pronouncements made clear that Osama had come to terms with the possibility that sooner or later the Americans might corner him, just as they had so many of his principal lieutenants. An American general in Afghanistan early in 2004 said Osama's days in his supposed hiding place somewhere near the Afghan–Pakistani border were numbered, even predicting that he would be captured by the end of the year. Intelligence agents fresh from their capture of Saddam Hussein in December 2003 were shifted back to Afghanistan; after their initial failure to grab Osama, many intelligence officers had been withdrawn to prepare for the March 2003 invasion of Iraq. Lieutenant General David W. Barno, the incoming commander of some 12,000 American and coalition forces in Afghanistan, said, "We have a variety of intelligence, and we're sure we're going to catch Osama bin Laden and Mullah Omar this year."[3] To the degree that such talk was based on more than braggadocio, cynics suggested that Osama's capture was simply a question of timing. With an eye to the 2004 elections, President George W. Bush, they said, knew exactly where Osama was hiding. Bush would capture Osama in time for an "October surprise" sure to appeal to late-to-decide voters. Some fanciful articles assumed that the United States already had Osama in custody and was simply waiting for a politically opportune moment to announce his capture. The Iranian news agency put out one such story in February 2004, but it was immediately denied by American and Pakistani officials.

General Barno's proclaimed optimism in fact had some connection with stepped-up Pakistani security sweeps that started in early 2004 in South Waziristan and other tribal areas along the Afghan border. That timing coincided with the two near-miss attempts on Musharraf's life and with America's indulgent acquiescence in Pakistan's transparently contrived solution when it was finally obliged to acknowledge years of illicit sales of nuclear secrets and equipment to Iran, Libya and North Korea. When confronted in late 2003 with Libyan documents linking its nuclear program to Pakistani designs and equipment, Musharraf, in a carefully orchestrated maneuver, persuaded Abdul Qadeer Khan, the high-living "father of Pakistan's atom bomb," to confess that he alone was responsible and had acted out of personal greed and a desire to help Islamic countries to break the great powers' monopoly on nuclear weapons. Still, the apparent exchange of Pakistani nuclear know-how for North Korean Nodong (re-baptised Ghauri) missiles could not be justified on Islamic grounds. Nonetheless, Khan was immediately pardoned, and his friends' earlier accusations that the ISI and the army were witting partners were neatly glossed over. The Bush administration was on record as threatening proliferators of weapons of mass destruction ultimately with preemptive war—and had toppled President Saddam Hussein in Iraq less than a year earlier on the premise, which proved unverifiable, that his regime possessed them.

Indeed, much of Bush's ideological commitment to the radical doctrine of "preemption"—arrogating to the United States the right to take unilateral military action without benefit of UN Security Council approval—linked possession of weapons of mass destruction to his "global war on terrorism." The administration argued that Saddam, out of anti-American hatred shared with Al-Qaeda, could hand Iraq's purported WMD to the jihadis. In the fall of 2002 National Security Adviser Condoleezza Rice first said that the United States could not risk allowing a "smoking gun" to turn into a "mushroom cloud," in a much-repeated justification for going to war against Saddam. Critics had argued that cooperation between the volatile jihadis and the secular Iraqi regime they abominated made little sense. Even the White House was obliged to concede after the invasion of Iraq that a much-weakened Saddam had been hanging on by the skin of his teeth and lied rather than admit he possessed no WMD. Given his vulnerability, Saddam was not about to enter into a partnership with jihadis who might precipitate a war with the United States he sought to avoid.

Soon after the United States invaded Iraq in March 2003, the messy aftermath began to chasten the administration and make it realize America lacked troops and international backing to force North Korea to abandon its demonstrably more advanced and threatening nuclear weapons program. Slowly Washington gave signs of appreciating anew the awkward compromises that had governed relations among states since the Treaty of Westphalia in 1648. Thus, in the name of catching Osama, President Bush opted to overlook Pakistan's nuclear sins. The White House understood that getting to the bottom of Pakistan's nuclear proliferation would endanger Musharraf and embolden the powerful Islamist political parties in the government and their militias with long-standing associations with Al-Qaeda. As in Saudi Arabia, the most likely alternative to the questionable regime in Pakistan were the very jihadis that had been tolerated for so long.

In fact, Bush was continuing what previous administrations had done over two decades: by and large ignoring Pakistan's dirty little nuclear secret. In the 1980s the top priority the United States assigned to defeating the Soviets in Afghanistan allowed Abdul Qadeer Khan and the Pakistani establishment to pursue their drive to produce nuclear weapons and delivery systems. By the time Pakistan exploded its first nuclear bomb in May 1998, the consequences of such forbearance had metastasized throughout Pakistani society. Successive governments encouraged (or were powerless to stop) the emergence of jihadi militias programmed to further Pakistani policy in Afghanistan and in the disputed Indian state of Kashmir, where their violence tied down New Delhi's army. At considerable domestic political risk, arguably 9/11 saved the Pakistani state from the consequences of its own foolish tolerance of Al-Qaeda by forcing Musharraf to make a 180-degree turn.

Such calculations about Pakistani policy past and present, of course, would become secondary in domestic American political terms if Osama were caught or killed. The deepening Iraqi quagmire would be sidelined on the evening television news. Turning the Pakistani nuclear proliferation scandal to its advantage, for the first time the United States could reasonably hope to force a much more vulnerable Musharraf to comply, despite Pakistani jihadis' threats. Americans would rejoice no matter how Osama was taken out of circulation, but Washington had to weigh the possible repercussions in Pakistan, where there were logical limits to Islamabad's cooperation. No Pakistani government would likely survive if it allowed American ground troops to operate openly inside Pakistan. Even the reinforced presence of FBI and CIA agents caused unease.

Beyond Americans' pleasure in punishing a foe they equated with pure evil, it remained far from sure that Osama's removal would provide any durable relief. (Similar hopes had been expressed when American troops captured Saddam Hussein near his hometown of Tikrit. But resistance to the U.S. occupation of Iraq failed to subside, perhaps because it was no longer freighted with Saddam's terrible legacy and could concentrate on opposing a foreign, and Western, occupation.)

Osama had no intention of making his seizure easy. There were persistent suggestions in jihadi circles that he had instructed his bodyguards to "martyr" him rather than allow his capture. Not for him the videotaped humiliation of Saddam's medical inspection for lice at the hands of an

American military doctor. He had no desire to finish his days as a caged prisoner to be exhibited in his enemy's capital. Washington also might well prefer to have him dead rather than on trial in an American court, spinning his story and inspiring the world's 1.2 billion Muslims with tales of bravado. At stake was the future of his myth and of the movement he had come to symbolize. Beyond the mechanics of perpetuating his legend, Osama had succeeded in isolating the United States internationally in ways the Soviets never managed in their heyday. Even the Bush administration was obliged to acknowledge that its muscular post–9/11 foreign policy and military interventionism had damaged American prestige abroad so thoroughly that "it will take us many years of hard, focused work" to restore America's international standing.[4]

OSAMA'S COMMITMENT to jihadi Islam certainly branded him an adept of ideology every bit as much as of religion. Indeed, Muslim critics questioned his understanding of Islam and his right to issue religious edicts. But in its war on terrorism the United States, only a generation after its involvement in the Vietnam War, also had chosen ideology, this time against the world's fastest-growing religion rather than "international communism." Bush certainly did not start out wanting to be seen doing so. His heart had been in the right place. He never again repeated his early use of the term "crusade" (although jihadi propaganda kept repeating it). Even after the invasion of Iraq he tried to reach out to America's 5 million Muslims by inviting their religious representatives to the White House for a traditional *iftar* meal breaking the daylight-hour fast during the holy month of Ramadan.

But Osama and even many moderate Muslims were having none of it. What they saw constantly on Arab satellite television were American-made helicopters and fighter-bombers in action against poorly armed Palestinians or Iraqis fighting an American army of occupation (often using urban-warfare tactics gleaned from the Israelis.) Osama was a latecomer to the Palestinian cause. But he came to appreciate it as the single most effective unifying force not just for Arabs, but for Muslims from Morocco to the Philippines. In much of the world, both Osama and Bush were seen as fundamentalists, one totally committed to uncompromising jihadi Islam, the other in thrall to his born-again Christian hard-core supporters in league with neoconservative political appointees. Many were ardent long-term backers of the Israeli right wing and its powerful friends in the United States. To complete this ideological dialogue of the deaf, neither faith-based protagonist admitted to any similarity in the other's language or behavior.

Given the seemingly unequal battle between the world's only super-power and the jihadis, that perceived rough equivalency was no small accomplishment for Osama, a man some critics labeled a nihilist. Aiding him were not just his considerable organizational skills and his proven ability to hurt the United States. He also had one clear advantage over Bush. While the president was often an awkward public speaker, Osama possessed a gift of eloquence in a language renowned for the beauty and poetry of the Koran. No outsider can appreciate fully the power and dangers of Arabic. Arabs of an older generation never forgot the speeches of Gamal Abdel Nasser, broadcast on Cairo's Voice of the Arabs radio—and the sense of desolation and humiliation when his heady words helped trap him into the Six-Day War in 1967, which Israel won handily. Osama's low-key, classical Arabic had a similar mesmerizing impact on a younger generation, even those brought up in the Western mold and addicted to Arab satellite television stations, especially Al-Jazeera.

A few years ago I asked a young Moroccan secretary working for Al-Jazeera in Paris for her impressions of an Osama interview. She looked, talked and acted like a sophisticated, professional Parisienne. Yet she said she was spellbound by his words, words she conceded she did not always fully comprehend, but which reminded her of her parents and grandparents. I suspect her reaction was written in her genetic code. In almost every Muslim slumbers the memory of Islamic glory in the arts, sciences and governance. Western colonization and its humiliations, Western education, Western capital, Western know-how and Western military might only serve to measure the distance from past preeminence and present perceived subservience. (History, in that unfortunate catchphrase, may be dead for the West, but not in the lands of Islam.) Compared with Osama, President Bush possessed no such gift, and his occasional efforts defining Islam as a great religion went largely unnoticed at home and abroad. He also played into his adversary's hands. By deliberately sidelining those few specialists inside and outside government who did understand Islam and the Islamic world, the White House, during its long preparation for the invasion of Iraq, flaunted its ignorance—and paid dearly for it. Such were the wages of spin in a faith-based administration.

The White House also displayed a curiously tin ear when it came to tolerating its American fundamentalists' mean-spirited views of Islam. Americans were not alone. Italian Prime Minister Silvio Berlusconi could be equally dismissive of Islam. Willy Claes, while briefly NATO secretary general in the middle 1990s, promoted Islam as NATO's next big threat, in what critics denounced as an oversimplified effort to replace recently redundant Communism as a way to keep the alliance vibrant. Born-again Christians close to the White House and the president's wing of the Republican Party at times seemed to be competing in insulting Muslims. The Reverend Jerry Vines, a former president of the Southern Baptists, America's largest Protestant denomination, said the Prophet Mohammed was a "demon-possessed pedophile." Televangelist Reverend Jerry Falwell said, "I think the Prophet Mohammed was a terrorist," on CBS's *60 Minutes,* portraying him as well as "a violent man, a man of war."[5] His fellow televangelist, the Reverend Benny Hinn, described the Arab–Israeli conflict "not as a war between Arabs and Jews, but as war between God and the devil." Franklin Graham, evangelist Billy Graham's son, who had delivered the benediction at the 1996 and 2000 Republican conventions and the invocation at President Bush's inauguration, dismissed Islam as a "very evil and wicked religion."

Paul Weyrich, an influential conservative, considered Islam a "threat" and said "Muslims should be encouraged to leave" the United States because they represented a "fifth column in this county."[6] Right-wing columnist Ann Coulter proposed to "invade their countries, kill their leaders and convert them to Christianity." Christian fundamentalist groups expressed the hope of sending missionaries to Iraq to do just that. Lieutenant General William G. "Jerry" Boykin, a born-again Christian who became under secretary of defense for intelligence in June 2003, appeared before church congregations in uniform and jump boots to proclaim his disdain for Islam. Other had "lost their morals, lost their values, but America is still a Christian nation," he contended, and the "only way to defeat the terrorists was to come against them in the name of Jesus." Recalling an encounter in the 1990s with a Somali warlord who had said, "Allah will protect me," the general replied, "I know my God was bigger than his." He was taped telling a congregation that Bush's war pitted the Judeo-Christian tradition "against a guy named Satan." The *Los Angeles Times* broke the Boykin story in October 2003. Defense Secretary Donald Rumsfeld and General Richard Myers, the chairman of the Joint Chiefs of Staff, played down the hard-charging combat hero's injudicious language, and he was allowed to keep his job after making a pro forma apology.

Such boys-will-be-boys indulgence was not lost on Bush's core constituency—or the Muslim world. Many Muslims seized on the general's remarks and his superiors' reaction as condoning and extending the evangelical preachers' barbs. The superpower shrugged. But what was good for the goose was not deemed good for the gander. When, in October 2003, Mahathir Mohammed, Malaysia's prime minister, paid Jews the left-handed compliment of saying they punched above their numerical weight in world affairs, all hell broke loose in the West, especially in the United States.[7] His remarks made clear he felt a grudging admiration for the Jews, who had prospered despite persecution historically at the hands of Europeans, not Muslims. Indeed, a close reading of his address to the fifty-seven-nation Organization of the Islamic Conference meeting in his capital, Kuala Lumpur, showed he was exhorting his fellow Muslims to join the modern world, use their brains, make peace and end suicide bombings.

Still, his words were rough to many Westerners accustomed to atoning for the Nazi Holocaust and millennial Christian persecution of the Jews and to soft-pedaling criticism of Israeli excesses for fear of being labeled anti-Semitic. "The Europeans killed 6 million Jews out of the 12 million, but today the Jews rule the world by proxy," the prime minister told his enraptured audience. "They get others to fight and die for them." "We are up against a people who think," he said. "They survived 2,000 years of pogroms not by hitting back, but by thinking. They invented and successfully promoted socialism, communism, human rights and democracy so that persecuting them would appear to be wrong. . . . They now have gained control of the most powerful countries and they, this tiny community, have become a world power." As uncomfortable as his remarks were to Western ears, Mohammed was no jihadi and had proved it by cracking down hard on local Muslim radicals. For him, the Palestinian struggle was "not religious at all; it is territorial. You take somebody's land and he will fight for it."

WHEN BUSH VISITED Indonesia that same month, he appeared genuinely puzzled by the questioning of his motives during an hour-long meeting with moderate Islamic leaders on the island of Bali. He asked his staff, "Do they really believe that we think all Muslims are terrorists?"[8] His surprise reflected the cocooned world of presidential travel since 9/11 and a disinclination to read much beyond his daily one-page intelligence briefing. Bush and his team seemed unwilling to acknowledge the resentment caused abroad by American policies and the intolerant words of their Christian fundamentalist friends at home. His mind-set mirrored that of many everyday Americans who, despite 9/11, remained incurious about the causes of jihadi anger and why so many moderate Muslims privately approved their violent deeds.

"They hate us for what we are" was an understandable American gut reaction in the immediate wake of the September 11 attacks, but it went only so far. The administration never really progressed much beyond that simplistic mantra. Bush and his colleagues insinuated repeatedly that Saddam Hussein's Iraq was poised to transfer weapons of mass destruction to Al-Qaeda. Indeed, opinion polls established that such unproven assertions provided the single most telling argument with everyday Americans to justify the war to unseat the Baghdad regime. Still, little self-examination or effort was expended to spell out to Americans how and why U.S. policy toward the Muslim world engendered such profound rejection. The administration line was that American soil had been attacked, and in and by itself that sufficed to justify open-ended war on terrorism. Underlying this uncompromising view was neoconservatives' belief that the American superpower was going to change the rules and bend Muslims and their undemocratic regimes to Washington's will.

While visiting London in November 2003, in a well-wrought speech aimed at the Middle East, Bush extolled the virtues of democracy, castigated previous administrations for sacrificing ideals to expediency and swore such demeaning distortions were at an end. Middle Easterners remained unconvinced. They knew that Washington still relied on autocratic regional regimes to maintain stability, even if Bush gently criticized key allies Egypt and Saudi Arabia by name on that score. As the Iraqi war soured, so did Muslims' faith in the administration's ability to make good on its promises. The limits in favor of democracy became transparent with the administration's policy in Iraq. The occupation authorities refused to approve Shi'a demands for direct elections before handing over formal sovereignty on June 30, 2004, for fear the Shi'a majority would vote in an Islamic Republic.

Such were the lessons of the "one man, one vote, one time" elections that ushered in Iran's Islamic republic. If anything, American tolerance of

undemocratic regimes increased. The United States stepped up cooperation with the intelligence organizations of its close traditional allies and for
the first time embraced others—such as Algeria and Tunisia—it previously
had kept at arms' length because of their questionable human and civil
rights practices. Realists argued that such were the constraints of the war
on terrorism.[9]

Washington treated these discrepancies as something solvable by advertising techniques and psychological warfare. It created for the Middle East
a new radio station—and later a television service—designed to get its
message across to Muslims. Pop music and upbeat items extolling the
American way of life feature prominently. Improved packaging was the
watchword. Questioning the connection between Saddam's Iraq and Al-
Qaeda was not encouraged. The neoconservative creed, gussied up with
Wilsonian glorification of elections and democracy, did not admit of
doubts. Conspicuously absent from most mainstream American discussion of terrorism was the central role that Israel played in most Muslims'
perception of the problem. Even many Muslims who welcomed Saddam's
overthrow were convinced that the war against his regime also sought to
control Baghdad's oil and weaken the Arab world's most outspoken critic
of Israel.

Such suspicions only added to traditional uneasiness. For most of the
twentieth century the Palestinian problem had nurtured Muslims' sense of
injustice and humiliation, born of accumulated defeat at the hands of ex-
pansionist Israel and the money, weapons and diplomatic support the
West, especially the United States, lavished on it. Palestine long since had
become the touchstone for centuries of Islamic decline, brought into sharp
focus by failed efforts at Westernization, beginning with Napoleon's campaign in Egypt and culminating for jihadis, if not all Muslims, in Ataturk's
abolition of the caliphate. Years earlier, an Israeli government spokesman
who disapproved of my reporting in the Middle East told me Israel had
"nothing to worry about as long as Americans read the Bible rather than
the Koran." Osama's lieutenant, Ayman al-Zawahiri, stood that logic on its
head.

In a book entitled *Knights Under the Banner of the Prophet*, serialized in
a Saudi-owned newspaper just after the collapse of the Taliban in 2001, Zawahiri argued that Palestine year in and year out had proved the jihadis'
best recruiting sergeant. In Nasser's day, his powerful Sawt al-Arab radio
station beamed Cairo's message to the smallest village in the Arab world.

But the impact of Voice of the Arabs was nothing compared with the real-time video footage of violence broadcast from the Israeli-occupied West Bank and Gaza or Iraq by Al-Jazeera and its satellite television rivals based in Abu Dhabi and Dubai. When Osama, Zawahiri or other Al-Qaeda leaders denounced the Americans as crusaders, they were, of course, historically inaccurate since the Crusades were a European endeavor that happened hundreds of years before Columbus discovered America. But Muslim viewers long since had taken on board Al-Qaeda's condemnation of the American "crusaders" and "Zionists." They were code words, emotional buttons to be pushed.

AL-QAEDA and other jihadis had few acolytes in preinvasion Iraq, and they were confined to the Kurdish buffer zone along the northern stretches of the Iran–Iraq border, where Tehran found them an effective way to keep Kurdish nationalists off balance. But post-Saddam Iraq provided a new battlefield for jihadis, attracting volunteers itching to embarrass the United States and undermine its designs for the region. Even before the American invasion, Osama and Zawahiri had called for jihadis to resist not in the name of defending Saddam's regime (whose secular politics they considered apostasy), but to protect Baghdad as a seat of the caliphate laid low by conquering Mongols in 1258. In one of the major ironies of Bush's war of choice against Iraq, the United States, which had been unable to prove an Al-Qaeda connection with Saddam before the war, within months of his removal faced a cascading series of suicide bombings bearing the jihadis' trademark willingness to sacrifice themselves. Western intelligence officers clocked hundreds of volunteers being recruited in Europe and infiltrated into Iraq from neighboring Iran, Jordan, Saudi Arabia, Syria, Kuwait and Turkey. For some of those states, the jihadis were a tool to wear down the Americans while exacerbating tensions among Iraq's Kurds and Sunni and Shi'a Arabs.

Some of these recruits dispatched from Europe were connected to Ansar al-Islam, a mainly Kurdish jihadi group established along the Iran–Iraq frontier in 2001. They then were geographically dependent on Iran for access and supplies. Their initial mission was to create problems for Iraq's Kurds, who then controlled an autonomous enclave thanks to the protective air umbrella Washington and London had maintained since 1991. In its efforts to convince Americans to go to war against Saddam, the Bush administration had tried mightily, but failed, to produce convincing evidence linking Saddam to Ansar. Some Ansar cadres had trained in Al-Qaeda camps in Afghanistan. But at most they and Saddam shared a common enemy in the Kurdish nationalists. Saddam feared any collaboration with them would drag him into the war with the United States he ardently sought to avoid. As part of its 2003 war in Iraq, the United States massively bombed entrenched Ansar positions, killing hundreds of jihadis. Others escaped across the nearby border into Iran.

Despite the punishment they had endured, Ansar survivors within months were reported infiltrating back from Iran to Iraq. Ansar and full-fledged Al-Qaeda cadres in Iran constituted a potential bargaining chip for Tehran, which was interested in the 3,000-plus armed members of the People's Mujahedeen, the anti-mullah Iranian organization Saddam bankrolled and stationed near the Iran–Iraq border; it had been on the State Department list of terrorist organizations for years. But administration neoconservatives toyed with using this force against Tehran. They accorded the organization special status in the months after the war, despite Washington's official doctrine refusing to draw distinctions between "good" and "bad" terrorists, notably blacklisting the Palestinian Islamic Jihad and Hamas, although they did not target Americans or their interests.

A relatively small force, these jihadis had their uses. Few Iraqi Sunnis resisting the American occupation were willing to conduct suicide bombings. But by August 2003 such attacks began in earnest, and Ansar's proven willingness to sacrifice its members' lives pointed to its involvement in lethal car-bomb assaults on various Western military contingents, the United Nations Baghdad headquarters and leading Shi'a religious leaders in An Najaf and An Nasiriyah. Ironically, Ansar jihadis, many of them foreign Arabs, overcame their long-standing distaste for Saddam and his secular regime and began cooperating with diehard Iraqi Sunnis who had remained loyal to him. Thus did the American invasion to unseat Saddam succeed in creating the deadly reality that the administration in far-fetched allegations months earlier, had invoked to justify extending the war on terrorism to Iraq.

To the embarrassment of the White House, Richard A. Clarke, the long-serving counterterrorism czar in three administrations, forcefully got that point across in testifying on March 24, 2004, before the independent commission investigating 9/11. He had resigned in October 2002, citing Bush's greater interest in toppling Saddam than in prosecuting the war against Al-Qaeda. "The reason I am strident in my criticism of the president of the United States is that by invading Iraq, the president of the United States has greatly undermined the war on terrorism."[10]

An Al-Qaeda messenger, Pakistani Mohammed Ghul, was captured by Kurdish forces near the Iranian border in mid-January 2004 carrying a CD disk containing a seventeen-page letter said to have been written by Abu Musab Zarqawi. The letter purportedly sought Al-Qaeda's approval for attacks on Shi'a in the hope of setting off hostilities with the country's Sunnis and plunging Iraq into full-fledged civil war before the Americans could cement their presence by handing over formal sovereignty on June 30, 2004. Zarqawi, a Jordanian of Palestinian extraction, had been repeatedly mentioned by administration officials (including Secretary of State Colin Powell in his February 5, 2003, address to the UN Security Council) as an Al-Qaeda associate who had received medical treatment in Baghdad after the 2001 Afghan fighting. No evidence was produced to back up that allegation, which represented the administration's strongest claim of Al-Qaeda–Saddam cooperation. In any case, less than a month after word of the letter was leaked, more than 150 Shi'a died on Ashura, the Shi'a day of atonement, in coordinated suicide-bomber attacks in Iraq.

The French warn of the dangers of "insulting the future." It is too early to draw up a definitive balance sheet for Osama and jihadi Islam. But he arguably has changed American society as much as, perhaps more than, any single foreigner in contemporary times. There's an edginess in American life, bordering on paranoia. The USA Patriot Act and its restrictions on civil liberties, hostile attitudes toward suspect immigrants, many of whom were held incommunicado for extended periods after September 11, and a general public fixation on security in what had prided itself as the world's most open society—all this can be laid at Osama's door.

As for terrorism itself, until March 11, 2004, it was tempting to think that steady international police work, improved cooperation among intelligence organizations and good luck will confine jihadi terrorism to soft targets in parts of the world peripheral to the real centers of power. That may sound heartless and ethnocentric. The half-century-long Cold War was fought in dozens of peripheral conflicts and almost never involved actual shooting between the Soviet Union and the United States and its European NATO allies.

On Thursday, March 11, 2004, thirteen bombs exploded on four morning rush-hour commuter trains in Madrid, killing 191 and wounding almost one thousand. Had the bombs exploded only a minute or so later, experts calculated, the glass roof of the main Atocha station might well have collapsed, resulting in many more casualties. The operation was astutely and symbolically timed—on the 911th day after the attacks in America and just three days before Spain's legislative elections. Prime Minister José María Aznar at first sought to blame ETA, the Basque separatist terrorists who had long been his special bugbear. But within hours the telltale traces of jihadi handiwork appeared—a communiqué to an Arabic-language newspaper in London claiming responsibility and the discovery of a van containing detonators and a cassette of Koranic verses near a suburban station where two of the trains had originated.

Aznar's tactics boomeranged. His strong law-and-order record might have helped his party had he not been perceived as trying to pin all the blame on ETA. Enraged crowds gathered outside Aznar's Partido Popular headquarters to protest his perceived effort to manipulate the vote. Voters turned out in higher-than-expected numbers. The underdog Socialists staged a surprise election upset with the prime minister designate José Luis Rodríguez Zapatero announcing he would honor his long-standing pledge to withdraw the 1,300 Spanish occupation troops from Iraq unless, in essence, the United States ceded control in Baghdad to the UN. He made no bones about denouncing Aznar's stubborn involvement in America's "fiasco" of a war in Iraq, which nearly 90 percent of Spaniards had opposed from the start. Aznar, who had spent the previous month giving self-congratulatory interviews, looked both a fool for having allied himself with President Bush over Iraq and a knave for favoring repression of ETA, neglecting the inroads made by Islamist terrorism and trying to manipulate the March 11 bombings for his party's benefit.[11] A message from the self-styled military spokesman of Al-Qaeda in Europe, said, "You love life and we love death," a not-so-subtle reworking of the old Falangist cry of "¡Viva la muerte!" The attacks "were in response to your collaboration with the criminal Bush and his allies," the message continued, "specifically in Iraq and Afghanistan."

American neoconservatives denounced what they construed as Zapatero's appeasement of the jihadis, alleging he was showing the white feather by threatening to withdraw from Iraq. What really bothered the White House was the first breach in coalition ranks; Spain's attitude would raise awkward questions for Bush only months before the American presidential election. British prime minister Tony Blair, who had also defied his public's wishes to participate in the Iraqi adventure, was further weakened. South Korea abruptly refused to station its contingent of troops around Mosul, which was judged too dangerous. In mid-April, Zapatero announced Spanish troops would be withdrawn over six weeks, and the much smaller Honduran and Dominican Republic contingents serving under Spanish command followed suit. Suddenly, Bush's painstaking efforts to work with new allies in Iraq looked to be in serious trouble.

But for counterterrorism specialists the real lessons lay elsewhere. For the first time the jihadis had struck western Europe. The choice of Spain was not a complete surprise. Spain had rolled up a major Al-Qaeda cell in late 2001, and it had served as a rendezvous for Mohammed Atta and Ramzi bin al-Shibh to put the final touches on the 9/11 operation the previous summer. Al-Qaeda had recently warned Madrid of the consequences of stationing troops in Iraq. And it had made plain that for jihadis Spain remained legitimately part of Dar al-Islam, or Islamic land, even 500 years after the Catholic monarchy had driven out the last Moor from Al Andalus, today's Andalusia, in 1492 and ended almost eight centuries of Muslim rule.

Equally ominous was the terrorists' modus operandi. For the first time they had found a way to carry out Al-Qaeda's trademark simultaneous attacks without conducting a suicide operation. Thanks to a doctored cellphone detonator found in an unexploded backpack aboard one of the commuter trains, investigators were able to quickly arrest a Moroccan immigrant, Jamal Zougam, originally from Tangier. He had been questioned in the wake of 9/11, largely at the request of the French who had been keeping string on him since 2000, but he had been released for lack of evidence. Zougam had started a hole-in-the-wall cell-phone shop in a largely immigrant neighborhood in Madrid.

Moroccan police quickly established that the previous year Zougam had visited Tangier, where he had met a well-known jihadi veteran named Abdelaziz Benyaich at whose home was found a prototype cell-phone detonator. A Benyaich brother was arrested in the wake of the Casablanca terrorist attacks in May 2003. Investigators were struck by the technical progress between the crude operation in Casablanca and the sophisticated

Madrid assaults. Such police cooperation after the fact only served to underline the lack of intelligence sharing among European security officials since 9/11. Bureaucratic and national rivalries played a role, as they did in counterterrorism in the United States. European Union security officials held an emergency meeting to tighten up procedures, and even decided to name a counterterrorism czar. What remained unclear was whether the Madrid operation was Al-Qaeda directed or the work of local Islamists who either had been encouraged to act or decided to do so on their own now that Osama was on the run. Judge Bruguière nicely defined the Western dilemma when he compared the Islamist threat to a constantly mutating AIDS virus.

IN ANY EVENT, it is illusory to think that the European Union measures or even the draconian regulations in the United States will stop terrorism. Terrorism has ever been part of the world and there is no reason to think that it will disappear from the face of the earth any more than poverty, disease or evil will. Other contemporary democratic societies have learned to live with terrorism without allowing their citizens' lives be totally disrupted. Where Americans seem determined to solve terrorism, Europeans seem resigned to muddling through and managing. This reflects neither resignation nor appeasement, no matter what neoconservatives and their columnist friends say and write in the United States. Britain put up with thirty years of Irish Republican Army bombs and assassinations before finding a delicate, if still vulnerable, political compromise in Northern Ireland. Germany and Italy, both societies with questionable political legitimacy because of their fascist pasts before and during World War Two, survived radical left-wing violence in the 1970s and 1980s. What is clear is that on 9/11 Americans lost their unique sense of invulnerability for the first time since the British burned down the White House in 1814 (or the Japanese succeeded in sending in a few balloon bombs over the West Coast in World War Two).

But Americans are resilient and over time are likely to understand that other priorities should be accorded pride of place. After all, there are many other problems competing for attention and funds. It would be no small accomplishment if Americans do come to that realization and if jihadi terrorism is contained in the peripheries. Think back only a few years. Thanks to 9/11 and the decades of neglect that preceded it, jihadi terrorism had entertained wider ambitions. Reducing Osama and his acolytes to terrorist activities in the Third World arguably could be a first step toward decreasing their impact everywhere. Terrorism thrives on publicity and its proven ability to strike not just Western interests—any targets in the West itself exercise a powerful attraction for angry young Muslims. So if suicide bombers fail to launch other "spectaculars" against the United States or another major Western country, the attraction of jihad may wane in and of itself.

Smarter policies in dealing with the Muslim world are essential to curb terrorism, starting with Palestine, but including Kashmir and Chechnya, which have been allowed to fester for far too long. Again, the United States should understand the cost of shirking its responsibilities. The unfinished war and unfinished peace in Afghanistan stand as a rebuke to the world, and especially the United States, which twice in a decade walked away from the ruins it helped create, despite abundant evidence of the terrible lessons such neglect produced. After 9/11 the cost of forgetting about far-off buffer states should no longer be acceptable.

I am not sure I agree with some Arab-world experts who estimate that as much as 70 percent of Muslim anti-Americanism (and violence) would disappear if only Washington would help bring about a viable Palestinian state alongside Israel, as Bush promised in 2002. Yet, whatever the percentage, the Palestinian problem remains the single greatest irritant in Muslim–American relations and an encouragement for jihadi terrorism. That is a stubborn enough perception to deserve serious and prolonged testing. Despite its occasional rhetoric and spurts of diplomatic activity, the Bush administration has shown no serious disposition to do so. Indeed Vice President Dick Cheney in his visit to the Middle East in the winter of 2002 gave every sign of espousing Prime Minister Ariel Sharon's systematic dismantling of fledgling Palestinian institutions. The unspoken agreement stipulated that the Palestinians could be ignored long enough for the United States to conduct the war against Iraq and impose a settlement on them—and other Arabs—in line with shared U.S. and Israeli interests.

The aftermath of the invasion of Iraq showed up such thinking for the wool-gathering it was and discredited the neoconservatives, who knew next to nothing about Iraq or the Arab world at large and had sidelined the specialists who questioned their war. Clearly, both Israelis and Palestinians repeatedly have demonstrated their inability to find a way out of their own increasingly nasty shared history. Palestinian suicide attacks against Israeli targets reflect not just the frustration of the weak whose land is being colonized. They also betray a dangerous deficit in rationality, since their targets are no longer confined to conceivably legitimate military targets—such as Israeli soldiers and armed settlers in territory Israel occupied in the 1967 Arab–Israeli war—but now include civilians living inside the Jewish state's internationally recognized frontiers. Israel's own use of force (often with American-built and donated aircraft and helicopters) is just as self-defeating. Much of the world considers America's honor stained because of its failure to rein in its Israeli protégé. For the United States to be perceived as going along with almost every Israeli excess is, I suspect, counterproductive for Israel, devastating for the Palestinians and inimical to proclaimed American interests for a more open and less angry Middle East.[12]

At this writing it is unwise to do more than speculate about the lasting repercussions of the Bush administration's invasion of Iraq, probably America's rashest political adventure in the Middle East, where for most of a century the United States somehow managed (albeit with increasing difficulty) to protect Israel and placate the Arabs controlling most of the Persian Gulf's oil. It is not impossible that Americans eventually may draw lessons of their own about the dangers of overextended dominion. Only a power confident to the point of arrogance and so closely identified with the Muslims' Israeli adversary would so insouciantly have invaded an Arab country so centrally located and so rich in oil.

Bush's war was a cosmic roll of the dice. It is legitimate to worry that its lofty aim of bringing open democratic society to the Muslim world may prove too much for a superpower subject to its own regular elections and an electorate questioning the cost in blood and treasure. Somehow forgotten since September 11 is the notion that radical political Islam (as opposed to jihadi violence) has been on the decline for at least a decade. But this war can reverse that. Doubtless Osama and the jihadis he has inspired are doing their utmost to humiliate the United States in Iraq, hoping that a setback there may help them seize power in Saudi Arabia and elsewhere in the Muslim world. It is not the least of Osama's surprises that jihadis have had a hand in turning Iraq into a battleground for the Middle East's soul and riches. But that was an opening the Bush administration served them on a silver plate; in any case, the Cheshire Cat's smile will be with us for quite some time.

Notes

PREFACE

1. *Le Soir,* Brussels, September 30, 2003.

BUG IN THE ELEPHANT'S EAR

1. *Washington Post,* April 15, 2002. Seven months after 9/11, Al-Jazeera, the free-swinging satellite network based in Qatar and watched by millions of Arabs in preference to their own often-censored national stations, broadcast a cassette showing Saudi hijacker Ahmad Alghamdi announcing in a March 2001 "last will and testament" that he knew his forthcoming martyrdom—or suicide—mission would be against a target in the United States. "It is high time we killed Americans on their own turf," he said. Al-Jazeera news editor Ibrahim Hilal remarked, "This tape closes the door of suspicion. It is the final say that Al-Qaeda is behind it."

2. *New York Times,* April 19, 2002. Paul Bucherer, a Swiss authority on Afghan art, said a special Al-Qaeda squad methodically smashed a storeroom full of ancient Buddhist and Gandharan statuary originally from Kabul's National Museum shortly before the Buddhas were blown up in March 2001. He said the Al-Qaeda squad of non-Afghans expertly carried out the destruction after local Taliban leaders refused to participate. Letters Western journalists found in Kabul after the Taliban fell described how Osama and top aides had convinced Mullah Omar to destroy the Buddhas.

3. *The Sociology and Psychology of Terrorism: Who Becomes a Terrorist and Why?,* Federal Research Division of the Library of Congress, 1999.

4. Bernard Lewis, *The Assassins,* Al Saqi Books, 1985, p. 47.

5. For example, Jamal Kashoggi, deputy editor of the *Arab News,* published in Jeddah, wrote an article on the first anniversary of the attacks bravely dissecting Arab attitudes.

6. *Newsweek,* April 28, 2002; *Washington Post,* May 1, 2002.

7. Julie Sirrs, a CIA analyst who visited Massoud, was chided for her trouble and decided to leave government employment. (interview, Washington, D.C., Dec. 21, 2000)

8. Whatever his personal misgivings, Arafat waited until December 2002 to make his first forthright attack on bin Laden. In an interview with the *Sunday Times* (London), Arafat said, "I'm telling him directly not to hide behind the Palestinian cause." "Why is bin Laden talking about Palestine now?" he said. "He has never helped us," Arafat added. He accused bin Laden of "working in another, completely different arena, and against our interests." Prompting Arafat's ire was a purported Al-Qaeda statement claiming responsibility for the suicide bombing the previous month of an Israeli-owned hotel near Mombasa in Kenya and championing the Palestinian cause. Ariel Sharon had seized on the claim, made public on a Web site established by a previously unknown group calling itself the Islamic Al-Qaeda Organization in Palestine, to renew his charge that bin Laden's operatives were active in the Israeli-occupied Gaza strip. (*Sunday Times* [London], December 15, 2002)

9. Al-Jazeera, in its early days a Washington favorite for its trailblazing courage in opening up long-censored Arab-world broadcasting, was subjected to undisguised Bush administration pressure for repeatedly airing Osama's statements, especially after September 11. With nary a protest, the administration persuaded surprisingly subservient U.S. television companies to limit airing these statements, then prevailed upon the Qatari emir, Sheikh Hamad al-Khalifa al-Thani, to rein in Al-Jazeera back home. Washington settled its scores with Al-Jazeera by dropping a smart bomb on its office and equipment in Kabul, albeit after the Taliban and Al-Qaeda had fled the capital in November. To its credit, Al-Jazeera continued to broadcast audiotapes and video provided by Al-Qaeda, but did exercise greater discretion in their presentation and editing.

10. The Russians boasted they killed Chechen President Djokar Dudayev in 1996 by targeting him with a smart missile guided to its target by emissions from his often-used satellite phone. There were anecdotes claiming that Osama indeed kept his satellite phone but had rigged up remote wiring so that he was safely far away from the person actually doing the dialing and holding the receiver.

11. Ramzi bin al-Shibh did so in an Al-Jazeera documentary aired for the anniversary, as did Osama's lieutenant Ayman al-Zawahiri less than a month later. Both spoke on audiotapes. Al-Jazeera also broadcast an audiotape purportedly from Osama himself, but the date was impossible to establish.

12. Not everyone was convinced the tape was authentic. Hervé Bourlard, director of a Swiss research institute called IDIAP, suggested the tape could be a fake. Comparing the recording with ninety minutes of earlier Osama voice samples, he said, "The authenticity is certainly questionable, there is doubt." Bourlard was interviewed by the French television network France 2, Nov. 28, 2002.

13. Britain's elite Special Boat Service was involved in the botched operation and scathingly blamed the Pentagon.

14. Sharon was the object of an eventually unsuccessful effort to bring him to trial in Belgium for war crimes, specifically the deaths of many hundreds of Palestinian civilians in Beirut's Sabra and Chatila camps in 1982. Only in 2002 did a Belgian court

rule that a law that had earlier tried and convicted Rwandans charged with genocide did not apply in Sharon's case.

15. Charles de Gaulle, *The Complete War Memoirs of Charles de Gaulle*, trans. Richard Howard, Carroll & Graf, 1998.

GROWING UP WITH THE BUMBLEBEE

1. That was before Pakistani Islamist extremists in January 2002 kidnapped and murdered *Wall Street Journal* correspondent Daniel Pearl in Karachi, a very nasty place that is always to be avoided if possible.

2. In some cases—in Bosnia, for example—the Saudis have desecrated surviving mosques and parts of damaged mosques in the name of their unadorned aesthetics.

3. Freya Stark, *The Coast of Incense*, John Murray, 1953, p. 67.

4. Yeslam bin Laden, one of Osama's half brothers, *Newsweek*, Nov. 9, 2001.

5. *Al-Hayat*, Nov. 6, 2001; *Los Angeles Times*, Nov. 13, 2001.

6. *Daily Telegraph*, Oct. 10, 2001.

7. Osama twice mentions Ibn Taymiyah by name in "Declaration of War Against the Americans Occupying the Land of the Two Holy Places," issued within months of returning to Afghanistan in May 1996, to justify the killing of all Americans, civilian or military. Ibn Taymiyah became Al-Qaeda's vital Islamic reference, justifying the deaths of innocents in the August 1998 bombings of the U.S. embassies in Kenya and Tanzania, in which 90 percent of the victims were local Africans and, of course, in the September 11 attacks. Shorn of Islamic theology, the "kill-them-all" argument was simple: if the victims are innocent they will go to paradise; if they are guilty they deserve a violent death. In the twelfth and thirteenth centuries the Pope's followers invoked identical reasoning in slaughtering adepts of the Albigensian heresy, known as Cathars, in southwestern France. "Kill them all," ordered papal legate Arnaud Amaury at the siege of Béziers in 1209. "God will recognize his own."

8. As late as 1993, Sheikh bin Jibreen, second-in-command of the government-appointed Council of Ulemas, declared, "The Shi'a is a heretic and idolater who should be eliminated." Shi'a are still second-class citizens, denied the right to join the armed forces and police and to build mosques in their villages, which are still often without running water. (Said K. Aburish, *A Brutal Friendship: The West and the Arab Elite*, Victor Gollancz, 1997, p. 243)

9. *Mut'a* (literally, "pleasure") marriages legalize short-term relationships between men and women in Shi'a jurisprudence. And in the Gulf, *misyar*, a less-well-known Sunni variation practiced by Wahhabis and other followers of the strict Hanbali school of Islamic jurisprudence, provides legal approval for similarly temporary arrangements theoretically contracted while a man is away from home.

10. *Correo de Bilbao* and *Daily Telegraph*, Oct. 12, 2001.

11. *Newsweek*, Nov. 19, 2001.

12. *Newsweek*, Nov. 19, 2001.

13. *Los Angeles Times*, Nov. 13, 2001.

14. Taki, Taki's Top Drawer, "The Lives & Loves of Osama bin Laden," *The New York Press*, Sept. 1–7, 1999.

15. *Newsweek,* Nov. 19, 2001.

16. *Newsweek,* Nov. 19, 2001.

17. France 3, "Pièces à Conviction," Oct. 18, 2001.

18. Interview, Jeddah, Dec. 1, 1999.

19. Interview with Jamal Kashoggi, Jeddah, Dec. 3, 1999.

20. Interview with Abul Anas, London, 2000.

21. Interview, Amman, May 3, 2000.

22. Robert Fisk, *Independent,* 1993.

23. Syria's abiding interest in Islamist radicals paid off after 9/11, when Damascus shared its vast database with the United States and gained temporary respite from Washington's pressure. But the neoconservatives ended the arrangement much to the displeasure of the CIA, which valued the Syrian database of 60,000 listed Islamic radicals, some belonging to the Muslim Brotherhood. Those who ended up in Spain turned out to have ties with the Madrid bombers and to have met with Mohammed Atta.

24. France 3, "Pièces à Conviction," Oct. 18, 2001. Prince Turki al-Faisal, the long-serving former Saudi intelligence chief, put the amount at $40 to $50 million. (*Arab News,* Nov. 8, 2001)

25. *New York Times,* Oct. 9, 2001.

AFGHANISTAN: STIRRED-UP MUSLIMS AND THE END OF THE COLD WAR

1. In May 2002, the United States tried to assassinate Hekmatyar with a missile-armed Predator drone shortly after the discredited warlord left his sanctuary in Iran under U.S. pressure and returned to Afghanistan. He had sought refuge in Tehran after the Taliban in 1996 drove him out of Kabul, much to the relief of its citizens. (*New York Times,* May 8, 2002)

2. Voice of America correspondent Don Larrimore, based in Islamabad in the 1980s, recalls playing poker with various American covert intelligence operatives who privately hinted they were "listening in" to Soviet military communications from mountainous points in the Northwest Frontier Province. Islamabad-based journalists, he said, were grateful to Australian, British and Canadian intelligence officers who followed the war as best they could. (interview, Paris, Nov. 24, 2002) But I still have my doubts. More than a decade after my first meeting in 1988 with a helpful U.S. diplomat stationed in Peshawar, I ran into him again. I asked him about the source of a particular bit of fascinating information he had given me then about the situation inside Afghanistan. "Almost everything I knew about what was going on inside then," he said, "was gleaned from a close reading of what journalists wrote after their forays across the border and talking to them about their experiences."

3. WBC, five-part interview, Nov. 2002.

4. Interview with Ahmad Muaffaq Zaidan, Islamabad, Oct. 7, 2000.

5. Interview with Anders Fange, Peshawar, Oct. 2, 2000.

6. *Nouvel Observateur,* Jan. 15–21, 1998.

7. Weaver, *A Portrait of Egypt,* Farrar, Straus & Giroux, 1999, p. 174.

8. Interview with Richard Murphy, New York, Dec. 14, 1998.

THE MAKING OF A LEADER

1. Barnett R. Rubin, *The Fragmentation of Afghanistan: State Formation and Collapse in the International System,* Yale University Press, 1995, p. 187.

2. Robert Fisk, *The Independent,* Nov. 1993.

3. Interview with Tariq al-Fadhli, Abyan, Yemen, Sept. 23, 1999.

4. *Time* correspondent Scott MacLeod in 1996 quoted Palestinian Hamza Mohammed, who fought in Afghanistan and worked for Osama in Sudan, as saying that bin Laden "not only gave his money, but he gave himself. He came down from his palace to live with Afghan peasants and the Arab fighters. He cooked with them, ate with them, dug trenches with them." (*Time,* May 6, 1976.)

5. Ibid.

6. Interview with Khaled Batarji, Jeddah, Dec. 12, 1999.

7. Interview with Jamal Kashoggi, Riyadh, Dec. 4, 1999.

8. Interview with Jamal Ismail, Islamabad, July 18, 1999.

9. Interview with Bounoua, London, Feb. 20, 2001.

FROM HERO TO TROUBLEMAKER

1. Interview with Tariq al-Fadhli, Abyan, Yemen, Sept. 23, 1999.

2. Bob Woodward, *Veil: The Secret Wars of the CIA 1981–1987,* Simon & Schuster, 1987, p. 215.

3. Prince Turki al-Faisal, in a Saudi WBC 5-part television interview and in *Arab News,* starting Nov. 3, 2001.

4. WBC interview, as above.

5. *New York Times,* Nov. 22, 2001.

6. *New York Times,* Dec. 27, 2001.

7. Gen. H. Norman Schwarzkopf, *It Doesn't Take a Hero,* Bantam Books, 1993, p. 379.

8. Osama and like-minded Saudis were not won over by scholars who argued that the prohibition against non-Muslims extended only to Mecca and environs, not the entire Kingdom.

9. Interview with Yemeni sheikh who regularly visited Jeddah to see bin Laden in 1990, Sanaa, Sept. 19, 1999.

10. Interview with Jamal Ismail, Islamabad, July 19, 1999.

SUDAN, THE ISLAMIC HAVEN

1. *Africa Confidential,* Oct. 13, 2000, Turabi is quoted as having said on December 18, 1999: "He [President Omar Hassan Ahmad al-Bashir] went to the Palace and I went to prison so that the Movement [the National Islamic Front] would not be exposed."

2. Testimony, New York trial of East African terrorists, Southern District of New York, *United States of America v. Usama bin Laden et al.,* S(7) 98CR.1023, Feb. 7, 2001.

3. U.S. State Department, *Foreign Terrorist Organizations,* Oct. 8, 1999.

4. Testimony, New York trial of East African terrorists, Feb. 7, 2001.

5. Sudan's radical credentials pre-dated NIF rule. The Palestine Liberation Front opened shop in Khartoum in 1969. U.S. Ambassador Cleo Noel, his number two, Curtis Moore, and the Belgian chargé had been assassinated there in 1973 by Black September in an operation that estranged Washington and contributed to delaying official recognition of the PLO for two decades.

6. In 1993 Osama financed the travel of between 300 and 480 Afghan Arab veterans from Peshawar to Khartoum, according to the State Department fact sheet dated August 14, 1996.

7. Turabi, convinced Sunni that he was, never hid from trusted foreigners his deeply felt contempt for Shi'a interpretations of Islam. (interview in Paris with Jean Gueyras, former *Le Monde* correspondent, June 23, 2002)

8. These pressures sometimes had perverse effects. Facing prison terms or worse if they returned home, many jihadis found temporary shelter in Sudan and Yemen, where Egypt kept demanding their extradition. Others headed for the wars in Bosnia and Chechnya to fulfill their perceived jihadi duties or simply to keep out of the clutches of their unforgiving home governments.

9. U.S. officials held Erwa responsible for the deaths of two Sudanese employees of USAID in the southern capital of Juba in 1992, an act that helped trigger U.S. sanctions against Khartoum the following year.

10. David Shinn, then in charge of East Africa at the State Department and a participant in Carney's farewell dinner, said he had been "skeptical the [perceived dinner table] offer would result in anything tangible and was pleasantly surprised at the proposal to get rid of Osama bin Laden." (communication with Shinn, May 31, 2003)

11. Telephone conversation with Ambassador Carney, June 2, 2002.

12. The Al-Saud had revoked Osama's citizenship in 1994, thus disowning him and making sure he would be unwelcome in the Kingdom. (interview with a Sudanese diplomat intimately involved in the negotiations, New York, June 11, 2002)

13. Conversation with an American diplomat involved in counterterrorism at that time, Paris, Sept. 12, 2001.

14. Conversations with Western ambassadors in Khartoum, Sept. 1999.

15. The prosecution in the New York trial never called Mohamed as a witness, instead relying on an affidavit. Mohamed became a prosecution witness in return for a reduced sentence.

16. Interview with a senior French police source, Paris, Feb. 23, 2002.

17. Osama bragged in public and private that Al-Qaeda fought against Americans in Somalia, according to Saudi journalist Jamal Kashoggi, who did not have the impression that Al-Qaeda's participation had been important. (telephone interview, London, Nov. 28, 2003) The only public record of Al-Qaeda military involvement concerned a training mission near the Kenyan border far from the main combat zones in Mogadishu and other major population centers. One Al-Qaeda trainer worked with Al-Ittihad, an Islamist group violently opposed to Mohammed Farah Aideed's militia that destroyed the helicopters. Moreover, Ambassador Robert Oakley, a veteran U.S. diplomatic troubleshooter who was dispatched to Mogadishu and enjoyed access to U.S. and UN intelligence, insisted that he thoroughly investigated all the evidence and

found no corroboration of claims of Al-Qaeda involvement. (interview in Washington, D.C., Oct. 16, 1999) Scott Peterson of the *Christian Science Monitor,* who reported on the UN operation and returned years later to check rumors of Al-Qaeda participation, said Aideed aides were indignant at suggestions they needed military instruction from any quarter and insisted they first heard of Osama and Al-Qaeda only after the 1998 attacks on the East African embassies. (interview, Amman, Nov. 25, 1999) Al-Qaeda action in Somalia against the United States featured in the indictments against Osama, but the prosecution in the New York trial did not belabor the point.

18. Testimony, New York trial of East African terrorists, 2001.

19. Interview with Sudanese diplomat, New York, June 11, 2002.

20. Ibid.

21. Interview with Abdel Bari Atwan, editor of *Al-Quds al-Arabi,* London, June 23, 1999.

22. Interview, Khartoum, Sept. 7, 1999.

23. Internal State Department talking points in August 1996 describe Osama not as a terrorist himself, but rather as "one of the most significant financial sponsors of extremist Islamic activities in the world today." Terrorism was not spelled out even there. (*Washington Post,* Oct. 3, 2001)

24. Ibid.

25. Still, a CIA report dated July 1, 1996, indicated that Fadl's "gold mine" insights had not percolated; it lamented, "We have no unilateral sources close to bin Laden." Bill Gertz, *Breakdown: The Failure of American Intelligence to Defeat Global Terror,* Plume, 2003, p. 10.

26. Cofer Black, former head of CIA counterterrorism and a onetime Khartoum operative, testified to the joint congressional panel investigating intelligence failures that the CIA had thwarted an attempt by "Osama bin Laden's thugs" to assassinate him in Khartoum in 1995. (*Washington Post,* Sept. 27, 2002) Black later became the State Department's Director of Counter-Terrorism. Other sources mentioned aggressive surveillance of CIA agents and two attacks—one with a claw hammer, another with a knife—that collectively were taken as demonstrating the Khartoum government's inability to provide adequate security for those with diplomatic status.

27. Telephone conversation with former official, Washington, D.C., Sept. 20, 2002.

28. Much of that aid never arrived. Its most important component comprised four refurbished C-130 transport planes. Only two were delivered because Ethiopia used them in its war with Eritrea starting in 1990. (communication with David Shinn, May 31, 2003)

29. Ijaz denies he was interested in Sudan's oil, but others well versed in Sudanese affairs have their doubts.

30. Telephone interview, Washington, D.C., Nov. 2, 1999.

31. *Vanity Fair,* Jan. 2002.

32. Telephone interview with former Clinton administration official, June 9, 2002. A senior State Department official recalled that in late 1999, the CIA swung around to Pickering's view and agreed to restaff the Khartoum station. The State Department in-

sisted one of its diplomats be in charge of the post at all times. (telephone conversation, Jan. 19, 2004)

33. Interview with Qutbi al-Mahdi, director of the External Intelligence Department, Khartoum, Sept. 8, 1999.

34. In fact, Richard Clarke said Clinton angrily rebuffed his suggestions that a missile attack might be misconstrued on those very grounds. Waving aside the messy fallout from the Lewinsky affair—"Don't you fucking tell me about my political problems, or my personal problems"—he asked Clarke if the strikes were warranted for national security reasons. Assured they were, Clinton then said, "Then just fucking do it." (telephone conversation with Clarke, Washington, D.C., Dec. 8, 2003)

35. Interviews with McElligott, Washington, D.C., 1999, 2000, 2001, 2002, 2003. McElligott served as Sudan's public relations and official representative in Washington until UN sanctions took effect in 1997, barring her from that formal role. By her own admission, she was not popular with Clinton administration officials. The feeling was mutual; she acknowledged eventually taking a "huge bundle of documents" to Special Prosecutor Kenneth Starr's office in Washington during the impeachment (although nothing came of it). She remained an adviser to Khartoum, albeit in an unofficial capacity, braving the administration's displeasure. She said she was threatened with jail at one point by a member of the State Department's Bureau of African Affairs for conducting prohibited private diplomacy. She told her tormentor to "go ahead and have me arrested . . . after you arrest Jimmy Carter and Jesse Jackson," who both intervened in Sudanese-American relations and in a more embarrassing, because public, way.

36. Telephone conversation, Dec. 8, 2003.

37. Telephone conversation with a former senior official who approved the strikes, Washington, D.C., Dec. 23, 2003.

38. Interview with senior Sudanese official, New York, June 11, 2002, and conversation with ABC producer Christopher Isham, who discussed the situation with O'Neill.

39. Telephone conversation, Washington, D.C., Dec. 22, 2003.

40. In Washington, CIA officials suggested Osama left the camp barely sixty minutes, according to Clarke, or ninety minutes, according to another senior policy-maker, before the strike. But a senior CIA operative based in the region at the time told me he remains convinced Osama went to ground right after the embassies were attacked and was nowhere near the targeted camp on August 20. (telephone conversation, Washington, D.C., Nov. 11, 2003) Although the same source is adamant that the Pakistani government was not told in advance of the strike, Clarke claimed his "best post facto intelligence" led him to believe a retired head of ISI, presumably Gen. Hamid Gul, somehow had found out about its imminence and warned Osama an attack was coming. (*New Yorker,* Aug. 8, 2003)

41. Telephone conversation with former senior official, Washington, D.C., Sept. 20, 2002.

42. Conversation, Washington, D.C., Feb. 25, 2000.

43. Rice bristled at suggestions that anyone in the administration could have demonstrated such culpable indifference to the nation's number-one priority by

turning down even a slim chance to learn more about the terrorist attacks in which her State Department colleagues died. Almost four years later she told me, "It's inconceivable in the midst of all the pain and suffering of our people who had been killed that the State Department, or any other U.S. government organ, would not be interested in pursuing any leads, no matter where they came from." (telephone conversation, Washington, D.C., June 8, 2002)

44. Telephone conversation with former senior official, Washington, D.C., Dec. 22, 2003.

45. A senior French intelligence official noted that such proferred raw intelligence could always be tampered with. The real problem, however, he noted, was that "unless you have someone who knows the scene, how do you make sense of all those thousands of pages?" Interview, Paris, August 14, 2002.

46. *Washington Post,* March 17, 2000.

47. A much-respected retired senior CIA official said Egyptian intelligence supplied the earth sample containing EMPTA. At the time, Egypt was fuming about the Mubarak assassination attempt, but quite quickly decided to make up with Khartoum. (e-mail correspondence with former official, March 16, 2003)

48. *Dateline,* Dec. 29, 1999.

49. Interview, June 11, 2002.

50. Telephone conversation, Washington, D.C., Jan. 20, 2004.

51. Telephone and e-mail exchanges, Washington, D.C., starting Nov. 11, 2003.

52. Reinforcing assertions that the U.S. government in fact never interrogated the two men, the Sudanese official said, "The FBI let it be known that they would die to see these two guys—until this day they know they missed one big chance and regret it." He said talks with the New York FBI had advanced. Interview, New York, June 11, 2002.

53. E-mail messages and telephone interview with Kamal Heyder, Islamabad, Dec. 7, 2003.

54. E-mail exchange and telephone conversation with Janet McElligott, Washington, D.C., Nov. 25, 2002.

55. Egypt, however, soon stopped threatening the NIF, apparently for fear its demise would somehow encourage the south to secede and entail even greater chaos.

56. *Vanity Fair,* Jan. 2002. Ambassador Carney later presented a similar "nonpaper," but it mentioned neither Al-Qaeda nor Osama. (communication with author, Nov. 20, 2002)

57. Turabi's Machiavellian disposition of the case provided clues to how he dealt with Osama less than two years later. Turabi told me that once the French confronted him with the evidence, "I told Carlos to leave as soon as possible." Turabi knew full well Carlos had nowhere to go. But he nonetheless feigned shock when he later learned Carlos was still in Khartoum. Turabi told me, "I said, 'Since he refused to understand, give him to the French.' It was not a difficult decision." Turabi nonetheless came in for serious criticism for betraying Carlos. But, after all, Turabi argued, Carlos was not a Muslim, and his far from discreet boozing and womanizing scarcely qualified him as a model citizen of a militantly Islamic country. Turabi was suggesting that handing over a non-Muslim, of course, involved no problem of conscience. This kind of reasoning

was the complement of Saudi and Yemeni refusal to allow nonbeliever Americans to interrogate Muslims suspected of participating in various terrorist operations involving U.S. deaths. (interview, *Washington Post,* May 3, 1995) The French were said to have thanked the NIF by delivering arms and satellite reconnaissance pictures of rebel positions in the south. As an extra dividend, Gen. Philippe Rondot, who tracked Carlos for years and negotiated for him with Turabi, was rewarded with a full rundown on Osama. The French knew the most of any Western intelligence service. (interview with a senior French official, Paris, Aug. 14, 2002)

58. *Washington Post,* Aug. 27, 1998.

59. Interviews with *Arab News* and WBC Television, Nov. 2001. Osama returned the compliment, blaming the Al-Saud.

60. Interviews, Islamabad, July 18, 1999, and Oct. 14, 2000.

61. Testimony, New York trial of East African terrorists, 2001.

62. Telephone conversation with former official, Washington, D.C., Sept. 20, 2002.

63. Testimony, East African terrorism trial, Feb. 2001, New York.

64. Osama did not, as sometimes stated, own shares in Al-Shamal because Islamic banking specifically eschews interest in favor of partnerships formed for separate transactions, in keeping with the *sharia.*

65. But many indeed were, according to Timothy Carney, who recalled trying to run down the strays when he was deputy assistant secretary of state in the South Asia bureau in 1995. (communication, Nov. 18, 2002)

66. Jamal Ismail, Peshawar, July 13, 1999.

67. The memorandum's other points did pinpoint the very kind of intelligence that the Clinton administration decided to forgo pursuing in breaking off contact with the NIF later in 1996: "Provide us with names, dates of arrival, departure and destination and passport data on mujahedeen that Osama bin Laden brought into Sudan." (*Washington Post,* Oct. 3, 2001)

ALGERIA: SPORT ET MUSIQUE

1. Interview, Washington, D.C., Jan. 5, 2000.

2. President Houari Boumedienne, as part of an ill-starred plan to replace French with Arabic as the language of instruction in Algerian schools in the 1960s, imported teachers from Egypt and other countries of the Middle East. Some of the Egyptian teachers were Muslim Brothers whom the Cairo regime was happy to get rid of. The program produced a generation of Algerians said to be "illiterate in both languages."

3. A travel warning from the U.S. embassy in effect in early 2001, a good half-decade after terrorism in the capital itself had subsided, noted that "official travel within Algiers is by armored car with appropriate security." The advisory told private American citizens they "should not move anywhere in Algeria unless accompanied by a known Algerian companion" and noted "this measure applies to walking the streets of Algiers and other cities."

4. Testimony, *Libération,* July 4, 2002, and *Le Monde,* July 5, 2002.

5. The most complete accounts of the regime's excesses are found in *La Sale Guerre* (The Dirty War), by Habib Souaidia, Éditions La Découverte, 2001, and in Samraoui's *Chronique des années de Sang* (Chronicle of the Years of Blood), Denoël, 2003.

6. *Libération*, Dec. 24, 2002.

7. In a statement in 1997 Prime Minister Lionel Jospin said his government "had to weigh its words" in dealing with Algeria, where France faced Islamist "opposition which is fanatical and violent against the regime, which also uses violence." Since "we have already been hit" in previous terrorist operations, "we must be careful," he said.

8. But Interior Minister Jean-Louis Debré that September said, "It cannot be excluded that Algerian intelligence services may have been implicated in the first" and most serious of the bomb outrages. (*Libération*, Nov. 1, 2002)

9. "We knew all the networks," boasted Jean-Louis Bruguière, the top counterterrorism judge. (*Washington Post*, Nov. 23, 2001)

10. Jean-François Clerc, second-in-command of the Direction de la Surveillance du Territoire (DST), the French counterespionage organization, insisted in court that France had "never been taken in" by a Sport et Musique only too willing, he acknowledged, "to say that Islamists are all terrorists, which is why we sort things out" carefully. He also bristled at published suggestions that the DST had used Ali Touchent. "Supposing Touchent had been an informer of ours, do you think we would have allowed him to carry out, against our interests, the terrorist operations" that followed the first explosion at the St. Michel express metro station near Notre Dame Cathedral? "We do protect our sources, but not to that extent." He also dismissed out of hand the defense lawyer's suggestion that Touchent was an Algerian agent. (*Libération*, Oct. 10, 2002) But more than a year later, Samraoui insisted that Touchent was a Sport et Musique "agent tasked with infiltrating Islamist ranks abroad and the French knew it," although they "probably did not suspect their Algerian counterparts were prepared to go so far." He suggested France lacked the motivation to find out who was giving the orders. "Apparently," he said, "the French authorities were satisfied with arresting and sentencing Boualem Bensaid, a subaltern who thought he was working for the GIA and never imagined he was working for the Direction du Renseignement et de la Sécurité," as Sport et Musique was formally known starting in 1990. (*Libération*, Nov. 15–16, 2003)

11. They replaced the notorious State Security Court, which President François Mitterrand and his Socialists had promised, upon taking power in 1981, to end. A rash of terrorism cases in 1985 and 1986, involving revolutionary Iran, led a right-wing government under Mitterrand to establish the new courts.

12. Demonstrably pleased with the wide reach of his combined intelligence, police and judicial functions, Bruguière boasted, "I can move fast—within two hours—and I do not need another judge's permission." (conversation, Paris, June 21, 1999)

13. One famous example was Richard Reid, the would-be British "shoe bomber" convicted for trying to blow up a Paris-to-Miami flight over the Atlantic in December 2001. While serving time as a juvenile offender in South London's Brixton Prison, Reid was converted by a radical prison chaplain and later gravitated to a Finsbury Park mosque and other jihadi mosques in London before traveling to Afghanistan for Al-Qaeda training and indoctrination.

14. Later Abu Zubaydah also selected Djamel Beghal, a thirty-five-year-old Algerian with dual French citizenship, to mastermind a terrorist attack on the American Embassy in Paris, in the spring of 2002. On his way back from Afghanistan, Beghal was arrested in Dubai on July 28, 2001, apparently at American request, but since he had figured on Bruguière's wanted list for two years, the judge rushed there and had him extradited to France. The French are convinced the Americans intended to hand Beghal over to the Algerians for questioning. Beghal, in a confession extracted in Dubai that he later denied, said Abu Zubaydah had asked him at the end of his training course if he would undertake a "martyr's mission." "He asked me if I was ready and I said I was." In March 2002 Abu Zubaydah was the first senior Al-Qaeda cadre caught after September 11, thanks to a joint U.S.–Pakistani raid in Faisalabad, Pakistan. He soon began cooperating with the Americans, who transferred him to an interrogation center at an undisclosed location.

15. Ressam also contributed to at least four indictments against terrorism suspects in Britain. He helped German investigators convict Mounir al-Motassadeq, a Moroccan member of the Hamburg Al-Qaeda cell that masterminded the September 11 attacks. It was thought that Ressam might be asked to testify against Zacarias Moussaoui, the Frenchman of Moroccan descent arrested in August 2001 after arousing suspicions at a Minnesota flight school. (*Seattle Times*, Feb. 26–27, 2003) Ressam's testimony was also possible against such suspected Al-Qaeda prisoners as Abu Zubaydah and Abu Doha, as well as the London firebrand preacher Abu Hamza al-Masri. Betraying annoyance with the Justice Department's repeated postponement of Ressam's sentencing, John Coughenour, the U.S. district judge who presided over this case, questioned why he had not been rewarded for providing "startlingly helpful information." Assistant U.S. Attorney Jerry Diskin told the judge, "Frankly, the government needs the leverage to ensure the cooperation of the defendant." (*Seattle Times*, Feb. 27, 2003)

16. Since the Algerian regime had a track record of manipulating French public opinion and policy-makers, using Dahoumane to provoke a terrorist operation in the United States traceable to Algerian Islamists might just persuade long-wary American officials to help the "eradicators." September 11 accomplished the same purpose, with the United States supplying materiel and diplomatic support that long had been denied the Algiers regime. Such thoughts apparently occurred to American officials who interviewed a suspiciously well-fed Dahoumane in Algiers. (Indeed, by mid-1992, the U.S European Command was welcoming six Algerian colonels and weighing supplying night-vision technology, according to the *Washington Post*, June 13, 2002.)

17. The handover was officially thwarted by legal niceties in both countries. Washington refused to deliver Anwar Haddam, an ex-FIS member of parliament who for all intents and purposes had benefited from political asylum in the United States. The Algerians considered him the GIA's top agent in America. But Algeria had condemned Haddam to death in absentia, and U.S. law prevented extraditing anyone facing a death penalty in their native land. In turn, Algeria declined to deliver Dahoumane on grounds the Algerian constitution forbade extraditing Algerians for trial abroad. Possibly reflecting these legal complications, a senior counterterrorism official I saw in Washington roughly a year after Ressam's arrest said the FBI was interested only in

gaining access to Dahoumane. He enigmatically remarked, "It is better for us if he stays there." The official seemed to be suggesting that the United States was likely to learn more if Sport et Musique's efficient interrogators worked on Dahoumane than had Algeria waived its extradition law and turned him over to the FBI. In U.S. custody he would have been spared muscular questioning and, in those pre–September 11 days, enjoyed access to a lawyer. Or was the official hinting he'd become convinced that Dahoumane might be an agent provocateur? In any case, in Washington suddenly Dahoumane, who the year before had warranted a $5 million reward if taken into U.S. custody, no longer seemed important.

18. Over the years, disgraced Russian oligarch Boris Berezovsky, from the safety of his London exile, charged repeatedly that the Russian intelligence services deliberately organized the terrorist attacks to help Putin.

19. He got his wish—and escaped from a jail in Sarajevo just days before he was to be sent to France. He was rearrested in Munich on December 13, 2003.

20. Under pressure from the United States and continental Europe even before September 11, draconian anti-terrorism legislation was enacted. By early 2003 Abu Hamza had been removed from his North London mosque and reduced to preaching on the pavement outside its doors, his citizenship, acquired through marriage, revoked and his deportation to Egypt threatened. The rumor nonetheless persisted that he had been cooperating with British intelligence for years.

21. I spent a long afternoon in Brussels in the spring of 2001 with Tarek Maaroufi, a Tunisian-born Islamist who insisted his only ire was directed at the Tunisian government. Later that year he was arrested on charges of involvement in the assassination of Ahmad Shah Massoud, which was carried out by two men with stolen Belgian passports. Maaroufi was said to have recruited one of them. He understood he was under police surveillance. But he made no secret of a visit the previous summer to Iran, where he said he met Gulbuddin Hekmatyar, the most outspokenly anti-American of the Afghan leaders during the anti-Soviet jihad, and to Afghanistan, where he claimed to have tried but failed to meet Osama. In the context of our conversation I took his very mention of Osama to mean that he indeed had met him.

22. The Netherlands refused to adopt repressive methods. In 2003 a Dutch court ordered the release of Jerome Courtailler, a French convert to jihadi Islam, pointedly refusing to accept intelligence reports as evidence implicating him and other defendants in an Al-Qaeda plot masterminded by Beghal to attack the American embassy in Paris.

23. The French first asked in 1995 for the extradition of Rashid Ramda, an Algerian accused of financing the 1995 campaign of terror in France. Osama allegedly wired funds to Ramda from Khartoum. He remained in jail in London, but by 2002 his lawyers virtually ensured he would not be handed over to France by invoking beatings allegedly meted out to other jihadis in French jails. Shortly after the destruction of the American embassies in East Africa in August 1998, the U.S. government asked for the extradition of Khalid al-Fawwaz and two other Islamists accused of belonging to Al-Qaeda. As of this writing they had not been handed over.

24. From his cell at Fleury-Mérogis Prison south of Paris, he wrote three essays for France 2, the main state-owned television station, from which the following information is drawn.

FLOOS

1. In the early 1960s the ruler of Kuwait, who was summering in the Lebanese mountain resort of Aley, abruptly summoned prominent Palestinian banker Youssef Beidas from Beirut, demanding to see the $5 million he had deposited with Beidas's Intra Bank. Beidas scurried around rounding up the cash, drove to Aley and began laboriously counting it out for the ruler to see. Halfway through, the ruler declared himself satisfied. But the banker was so irate that he told the ruler to keep his money.

2. Although rich Saudis were major investors (and quite often silent partners) in Islamic banks, in fact the Kingdom authorized them well after Sudan and Egypt. Prominent Islamic banks include Dar al-Mal al-Islamiyya, Dubai Islamic Bank, Tadamon Islamic Bank, Faisal Islamic Bank and Sudan's smaller Al-Shamal Islamic Bank, which, according to an August 14, 1996, State Department fact sheet, Osama entrusted with $50 million soon after he arrived in Khartoum in 1991. Islamic banks were not generally considered to be especially well managed or profitable. They initially were most influential in Sudan. Starting in the early 1980s, they were instrumental in enriching the National Islamic Front at the expense of more-established Sudanese banks identified with the traditional Democratic Unionist Party, and the Umma Party, which were swept from power in the NIF coup d'état in June 1989.

3. And after the September 11 attacks, when they did, the United States was unable to prosecute them successfully on money-laundering or terrorist-financing charges. (*Times* [London], Oct. 8, 2003)

4. In Iraq in 2003 American soldiers searching for pro–Saddam Hussein suspects systematically confiscated considerable amounts of cash found in private homes. The soldiers were convinced the cash was proof of payoff money either from—or for—the armed resistance to the American occupation. They could not comprehend that Arabs innocently kept their savings at home in cash as a hedge against the regime's chronic unpredictability, often in dollars correctly seen as less volatile than constantly devaluating Iraqi *dinars*. The confiscations were considered as theft and helped increase Iraqi suspicions of the occupation. The soldiers no doubt had in mind the hundreds of millions of dollars in $100 bills that Saddam's family removed by the truckload from the central bank just before Baghdad fell on April 9. That Saddam kept such an enormous number of dollars stashed there and elsewhere in Baghdad, of course, may have reflected less a supposed fascination with cash than a prudent husbanding of a universal currency for eventual use in times of personal need . . . or for funding the resistance.

5. Similarly, in the 1950s and 1960s the *Daily Mail*, a Fleet Street newspaper with a string of foreign correspondents, issued them cigarette cases whose inside lids were engraved with a message to the far-flung branches of travel agents "Thomas Cook to pay the bearer 500 pounds sterling," a very considerable sum in those days.

6. *Economist,* April 14, 2001.

7. The CIA was a longtime believer in cash, most recently in buying loyalties in its campaign against the Taliban and again in Iraq two years later. Back in the 1950s, the agency memorably tried to buy Egyptian President Gamal Abdel Nasser's affections with a gift of $3 million in cash. Nasser showed his disdain by using the money to build an otherwise useless tower in Cairo, known to local wags as "Roosevelt's erection" to honor CIA operative Kim Roosevelt, who delivered the bribe. (Miles Copeland, *The Game of Nations,* Simon & Schuster, 1970)

8. They were not alone, according to Siyamend Othman, then Amnesty International's man for the Arabian peninsula. He meticulously checked reports of these assassinations at the time and told me American diplomats he visited in Sanaa expressed no surprise—or concern. (interview, London, June 16, 2000)

9. Saudi Arabia, which long had used the border dispute as a lever against Yemen, agreed to its delimitation only after 9/11. Previously even the lines on the maps varied according to the map one was looking at.

10. Intelligence reports said some of the Al-Qaeda operatives who took part in the deadly May 13, 2003, attack on living quarters favored by foreign residents in Riyadh had infiltrated into the Kingdom from Yemen.

11. That didn't stop Taliban immigration and customs officials from methodically going through my belongings a few months before they fell from power. No doubt their inspection at the border post at Torkham near the Khyber Pass was a welcome distraction from an otherwise dull job, since no Afghans or Pakistanis warranted the same attention lavished on me.

12. Interview, Washington, D.C., Feb. 24, 2000.

13. Similarly, Yasser Arafat was credited with keeping the details of the budget of the Palestinian Liberation Organization (and later the Palestinian Authority) in the breast pocket of his trademark uniform. Sunni leader Rashid Karáme, a prominent fixture of many Lebanese governments from the 1940s to his assassination in 1987, always insisted on retaining the finance portfolio when he was prime minister.

14. Indicative of the Kingdom's predicament was its treatment in a 900-page congressional report on September 11, issued July 24, 2003, after a seven-month delay due to prolonged haggling with the Bush administration. Interest in the joint House and Senate report centered on twenty-eight pages blacked out by the administration that dealt with financial and other involvement of foreign governments, especially Saudi Arabia. Some of those claiming to have read the redacted pages said they accused senior Saudi officials, indeed members of the royal family, of having funneled hundreds of millions of dollars to jihadi terrorists. Among the principal suspects were prominent Saudis linked to Islamic banks and Islamic charities, including some operating in the United States and many other countries. Others claiming access to the material said the pages produced no convincing evidence to sustain such accusations. Somewhat understandably, the Al-Saud felt they were victims in an international diplomatic version of "Have you stopped beating your wife?" Prince Saud al-Faisal, the Saudi foreign minister, insistently asked the United States government to publish the controversial pages to clear the good name of the Kingdom, which did not enjoy sharing the legal fate of some 680 detainees at Guantanamo Bay, many of them Saudi nationals, who were de-

nied access to the evidence against them. The Prince flew to Washington to appeal in person to President Bush. But hours before he was to be received, the White House announced it would not publish the material on the grounds that intelligence sources required protection. Thus did "open society" Washington and "secretive" Riyadh swap roles in mid-2003. Cynics suggested Washington and Riyadh agreed to this scenario to look responsible in the eyes of their domestic audiences. (*New York Times*, July 27, 2003)

15. A former British ambassador to Saudi Arabia said that after the 1991 Gulf War the Saudis resented American pressure to buy more commercial airliners. The royal family had paid the United States handsomely to offset costs for the war to liberate Kuwait from Iraq. They were also peeved about having to choose Boeing rather than Airbus when they believed the American planes were no longer the cheapest, most modern or most efficient. "The terms couldn't have been clearer," the former diplomat said: "Either you buy Boeing or we won't protect you." (conversation, London, May 27, 1999)

16. The computer belonged to Ramzi Youssef, who masterminded the first attack on New York's World Trade Center in 1993. The letter was signed by Khaled Sheikh, his uncle Khaled Sheikh Mohammed's first two names, albeit fairly common Arab ones. (*Los Angeles Times*, Dec. 12, 2002)

17. *Foreign Terrorist Organizations*, Department of State, Oct. 8. 1999.

18. Bill Gertz, *Breakdown: The Failure of American Intelligence to Defeat Global Terror*, rev. ed., Plume, 2003, p. 15.

19. In a *Wall Street Journal* op-ed article Louis Freeh credited the change of heart to the direct intervention of the first President Bush, beloved by the Al-Saud for having saved the Kingdom in 1990. (May 20, 2003)

20. For details, see the Southern District of New York's November 1998 indictment of Osama and other Al-Qaeda leaders, as well as of four men charged with the Nairobi and Dar es Salaam embassy bombings, plus subsequent documents entered in their trial, which began in January 2001.

21. Belated realization of the danger Osama represented prompted FBI and CIA investigators to enlist Kenyan cooperation in raiding the Nairobi cell in the summer of 1997, although they overlooked key documents. Only on June 10, 1998, was a sealed indictment against Osama handed up by a federal grand jury impaneled in the Southern District of New York.

22. Court documents produced during New York trial of four men accused of participating in the 1998 Nairobi and Dar es Salaam bombings.

23. Only a good month after 9/11 did the administration partially lift the veil on what it knew about Muwafaq. In freezing suspected Saudi terrorist financier Yasin al-Qadi's assets, a government press release said: "He heads the Saudi-based Muwafaq Foundation" which is "an al-Qaeda front that receives funding from wealthy Saudi businessmen" estimated in the "millions of dollars."

24. The *Africa Confidential* case blazed a trail for wealthy Arab businessmen who sought redress under notoriously claimant-friendly English libel law over allegations they may have helped finance Al-Qaeda networks. The *Guardian* quoted a London libel lawyer: "Say what you will about Osama bin Laden, but he's done wonders for the

defamation bar." The Arab businessmen, the *Guardian* noted, were not discouraged by lower libel awards in recent years. Their main aim was "obtaining a judgment protecting their reputations that will be accepted internationally by governments, court, media and business." Among those involved in these suits were the *Wall Street Journal Europe,* published in Brussels, and the London newspapers the *Sunday Times* and the *Mail on Sunday,* as well as a book published in France, Germany and the United States, *The Forbidden Truth,* by Jean-Charles Brisard (Thunder's Mouth Press, 2003). (*Guardian,* Oct. 16, 2003)

25. *Washington Post,* Oct. 24, 2001.

26. *Economist,* April 14, 2001.

27. For example, the Caribbean island of Antigua, once an important tax haven and money-launderers' favorite, in 2003 hosted five banks, compared with ninety-one five years earlier. Offshore banks in the Bahamas underwent similar shrinkage. Almost all offshore banks now refuse cash deposits exceeding $5,000 and require a third-party reference to open an account. Some offshore banks issuing credit cards are asked by U.S. tax authorities to identify their customers. (*International Herald Tribune,* March 15, 2003)

28. Conversations with senior official at the Financial Action Task Force, Paris, 2000, 2001, 2002, 2003.

29. *Le Monde* reports that the bank, even as late as 2002, was said to maintain some twenty accounts for Al-Qaeda. (*Le Monde,* Feb. 26, 2003)

30. *New York Times,* Dec. 12, 2002.

31. Bearden claimed that *pushtunwali* didn't protect an Afghan at one end of a valley from betraying the foreign guest of a fellow Afghan at its far end. (*New York Times,* Dec. 12, 2002)

32. Turabi never came through with the cash to pay for the road. Instead Osama was given a bankrupt tannery, land and the concession to export commodities such as sesame and gum Arabic.

33. An Al-Qaeda defector in charge of receiving volunteers estimated that bribes, cheap guest house, purchase of *shalwar kameez* outfit and taxi fare across the border came to $30 a head. (telephone conversation with an Afghan defector who requested anonymity, Oregon, Aug. 20, 2001)

34. Under the Taliban, Afghanistan was credited with producing some 4,000 metric tons of opium a year, roughly three-quarters of the world total. In 2000 they effectively banned all opium planting. It was a telling demonstration of their power, gaining them kudos from the United Nations and even $43 million from Washington, while allowing them to sell off accumulated stocks and maintain prices. Narcotics experts believe a sizable portion of the opium and heroin produced from the poppy, which continued to be exported, was shipped through territory controlled by Ahmad Shah Massoud and his Northern Alliance and then across the former Soviet Central Asian republics. By 2003 the opium poppy crop reached some 4,000 tons, back to its pre-ban level, and amounted to $2.3 billion, or a bit more than half the country's estimated legitimate gross domestic product of $4.6 billion, according to the director of the UN Office of Drugs and Crime. He estimated Afghanistan supplied 90 percent of the heroin con-

sumed in Russia, Central Asia and Europe. (*International Herald Tribune*, Nov. 8–9, 2003)

35. *Le Monde*, Sept. 11, 2003.

36. *Economist*, Sept. 27, 2003.

37. Following the UN sanctions grounding Afghanistan's national carrier, Ariana Afghan Airlines, the Taliban briefly ran charters from the U.A.E. to Kandahar until that service was shut down under U.S. pressure.

38. In announcing the larger amount, Dennis Lourmel, the FBI official in charge of the financial side of the attacks, suggested other sources of financing had not yet come to light. (*New York Times*, Oct. 17, 2002) The smaller amount was mentioned by John Lumpkin of the Associated Press, on July 31, 2003.

39. One reason they do not know for sure is that Rashid Ramda, the London-based Algerian the French accuse of having wired funds to the bombers in Paris, for nearly a decade has managed to avoid extradition by exhausting one procedure after another from his jail cell in England.

40. Truck and car bombs, with or without suicide drivers, have been a standard terrorist tactic for decades. They were widely used in the Lebanese conflict between 1975 and 1990, specifically with devastating effect by Hezbollah against the U.S. embassy in Beirut and American and French troops there in 1983. Syrian Muslim Brothers employed car bombs in the late 1970s against President Hafez Assad's regime in Damascus. Syria pioneered the use of now-standard setback obstacles, often sections of concrete irrigation pipes filled with earth and decorated with flowers, to protect key buildings.

41. Simon Reeve, *The New Jackals: Ramzi Youssef, Osama bin Laden, and the Future of Terrorism*, André Deutsch, 1999, p. 108.

42. *New York Times*, Oct. 17, 2001.

43. Famously, two of the nineteen men involved in the plot were on a CIA watch list that, until after they were in the United States, was not shared with immigration officials; FBI higher-ups vetoed a suggestion by an agent in Phoenix to investigate Arabs enrolled in flight schools; and FBI headquarters thwarted the Minnesota office's efforts to examine the computer of Zacarias Moussaoui, the Al-Qaeda operative arrested after arousing suspicion in flight school.

44. *New York Times*, Nov. 5, 2001.

45. On October 14, 2003, Raissi won undisclosed damages and an apology in a London court from the *Mail on Sunday*, which had printed the U.S. charges.

46. *Washington Post*, Oct. 8, 2002.

47. *International Herald Tribune*, Oct. 19–20, 2002.

48. *New York Times*, Dec. 19, 2002.

49. *Washington Post*, Dec. 18, 2002.

50. Said to be in ill health, Khalid was relieved of his duties at the bank in 1999 and since has been reported in a Saudi military hospital in the mountain resort of Taif, where he is staying virtually incommunicado.

51. Known throughout the Muslim world as Rabita for its Arabic name, Rabita al-Alam al-Islami, the League was established in 1962 to counter the influence of Presi-

dent Gamal Abdel Nasser of Egypt and came to be influenced by Muslim Brothers who had fled to the Kingdom to escape his rule. Said Ramadan, son-in-law of the Muslim Brothers' founding father, Hassan al-Banna, was himself was one of Rabita's nine founders.

52. A similar confrontation between the Al-Saud and the Grand Mufti, Abdulaziz bin Baz, took place in the wake of the war to end Iraq's occupation of Kuwait in 1991. King Fahd gave way when American troops remained in the Kingdom after the hostilities, despite bin Baz's understanding that they would leave promptly.

53. E-mail exchange with New York–based private investigator and specialist on money laundering John Fawcett (2003).

54. In August 2003 the Bush administration further cracked down on Hamas's purely humanitarian activities, and the long-reluctant European Union the following month agreed to freeze funds of Hamas, Palestinian Islamic Jihad and other Islamist Palestinian charities. But *Le Monde* reported that in fact the EU watered down the application (Sept. 18, 2003).

55. Haddad's lawyer, Ashraf Nubani, said, "The government never established, other than with smoke screens and innuendo, that he was linked to terrorism." Prosecutors, by way of justification, said some evidence was kept secret to protect terrorism investigations. (*New York Times*, July 16, 2003)

56. *New York Times*, Aug. 2, 2003.

57. *New York Times*, March 25, 2002.

58. *New York Times*, March 15, 2002.

59. The FBI was given jurisdiction over all terrorism-financing investigations in March 2003. But the newly minted Department of Homeland Security's Customs Service, which initiated the case, refused to hand over its files. (*Washington Post*, Oct. 11, 2003)

60. Released at the request of the *Wall Street Journal*, the affidavit said $26 million of $54 million collected between 1996 and 2000 were sent to the Isle of Man, a tax haven whose secrecy laws make tracing the final destination of funds impossible. The purpose, Homeland Security agent David Kane said, was "to route money through hidden paths to terrorists, and to defraud the United States by impeding, impairing, obstructing and defeating the lawful government functions of the IRS." The affidavit said the Safa Group had supported Hamas and Palestinian Islamic Jihad, and senior investigators said the group also put millions of dollars into banks and companies financing Al-Qaeda. Defense lawyer Nancy Luque, representing many of those cited in the affidavit, said it reflected "rank speculation by agent Kane." "It doesn't show that one penny went to a terrorist or a terrorist organization." That, she said, explained why the government affidavit was released, "which to me means the case is at a dead end. . . . They can leave it out there to smear everyone." (*Washington Post*, Oct. 18, 2003)

61. Unnamed UN report cited in *Newsweek*, July 30, 2003.

62. *Economist*, Sept. 6, 2003, and *New York Times*, Oct. 15, 2003.

63. To appreciate the ins and outs of this traffic, spanning West Africa, Latin America, the Middle East, the Antwerp diamond traders and beyond, see Douglas Farah, *Washington Post*, Nov. 2, 2001, and Dec. 30, 2002.

64. *Washington Post,* Aug. 3, 2003.

65. In fact, diamonds had been part of the Middle East scene for many decades. Following an abortive coup in Lebanon in the 1960s by the Parti Populaire Syrien, an authoritarian pan-Arab political movement based in Beirut, key cadres fled abroad and were eventually welcomed and fitted out with Jordanian diplomatic passports. They were sent to West Africa, where they served as couriers moving "hot" diamonds to Europe.

66. *Washington Post,* Oct. 18, 2002.

67. *Washington Post,* Oct. 8, 2003.

68. *New York Times,* Dec. 12, 2003.

69. Some Western intelligence analysts viewed that number as exaggerated. So, apparently, did Richard Clarke. In a conversation in Washington, D.C., on December 21, 2000, he wryly suggested the CIA estimate was accurate "within 10,000."

70. *Washington Post,* Sept. 16, 2002.

71. Government witness Ali A. Mohammed mentioned Zawahiri's unsuccessful trip in testimony during the 2001 trial in New York of the four men eventually sentenced to life imprisonment for their parts in the bombing of the U.S. embassies in East Africa.

72. *Asian Wall Street Journal,* Feb. 1, 2002.

73. Al-Farouq, on Brooklyn's Atlantic Avenue, first achieved prominence for recruiting and for raising money for the anti-Soviet jihad in Afghanistan in the 1980s. Members of the mosque were involved in the 1993 terrorist attack against the World Trade Center.

74. Pakistan in 2003 established a financial intelligence bureau to analyze suspect transactions and liaise with internationalize financial intelligence agencies. (*Times* [London], Oct. 8, 2003)

75. Even freewheeling Dubai by 2003 had heeded U.S. advice and gone along with formally registering its *hawalas* and promising to keep them under loose surveillance. Only a year earlier, a despairing U.S. team had toured the Gulf, lamenting that *hawalas* constituted "the biggest problem for all of us" and warning "it could take a generation" to bring them under control.

76. Earlier, according to David Aufhauser, general counsel of the Department of the Treasury, Saudi cooperation was "always responsive, never pro-active, . . . not based on conviction, but necessity and based on the evidence we presented them. . . . Post May 12, it was like a light switch went off," he added. (*New York Times,* Oct. 8, 2003)

77. A typical abuse was a gift of $2.7 million to pay for the purchase of land and the construction of a mosque, a school and two soccer fields in Baluchistan, near the Afghan border. Saudi researcher Nawaf Obaid said an on-site inspection more than a year later revealed that only the land had been purchased, and the rest of the money most likely ended up with Al-Qaeda. He estimated that Al-Qaeda pocketed between $40 million and $58 million diverted from such operations over the years. (telephone conversation, Geneva, April 15, 2003)

78. Even a doubting Thomas like Prince Nayef ibn Abdul Aziz al-Saud appeared determined to bring the full rigor of Wahhabi Islam to bear on Osama's homegrown acolytes. But as late as August 2003, in an interview in a Kuwaiti newspaper, the Prince

perpetuated the canard that the Zionists were responsible for September 11 and had it posted on the royal family Web site, ainalyaqeen.com. The Web site is now closed. Hamid Gul, the ISI general toward the end of the anti-Soviet jihad who later turned into a radical jihadi firebrand in Pakistan, was responsible for launching that whopper within days of the attacks. It proved to have deep resonance, convincing many Egyptians, for example.

79. These measures were the outcome of yet another high-level U.S. government mission drawn from the NSC, FBI and Treasury and State Departments. (*New York Times,* Sept. 14, 2003)

80. *New York Times,* Dec. 12, 2003.

81. Conversation with official, who requested anonymity, at the Financial Action Task Force, May 23, 2003.

82. The dealer planned to sell fifty missiles at $500,000 apiece. (*New York Times* and *Washington Post,* July 13–14, 2003)

83. Larry C. Johnson, former CIA analyst and State Department counterterrorism official, and John F. Moynihan, former Drug Enforcement Agency (DEA) official, testimony before the House Committee on Financial Services, Washington, D.C., March 11, 2003. USA Patriot Act provisions effectively already had made banks into surrogate gendarmes policing an ever-cascading number of transactions at a cost estimated to reach $700 million by 2005. (*Economist,* Sept. 6, 2003)

84. *New York Times,* Aug. 6, 2003.

85. *New York Times,* July 16, 2003.

"THE BEHINDER WE GET"

1. *Independent,* Aug. 10, 1996.

2. As various Taliban leaders confirmed after the regime collapsed in 2001.

3. Telephone conversation, Washington, D.C., Dec. 8, 2001.

4. India was quick to trumpet these links when senior Al-Qaeda leaders were captured in houses belonging to Pakistani Islamist militants active in the Kashmir struggle. And in March 2002 Abu Zubaydah, the first major Al-Qaeda cadre arrested, was caught in Faisalabad in the home of an activist belonging to Lashkar-e-Taiba, a militant group the United States suspected was an ISI creation. Almost a year to the day later, Khaled Sheikh Mohammed, the planner and overseer of the September 11 operation, was seized in a Rawalpindi villa belonging to a Jamaat-e-Islami militant.

5. Telephone conversation with former senior CIA official, Washington, D.C., Nov. 11, 2003.

6. Ibid.

7. These doubts were not shared by various American intelligence specialists who visited Massoud on their own hook. Reuel Marc Gerecht, a Farsi-speaking former CIA field officer who saw Massoud in late September 1999, interviewed prisoners whose bearing and conversations persuaded him they were professional military men. (conversation, Paris, Nov. 3, 1999) Julie Sirrs, a CIA employee who visited Massoud in 1998 and 1999 and was fired for her initiative, came away with the same impression. (conversation, Washington, D.C., Dec. 23, 2000)

8. *New York Times,* Nov. 27, 2001.

9. A Belgian counterterrorism official told me his group seized a version in 1995 in a raid on North African radicals, but passed it on to Israel's Mossad because his small organization lacked funds to translate it. (interview, Brussels, Feb. 12, 2000)

10. The exact number of Osama's men in the 055 brigade at any one time remains unclear. In the fighting in 2001, several thousand Al-Qaeda jihadis fought alongside their more numerous Taliban allies. Massoud told Gerecht that between 750 and 1,000 Al-Qaeda jihadis were facing his front lines. The real number may have been smaller since it was in the Northern Alliance leader's interest to exaggerate their strength. Nonetheless, he credited the 055 brigade with great motivation, courage and night-fighting skills, calling them the "glue that held the Taliban together." (conversation with Gerecht, Paris, Nov. 23, 1999)

11. Indeed the Pakistan CIA station's first priority was capturing Kansi, a mission accomplished when "the price became right" and he was sold out by another Baluchi in June 1997. Only thereafter did the Islamabad station begin focusing on Osama. (telephone conversation with former senior CIA officer, Washington, D.C., Nov. 11, 2003)

12. The *fatwa* announced the creation of the Islamic Front Against the Crusaders and Jews in Feb. 1998.

13. Report of International Crisis Group, Sept. 2003.

14. Qaddafi claimed to have been targeted by Osama and indeed took the first known legal action against Al-Qaeda by filing a formal complaint with Interpol in 1998. The so-called red notice, file 1998/20032, was basically an international warrant for his arrest. It accused Osama of involvement with the Libyan Islamic Fighting Group, which allegedly killed a German counterterrorism specialist and his wife in 1994 in Libya and tried to assassinate Qaddafi himself. Britain's MI5 was rumored to have used the same group in an unsuccessful plot to eliminate Qaddafi in 1996. (*New York Times,* Nov. 12, 2001)

15. CIA analysis memorandum, reported in *Breakdown: How America's Intelligence Failures Led to September 11,* by Bill Gertz, Regnery, 2002, p. 107.

16. Gerecht's near-obsession with Iran prompted him, once free of the CIA, to embark on a reckless week of travel to Iran hidden in a Kurdish truck driver's secret compartment. Borrowing the name of a much earlier clandestine British traveler, Edward Shirley, he recorded his impressions in *Know Thine Enemy: A Spy's Journey into Revolutionary Iran,* Farrar, Straus & Giroux, 1997.

17. *Atlantic Monthly,* Aug. 2001.

18. See the disabused views of Robert Baer, a veteran CIA field hand in the Muslim world, about his former employer's mind-set while he was assigned to Central Asia in the mid-1990s: *See No Evil: The True Story of a Ground Soldier in the CIA's War on Terrorism,* Crown, 2002.

19. To beef up its thin ranks of Arabic-speakers, the post–9/11 State Department started giving such native speakers priority among recruits. The State Department in 2003 formally reported fifty-four "fully proficient or bilingual" Arabic-speakers, but insiders insisted fewer than a dozen possessed anything approaching full command of the language. The CIA's stock was of roughly like dimension. (*Washington Post,*

Oct. 2, 2003) Newspaper reports in late 2003 suggested that recruiting sufficient native Arabic-speakers was still proving difficult.

20. I first stumbled on the problems posed by such labor-intensive work when Soviet-led armies invaded Czechoslovakia and ended the "Prague Spring" in August 1968. The Soviets had to assign an entire signals and intelligence battalion to Bratislava, the capital of the smaller and poorer Slovak part of Czechoslovakia, which had perhaps 3 million citizens and relatively few telephones.

21. For a detailed, if sometimes self-serving, account of Pentagon foot-dragging and FBI bumbling as seen through the eyes of members of Clinton's National Security Council, see Daniel Benjamin and Steven Simon, *The Age of Sacred Terror,* Random House, 2002.

22. The USS *Cole* was towed back to the United States for repairs and returned to active duty in November 2003.

23. The Navy inquiry ended in a systematic whitewash.

24. Soon after World War One a Pakistani Pashtun in the Northwest Frontier Province killed a British district officer and his wife and kidnapped their daughter before taking her across the border into Afghanistan. Amanullah handed the fugitive over to the British, thereby setting off a revolt among Afghan Pashtuns in the Khost region.

25. *Washington Post,* April 17, 2002, and terrorist expert Rohan Gunaratna, quoted in *The New Yorker,* Aug. 4, 2003. All manner of American aircraft, including Vietnam-era B-52s, bombed the Afghan redoubt pretty much around the clock for two weeks starting on November 30, 2001.

26. *New York Times,* Dec. 16, 2001.

27. *Daily Telegraph,* Feb. 23, 2002.

28. *Sunday Times* (London), July 7, 2002.

29. Ibid.

30. *New York Times,* Sept. 30, 2002.

31. *New York Times Magazine,* July 20, 2003.

32. But even his favored warriors could prove hidebound. Within the Special Forces, critics complained that nearby Green Beret units in Afghanistan were prevented from acting immediately on tips, specifically locating Zawahiri near Gardez in 2002 and Mullah Omar in a Kandahar mosque in 2003, in favor of specially designated Delta and SEAL Team Six hunter-killer teams. The latter were located farther afield, and by the time they got organized Zawahiri and Omar had escaped. (*Washington Post,* Jan. 5, 2004)

33. When U.S. and Al-Qaeda troops fought at close quarters in the follow-up Operation Anaconda in the Afghan mountains in March 2003, the Americans recognized their foe as cool, dedicated, well-trained and courageous fighters who, despite constant bombing from the air, stood their ground and gave as good as they got.

34. The estimate of the winnowing of ISI ranks is from a senior French counter-intelligence official (interview, Paris, Aug. 8, 2002). Suggestions of ISI protection for the perpetrators of the assassination of *Wall Street Journal* correspondent Daniel Pearl reinforced such doubts.

35. By early spring, Bush insisted that the war on terrorism was "bigger than one person," describing Osama as someone who had "met his match" and was now "marginalized." "I truly am not that concerned about him," he said. (*Washington Post,* April 17, 2002)

36. Comments in connection with Ron Suskind's book *The Price of Loyalty: George W. Bush, the White House and the Education of Paul O'Neill* (Simon & Schuster, 2004), in the *Washington Post,* Jan. 11, 2004.

37. Kathleen and Bill Christison, *CounterPunch,* Dec. 13, 2002.

38. Poll conducted by Pew Research Center for the People and the Press, March 18, 2003.

39. Reuters, Jan. 22, 2004. A *Washington Post* editorial on February 2, 2004, noted Arar had not been sent to Canada or detained in the United States as an enemy combatant and asked, "What was the goal, if not to delegate to the Syrians torture that Americans cannot engage in?"

40. *Washington Post,* June 26, 2003.

41. 75 percent estimate is from John McLaughlin, deputy director of intelligence, *Washington Post,* Jan. 8, 2004.

42. Abu Zubaydah fingered KSM, but his American interrogators did not believe him for an additional three months. Rohan Gunaratna, *Inside Al-Qaeda: Global Network of Terror,* Berkley Books, 2003, pp. xxvii–xxviii.

43. Gunaratna, *Inside Al-Qaeda,* p. xxii.

44. *New York Times,* July 23, 2003.

45. View on funding, telephone conversation with Clarke, Washington, D.C., Dec. 8, 2003.

46. The only known exception in Al-Qaeda annals concerned Sheikh Omar Abdel Rahman, the blind Egyptian jihadi cleric who was sentenced to life imprisonment in 1996 in a New York trial, thanks to the rare use of a seditious conspiracy law dating from the decade after the American Civil War. Osama, and especially Zawahiri and the other Egyptian members of his Gama'a al-Islamiyyah, early on demanded Omar's release. When Al-Qaeda proved powerless to bring that about and was unwilling to stage specific terrorist operations to help obtain his freedom, some members left Osama's organization.

47. *New Yorker,* Aug. 4, 2003.

48. Neoconservatives, for months on end, kept insisting that Atta was in cahoots with an Iraqi intelligence agent in Prague despite mounting evidence that this was a red herring. The neoconservatives were not deterred by the agent's arrest in Iraq and the fact his American captors made no mention of the purported Atta connection.

49. *New York Times,* June 10, 2003.

50. In so doing, his neoconservative adversaries noted, Powell contradicted his own crucially important statement before the UN Security Council on February 5, 2003: "Iraqi officials deny accusations of ties with Al-Qaeda. These denials are simply not credible." (*New York Times,* Jan. 9, 2004)

51. Kenneth Pollack, *Atlantic Monthly,* Jan.-Feb. 2004.

52. *Washington Post,* Nov. 9, 2003.

53. *Washington Post,* March 16, 2003.

54. *New York Times* and *Washington Post,* Jan. 14, 2004.

55. The royal family officially had announced the base would not serve to attack Iraq, then quietly allowed the U.S. Air Force to do just that. U.S. Special Forces troops also operated from jumping-off places on Saudi soil near the Iraq border.

56. *Washington Post,* Aug. 5, 2002.

57. *New York Times,* Nov. 25, 2002.

58. Interview in *Der Spiegel,* quoted in the *Washington Post,* Dec. 12, 2001.

59. *New Yorker,* Jan. 5, 2004.

60. See the detailed article by Michael Scott Doran, assistant professor at Princeton: "The Saudi Paradox," *Foreign Affairs,* Jan./Feb. 2004, from which this quotation is taken.

61. *New York Times,* May 16, 2004.

62. *Washington Post,* June 3, 2003.

63. One of the captured alleged leaders, Adnan Ersoz, confessed, according to the Turkish press, that he had met Osama just before the September 11 attacks at a breakfast in Kandahar. Subsequently, some 450 Turks underwent training at an Al-Qaeda camp in Afghanistan. (*Libération,* Jan. 27, 2004)

64. Identical messages were sent to Al-Quds al-Arabi and Al-Majallah in London. (*Washington Post,* Nov. 17, 2003)

65. *Washington Post,* Jan. 14, 2004.

66. *New York Times,* Jan. 21, 2004.

67. Reuters, Dec. 17, 2003.

EPILOGUE

1. "I am ready to die. My cause will continue after my death." (*New York Times,* Nov. 10, 2001)

2. Quoting Dr. Amer Aziz, who did not see "any evidence of kidney disease" or "dialysis."

3. Interview with British official, Martha's Vineyard, Mass., Aug. 12, 2000. Conversation with Palestinian engineer, Amman, May 5, 2000.

4. Margaret Tutwiler, in discussing her new State Department job in charge of public diplomacy. Edward Djerejian, former American ambassador to Israel and Syria, concluded that "the bottom had indeed fallen out of support for the United States" after submitting a report on the problem the previous October at congressional request. (*New York Times,* Feb. 5, 2004)

5. *New York Times,* Oct. 4, 2002.

6. *New York Times,* July 9, 2002.

7. *New York Times,* Oct. 16, 2003.

8. *New York Times,* Oct. 24, 2003.

9. Irene Kahn, General Secretary of Amnesty International, noted that "it is not undemocratic regimes but liberal democracies which favor adopting draconian mea-

sures to limit civil liberties in the name of public safety." (*New York Times*, May 29, 2002)

10. *New York Times*, March 25, 2004.

11. Spanish counterterrorism forces devoted only between one quarter and one third as many agents to keeping track of Islamist militants as were earmarked to hunt down ETA. *New York Times*, March 22, 2004.

12. Consider the principal theses of David Frum and Richard Perle, who in a 2003 book, *How to Win the War on Terrorism*, favored getting tough on Saudi Arabia, forcing Syria to withdraw from Lebanon, blockading North Korea, revising the UN charter and widening the use of preventive war. Midway through 2004, the administration was as dependent as ever on Saudi oil, the Shi'a were causing major problems in Iraq, Washington was begging the UN Security Council to bail it out of Iraq and happy to negotiate North Korea's nuclear threat.

Bibliography

Anonymous. *Through Our Enemies' Eyes, Osama bin Laden, Radical Islam and the Future of America.* Washington, D.C.: Brasseys, 2002.

Bear, Robert. *Sleeping with the Devil.* New York: Crown, 2003.

———. *See No Evil.* New York: Crown, 2002.

Benjamin, Daniel, and Steven Simon. *The Age of Sacred Terror.* New York: Random House, 2002.

Bergin, Peter L. *Holy War Inc.* New York: Free Press, 2001.

Bodansky, Yossef. *Bin Laden: The Man Who Declared War on America.* Rocklin, Calif.: Forum, 1998.

Clarke, Richard A. *Against All Enemies: Inside America's War on Terrorism.* New York: Free Press, 2004.

Cooley, John K. *Unholy Wars: Afghanistan, America and International Terrorism.* London: Pluto Press, 1999.

Follain, John. *Jackal: The Secret Wars of Carlos, the Jackal.* London: Weidenfeld & Nicolson, 1998.

Girardet, Edward, and Jonathan Walter. *Afghanistan, Geneva.* Essential Field Guides, 1998.

Gul, Imtiaz. *The Unholy Nexus: Pak-Afghan Relations under the Taliban.* Lahore, Pakistan: Vanguard, 2002.

Gunaratna, Rohan. *Inside Al Qaeda.* New York: Berkley Books, 2003.

Jacquard, Roland. *Fatwa contre l'occident.* Paris: Albin Michel, 1998.

Kepel, Gilles. *Jihad: Expansion et declin de l'islamisme.* Paris: Gallimard, 2000.

Khosrokhavar, Farhad. *L'islam des jeunes.* Paris: Flammarion, 1997.

Labévière. *Les dollars de la terreur.* Paris: Grasset, 1999.

Laidi, Ali. *Le jihad en Europe.* Paris: Editions du Seuil, 2002.

Lewis, Bernard. *The Assassins.* London: Al Saqi Books, 1985.

Lippman, Thomas W. *Inside the Mirage: America's Fragile Partnership with Saudi Arabia.* Boulder, Colo.: Westview Press, 2004.

Maley, William. *Fundamentalism Reborn? Afghanistan and the Taliban.* Lahore, Pakistan: Vanguard, 1998.

Palmer, Nancy. *Terrorism, War, and the Press.* Cambridge, Mass.: Harvard University Press, 2003.

Posner, Gerald. *Why America Slept: The Failiure to Prevent 9/11.* New York: Random House, 2003.

Rashid, Ahmed. *Taliban, Islam, Oil, and the New Great Game in Central Asia.* London: I. B. Tauris, 2001.

Reeve, Simon. *The New Jackals.* London: André Deutsch, 1999.

Roy, Olivier. *L'islam mondialisé.* Paris: Editions du Seuil, 2002.

Seale, Patrick. *Abu Nidal: A Gun for Hire.* New York: Random House, 1992.

Robinson, Adam. *Bin Laden: Behind the Masque of the Terrorist.* Edinburgh: Mainstream Publishing, 2001.

Shirley Edward. *Know Thine Enemy: A Spy's Journey into Revolutionary Iran.* New York: Farrar, Straus & Giroux, 1997.

Souaidia, Habib. *La sale guerre.* Paris: Editions la Découverte, 2001.

Sprinzak, Ehud. *Brother Against Brother: Violence and Extremism in Israeli Politics from Atlalena to the Rabin Assassination.* New York: Free Press, 1999.

Stark, Freya. *The Coast of Incense: Autobiography 1933–1939.* London: John Murray, 1953.

Suskind, Ron. *The Price of Loyalty: George W. Bush, the White House, and the Education of Paul O'Neill.* New York: Simon & Schuster, 2004.

Teitelbaum, Joshua. *Holier Than Thou: Saudi Arabia's Islamic Opposition.* Washington, D.C.: Washington Institute for Near East Policy, 2000.

Weaver, Mary Anne. *A Portrait of Egypt.* New York: Farrar, Straus & Giroux, 1999.

Yallop, David. *To the Ends of the Earth: The Hunt for the Jackal.* London: Jonathan Cape, 1993.

Yousad, Muhammad, and Mark Adkin. *The Bear Trap.* Lahore, Pakistan: Jang, 1992.

Woodward, Bob. *Bush at War.* New York: Simon & Schuster, 2002.

Al-Zawahiri. *Knights Under the Prophet's Banner.* Cairo: al-Sharq al-Awsat, 2001.

Index

NOTE ABOUT THE AUTHOR

Jonathan Randal was born in 1933 in Buffalo, New York, and educated at Exeter and Harvard. He spent his junior year in France, and after serving as a private in the U.S. Army in Europe, he started out as a foreign correspondent in the mid-1950s in Paris and over the decades has worked for United Press, the old *Paris Herald, Time,* the *New York Times* and, for nearly thirty years, the *Washington Post.* As a war correspondent he reported the Algerian War of Independence from France, followed by wars and crises in the Congo, Vietnam, Iran, Lebanon, Kurdistan, Bosnia, Liberia and a dozen other combat zones. He considers himself privileged to have witnessed these events and lucky to have survived when so many of his colleagues did not. Randal is the author of *Going All the Way: Christian Warlords, Israeli Adventurers and the War in Lebanon* and *After Such Knowledge, What Forgiveness? My Encounters with Kurdistan.*

ALSO BY JONATHAN RANDAL

After Such Knowledge, What Forgiveness?
My Encounters with Kurdistan

Going All the Way: Christian Warlords,
Israeli Adventurers and the War in Lebanon